African American Studies

D0809290

Introducing Ethnic Studies

General Editor: Robert Con Davis-Undiano

Titles in the series:

Native American Studies
Clara Sue Kidwell and Alan Velie

African American Studies
Edited by Jeanette R. Davidson

Asian-American Literary Studies
Edited by Guiyou Huang

African American Studies

Edited by Jeanette R. Davidson

Edinburgh University Press

© in this edition, Edinburgh University Press, 2010
© in the individual contributions is retained by the authors

Edinburgh University Press Ltd
22 George Square, Edinburgh

www.euppublishing.com

Reprinted 2012, 2014

Typeset in Monotype Ehrhardt
by Servis Filmsetting Ltd, Stockport, Cheshire, and
printed and bound in the United States of America

A CIP record for this book is available from the British Library

ISBN 978 0 7486 3714 0 (hardback)
ISBN 978 0 7486 3715 7 (paperback)

The right of Jeanette R. Davidson to be identified as editor
and of the contributors to be identified as authors of
this work has been asserted in accordance with
the Copyright, Designs and Patents Act 1988.

Contents

Part III   International Perspectives

Part IV   Selected Areas of Scholarship

Part V   Commentary

To J. James Carlisle and Elizabeth Carlisle,
Tim Davidson, Zach Davidson, and Corey Davidson

Acknowledgements

I want to thank, first, the contributors and interviewees who are included in this text. It is an honor to be able to present their valuable contributions here. I want to thank R. C. Davis, Neustadt Professor of English at the University of Oklahoma, editor of *World Literature Today* and the managing editor of this *Ethnic Studies Series*. He is a wonderful friend and colleague, and I can always count on his support and encouragement. Thanks go also to Mairead McElligott, Jackie Jones, and Daniel Bourner of Edinburgh University Press for their assistance in helping this work come to fruition. The support for this text given to me by my staff at the University of Oklahoma African and African American Studies Program (AFAM) is greatly appreciated. I am blessed to have them in my life every day! My sincere thanks go to Sharri Coleman, Ruth Gomez, Patience Sijuola Ogunsanya, and Monica Flippen-Wynn. I want to also thank University of Oklahoma President David L. Boren and Dean Paul Bell, College of Arts & Sciences for entrusting me with the directorship of AFAM and for their support and belief in the importance of the program. I am extremely indebted, of course, to the students and the faculty members of the AFAM program. They inspire me every day and serve as constant reminders of why this work is so vital to the academy. My deepest appreciation goes to my husband Tim Davidson and our sons, Zach and Corey, for the love, support, encouragement, and validation they give me every day (and to Zach for his cover design), to my sister, Aileen Franssen, who was my earliest role model, and to my mum and dad, Elizabeth and J. James Carlisle, who first taught me about all that is righteous and matters in life.

Jeanette R. Davidson

Series Editor's Foreword

Jeanette R. Davidson's volume marks a valuable moment for recognition of the status that African-American Studies has achieved as a body of knowledge and a field of studies. This is a book about accomplishments in African American Studies and, in some cases, about recognizing that fundamental cultural issues do not get resolved so much as reframed. This book marks a point of maturity in which, for the first time, it is possible to see African American Studies—with nearly half a century of history behind it—in the act of renewing itself for the twenty-first century.

This renewal is strengthened by the presence in this volume of figures synonymous with innovative inquiry. Molefi Asante is the principal figure who has defined Afrocentricity in African American Studies. The actor and director Danny Glover reflects on African Americans in film and the arts. Manning Marable, Charles Jones, and Nafeesa Muhammad explore the dimension of social activism that is inextricable in African American Studies, and they are joined by a cadre of talented scholars who investigate the arts and social thought in a manner in keeping with the Black intellectual tradition.

This volume also shows that, beneath the interpretation of the social sciences and the arts in African American Studies, is a deeper concern. This volume demonstrates that the great power of African American Studies has never been limited to its choice of areas to investigate, but includes a commitment to critique the relationship of race and power in America—the relationship of the African American community and American society at large. From the *Narrative of the Life of Frederick Douglass, An American Slave, Written by Himself* (1845) through the recent work of bell hooks and

Cornel West, that drive has been to interrogate the underlying assumptions about race that too often artificially limit American society and culture. The commitment to this critical inquiry has been the primary engine of African American Studies, and an articulation of that critique runs anew throughout each and every chapter of this book.

In her Introduction and (with Tim Davidson) in the volume's concluding chapter, Davidson focuses incisively on African American Studies' engagement with race and power and maps the lines of a critique that reveals nothing less than, in Cornel West's words, "what it means to be human, what it means to be modern, and what it means to be American." In its manner of engaging with these issues, this book is a celebration of renewal for African American Studies and a gesture of faith in what is to come—the critical remapping of a field of inquiry that is committed to understanding and helping to shape the future.

Robert Con Davis-Undiano

CHAPTER I

Introduction

Jeanette R. Davidson

University of Oklahoma

The story of African American Studies is one of strength, resilience, accomplishment, and empowerment. African American Studies scholars have, and will continue to have, unique and far-reaching contributions within universities—intellectually, aesthetically, spiritually, politically, and culturally. At the same time, in many ways, African American Studies exemplifies the quintessential story of race in the United States, with all the challenges, power dynamics, and hard-fought successes too long in coming. As with the larger national context, so goes it for African American Studies. We have come a long way, but still have a long way to go.

With a history reaching back to Black intellectual education pioneers like W. E. B. Du Bois, Mary McLeod Bethune, E. Franklin Frazier, and many others, within the field of education and in other professional arenas, and reaching beyond to scholars, activists, and artists in Africa and the Diaspora, African American Studies has a remarkable foundation.[1] Building on that foundation, professors and students, and people from the community, in the late 1960s demanded that education within the "ivory towers" become relevant to Black students and other students of color, with their efforts coming to fruition in the birth of formal Black Studies.[2] Since then, African American Studies has continued to grow. In measurable ways, development in scholarship, curriculum building, and creative production has been extraordinary.

To understand African American Studies, one must understand the historical context, the ongoing political and institutional struggle existing for programs and departments. One must also recognize how these dynamics have shaped curricula, the development of varied theoretical perspectives and worldviews, faculty composition, and the institutional prestige accorded to the discipline. African American Studies departments and programs have from their inception been under intense scrutiny. While the discipline has gained a "good press," and some would argue has experienced a "second Renaissance," obstacles like racial bias and White Supremacy have often prevailed and have influenced external perceptions of academic legitimacy.

Today, African American Studies' status has made tremendous ground in universities within the United States, even where previously unwelcome. Universities are now responding to changes in the world. Appreciating that Black Studies is important to all people, not only scholars and students of African descent, Cornel West notes that the heart of African American Studies was never solely for African Americans, but "was meant to try to redefine what it means to be human, what it means to be modern, what it means to be American," adding, "because people of African descent in this country are profoundly human, profoundly modern, profoundly American."[3] Many (not all) departments and programs have endured, even thrived, and, in spite of the extraordinary challenges, faculty scholars have transformed the learning experience for students of all races by envisaging new paradigms, forcing a reexamination and new understanding of history and past works, and creating substantial bodies of knowledge, literature, and the arts. Over time, universities have been positively impacted by African American Studies and they will continue to change for the better because of the value of the discipline.

This volume introduces students and scholars to the large and rich area of inquiry and scholarship known as African American Studies (also called Black Studies, Africana Studies, African and African American Studies, Diaspora Studies, and Pan-African Studies). It is designed for use with undergraduate students in African American Studies programs and American Studies and Ethnic Studies programs, as well as beginning graduate students in these fields of study. It will also be of use to faculty members and university administrators as they work together to strengthen African American Studies in their respective institutions of learning.

At the center of what we do in African American Studies are our students. In our program at the University of Oklahoma one of the great joys for us is being able to present a rich curriculum, including (from a roster of core and elective courses totaling over forty in number), courses as varied, yet as connected, as African American Gospel Choir Traditions,

African Dance, the African American Family, Africa and the Diaspora, African Aesthetics, The Digital Divide, African Art, African American Military History, Civil Rights Law, Blacks in Oklahoma, African American Visual Culture, African American Religious Traditions, and the most recent additions, the Prison Industrial Complex and Africana Thought. Some classes are taught by African and African American Studies core faculty or suitable faculty from traditional disciplines in the university, while other courses give us the opportunity to bring experts from the community into the classroom each semester to share their knowledge, wisdom, expertise, and activist experiences—among them, local social workers, the pastor of the largest local Black church, and a high-profile attorney.

Students benefit from a diversity of subject matter, service learning opportunities, and instructors. They enjoy being exposed to new, stimulating, inspiring content that "opens their eyes." As their instructors, we are blessed by being able to provide an intellectual and physical space for our students where we nurture, support, and mentor them, and see that they feel valued and welcome.

This volume exemplifies African American Studies' characteristic of promoting many different voices. Alexander and Austin, for example, give voice to "ordinary" people in their chapter: Bea Jenkins picking cotton, who speaks from the heart about her anguish over Emmett Till's death and Harold Taylor speaking about the invisible wounds inflicted on him through torture, all the while maintaining that he will keep working for his people.

The voice of an artist committed to being proactive in challenging injustices in the world is also heard in the interview with actor-activist Danny Glover. We hear this world-renowned artist, who has lived a life pursuing values established in him as a "child" of the Civil Rights Movement, as he voices his purposeful desire to share "the people's stories"—stories of people about whom you would not normally hear; stories about people transforming from ordinary to extraordinary; important stories about relationships and living; and of people transcending against the odds.

We hear the voices too of great scholars like Molefi Asante, Perry Hall, and Charles Jones, who know what it was like to push for Black Studies "back in the day," and of Manning Marable, a brilliant "public intellectual" committed to sharing Black Studies with the public. These voices of long experience in the field are juxtaposed with those of the other authors, including an American Ambassador, a graduate student, authors born outside the US, and those representing various areas of expertise and longevity in Black Studies.

PART I: HISTORY AND THEORETICAL PERSPECTIVES IN AFRICAN AMERICAN STUDIES

Part I provides essential background knowledge about the history and development of the field. Much of this text honors the idea of looking back to see and learn from where we have come, at the same time as we move forward (Sankofa). In Part I and throughout the text there are frequent references to educational pioneers of the late nineteenth and early twentieth centuries and to scholars, activists, and students of the 1960s, all to whom we owe an immeasurable debt. An examination of a variety of theoretical paradigms used in African American Studies is also presented in this Part. Set in historical context and within the developmental frame of Black Studies, theory is presented as central and inextricably linked to history.

Clearly, there is no one way to conceptualize African American Studies. Ronald Bailey highlights, "We do not have to be the same or think the same to carry on collective work aimed at one or more common objectives. And we do not have to have the same objectives."[4] Thus Perry Hall's chapter, "African American Studies: Discourses and Paradigms," presents the range and differences of intellectual and ideological perspectives in the field, and the variations in paradigms and theoretical perspectives past and present. Reflecting on history, societal contextual factors, and the evolution of African American Studies, Hall speaks from a long history of experience in the field. Following a discussion of the integrationist/inclusionist framework, Black Feminist discourse, Marxist and Black Nationalist discourses on race and class, the Afrocentric paradigm, and Gender and Women's Studies perspectives, he presents the "transformationist" approach, which he describes as a "range of alternative perspectives." Hall indicates that such an approach is helpful in the way it "connects and contextualizes classical and contemporary African American experiences to the wider, global human experiences."

While Hall's chapter illustrates the diversity of approaches taken in African American Studies, it is reasonable to say that one approach that has garnered a giant share of attention is Afrocentricity. This bears testament to the tremendous impact of Afrocentricity and the work of Molefi Kete Asante in the field of African American Studies.

Molefi Kete Asante's chapter, "Afrocentricity and Africology: Theory and Practice in the Discipline," presents a clear and straightforward discussion of the philosophical paradigm of Afrocentricity. He highlights its origins as theory and practice, rooted in an intellectual idea written from activism, observations, and notions of social transformation, and discusses in detail its emphases on the centrality and agency of the African person. Important constructs and characteristics of Afrocentricity are delineated, and assertions corrective to common misunderstandings about the approach are presented. Throughout the chapter, Asante, arguably the foremost articulator of Afrocentricity, references Afrocentric scholars past and present, and clarifies, alongside his discussion of the importance of their work, that it is *consciousness* and *orientation* rather than race *per se* that define them. Thus he dispels the misconceptions that Afrocentric scholars must be African or of African descent, or that all Black scholars are necessarily Afrocentric.

PART II: COMMUNITY SERVICE, SOCIAL ACTIVISM AND THE ACADEMY

Part II calls to the forefront the traditional emphasis placed on the link between community service, social activism and the academy in Black Studies. This has been a defining characteristic articulated in the discipline and should remain so. Though debated by some scholars,[5] it is generally understood to be indispensable to Black Studies scholarship. In *Beyond Black and White*, Manning Marable expresses his view in no uncertain terms:

> It is insufficient for black scholars to scale the pristine walls of the academic tower, looking down with calculated indifference on the ongoing struggles of black people. We must always remember that we are the product and beneficiaries of those struggles, and that our scholarship is without value unless it bears a message which nourishes the hope, dignity and resistance of our people.[6]

While a focus on praxis threads through the text, the chapters in this Part, particularly, highlight African American Studies' responsibility to communities. Today most undergraduate students who have elected to major or minor in African American Studies state that they are motivated to be of service and give back to their communities. Other students who attend our classes, but major in other disciplines, often voice a similar desire, with the objective of serving as culturally competent journalists, social workers, lawyers or teachers. These chapters champion service to the community as an essential ingredient of African American Studies.

In "Town and Gown: Reaffirming Social Responsibility in Africana Studies," Charles Jones and Nafeesa Muhammad focus on the "social imperative" of Africana Studies as conceptualized originally by scholars and activists who shaped the earliest formal programs. They write of the early days when Black Studies units were characterized by an adherence to the "dual mission" of education and activism, with goals of community empowerment and the development of students. Jones and Muhammad present their recent research concerning the current status of graduate programs and their commitment to working with the community. Their findings indicate a general demise in the attention given by graduate Africana programs to community service and the authors then postulate reasons, both internal and external, for such a change over time. Still, Jones and Muhammad are able to present a number of examples of creative programs of outreach from Black Studies programs to the community that should serve as models and will prove inspiring to students.

In an exclusive interview, "Reflections on the Journey," Danny Glover, internationally acclaimed actor, activist, and former student at San Francisco State College, describes the social and political environment of San Francisco at the time the first Black Studies program was established. Glover gives an in-depth account of his activities and those of his peers when, together with external community supporters, they fought for Black Studies to be added to the curriculum. Glover talks passionately about his commitment to social justice and shows clearly that his art and activism are inseparably merged in his life.

The September 2008 interview with Manning Marable, "Black Studies for the Public," presents the insights of one of the foremost Black intellectuals of contemporary times. He insists that Black Studies must be for the public and illustrates this in his discussion of efforts he has made and examples of research by many other scholars past and present. Linking his belief that Black Studies must open new vistas of understanding and serve the public, he highlights the importance of advocacy and the pursuit of social justice in this field of studies. He maintains the importance of Black Studies scholars involving ourselves in political projects with the goal of providing solutions to real problems, experienced by Black people in their daily lives in the United States and the Diaspora, such as the incarceration of excessive numbers of Black men and women, inadequate healthcare, and poverty. Marable makes it clear that the interdisciplinary approach of Black Studies is best suited for these complex tasks at hand and applauds the exciting work of contemporary Black intellectuals endeavoring to make a real and significant difference to the lives of people with their scholarship.

PART III: INTERNATIONAL PERSPECTIVES

The world has changed in many ways since the beginning of formal university programs and departments in Black Studies. With these developments have come inevitable changes in content in the curricula, student demographics, scholarship foci, and international educational and service partnership possibilities. Studies in the field are no longer conceptualized as pertinent solely to the United States and focused only on that country's concerns.

In Part III, the opening chapter discusses Africa's centrality to African American Studies and demonstrates the importance of our having dialogue and relationships in the international arena. Former US Ambassador Tibor Nagy reflects his twenty-five years' experience and service to several countries in Africa, including posts as Ambassador to Guinea and Ethiopia, in his chapter, "Africa and its Importance to African American Studies." He asks African Americans to become more involved in Africa and to make loud demands for the United States to make the continent much more of a priority in international policy and relations. Outlining the very great challenges of Africa—poverty, HIV/AIDS, human rights violations, war, the list goes on—he also highlights its great strengths and describes it as currently being "in transition." His call to action of African American Studies scholars reflects his considered opinion that non-African scholars and "experts" are too often tainted by colonial biases. He indicates that African American scholars offer more positive outlooks, higher expectations, and cultural understanding and therefore are understandably better equipped to work in partnerships with Africans in developing new models for their success, in keeping with their systems, history, traditions, and cultures. Nagy's chapter views African countries also as being full of potential for increased partnerships with African American Studies students and faculty with regard to institution travel abroad exchange agreements, research, distance learning, and service learning opportunities.

The second chapter in Part III examines the situation of Black Studies in the United Kingdom, illustrating another international perspective. Mark Christian's chapter offers the rare insights of someone who has been involved in, and has taught, Black Studies in both the United Kingdom and the United States. In "Black Studies in the UK and US: A Comparative Analysis," Christian compares the development of Black Studies in both countries and focuses on historical and social differences and the result-ant structural differences in the educational systems. Christian's discus-sion of the UK focuses mostly on his personal experiences in Liverpool, England, and he presents the situation there as a case study of grassroots, community-based Black Studies. Throughout, he presents a harsh but fair criticism of the commentaries by White British "experts" on race who have presumed to evaluate the worth (or lack thereof) of Black Studies in the UK. While understanding the many challenges faced by educators in the United States, Christian still concludes that the situation there for Black Studies is far advanced in comparison to the United Kingdom.

PART IV: SELECTED AREAS OF SCHOLARSHIP

It would be impossible to present a fair representation of recent African American Studies scholarship in any single volume. The strength of the selections made for Part IV lies in their differing areas of subject focus, sty-listic variation, diverse pedagogical approaches, and theoretical viewpoints. As such they *point to* the diverse and expansive nature of Black Studies, albeit within a small sample. At the same time, these chapters illustrate certain areas of convergence in substance and approach, illustrating the characteristic interdisciplinarity and intradisciplinarity of writers in the Black intellectual tradition. As noted previously, for students one of the joys of participating in African American Studies is that classes and courses offer such diversity of subject matter. In one class they may be engaged in deep discussion with a scholar on African American religion; in the next they are learning the theory and artistic formulations of African dance and, dressed in their *lappas*, are dancing on the floor borrowed from "Fine Arts." Later in the day they are engaged in vigorous discussions about the literature written by brilliant Black women. Yet at the end of the day they are able to see how their teachers have presented them with an holistic approach with which to view the subject matter at hand *and* a means to link it with other courses on the curriculum.

Leslie M. Alexander and Curtis J. Austin, in "Africana Studies and Oral History: A Critical Assessment," describe and explain the importance and indispensable value of oral traditions to African people, throughout history, in telling stories and expressing their social, cultural, and political realities. Alexander and Austin contend that oral history is just as significant today and argue that oral history methods should be central to Africana History and Africana Studies. The authors present a searing first-person account of torture from Harold Taylor, a recently freed member of the San Francisco 8[7] and make a compelling case that access to such living history is most likely made using the methodology they suggest.

In "African American Philosophy: Through the Lens of Struggle," George Yancy emphasizes philosophical themes and assumptions that put the social and historical struggle of Black people at the center. Coming from this vantage point, he provides an approach to African American philosophy that is clearly oppositional to the norms and narrowness generally held in the discipline of philosophy at large. He is careful to note that he is not implying that African American philosophers do not share concerns with other philosophical traditions and paradigms, but highlights the need to address the biases generally infused in mainstream philosophical thought that ignore the impact of White Supremacy, power and oppression, anti-Black sensibilities, and racist thinking. He advocates the need to be oppositional and transgressive as an African American philosopher and notes the ongoing challenges the group has faced in the past and in contemporary times with their "outsider" status. Yancy highlights the importance of creating a community of African American philosophers who will challenge the hegemony of typical Philosophy departments and discusses philosophy in terms of working in the struggle for liberation, inspiring hope and self-validation, affirming agency, and moving forward in the quest for equality and social transformation.

In her chapter "Song and Dance Nexus in the Africana Aesthetic: An Approach," Melanie Bratcher begins with Marimba Ani's definition of Africana Aesthetics and then guides the reader through the process she follows when teaching in the classroom. Coming from an Afrocentric perspective, Bratcher, an accomplished dancer in the Umfundalai technique of Contemporary African Dance and jazz singer, carefully describes her practices in pedagogy, paradigm construction, and applied aesthetics. An engaging example of Nina Simone's *Four Women* is central to Bratcher's discussion and analyses. As a teacher, Bratcher operates with the goal of influencing the lives of her students in a way that will transform their actions and has evidence that they have indeed been inspired to apply what they have learned in the classroom to various fields of professional employment.

Maria D. Davidson and Scott Davidson's chapter, "Perspectives on Womanism, Black Feminism, and Africana Womanism" highlights similarities and differences between the three, while demonstrating how they all give voice to Black women, are not mutually exclusive, and in many ways complement each other. The authors specify some of the shortcomings of White Feminism in addressing the oppression experienced by women of color, thereby shedding light on sources of tension between these groups of women. At the heart of the chapter, the authors look at selected works, analyzing them within the category of Womanist literature. Davidson and Davidson highlight that Womanism, Black Feminism, and Africana Womanism are all praxis-oriented in ways that are important to the lives of Black women seeking to gain agency, have a voice, be activist in their responses, and become empowered.

The final chapter in this Part is Victor Anderson's "Theorizing African American Religion." Anderson delves into significant historical content as he discusses methodology and debates about formations of African American religious experiences and questions about the extent African presence contributes to African American religion. Included in this chapter are discussions about the Negro Church, the Black Church, Black Theology of Liberation, and Black Womanist Theology. Anderson concludes with an examination of the "divide" between Black Church Studies and African American Religious Studies, which he believes causes African American Religion to have a peripheral position in African American Studies. Anderson presents a methodological position that he describes as "African American Religious Cultural Criticism" for moving past this divide.

PART V: COMMENTARY

In the final chapter, "African American Studies: Vital, Transformative and Sustainable," Tim Davidson and I present an unvarnished picture of African American Studies programs and departments as they function today in many predominantly White universities. Highlighting the many great strengths in this area of studies and the challenges that still exist, especially for some of the smaller, under-funded programs and departments, we make the case that African American Studies is vital to the academy, that it is transformative for students, communities, and universities, and that it is eminently sustainable.

African American Studies is positioned today within the university system to contribute greatly to the overall mission of the academy. A few symbols from Akan culture and Ghanaians as a whole[8] remind us to move forward with a strong spirit of peace and determination:

1. *To value our rich heritage of wisdom and knowledge*
   Sankofa ("go back to fetch it") is a powerful reminder that it is necessary to learn from the past in order to build for the future. The symbol depicts a bird turning its head backward with its long beak facing its tail feathers, which represents (among several meanings) the idea that a person should collect all the data and wisdom of previous learning experiences to strengthen the quest for knowledge in the present and future. This most popular symbol represents reflection and vision, and captures an individual and collective sense of spirit and identity for people of African descent.

2. *To remind ourselves that, even if we are marginalized in some university systems, being small does not mean we are unable to fulfill our destiny as a discipline*
   The spiders' web (*Ananse Ntontan*) is a symbol of wisdom, creativity, and craftiness in the face of life's complexities. In Akan folklore, the spider demonstrates how something small can use its resources to survive and create something good from its ingenious design.

3. *To embrace our theoretical breadth and divergent paradigms as a discipline, recognizing our diverse points of view and our common purpose*
   Funtummireku-Dɛnkyɛmmireku is the popular Ghanaian mythical symbol of a two-headed crocodile with a single stomach. It is a symbol for unity in diversity. Its application includes the idea that even though members of a group are different, they can still achieve mutual goals, be unique and creative, and function as a collective.

4. *To prompt us that we need to hold on to what we study and then translate that knowledge into a better world*
   Mate Masie is a symbol indicating that what is heard has been understood and will be retained, therein representing an important part of listening to teaching and incorporating that wisdom into everyday life.

5. *To encourage us to be strong but not to be inattentive to the need to adapt to the twenty-first-century challenges for our discipline*

Nkyinkyin ("twisting") is a symbol for toughness and adaptability, reflecting the Akan people's admiration of the ability to withstand hardship and recognizing that a change of strategies is sometimes the best way to improve outcomes.

6. *To provoke in us a firm resolve and steadiness as we move our discipline forward*

   Tabono is a paddle used in a canoe. The symbol refers to how a steady paddle will inspire confidence and how, if the canoe is to stay afloat in difficult waters, the paddler will need to be persistent and strong.

NOTES

1. For a few examples, see W. E. B. Du Bois, *The Souls of Black Folk* (New York: Penguin Books 1989; first published 1903); and *The World and Africa: An Inquiry into the Part Which Africa has Played in World History* (New York: International Publishers, 1965). See also Stephanie Y. Evans, "Mary McLeod Bethune's Research Agenda: Thought Translated to Work," *African American Research Perspectives*, vol. 12 (2008), 2–39; James B. Stewart, "Social Science and Systematic Inquiry in Africana Studies," in *Afrocentric Traditions: Africana Studies*, Vol. 1, ed. J. Conyers, Jr. (London: Transaction Publishers, 2005); and "The Legacy of W. E. B. Du Bois for Contemporary Black Studies," *Journal of Negro Education* 53 (1984): 296–311; and Cheikh Anta Diop, *The African Origin of Civilization: Myth or Reality*, transl. Mercer Cook (New York: L. Hill, 1974).

2. See Perry A. Hall, *In the Vineyard: Working in African American Studies* (Knoxville, TN: The University of Tennessee Press, 1999).

3. Cornel West, *The Cornel West Reader* (New York: Basic Civitas Basic Books, 1999), 542.

4. Ronald W. Bailey, "Black Studies in the Third Millennium: Reflections on Six Ideas That Can Still (and Must) Change the World," *Souls* (Summer 2000), 88.

5. See Henry Louis Gates, Jr. and Manning Marable, "A Debate in Activism in Black Studies," in Manning Marable, ed., *Dispatches from the Ebony Tower: Intellectuals Confront the African American Experience* (New York: Columbia University Press, 2000), 186–91.

6. Manning Marable, *Beyond Black and White: Transforming African-American Politics* (London: Verso, 1995), 112.

7. See www.freethesf8.org.

8. W. Bruce Willis, *The Adinkra Dictionary: A Visual Primer on the Language of Adinkra* (Washington, DC: The Pyramid Complex, 1998).

PART I

History and Theoretical Perspectives in African American Studies

CHAPTER 2

African American Studies: Discourses and Paradigms

Perry A. Hall

University of North Carolina at Chapel Hill

BACKGROUND

African American Studies, like all academic disciplines, has been constituted from several paradigms or schools of thought evolving historically from specific intellectual and social contexts. The purpose of this
chapter is to show how a multiplicity of perspectives has developed in the
context of the creation of African American Studies and its maintenance
and development as an academic field. My task here is to frame those perspectives contextually among the many levels of confrontation and struggle
comprising and characterizing the social movement out of which the initiative for intellectual enterprise of African American Studies was impelled.
Reflecting the historical evolution of African American Studies, as well
as the current variation among Black Studies scholars and those in the
community in general, the multilayered nature of this struggle reflects
the variety of intellectual and ideological perspectives involved in creating
the field that has taken shape, as well as the variations in paradigms and
theoretical perspectives that have emerged to constitute the field.

African American Studies (originally called Black Studies) emerged as a
consequence of the quantum leap in the numbers of African Americans on
predominantly white, public, and private college and university campuses,
all of which resulted from the gains and pressures of the Black Freedom
Movement in the mid-1960s.[1] Their campus tenure was profoundly
shaped by important events that startled history and disrupted social order.
Bloody confrontations in Selma, Alabama eventually yielded the Voting
Rights Act, an historic victory that capped a phase of the Black Freedom

Movement while, in nearly the same timeframe, the violent deaths of Malcolm X, Martin Luther King, Jr., and Robert Kennedy, leaders and allies who helped inspire those historic mobilizations, suggested impending instability and social erosion. The Black Power and Black Arts Movements emerged in the midst of the major civil uprisings in Watts, Detroit, and more than a hundred other American cities. The Vietnam War escalated— as a military event, as a highly divisive social issue, and as a phenomenon affecting the course of the Black experience.

THE STRUGGLE FOR BLACK STUDIES: DISCOURSES ON RELEVANCE AND LEGITIMACY

In this context of disruption and activism, a confrontation of cultural sensibilities, political imperatives, and intellectual perspectives ensued, leading to the creation of African American Studies as an academic discipline. Certain recent attempts to document the early history of Black Studies characterize the motivations of the ensuing campus movements as "disillusionment" with the Civil Rights Movement. This obscures and oversimplifies the fact that the presence of these cohorts and the movements, and the changes they precipitated, resulted directly from the successes of the Civil Rights Movement and reflected its development to a new stage.[2] Any sense of "disillusionment" arguably stemmed more from the conditions black students found in the newly accessible integrated settings, and less from the movement that brought them there—a movement whose spirit, thrust, and tactics they embraced in subsequent efforts to transform those conditions.

These recent efforts to historicize the field are also notably clumsy in their characterization of various elements involved in the creation of the field. In particular, the most activist elements, students and activist scholars whose actions usually initiated program activities, are invariably tagged with the undefined labels of "nationalist" "separatist," or "political," and opposed binarily with programs and individuals characterized as more "academic" and more "savvy" about university standards and procedures.[3] Aside from implying that "nationalist" or "political" people couldn't also be "academic" or "savvy" (and that "academic" and "savvy" actors were not "political"), labeling these activists as "nationalist" or "separatist" obscures the epistemological basis of the confrontation, while conflating the multiplicity of ideological and intellectual perspectives represented in the emerging and evolving ideas of those students and activist scholars. Those students and scholars were the ones whose collective voice indicated the vacuum in educational practice that erased, silenced, and marginalized the histories and humanities of black peoples, as well as articulated the substance that would fill that void in the name of Black Studies.

These varying perspectives coalesced around the core insight that current knowledge production and transmission processes did not address, and were not "relevant to," the exigencies of black individuals and communities in that juncture. Black humanity was invisible, whether absent altogether or considered only in the marginalized, "othering" context of concerns peripheral to existing disciplines and practices. Activists used a variety of methods to press their struggle outward and create the space to establish Black Studies in academia, while an inward struggle ensued to define the nature and substance of the space. The circumstances through which these components were mediated varied dramatically in this context of tumultuous social change. At Cornell, black students (who had received threats from local vigilantes) were photographed for national magazine covers bearing rifles and ammunition belts.[4] Then, there was a host of situations that, while not involving the display of arms, were nearly as militant and bitter, such as the movements at San Francisco State and Harvard. In some places there were conferences similar to the one initiated by students at Yale in 1968, while many institutions, especially small liberal arts colleges, instituted courses in black history, literature, and other areas with little fanfare.[5] Characterizing programs originating in militant circumstances as "political," to separate them from those emerging in more moderated contexts, does not alter the underlying fact that the impetus—recognition or acceptance of the need for curricular alternatives for studies of black life—was fundamentally the same for all.

The academic establishment responded in complex ways, quelling or suppressing disruption, accommodating new approaches and ideas, and maintaining academic values and standards. These negotiations were always mediated and sometimes distorted by institutional, bureaucratic, and ideological politics; however, the battle to establish Black Studies in the academy was ultimately fought and won on intellectual and epistemological grounds. In those terms, the fundamental issue was how to determine what constitutes valid knowledge about the subject—the experiences, conditions, and aspirations of black folks. The very premise that there could be an intellectually valid "black perspective" on matters of knowledge and truth was a fundamental challenge to the epistemological foundations on which universities functioned. While questioned, even ridiculed, during the period of confrontation, it now seems evident that this challenge to the universalist contentions of establishment academics has endured and gained legitimacy, establishing an epistemological path followed by women, peoples of color, and others whose multicultural voices broaden conversations and notions of humanity, modernity, and progress.

The space—the beachhead—established in academia to develop this basic idea was housed and structured in various ways on campuses across the nation, depending on how other factors figured in the negotiations that produced them. Thus, while most colleges and universities added courses on Afro-American life and history to their curricula, and most made efforts to include blacks on their faculties and administrative staffs, the scope, depth, and form of these changes have varied greatly.[6] A great many institutions merely added a few courses in history or literature, while some formed programs by developing new courses and coordinating curricular activities in existing disciplines and departments.

BLACK STUDIES ON CAMPUS: DISCOURSES ON INCLUSION AND SELF-DEFINITION

During African American Studies' formational period, this approach—where the erasure of black humanity is addressed by "inclusion" or "integration" of studies concerning relevant aspects of black life within existing disciplines and canons of knowledge—was most likely to be favored by the university administrators and established academics, and this tendency was also reinforced in the funding objectives of outside agencies like the Ford Foundation, which attempted, as early as 1969, to influence the evolution of the field.[7] Not only did this approach require minimal programmatic or structural adjustment, it also required only minimal epistemological adjustment. As Ronald Taylor observed, this approach did not favor "the wholesale abandonment of conventional theoretical constructs, but the reformulation of those conceptual frameworks with the greatest potential for illuminating various aspects of the Black experience."[8] Canons and premises were certainly not questioned or restructured. Information was "included," "integrated" or "added." In an influential 1992 essay, James B. Stewart labeled this the "value-added" approach.[9] Far from seeking to define a new discipline or field, the approach views special courses on, say, black history and literature, theoretically at least, as temporary and provisional. This view in its extreme was articulated by Nathan Huggins, when he stated, "The question . . . is not whether English departments offer courses in Afro-American literature, but whether works by black authors are taught in courses on American literature."[10]

This "integrationist/inclusionist" framework has been the context for the work of some Black Studies scholars and much of the work about blacks that comes from traditional disciplines. Notwithstanding the preferences of academic and funding establishments, however oppositional, alternate views and approaches have endured and continue to influence the character and evolution of the field. In the confrontation/formation period, activists among students and scholars who challenged the legitimacy of this "inclusionist/integrationist" approach were likely to press for more autonomous structures, such as the Black Studies departments formed at Harvard, Indiana, and Ohio State universities, and the nearly self-contained Institute for Africana Studies at Cornell. In turn, those Black Studies proposals that envisioned departmental or autonomous structures were likely to encounter more resistance from the university establishment, and succeeded only when considerable pressure was brought to bear. Often such outcomes were the result of relatively militant confrontations, giving rise to the application of the labels "political" and "separatist" to describe these campaigns. (In more recent years, however, programs of all orientations across the nation have successfully achieved departmental status.)

EPISTEMOLOGICAL CHALLENGE: DISCOURSES ON OPPOSITION AND DECONSTRUCTION

Given the politically charged atmosphere, it is not surprising that the academy's resistance to departmental autonomy was expressed (and remembered) in terms of "intellectual standards" and "academic principles." However, the preoccupation with scholarly "integrity" (an alleged integrity surely tainted by the racist neglect and marginalization of black life around which activists mobilized) obscures the fact that the political struggles over structure, departmental control, tenure, academic credit, and other tools of academic authority had a legitimate epistemological basis. Some were indeed "separatist" in the political sense, in the various ways that term might operate in the modern and postmodern contexts. But the principal "separatism" that united the activist element was the virtual unanimity with which they rejected the possibility that knowledge relevant to "black liberation" could come from the biased disciplinary canons created from traditional Western epistemology. They were "separatist" in the same sense that early sociologists were separatists when they endeavored to create a new discipline in order to address the issues and concerns they shared.

Thus, although the discourse around African American Studies was often framed in terms of political ideology and/or organizational structure, it was in fact a set of underlying epistemological issues—issues of determining what (and who), in fact, constitutes valid knowledge about black people and black communities—that united the various groups of the Black Studies Movement who opposed the integrationist/inclusionist model. For them, the necessary "epistemic renovation" required a totally restructured analytical framework. Mere inclusionism and contributionism regarding the experiences and achievements of blacks were insufficient for these purposes. A wholesale disruption of Eurocentric "master-narratives" would be required.

While opposition was virtually unanimous among activists, no single alternative was advocated by all. The processes involved in developing frameworks, approaches, paradigms, and epistemological structures to replace, challenge or augment the standard inclusionist approach produced lively and creative dialogue among the fledgling discipline's adherents and practitioners, while they struggled at the same time for institutional stability and structural legitimacy within the larger academic world. Alternate intellectual approaches and paradigms were informed from various strains, mixtures, and combinations of nationalism/Pan-Africanism, Marxism/socialism, and feminism/Womanism. Fundamentally, however, the dialogue tended to be masculinist in tone and was more centered on the tensions generated by nationalist and Marxist "tendencies" in the proceedings and productions of formations like the National Council for Black Studies, the African Heritage Studies Association, the Institute of the Black World, and the Association for the Study of Afro-American Life and History, and through the pages of publications like *The Black Scholar*, *Negro Digest/Black World*, *The Journal of Black Studies*, the *Western Journal of Black Studies*, and the *Journal of Black Political Economy*.

Radical feminist discourse such as that generated among the National Black Feminist Organization and the Cohambee River Collective during the 1970s took place in relative isolation from formations and discourses that comprised the Black Studies Movement (though there was overlap), a fact that has continued to affect and reflect the relationship between Black

Studies and Black Women's Studies. One of the earliest introductory texts, *Introduction to Afro-American Studies*, was produced by a well-known Marxist collective in 1977. Among nationalist productions, Maulana Karenga's *Introduction to Black Studies* (first published 1983) was probably the most widely circulated introductory text to appear in this period. The pioneering anthology *All the Women Are White, All the Blacks Are Men, But Some of Us Are Brave: Black Women's Studies* (Gloria T. Hull et al.) also appeared in 1982, during this period of debate and contention.

Dialogue along this spectrum focused on the tasks involved in deconstructing the overarching white-dominated system, or superstructure, which influenced and shaped reality for all people, including their mental processes and ways of knowing. The shared objective was to replace the existing system of thought that conceived no alternatives to the marginalization, or "othering," of black life-forces and activities, which allowed no possibility of new actualization, no expression of human potential. A new system of thought capable of unraveling the racist fabric of conventional Euro-American thought and ideology would have to be as forceful and compelling as the dominant Eurocentric mode. Around this shared goal, disparate factions forged a level of operational unity and discourse which has led to the competing intellectual frameworks that comprise the terrain of African American Studies today.

BLACK MARXISM AND BLACK NATIONALISM: DISCOURSES ON RACE AND CLASS

Marxism offered an alternative but equally powerful and well-developed system of thought informed by a vision of social transformation that allowed for the elevation of black humanity, along with that of the downtrodden workers of the world. A class-based political economy perspective to explain the emergence of slavery and racism corrected the conventional approach of social science disciplines, which in effect "expunges from the collective intellectual memory the major pathology of the American political economy as if it never existed" and thus fails "to clarify the issues which embody the essential description and explanation of how the system of capitalist political economy works itself out in the real world."[11] The language and methods of Marxist, class-based inquiry proclaimed a "scientific" level of precision and clarity which was often persuasive in framing and highlighting the historical and structural contexts of black existences and exigencies. A scheme for periodization of the African American historical experience developed by Marxists, specifically the Marxist collective known as Peoples College, has proved useful and enduring across many of the content areas comprising African American Studies as the field has matured.[12] For these reasons Marxist and socialist approaches became significantly influential in this discourse.

The value of Marxism, a system capable of both illuminating issues of race and class, and of opposing the traditional Eurocentric tendency to marginalize and pathologize blackness, was often acknowledged, even admiringly, by the nationalist camp, who were forced to admit that nationalist thought, with its sometimes hazy terms of discourse, "has not been as structured as it should have been."[13] There has even been a tendency toward stylistic appropriation of Marxist rhetoric, symbols, and concepts (for example, the notion that Pan-Africanism is the "highest form" of nationalism, mirroring the Marxist-Leninist assertion that imperialism is the "highest form" of capitalism[14]) as nationalist/Pan-Africanists sought to formulate frameworks that, like Marxism, could provide a methodology, a "systematicity," a disciplined and "scientific" approach that might potentially organize and unify a system of thought as effective in conceptualizing a liberated black humanity as the dominant system was in rationalizing its negation. While appropriating Marxist rhetoric to examine race and class, the terms were often reversed, with race rather than class becoming the "fundamental contradiction" that "scientific socialism" should address in building black nationalism and Pan-Africanism. Thus, an early articulation of "Systematic Nationalism" states:

> As Marx and Engels had done for the economically oppressed,
> Garvey and Muhammad did for the racially oppressed. That is
> why the systematic nationalist says socialism to deal with class
> contradictions; nationalism to deal with race contradictions.[15]

As a conceptual and analytical framework Marxism was, and remains, valuable in illuminating the real nature of "race relations" in the modern world. On the other hand, tendencies among some strains of Marxist discourse toward materialist determinism subordinated cultural and racial issues that were basic to the definition of Black Studies as a body of knowledge and to its formation as a field of study. Rejection of materialist tendencies toward minimizing the importance of "African" and "black" spiritual, cultural, and aesthetic matrices shaping the African American experience forced Marxists in the Black Studies Movement to continually rethink and restructure their theoretical statements on black culture. They also had to reconsider the importance of cultural phenomena in conceptualizing African American social cohesion. Furthermore, the Marxian ideal of cross-race working-class unity contradicted the naked reality of white working-class racism and conservatism. These incongruities reflected the more basic fact that any application of Marxian principles in this area had to embrace the motivation that brought a critical mass of African American students to assert themselves when they entered mainstream campuses and ignited the original campus confrontation in the 1960s.

So, while the Black Studies Movement was itself a vehicle for cultural nationalist sentiment, the oppositional standpoint of the Black Studies Movement, the presence of Marxists, and the sense of revolutionary consciousness that linked some local and international struggles were factors that pushed the movement's nationalism to the left at the outset in the late 1960s. During the 1970s, revolutionary struggles in Africa, the Caribbean, and elsewhere in the Third World linked easily with domestic radical and revolutionary sentiments, ideas, and movements creating much ground for commonality among Black Studies activists. For example, the movement led by Amical Cabral in Guinea provided a program that all sides could support in a way that illuminated principles and sensibilities emphasized by each. As noted by Phil Hutchings, reporting on the African Liberation Support Movement conference in 1974:

> Cultural nationalists in the movement like the attention Cabral gave to culture and identity in the national liberation movement. Black Marxists admire his dialectical and historical materialist approach to the problems of Guinea and struggle in general. And then there are those who like Cabral because he was a black man leading a successful armed struggle against Western colonialism in Africa.[16]

In this period, most who considered themselves nationalists agreed with Karenga that "it must be obvious to us by now that capitalism cannot and will not provide for us . . . that we of necessity [must] look further to the left to socialism."[17] And while a few nationalists found fault with capitalism only because it had not yet worked satisfactorily for them, most agreed with Marxist Tony Thomas's statement: "black liberation and socialism are directly linked, as are racism and capitalism . . ."[18]

THE AFROCENTRIC PARADIGM: DISCOURSES ON OWNERSHIP AND ORIGIN

Through the 1980s, however, international revolutionary fronts were undermined or derailed; radical and leftist voices were muted (for an analysis of the impact of leftist-nationalist dialogue, see Cedric Johnson's 2003 critique[19]), and the need for black "ownership," symbolic if not real, amid a rising conservative tide, became pronounced. In terms of Black Studies discourses, this need translated to a commitment to complete freedom from European or "white" categories of thought and analysis. Something as broad and pervasive as the dominant Euro-American modes of thought required a comparably broad and pervasive counter-discourse that reflected images of black humanity (not another European-derived system of thought). So, although radical Marxist critiques were prominent in shaping the dialogue during the 1970s and early 1980s, the later 1980s saw the rise of the form of cultural nationalism known as Afrocentrism. ("Afrocentricity" is the term preferred by Molefi Kete Asante, articulator of the most well-known strain; "Africentricity," "Afracentricity," "African-Centered," and "Africology" are embraced by others for this trend). With broad support among Black Studies scholars, Afrocentric perspectives have developed from some of the movement's activist founders. The appearance of Karenga's *Introduction to Black Studies* in 1982 represented a substantial step in the emergence of an Afrocentric paradigm shaped to address the epistemological issues raised while Black Studies evolved from a movement to an institutionalized field of inquiry.[20] The emergence of the first and largest Black Studies PhD program at Temple University under the leadership of Asante was another landmark for the Black Studies Movement.

Asante has subsequently emerged as a natural spokesperson, often representing the Afrocentric perspective. For example, during the 1990s debates about multiculturalism in education, two things stood out through the body of this work. First is a central concern with language as a linchpin in the construction of knowledge, meaning, identity, and culture. Second is the continual reference to African ideas, cultures, and histories as backdrops to the alternative construction of knowledge that emerges as Afrocentricity. Ultimately, this thrust focuses on the reclamation of the histories, philosophies, and monuments of dynastic Egypt (Kemet) as a cornerstone on which the project is to construct an Afrocentric worldview with as much historical depth and cultural legitimacy as Eurocentrism.

Claiming Egypt as a "classical African civilization," Afrocentric historiography connects the glory, wisdom, and knowledge of Egypt to the development of the rest of Africa. This counters, or deconstructs, ideologically distorted Western historiographies that either cut classical Egypt away from the roots of Western civilization and/or cut Egypt itself away from Africa in terms of racial characteristics and cultural and historical ties. Moreover, in this restored historiography it is Egypt rather than Greece and Rome that stands as the source of "high culture" and of Western civilization itself.

Clearly, the body of knowledge and information emphasized and highlighted by Afrocentrism has been essential in the reconstruction of intellectual perspectives and cultural sensibilities that challenge Eurocentric chauvinism, while affirming the historical and cultural legitimacy of blacks—routinely referred to as "without history" and "without culture" in conventional discourses. Afrocentrism's significant contribution has been its fundamental deconstructive drive toward dismantling prevailing Eurocentric bias, seminal in the historical construction of Western social science and aesthetic studies, which have regularly distorted, marginalized, or negated the agency and humanity of blacks and all marginalized "others." Aspiring to fill the need for development of paradigms free of this burden, forms of this "Afrocentric perspective" have been widely embraced as an "antidote" to the biases of Eurocentrism, which are among the many odious legacies of Western imperialism.

For these and other reasons, Afrocentricity emerged during the 1980s as the most visible alternative to the "integrationist" paradigm while aspiring to be embraced as the central theoretical perspective around which to organize the discipline. Indeed, a presumption developed, both inside and outside the field, that Afrocentricity and African-American Studies were synonymous. For several years in the late 1980s, for example, the terms "Afrocentricity" and "Afrocentric" were used to frame the theme of the National Council for Black Studies annual conference. However, while the deconstructive initiatives of the Afrocentric paradigm may be necessary, its reconceptualizations have not been sufficient in constituting a viable African American Studies disciplinary matrix that accounts for the full range of perspectives that have developed to constitute the field. The provocative contributions of Afrocentrists certainly have not come without controversy; some aspects have been critically questioned. The foregrounded emphasis on reconceptualizing the past and renaming the present is privileged over a concrete focus on those disruptions and limiting structures against which descendants of Africa have historically struggled. These potential weaknesses become self-reifying barriers between Afrocentrists, other Black Studies scholars, and other fields of study and areas of praxis.

In fact, Afrocentrism as a theoretical orientation has functioned in a context—normative for academic disciplines—where differing schools of thought coexist which are in some ways competitive with and in some ways complementary to one another. As one stream of thought among several that interact synergistically within the self-refining "black/Africana Studies disciplinary matrix," James B. Stewart (referencing terms developed by Thomas Kuhn) described how Afrocentrism's possible errors and distortions occur in context with a continuous stream of critical discourse, maximizing the possibility that useful insights will be produced in the process.[21] In other words, the presence of alternate perspectives promotes dialogue, which in turn promotes clarity, within the discipline. The prejudices, erasures, and silences of any perspective can be challenged or augmented from other perspectives in the process of creating greater clarity. Thus, Afrocentrism's inadequacies regarding class, gender, and static conceptions of culture, among other issues, have generated critical reflections from others who have been part of the activist discourse.

GENDER AND WOMEN'S STUDIES: DISCOURSES ON ERASURES AND SILENCES

It may be noted, however, that feminist perspectives have had vexed receptions, and gender issues have posed a particularly significant challenge in this pattern of discursive evolution. Women have been visible, indeed prominent, among Black Studies' intellectual and organizational leaders, and women and gender-related issues have always been among those addressed in the formations and publications associated with the field. Feminist perspectives, sometimes defined as "Womanist" to distinguish them from white feminists' ideological frameworks, remain visible within the field. For some feminists, however, it would appear that little alteration of the overall masculinist tone of the discourse has occurred. The founding of the National Black Feminist Organization (NBFO) in 1973 and the Cohambee River Collective in 1974 reflects the fact that feminist voices seeking to decenter the masculinist focus of Black Studies Movement discourse (and social and cultural commentary among blacks generally) and the focus on issues affecting black women needed to create venues and sites, apart from those comprising the Black Studies Movement. When Michele Wallace, a founding member of the NBFO, critiqued masculinist orthodoxy in civil rights formations and movements in *Black Macho and the Myth of the Superwoman*,[22] her views were marginalized, sometimes demonized, as counterproductive to "race" progress, complicit with forces that "endangered" the existence of black men and foils of the white Women's Movement. As part of this trend of separate sites for black feminist discourse, the pioneering 1982 Black Women's Studies anthology *All the Women Are White, All the Blacks Are Men, But Some of Us Are Brave: Black Women's Studies*, which embraced the Cohambee River Collective's "Black Feminist Statement" as its second selection, was a project whose support derived from feminist and Women's Studies resources.

Microcosmically, the emergence of issues related to gender, Black Women's Studies, and black feminism within and alongside the Black Studies Movement reflects the fact that black women's perspectives in particular, and gender issues in general, were subject to the same constraints, ambivalences, and ambiguities in conjunction with the Black Studies Movement that they have historically faced in the larger movements for black and women's equality. The creatively constructed anthology title suggests that black women in academia experienced great difficulty accessing channels for voicing their concerns as black women within either the Black or the Women's Studies' Movements and, like black women aspiring to leadership roles historically, had to perform singular acts of self-assertion to erase their invisibility. As Deborah King explains, "It is precisely those differences between blacks and women, between black men and black women, between black women and white women that are crucial to understanding the nature of black womanhood."[23]

The emergence of a distinct Black Women's Studies project has been analogous, in terms of raising new issues of perspective, validity, and authenticity, to the historic confrontation that inaugurated Black Studies as a distinct field of study. The embedded procedures, customs, and habits of thought that have led to the exclusion, marginalization and neglect of issues uniquely affecting black women have continued to sustain a separate Black Women's Studies initiative. Much of the initiative in shaping Black Women's Studies discourse has been taken by literary scholars, following the influence of Nellie McKay, Barbara Christian, Gloria Hull, and Claudia Tate, among others.[24] However, the strong imperative remains to challenge and balance masculinist biases in the field of African American

Studies itself. For example, Deborah King noted the manner in which selective presentation of issues (e.g., school drop-out rates, imprisonment rates, homicide rates, college attendance) suggests that the problems of black communities focus on the issue of the "decimation of the black male." As a result, she argues, "we learn that in the current conceptualization black women are either: (1) invisible, (2) advantaged, or (3) victimizers."[25] Meanwhile, issues especially affecting black women—domestic abuse, sexual assault, impoverished single-parent families, insensitive welfare policies, AIDS as a leading cause of death—are not necessarily seen as "race" problems in a comparable way.

King and Patricia Hill Collins are both social scientists who have worked toward developing a theoretical model for the study of gender issues. In addition, bell hooks' work is guided by the postmodern cultural studies paradigm that incorporates both social and literary studies.[26] A body of theory has developed from the work of such black feminist scholars that locates black women's experiences in a hub where race, class, and gender converge, like spokes in a wheel of social constructions, to shape the particulars of black women's lives. Moreover, these uniquely black feminist voices consistently point to the inextricable intersectionality of all these forms of oppression and to the necessity of addressing all dimensions of human oppression. As such, this body of theory particularizes a "black women's standpoint epistemology" at the same time that it universalizes black women's struggle as the epitome of the human struggle for freedom, dignity, and fulfillment.

CONTINUITY AND CHANGE: DISCOURSES ON TRANSFORMATION

The foci on interrelationships and complexities that these feminisms embrace are shared within a broader discourse in the field which, like Afrocentrists, is concerned with altering conventional canons and frameworks of knowledge production but also considers the dynamic relationships among cultural and structural factors that have continually transformed the experiences, identities, and communities of black peoples. While deconstructing conventional paradigms, these scholars remain cautiously aware that the moment we free our minds from previous conceptual prisons is precisely the moment when we are most vulnerable to new errors. Any new premises, new paradigms, and new perspectives must be scrutinized from the same "center" that led us, in the first instance, to challenge the imposed Eurocentric conceptual constructs. "Transformationist" is a term that has been used by this writer to refer to a range of alternative perspectives that maintain critical scrutiny of both the conventional epistemology of the "integrationist/inclusionist" approach and the emergent Afrocentrist alternative.[27] From this perspective, relevant Afrocentric insights and sensibilities are seen through a lens that clarifies their interaction, or transformation, in the context of more traditional Western forms and structures.[28] Therefore, in seeking alternative frameworks to establish and legitimate black perspectives, transformationists have been concerned to locate them in an inclusive human universe, to address the challenge of capturing the sometimes complex interplay of the particular and the universal, the local and the global, the struggle for both inclusion and self-definition, that characterizes aspects of black life and culture.

In this regard, the work and legacy of W. E. B. Du Bois has been foundational and a dominant guide in the task of disentangling and clarifying the complexities and contradictions in the variety of lived experiences among African Americans. Pervasive reference to the "double-consciousness" that Du Bois indicated forms African American self-awareness suggests that it is perhaps the perspective of "doubleness" or "duality" (and eventually other forms of multiple consciousness) in affairs involving black social, cultural, and political reality that most clearly distinguishes this alternative approach from others.[29] Manning Marable, for instance, notes, "The cultural orientation of the transformative vision is neither 'integrationist' nor 'nationalist.' It recognizes the enduring validity of the 'double-consciousness' formulation of W. E. B. Du Bois nearly a century ago."[30] In addition to Du Bois, precepts of this alternate paradigm are drawn from the radical tradition of black intellectual thought provided by such past thinkers as Walter Rodney, Eric Williams, C. L. R. James, and Frantz Fanon, whose work in each instance incorporates Afrocentric insights regarding the original, ancient or classical history, culture, and peoples of Africa within an analytical framework that also addresses 500 years of global transformation that created the postmodern world; a world in which Africa itself has been unalterably changed and its peoples dispersed.[31]

A key premise of this discourse is that any recovery of classical African culture and history does not negate the need to study and understand the rest of the world and the transformations those cultures and peoples have endured. The transformationist approach connects and contextualizes classical and contemporary African and African American experiences to the wider, global, human experiences, as Africa and its descendants, along with most of the rest of the world, have been transformed with the expansion of Eurocentric cultural, economic, and political systems to positions of global dominance. Building on this radical strain, the transformationist theoretical perspective has thus inherited some of the Marxian focus on economic, social, and structural factors. There is common acknowledgment that the expropriation of the technologies of destruction, production, and domination, the growth of colonial empires, the role of the slave trade, and the rewriting of history and science in service of the expansion of European imperialism define the legacy and impact of racism in the modern world, as well as the full context of critical issues, conditions, and problems that require comprehension. Work in African American Studies that has fused aspects and standpoints of black particularity, incorporating class, politics, gender, culture, and other reference points, along with structural factors and dynamics, follow from the radical scholarship of Cedric Robinson and Angela Y. Davis, among others, and is reflected across a range of contemporary work among scholars in the field.[32]

GLOBAL MODERNITY AND THE FUTURE:
DISCOURSES ON REPRODUCING THE FIELD

Fiscal strains and persistent institutional hostility notwithstanding, African American Studies experienced consolidation and a kind of resurgence in the 1990s and 2000s, when the full-fledged development of graduate-level studies emerged to train future scholars and perpetuate the field and its various schools of thought and, thus, entered the twenty-first century as a firmly established yet still fledgling discipline. While there are only eight PhD programs, a disproportionate number are in prominent and highly ranked private and public universities, including Berkeley, Harvard, Indiana, Massachusetts, Michigan State, Northwestern, Temple, and Yale, while the twenty-one Master's degree programs include Columbia, Cornell, Indiana, NYU, Ohio State, Syracuse, SUNY-Albany, UCLA, and Wisconsin. One might infer from this trend that prominent scholars and faculties are increasingly willing to combine their commitment to African American Studies as a distinct field with a determination to make it a fully functioning enterprise at these major research institutions, a goal that encompasses teaching and working with graduate students and training new scholars to carry on the process.

At Temple, where the first doctoral program began in 1988, the Afrocentric approach, seeking clear demarcation from other disciplines or paradigms, is dominant, if not hegemonic. As recently as 2006 Asante maintained,

> Afrocentricity is fundamental to the discipline as a critical theory. The locus of our work is neither gender as in women's studies nor class as in Marxist studies nor sexual preference as in queer studies but the emancipation of African knowledge and people from the hegemonic ideology of White racial domination. This does not mean that our analyses are not tempered and informed by our understanding, examination, and appreciation of gender, class, and sexual issues but rather that gender, class, and sexual issues might be more definitively interrogated in other disciplines.[33]

The inclusionist/integrationist approach that pairs or blends African American Studies with established disciplines endures at the doctoral level in separate iterations at Yale, where it has been most visibly modeled, and Harvard, where cultural studies paradigms are dominant. At Massachusetts, a program focused on the black experience in the United States bears the name of Du Bois and seeks to provide a setting where the rich potential of his legacy can be developed. Programs at Berkeley, Northwestern, and Indiana are framed by the concept of Diaspora and Diaspora Studies, reflecting how the multiple forces and changes referred to as "globalization" and an evolving discourse on "race" and its construction in the globalized twenty-first century have occupied scholars in African and African American Studies. In this trend the basis is being laid for a paradigm that deconstructs the historical separations between African Studies and Black (Africana/African American) Studies and unites scholars in those fields around a discourse that frames the global emergence of systems of modernity to connect the histories of Africa's descendants, a paradigm that disrupts conventional narratives of Western development by decentering the hegemonic Eurocentric approaches to knowledge production.

Thus, as dialogue and development have continued among proponents of the field's various perspectives—amid ongoing debates about post-modernism, multiculturalism, and the various impacts and implications of an emerging global culture—new configurations of human reality and possibility have emerged for Black Studies scholars to investigate and comprehend. Divisions between classes and generations among black communities which emerged in the 1970s continue to strain conceptions of black unity and collective agency. Discussions of identity and culture have expanded to incorporate the parameter of sexuality or sexual orientation along with race, class, and gender, among elements of construction and analysis.[34] New patterns of migration, communication, and interaction have complicated perceptions and relations among Afro-diasporic populations in the US national arena, as well as on the global stage. These are among the issues that shape the current field of discourse in which African American Studies scholars work, engaging, incorporating, developing, and synthesizing new ideas, concerns, and imperatives, constructing the role of the African American Studies scholar, while developing the concepts, capabilities, and structures to institutionalize and perpetuate it.

NOTES

1. See Marvin W. Peterson et al., *Black Students on White Campuses: The Impacts of Increased Black Enrollments* (Ann Arbor, MI: Institute for Social Research, University of Michigan, 1978), 31–7.
2. Fabio Rojas, *From Black Power to Black Studies: How a Radical Social Movement Became an Academic Discipline* (Baltimore, MD: Johns Hopkins University Press, 2007); Noliwe M. Rooks, *White Money/Black Power: The Surprising History of African American Studies and the Crisis of Race in Higher Education* (Boston, MA: Beacon Press, 2006).
3. "Black studies programs survived when they resonated with the culture of higher education. Other forms of black studies—such as 'inner-city studies' or nationalist black studies—failed because they were incompatible with the beliefs about what constituted legitimate teaching and research" (Rojas, *From Black Power to Black Studies*, 13). Little attention is given to how beliefs about legitimate knowledge were changed by "nationalists" and others who challenged the terms by which legitimacy was determined.
4. Steve Carr's Pulitzer Prize-winning photograph emblazoned the May 5, 1969 cover of *Newsweek*.
5. Nathan Huggins, *Afro-American Studies: Report to the Ford Foundation* (New York: Ford Foundation, 1985), 9.
6. Huggins, *Afro-American Studies*, 19.
7. See Rojas, *Black Power to Black Studies*, 130–66; also Rooks, *White Money/Black Power*, especially chapters 1 and 4.
8. Ronald L. Taylor, "The Study of Black People: A Survey of Empirical and Theoretical Models," *Urban Research Review*, vol. 2, no. 2 (1987); reprinted in Talmadge Anderson, *Black Studies: Theory, Method, and Cultural Perspectives* (Pullman, WA: Washington State University Press, 1990).

9. James B. Stewart, "Reaching for Higher Ground: Toward an Understanding of Black/Africana Studies," *The Afrocentric Scholar* (May 1992), 6.
10. Huggins, *Afro-American Studies: Report to the Ford Foundation*, 62.
11. Quoted in Gerald A. McWorter and Ronald Bailey, "Black Studies Curriculum Development in the 1980s: Its Patterns and History," *Black Scholar*, vol. 15, no. 2 (March/April 1984), 18–31.
12. Abdul Alkalimat and associates, *Introduction to Afro-American Studies* (Chicago: Peoples College Press, 1977).
13. Molefi Kete Asante, "Systematic Nationalism," *Journal of Black Studies*, vol. 9, no. 1 (September 1978), 118.
14. See, e.g., Mary Frances Berry and John W. Blassingame, *Long Memory: The Black Experience in America* (New York: Oxford University Press, 1982), 382.
15. Asante, "Systematic Nationalism," 123.
16. Phil Hutchings, "Report on the ALSC National Conference," *The Black Scholar*, vol. 5, no. 10 (July/August 1974), 51.
17. Maulana Ron Karenga, "Which Road: Nationalism, Pan-Africanism, Socialism?" *Black Scholar*, vol. 6, no. 2 (October 1974), 27.
18. Tony Thomas, "Black Nationalism and Confused Marxists," *Black Scholar*, vol. 4, no. 1 (September 1972), 47.
19. Cedric Johnson, "From Popular Anti-Imperialism to Sectarianism: The African Liberation Support Committee and Black Power Radicals," *New Political Science*, vol. 25, no. 4 (December 2003), 477–507.
20. Maulana Karenga, *Introduction to Black Studies* (Los Angeles, CA: Kawaida Publications, 1982).
21. Stewart, "Reaching for Higher Ground," 45. For full discussion of Kuhnian ideas regarding the phenomenon of "paradigm shift," see Thomas S. Kuhn, *The Structure of Scientific Revolutions* (Chicago: University of Chicago Press, 1962).
22. Michele Wallace, *Black Macho and the Myth of the Superwoman* (New York: Dial Press, 1979).
23. Deborah King, "Multiple Jeopardy, Multiple Consciousness: The Context of Black Feminist Ideology," *Signs: A Journal Of Women In Culture And Society*, vol. 14, no. 1 (Fall 1988), 42–72.
24. Beverly Guy-Sheftall, "Nellie Mckay and the Trajectory of Black Women's Studies," *African American Review*, vol. 40, no. 1 (2006), 20–1.
25. Deborah King, "Unraveling Fabric, Missing the Beat: Class and Gender in Afro-American Social Issues," *Selected Papers from the Wisconsin Conference on Afro-American Studies in the Twenty-First Century* (April 18–20, 1991), in *The Black Scholar*, vol. 22, no. 3 (Summer 1992), 36–48.
26. Patricia Hill Collins, *Black Feminist Thought: Knowledge, Consciousness, and the Politics of Empowerment: Perspectives on Gender*, Vol. 2 (Boston, MA: Unwin Hyman, 1990); bell hooks, *Talking Back: Thinking Feminist, Thinking Black* (Boston, MA: South End Press, 1989).
27. These terms also align closely with those employed in Marable's analysis of ideological and intellectual trends among black leadership and intelligentsia. Here he uses the terms "inclusionist," "nationalist/Afrocentrist" and "transformationist" to

describe "three overlapping, strategic visions about the nature of the contemporary political economy, the meaning of 'race' in the post-Civil Rights era, and what is to be done in the next century to address the problems of black people and to construct a multicultural democracy." Manning Marable, 'The Divided Mind of Black America: Racial Ideologies and the Urban Crisis." Paper presented at the "Race Matters: Black Americans, U.S. Terrain Conference," sponsored by the American Studies and Afro-American Studies Programs of Columbia University, April 30, 1994.

28. Perry A. Hall, "Paradigms in Black Studies," in Delores P. Aldridge and Carlene Young, eds., *Out of the Revolution: The Development of Africana Studies* (Lanham, MD: Lexington Books, 2000), 25–38.

29. W. E. B. Du Bois, *The Souls of Black Folk* (New York: Signet Books, [1903] 1982), 45.

30. Marable, "The Divided Mind of Black America."

31. Walter Rodney, *How Europe Underdeveloped Africa* (Washington, DC: Howard University Press, 1974); Eric Williams. *Capitalism and Slavery* (Chapel Hill, NC: University of North Carolina Press, 1944); C. L. R. James, *The Black Jacobins: Toussaint L'Ouverture and the San Domingo Revolution* (New York: The Dial Press, 1938); Frantz Fanon, *Black Skin, White Masks*, English trans. (New York: Grove Press, 1967; first published as *Peau noire, masques blancs*); and *Wretched of the Earth* (New York: Grove Press, 1968).

32. Including Manning Marable, Gerald Horne, Robin D. G. Kelley, Joy James, Barbara Ransby, Sundiata Cha-Jua, Nikhil Pal Singh, and James B. Stewart.

33. Molefi Kete Asante, "A Discourse on Black Studies: Liberating the Study of African People in the Western Academy," *Journal of Black Studies*, vol. 36, no. 5 (May 2006), 646–62.

34. Dwight A. McBride, "Toward the New Black Studies," *Journal of Black Studies*, vol. 37, no. 3 (January 2007), 428–44.

CHAPTER 3

Afrocentricity and Africology: Theory and Practice in the Discipline

Molefi Kete Asante

Temple University

A frocentricity is a philosophical paradigm that emphasizes the centrality and agency of the African person within an historical and cultural context. As such, it is a rejection of the historic marginality and racial alterity often expressed in the ordinary paradigm of European racial domination. What is more, Afrocentrists articulate a counter-hegemonic view that questions epistemological ideas that are simply rooted in the cultural experiences of Europe and are applied to Africans (or others) as if they are universal principles.[1] This may be discovered in the type of language, art forms, expressive styles, arguments, economic or social ideas within an interactive situation. Thus, the Afrocentric idea is critical to any behavioral activity that involves Africans or people of African descent.

In the field of African American Studies (or Africology), Afrocentricity holds a dominant paradigmatic place because it seeks to add substance to the idea of a black perspective on facts, events, texts, personalities, historical records, and behavioral situations. Thus, it is the critical turn that is essential for an intellectual to be fully committed to making a difference in the analysis and interpretation of situations involving people of African descent.[2]

Necessitated by the conditions of history that have seen Africans moved off cultural, expressive, philosophical, and religious terms, the Afrocentric idea in education seeks to reposition Africans at the center of our own historical experiences rather than on the margins of European experiences. This is a philosophical turn that is essential for the subject place of Africans as agents within the discipline called variously Black Studies, African American Studies or Africology. If Africans are not subjects in their own situation, then the old patterns of marginality adhere and consequently the interpretation cannot be authentic; it can only be subject to object, but never subject to subject. This can occur whether the viewer/researcher is black, Asian, Latino, or white so long as the active researcher operates from a Eurocentric base.

In its attempt to shift discourse about African phenomena from ideas founded in European constructs to a more centered perspective, Afrocentricity announces itself as a form of anti-racist, anti-patriarchal, and anti-sexist ideology that is new, innovative, challenging, and capable of creating exciting ways to acquire and express knowledge. The denial of the exploitative expression of race, gender, and class often found in older constructions of knowledge is at once controversial and a part of the evolving process of paradigmatic development. Afrocentricity confronts this marginality of Africans and critiques European patriarchy and sexism as a part of the baggage of the hegemonic tendencies frequently found in Western social and behavioral sciences.

SHIFTING THE WEIGHT

Because Afrocentricity is an intellectual perspective seeking the centrality of African people and phenomena in the interpretation of data, Maulana Karenga, a major figure in the Afrocentric Movement, was able to write that "it is a quality of thought that is rooted in the cultural image and human interest of African people."[3] Among the early adherents of the Afrocentric idea were Kariamu Welsh, C. T. Keto, Linda James Myers, J. A. Sofola, and others. Afrocentricity developed almost parallel to the Black Psychology Movement and there has always existed a critical synthesis between them. Thus, the names of Charles White, Bobby Wright, Amos Wilson, Na'im Akbar, Kobi Kambon, Wade Nobles, Patricia Newton, and others can be added to the list of compatriots in the idea that Africans should speak in their own authentic voices.[4] African American scholars trained in political science and sociology, such as Leonard Jeffries, Tony Martin, Vivian Gordon, James Turner, Marimba Ani, and Charshee McIntyre, greatly influenced by the works of Yosef Ben-Jochannon, Chancellor Williams, and John Henrik Clarke, supported the process of seeking a non-European way to conceptualize the African experience.[5]

On the other hand, Afrocentricity finds its inspirational source in the Kawaida philosophy's long-standing concern that the cultural crisis is a defining characteristic of twentieth-century African reality in the Diaspora, as the nationality crisis is the principal issue on the African continent. Afrocentricity sought to address these crises by repositioning the African person and African reality from the margins of European thought, attitude, and doctrines, to a centered, and therefore positively *located*, place within the realm of science and culture.

Afrocentricity finds its grounding in the intellectual and activist precursors who first suggested culture as a critical corrective to a displaced agency among Africans. Recognizing that Africans in the Diaspora had been deliberately de-cultured and made to accept the conqueror's codes of conduct and modes of behavior, the Afrocentrist discovered that the interpretative and theoretical grounds had also been moved. Thus, synthesizing the best of Alexander Crummell, Martin Delany, Edward Wilmot Blyden, Marcus Garvey, Paul Robeson, Anna Julia Cooper, Ida B. Wells-Barnett, Larry Neal, Carter G. Woodson, Willie Abraham, Frantz Fanon, Malcolm X, Cheikh Anta Diop, and W. E. B. Du Bois, Afrocentrists project an innovation in criticism and interpretation that relies on African centeredness.

It is, therefore, as Mazama contends, a paradigm, a framework, and a dynamic.[6] However, it is not a worldview and should not be confused with Africanity, which is essentially the way African people—any African people—live according to customs, traditions, and mores of their society. One can be born in Africa, follow African styles and modes of living, and practice African religion and not be Afrocentric; to be Afrocentric one has to have a self-conscious awareness of the need for centering. Thus, those individuals who live in Africa and recognize the decentering of their minds because of European colonization may self-consciously choose to be demonstratively in tune with their own agency. If so, this becomes a revolutionary act of will that cannot be achieved merely by wearing African clothes or having an African name.

SCHOOLS OF THOUGHT

On the continent of Africa, Chinweizu, Ngugi wa Thiong'o, J. A. Sofola, M. Bilolo, T. Obenga, and Aboubacry Moussa Lam have been keen activists in the movement to recenter Africans in their own historical and social terms. In the United States and the Caribbean, the work of Terry Kershaw, Mekada Graham, Jerome Schiele, Walter Rodney, Leachim Semaj, Danjuma Modupe, Kwame Nantambu, Ama Mazama, Errol Henderson,

Nah Dove, Marimba Ani, Theophile Obenga, and Oba T'shaka have been inspiring in defining the nature of the Afrocentric school of thought. The principal motive behind their intellectual works seems to have been the use of knowledge for the cultural, social, political, and economic transformation of African people by suggesting the necessity for a recentering of African minds in a way that brings about a liberating consciousness. Indeed, Afrocentrists argue that there could be no social or economic struggle that would make sense if African people remained enamored with the philosophical, linguistic, and intellectual positions of white hegemonic nationalism as it relates to Africa and African people. At base, therefore, the intellectual work of the Afrocentric school of thought is a political one in the sense that all social knowledge has a political purpose.[7] No one constructs or writes about repositioning and recentering merely for the sake of self-indulgence; none could afford to do so because African dispossession in material and cultural terms appears so great and the displacing myths so pervasive that simply to watch the process of African *peripheralization* is to acquiesce in African decentering.

The Afrocentrist contends that passion can never be a substitute for argument, as argument should not be a substitute for passion. Afrocentric intellectuals may disagree over the finer points of interpretation and some facts, but the overall project of relocation and reorientation of African action and data has been the rational constant in all Afrocentric work.

Interest in African people is not sufficient for one's work to be called "Afrocentric." Indeed Afrocentricity is not merely the discussion of African and African American issues, history, politics, or consciousness; any one can discuss these issues and yet not be an Afrocentrist. Furthermore, it is not a perspective based on skin color or biology and should not be confused with melanist theories, which existed before Afrocentricity and which tend to be based on biological determinism. In this connection, it should be pointed out that Afrocentrists usually refer to their field as Afrocentricity not Afrocentrism, since the latter term has been used by opponents of the Afrocentric idea to define a "religious" movement based on an essentialist paradigm which Afrocentricity is not.

Danjuma Modupe has posited *agency, centeredness, psychic integrity,* and *cultural fidelity* as the minimum four theoretical constructs necessary for a work to be called Afrocentric.[8] Thus, what is clear is that neither a discussion of the Nile Valley civilizations, an argument against white racial hierarchy, nor how to develop economic productivity in African American communities is sufficient for a discourse to be considered Afrocentric.

Operations that involve the Afrocentric framework, identified by the four theoretical constructs, represent an Afrocentric methodology. As in every other case, the presentation of theory and methodological considerations implies avenues for criticism. For criticism to be effective it must always derive from the definitions established by the proponents of Afrocentricity. For example, the debate over extraneous issues such as "Was Socrates black?" or "Was Cleopatra black?" has nothing at all to do with Afrocentricity. They may make good work for the history detective but are not Afrocentric positions. There can be a tendency for scholars in African American Studies itself to assume that the use of literary or philosophical terms to analyze African phenomena might be more important for understanding phenomena than Africological terms such as *position*, *line*, *centeredness*, *agency*, and *location*. What is more relevant for the Afrocentrist is the question, "What is the *location* of the person asking such questions or the location of the person needing to answer them?"

NARRATIVE INFLUENCES

Although writers and community activists growing out of the 1960s Black Power Movement increasingly saw the need for a response to marginality, Afrocentricity did not emerge as a critical theory and a practice until the appearance of Molefi Kete Asante's book *Afrocentricity*[9] in 1980. This was the first self-conscious marking along the intellectual path that had been suggested by Kwame Nkrumah in his work *Consciencism*. It was Nkrumah in 1960 who called for an African plan of research that would be "Afro-centric," and although there had been a journal published in 1973 as *An Afrocentric Review*, with no more than three issues, nothing concrete existed as a theoretical work before *Afrocentricity*. Using my own activism and community organizing, protracted engagement with the self-hatred in the African community, I consciously set out to explain a theory and practice of liberation by reinvesting African agency as the fundamental core of African sanity. Thus, *Afrocentricity* was the first time that the theory of Afrocentricity had been launched as an intellectual idea. It was written from activism, observations, and textual analyses of what guaranteed social transformation in community organizations. Rather than use political organization for the mere sake of organization, Afrocentricity envisions the cultural base as the major organizing principle. This had a more telling effect on and a more compelling attraction to African people. Based in the lived experiences of African people in the Diaspora, the Caribbean, and the African continent, the Afrocentric idea had to be concerned with nothing less than the relocation of subject-place in the African world after hundreds of years of living on the imposed and ungrounded terms of Europe.

Unlike the Negritude Movement to which the Afrocentric Movement is often compared, Afrocentricity has not been limited to asking artistic questions. Indeed, the cultural question as constructed by the Afrocentrists is not merely literature, art, music, and dance, but the entire process by which Africans are socialized to live in the modern world. Thus, economics is a cultural question as much as religion and science in the construction of the Afrocentrist. This is why Afrocentrists tend to pose three sets of questions regarding historical and contemporary societies. How do we see ourselves and how have others seen us? What can we do to regain our own accountability and move beyond the intellectual and cultural plantation that constrains our economic, political, social, and scientific development? Which allied theories and methods can be used to rescue the African ideas and ideals marginalized by Europe and thus in the African's mind as well?

FIVE DISTINGUISHING CHARACTERISTICS

One approach to teaching and researching in Africology, the Afrocentric study of African phenomena, is to use a cultural configuration distinguished by five characteristics. What I have done is to integrate Modupe's and Mazama's ideas into the final version of a construct for the scholar who wants to answer the question, "What characterizes the Afrocentric approach?" These are the five characteristics that are meaningful to the researcher.

There ought to be an intense interest in psychological location as determined by symbols, motifs, rituals, and signs. What this means is that the researcher is seeking to determine by icon, myth, motifs, symbols, etc., where the person, text or event is located. Is it a Eurocentric, Asiocentric or Afrocentric phenomenon? Is the person asking the question located in the proper place to ask a genuine question? For example, one could ask a Eurocentric question such as, "Is African religion monotheistic or polytheistic?" But if the question is asked in an African situation, it would have to be reoriented and interrogated for its location.

There should be a commitment to finding the subject-place of Africans in any social, political, economic, architectural, literary, or religious phenomenon with implications for questions of sex, gender, and class. There is no field or interest that is without some perspective and the Afrocentrist's commitment is to discovering the proper role of Africa or Africans in all situations involving Africans. A critique of inequality, injustice, marginality or other forms of off-centeredness is certainly pertinent in this research.

There has to be a defense of African cultural elements as historically valid in the context of art, music, education, science, and literature. One cannot assume that Africans have not spoken, commented or acted in all the ways that humans behave in the world of culture, science, and economics. To defend African cultural elements means that we must study African cultures, whether on the continent or in the Diaspora, in order to become expert in our field of inquiry.

There has to be a celebration of "centeredness" and agency and a commitment to lexical refinement that eliminates pejoratives about Africans or other people. Nothing pejorative or demeaning to Africans as humans can escape the attention of Afrocentrists. If someone uses the term "tribe" in a negative way or speaks of "minorities" when speaking or writing about African people in the United States, Brazil or anywhere else, that person must be checked—that is, located—before you can make a proper assessment of the situation.

There should always be a powerful imperative from historical and social sources to revise the collective text of African people. Since so much negativity about Africa has been written over the centuries, the Afrocentrist takes the position that the correcting of the collective text is a vital part of the reformative process of education and the only real way to a truly liberating knowledge.

Some scholars, such as Mekada Graham and Jerome Schiele, have seriously concentrated on the social transformative aspects of centrality, believing that it is possible to change the conditions of the socially marginalized by teaching them to see their own centrality and thus empower themselves to confront their existential and material situations.[10] Afrocentrists believe that there is a serious difference between commentary on the activities of Europeans, past and present, and the revolutionary thrust of gaining empowerment through the reorientation of African interests. There is no rush to discover in Europe the answers to the problems that Europe created for the African condition, psychologically, morally, and economically. Afrocentrists do not shun answers that may emerge in the study of Europe, but what Europeans have thought and how Europeans have conceived their reality can often lead to further imprisonment of the African mind, creating intellectual imitators who can only think within the framework of a hegemonic European theoretical or methodological tyranny. Thus, Afrocentrists call for the liberation of the mind from any notion that Europe is the teacher and Africa the pupil, believing that one must contest every space and locate in that space the freedom for Africa to express its own truths. This is not a biologically determined position; it is a culturally and theoretically determined one. That is why there are now Afrocentrists who are European and Asian, while simultaneously one can find Africans who are not Afrocentric. The new work on Du Bois by the Chinese Afrocentrist Ji Yuan and the work of Cynthia Lehman, a white Afrocentrist, on the Egyptian texts are examples of non-Africans exploring the various dimensions of centeredness in their analyses of African phenomena. It is consciousness, not biology, that decides how one is to apprehend the intellectual data because the key to the Afrocentric idea is orientation to data, not the data themselves. Where do you stand when you seek to *locate* a text, phenomenon or person?

More than 125 doctorates have been awarded by Temple's Department of African American Studies, and all of them, as of 2010, are gainfully employed, many as heads, chairs, distinguished professors, and directors. Given this record of success in the academy there is no school of thought in African American Studies as dominant as the Afrocentric school. Temple's graduates run more departments and programs in African American Studies than graduates from any other graduate program in African American Studies and have written more articles and scholarly books in African American Studies than any other group of scholars. They have begun to constitute the defining center of the field, largely because many are trained well in a closely argued, robust intellectual Afrocentric tradition.

OBJECTIVITY–SUBJECTIVITY

Perhaps because of the rise of the Afrocentric idea at a time when Eurocentric scholars seemed to have lost their way in a dense forest of deconstructionist and postmodernist concepts challenging the prevailing orthodoxies of the Eurocentric paradigm, we have found a plethora of challenges to the Afrocentric idea as a reaction to postmodernity. But it should be clear that the Afrocentrists, too, have recognized the inherent problems in structuralism, patriarchy, capitalism, and Marxism with their emphasis on received interpretations of phenomena as different as the welfare state and e. e. cummings' poetry. Yet the issues of objectivity and subject-object duality, central pieces of the Eurocentric project in interpretation, have been shown to represent hierarchies rooted in the European construction of the political world.

Afrocentrists claim that the aim of the objectivity argument is always to protect the status quo because the status quo is never called upon to prove its objectivity; only its challengers are asked to explain their objectivity. And in a society where White Supremacy has been a major component of the social, cultural, and political culture, the African, Native American, Asian, and Latino will always be in the position of challenging the white racial privileged status quo, unless, of course, he or she is co-opted into defending the economic, literary, critical, political, social or cultural status quo,[11] in which case the person will often be defending the constraining and hierarchical reality created by Eurocentrists.

It is the subversion of that configuration that is necessary to establish a playing field based on equality. One can never submit to anything less than equality. But to claim that those who take the speaker or the subject position *vis-à-vis* others seen as audiences and objects are on the same footing is to engage in intellectual subterfuge without precedence. On the other hand, it is possible, as the Afrocentrists claim, to create community when one speaks of subject-subject, speaker-speaker, audience-audience relationships. This allows pluralism without hierarchy.

As applied to race and racism, this formulation is equally clear in its emphasis on subject-subject relationships. Of course, the subject-subject relationship is almost impossible in a racist system or in the benign acceptance of a racist construction of human relationships as may be found in US society and is frequently represented in the literature of several scholars who have African ancestry but who are clearly uncomfortable with the fact.

White Supremacy cannot be accommodated in a normal society; therefore, when a writer or scholar or politician refuses to recognize or ignores the African's agency, he or she allows for the default position— White Supremacy—to operate without challenge and thus participates in a destructive mode for human personality. If African people are not given subject place in the thinking of Africologists (those practicing an Afrocentric analysis of phenomena), then we remain objects without agency, intellectual beggars without a place to stand. There is nothing essentially different from this enslavement than the previous historical enslavement, except our inability to recognize the bondage. Thus, you have a white-subject and black-object relationship expressed in sociology, anthropology, philosophy, political science, literature, and history rather than a subject-subject reality. It is this marginality that is rejected in the writings of Afrocentrists.

DIOPIAN INFLUENCE

The late Cheikh Anta Diop did more than anyone to reintroduce the African as a subject in the context of African history and culture. It was Diop's singular ambition as a scholar to reorder the history of Africa and to reposition the African at the center of her own story.[12] This was a major advance at a time when so many African writers and scholars were rushing after Europe to prove Europe's own point of view on the rest of the world. Diop was confident that the history of Africa could not be written without throwing off the falsifications of Europe. Doing this was not only politically and professionally dangerous, it was also considered to be impossible given the hundreds of years of accumulated information in the libraries of the West.

In the first place, Diop had to challenge the leading scholars of Europe, meet them on their intellectual home ground, defeat their arguments with science, and establish Africa's own road to its history.[13] The fact that he achieved his purpose has meant that scholars who declare themselves Afrocentrists have done so with the example of Diop marching before in splendor. His key contention was that the ancient Egyptians laid the basis of African and European civilization and that the ancient Egyptians were neither Arabs nor Europeans, but, as Diop would say, "Black Africans" to emphasize that there should be no mistake. These "Black Africans" of the Nile Valley gave the world astronomy, geometry, law, architecture, art, mathematics, medicine, and philosophy.[14] The ancient African Egyptian term *seba*, first found in an inscription on the tomb of Antef I from 2052 BCE, had as its core meaning in the *Medu Neter* the "reasoning style of the people."

What Diop taught his students and readers was that Europe pronounced itself the categorical superior culture, and therefore its reasoning often served the bureaucratic functions of "locking" Africans in a conceptual cocoon which seems, at first glance, harmless enough. Nevertheless, the prevailing, often anti-African, positions were supported by this bureaucratic logic. How can an African liberate himself or herself from these racist structures? Afrocentrists take the position that this is possible, and indeed essential, but can only happen if we search for answers in the time-space categories which are anti-hegemonic. These are categories which place Africa at the center of analysis of African issues and African people as agents in our own contexts. Otherwise, how can we ever raise practical questions of improving our situation in the world? The Jews of the Old Testament asked, "How can you sing a new song in a strange land?" The Afrocentrists ask, "How can the African create a liberational philosophy from the icons of mental enslavement?"

CORRECTIVE AND CRITIQUE

There are certainly political implications here because the issue of African politics throughout the world becomes one of securing a place on which to stand, unimpeded by the interventions of a decaying Europe which has lost its moral way in its reach to enslave and dispossess other peoples.[15] This is not to say that all Europe is bad and all Africa is good. To even think or pose the issue in that manner is to miss the point I am making. For Africans and Native Americans, Europe has been extremely dangerous; it is 500 years of dangerousness and I am not talking of physical or economic danger, though that history is severe enough, but psychological and cultural danger, the danger that kills the soul of a people. One knows, I surmise, that a people's soul is dead when it can no longer breathe its own cultural or spiritual air, speak its own language, and when the air of another culture seems to smell sweeter. Following Frantz Fanon, Afrocentrists argue that it is the *assimiladoes*, the educated elite, whose identities and affiliations are often killed first.[16] Fortunately, their death does not mean that the people are doomed, only that they can no longer be trusted to speak what the people know because they are dead to the culture, to the human project.[17]

Therefore, Afrocentricity stands as both a corrective and a critique. Whenever African people, who collectively suffer the experience of dislocation, are relocated in a centered place, that is, with agency and accountability, we have a corrective. By recentering the African person as an agent we deny the hegemony of European domination in thought and behavior and then Afrocentricity becomes a critique. On the one hand, we seek to correct the sense of place of the African, and on the other, we make a critique of the process and extent of the dislocation caused by the European cultural, economic, and political domination of Africa and African peoples. It is possible to make an exploration of this critical dimension by observing the way European writers have defined Africa and Africans in history, political science, anthropology, and sociology. Biko understood this quite clearly and put it in the context of a fierce struggle for definition when he wrote, "The most potent weapon in the hands of the oppressor is the mind of the oppressed."[18] The oppressed must resist all forms of enslavement and the founders of the Black Studies Movement in the 1960s were clear in their minds that the "Establishment" was not about to give up its position of dominance without a struggle—in this case, an intellectual struggle. To condone the definition of Africans as marginal and fringe people in the historical processes of the world, including the African world, is to abandon all hope of reversing the degradation of the oppressed.

Thus, the aims of Afrocentricity as regards the cultural idea are not hegemonic. Afrocentrists have expressed no interest in one race or culture dominating another; they express an ardent belief in the possibility of diverse populations living on the same earth, without giving up their fundamental traditions except where those traditions invade other peoples' space.[19] This is precisely why the Afrocentric idea is essential to human harmony. The Afrocentric idea represents a possibility of intellectual maturity, a way of viewing reality that opens new and more exciting doors on human understanding. I do not object to viewing it as a form of historical consciousness, but more than that, it is an attitude, a location, an orientation. To be centered is to stand somewhere and to come from somewhere; the Afrocentrist seeks for the African person the contentment of a subject, active, agent place.

PRINCIPAL CONCEPTS

Afrocentricity represents a reaction to several tendencies. It spurns the limited analysis of Africans in the Americas as Europeans, as well as the notion that Africans in the Americas are not Africans. Rather, it concentrates on activating the communal cognitive will by demonstrating cultural fidelity to the best traditions and values of African people.[20] Afrocentric consciousness is necessary for psychological liberation and cultural reclamation, and in Africology we must seek consciousness that will eradicate collective marginality if we are to be successful academics in the sense of transforming human lives.

There are four areas of inquiry in Afrocentricity: *cosmological, axiological, epistemological,* and *aesthetics.* A scholar seeking to locate a person, event or phenomenon should utilize one of these forms for inquiry. Accordingly, the Afrocentrist places all phenomena within one of these categories. Cosmological refers to the myths, legends, literatures, and oratures that interact at a mythological or primordial level with how African people respond to the cosmos. How are racial or cultural classifications developed? How do we distinguish between Yoruba and African Brazilian? How do gender, class, and culture interact at the intersection of science? The epistemological issues are those that deal with language, myth, dance, and music as they confront the question of knowledge and proof of truth. What is the rational structure of Ebonics as an African language and how does it present itself in the African American's behavior and culture? Axiology refers to the good and the beautiful as well as to the combination that gives us right conduct within the context of African culture. This is a value issue. Since Afrocentricity is a trans-generational and transcontinental idea, as understood by Winston Van Horne, it utilizes aspects of the philosophies of numerous African cultures to arrive at its ideal.[21] "Beauty is as beauty does" is considered an African American adage, but similar proverbs, statements, and sayings are found throughout the African world, where beauty and goodness are often equated. Aesthetics as an area of inquiry is closely related to the issue of value. Afrocentrists, however, have isolated, as in the work of Kariamu Welsh, seven senses of the Afrocentric approach to aesthetics: *polyrhythm, dimensionality and texture, polycentrism, repetition, curvilinearity, epic memory,* and *wholism.* Welsh contends that these elements are the leading aspects of any inquiry into African plastic art, sculpture, dance, music, and drama.[22] A number of Afrocentric scholars have delved into a discussion of ontology, the study of the nature of being, as another issue of inquiry.[23] This should not be confused with the idea of personalism in the original Afrocentric construction of philosophical approaches to Afrocentric cultural theory (critical methodology) and Afrocentric methodology (interpretative methodology).[24] In earlier writings on Afrocentricity, I contended that the European and Asian worlds might be considered materialistic and spiritualistic, whereas the dominant emphasis in the African world was personalism.[25] This was not to limit any cultural sphere, but to suggest the most prominent ways that large cultural communities respond to their environments.

Maulana Karenga has identified seven areas of culture. These are frequently used by Afrocentrists when conceptualizing areas of intellectual organization. They are: history, mythology, motif, ethos, political organization, social organization, and economic organization.[26] Used most often in the critical analysis of culture, these organizing principles are applied to the fundamental subject fields of social, communication, historical, cultural, economic, political, and psychological fields of study whenever a student wants to determine the relationship between culture and a given discipline.

Africology emerges from the various treatments of data from the Afrocentric perspective. Africology is defined as the Afrocentric study of African phenomena. It has three major divisions: *cultural/aesthetics*, *social/behavioral*, and *policy/action*. Under cultural/aesthetic the scholar can consider at a minimum three key elements to culture and aesthetics: *epistemic*, *scientific*, and *artistic*. In terms of epistemic dimensions the Afrocentrist examines *ethics, politics, psychology*, and *other modes of behavior*. The scientific dimension includes *history, linguistics, economics*, and *other methods of investigation*. The artistic dimension involves *icons, art, motifs, symbols*, and *other types of presentation*.

THE CENTRIC IDEAL

Afrocentricity as a substantive and practical research paradigm for graduate studies in African American Studies is traced to the quartet *Afrocentricity*; *The Afrocentric Idea*; *Kemet, Afrocentricity, and Knowledge*; and *An Afrocentric Manifesto*,[27] written by Molefi Kete Asante between 1979 and Ama Mazama's *The Afrocentric Paradigm* and *L'Imperatif Afrocentrique*, which appeared in 2003 and 2005 respectively, and added immensely to the theoretical and intellectual development of the concept. In addition, Mazama, originally from Guadeloupe and with a doctorate in Linguistics from the Sorbonne, helped to internationalize the idea of Afrocentricity as a paradigm-shifting philosophy. As members of the Temple Circle of Afrocentricity, Asante and Mazama have mentored numerous students who are experts in Afrocentric analysis and interpretation.

Others in what might be called the "centric" movement include the outstanding Japanese scholar Yoshitaka Miike, one of the principal architects of a multilayered and multifaceted approach to international communication theory and the leading theorist of Asiocentricity.[28] On the other hand, Afrocentricity became a discourse that thrusts the concept of agency into the intellectual arena as a perspective whose core was the interpretation and explanation of phenomena from the standpoint of subjects rather than victims or objects. It has found advocates in South Africa, Nigeria, Kenya, Zimbabwe, Senegal, Colombia, Cuba, Jamaica, France, England, Norway, China, Haiti, and many other nations.

Central to the Afrocentric idea is the fact that Africans were moved off intellectual, philosophical, and cultural terms by enslavement and colonization. In order to return to an authentic consciousness rooted in self-respect and affirming dignity, it is necessary for African people to see themselves in the midst of their own history and not as located in the margins of Europe. This means that it is essential to return to the classical civilizations of Africa for models of argument, construction, encounter, and ethics in much the same way as Westerners looked back to the ancient Greeks and Romans.[29]

Thus, the return to a discussion of the ancient African civilizations of Egypt and Nubia was essential for an appreciation of the role that Africans and Africa played in human behavior, communication, rhetoric, and world history. Afrocentrists were the first to see the overthrow in the African's mind of European domination by a return to classical Africa. Even this position, thoroughly grounded in the right of African people to discuss their own origins and cultures, was contested by Europeans, who insisted that what was black was not black and what was black had to be the creation of someone outside of Africa. In this vein a few books, notably Mary Lefkowitz's *Not Out of Africa*[30] and Stephen Howe's *Afrocentrism*,[31] were meant to reassert Eurocentric hegemony over African agency. Besides its acceptance of classical Africa, however, Afrocentricity was grounded in the historical reality of African people through the presentation of key intellectual ideas that demonstrated the interconnectedness of African cultures, even across the Sahara. This was not the concentration of Afrocentricity; it was only a place on the way to the destination of African agency. The point is that the Afrocentric idea in communication was not merely stuck in the fertile ground of ancient philosophies of Khunanup, Merikare or Duauf, but rather the theorists saw these philosophers as departure positions, not end places.

For example, it was important to contend that the Eurocentric view had become an ethnocentric view, which elevated the European experience and downgraded all others. For the Afrocentrists it was clear that Afrocentricity was not the counterpoint to Eurocentricity, but a particular perspective for analysis that did not seek to occupy all space and time as Eurocentrism has often done. All human cultures must be centered, in fact, subject of their own realities.

THE PRECEDENCE OF LOCATION

In the Afrocentric view, the problem of location takes precedence over the topic or the data under consideration. Two methodological devices have emerged to assist in the construction of a new body of knowledge: *reasonable plausibility* and *intelligent conclusion*. Both are common terms used in a definite and precise sense to deal with the issue of historical, social, and cultural lacunae in many discourses on African people.

Afrocentrists contend that human beings cannot divest themselves of culture, whether participating in their own historical culture or that of some other group. A contradiction between history and perspective produces a kind of incongruity called decenteredness. Thus, when an African American speaks from the viewpoint of Europeans who came to the Americas on the *Mayflower* when Africans really came on slave ships, or when literary critics write of Africans as "the Other," Afrocentrists claim that Africans are being peripheralized within their own narrative.

METAPHOR OF LOCATION

Metaphors of location and dislocation are the principal tools of analysis as events, situations, texts, buildings, dreams, and literary authors are seen as displaying various forms of centeredness. To be centered is to be located as an agent instead of as "the Other." Such a critical shift in thinking has involved the explanation of psychological mis-orientation and disorientation, attitudes that affect Africans who consider themselves to be Europeans or who believe that it is impossible to be African and human. Severe forms of this psychological attitude have been labeled extreme mis-orientation by some Afrocentrists.[32] Additional issues have been the influence of a centered approach to education, particularly as it relates to the revision of the American educational curriculum. Hundreds of dissertations and numerous books[33] and articles have been written extending the idea of Afrocentricity in communication, architecture, social work, religion, politics, historical and cultural analysis, criminology, and philosophy.

Afrocentricity creates, among other things, a critique of human communication and social history in the search for a unique standing place for agency. Such an action is at once a liberalizing and a liberating event, marking both the expansion of consciousness and the freeing of the mind from hegemonic thinking.

NOTES

1. Ama Mazama, "Eurocentric Discourse on Writing: An Exercise in Self-Glorification," *Journal of Black Studies* (March 1998).
2. Manning Marable, ed., *Dispatches from the Ebony Tower* (New York: Columbia University Press, 2000).
3. Maulana Karenga, *Kawaida and Questions of Life and Struggle* (Los Angeles, CA: University of Sankore Press, 2007).
4. Clinton M. Jean, *Behind Eurocentric Veils: The Search for African Realities* (Amherst, MA: University of Massachusetts Press, 1991).
5. Marimba Yurugu Ani, *An Africa-Centered Critique of European Cultural Thought and Behavior* (Trenton, NJ: Africa World Press, 1994).
6. Ama Mazama, ed., *The Afrocentric Paradigm* (Trenton, NJ: Africa World Press, 2002).
7. Ronald Walters, *Pan Africanism in the African Diaspora: An Analysis of Modern Afrocentric Political Movements* (Detroit, MI: Wayne State University Press, 1997).
8. Molefi Kete Asante, *Kemet, Afrocentricity and Knowledge* (Trenton, NJ: Africa World Press, 1990); Molefi Kete Asante, *The Afrocentric Idea Revised* (Philadelphia: Temple University Press, 1998). See Danjuma Modupe, "Afrocentricity: What it is and What it is Not." Paper presented at the Cheikh Anta Diop International Conference, Philadelphia (October 2000).
9. Molefi Kete Asante, *Afrocentricity: The Theory of Social Change* (Buffalo, CO: Amulefi Publishing, 1980).
10. Mekada Graham, *Black Issues in Social Work and Social Care* (Bristol: Policy Press, 2007); see also Jerome Schiele, *Human Services and the Afrocentric Paradigm* (New York: Routledge, 2000).
11. Jack D. Forbes, *Africans and Native Americans* (Urbana, IL: University of Illinois Press, 1993).
12. Molefi Kete Asante, *The History of Africa: The Quest for Eternal Harmony* (London: Routledge, 2007); see also Cheikh Anta Diop, *The African Origin of Civilization: Myth or Reality* (Chicago: Chicago Review Press, 1989; first published 1974).
13. Cheikh Anta Diop, *Civilization or Barbarism: An Authentic Anthropology*, transl. Yaa-Lengi Meema Ngemi, ed. Harold J. Salemson and Marjolin de Jager (New York: Lawrence Hill Books, 1991).
14. Asante, *The History of Africa*; see also M. K. Asante, *The Egyptian Philosophers: Ancient African Voices from Imhotep to Akhenaten* (Chicago: African American Images, 2000); and Chinweizu, *Decolonising the African Mind* (Lagos: Pero Press, 1987).
15. Ngugi waThiong'o, *Decolonising the Mind* (London: Heinemann, 1986).
16. Frantz Fanon, *The Wretched of the Earth* (New York: Grove Press, 1963).
17. Stephen Bantu Biko, *I Write What I Like: Selected Writings* (Chicago: University of Chicago Press, 1978).
18. Biko, *I Write What I Like*, 21.
19. Mazama, *The Afrocentric Paradigm*; see also Kobi Kambon, *The African Personality in America: An African Centered Framework* (Tallahassee, FL: Nubia Nation

Publications, 1992); and C. Tsehloane Keto, *The Africa-Centered Perspective of History* (Blackwood, NJ: K. A. Publishers, 1991).

20. Karenga, *Kawaida and Questions of Life and Struggle*.

21. Winston A. Van Horne, "Africology: Considerations Concerning a Discipline," in *Contemporary Africana Theory, Thought and Action*, ed. Clenora Hudson-Weems (Trenton, NJ: Africa World Press, 2007), 105–27.

22. Kariamu Welsh, *The African Aesthetic: Keeper of the Traditions* (Westport, CT: Praeger, 1994).

23. Linda James Myers, *Understanding the Afrocentric Worldview* (Dubuque, IA: Kendall-Hunt, 1988).

24. Asante, *Afrocentricity*.

25. Asante, *Afrocentricity*; see also Kambon, *The African Personality in America*.

26. Maulana Karenga, *Introduction to Black Studies* (Los Angeles, CA: University of Sankore Press, 2002).

27. Molefi Kete Asante, *An Afrocentric Manifesto: Toward an African Renaissance* (London: Polity Press, 2008).

28. Yoshitaka Miike, "Towards an Alternative Metatheory of Human Communication: an Asiacentric Vision," *Intercultural Communication Studies*, vol. XII, no. 4 (2003), 39–63.

29. Carter G. Woodson, *The Mis-Education of the Negro* (Trenton, NJ: Africa World Press, 1990).

30. Mary Lefkowitz, *Not out of Africa: How Afrocentrism Became an Excuse to Teach Myth as History* (New York: Basic Books, 1997); see also Molefi Kete Asante, *The Painful Demise of Eurocentrism: An Afrocentric Response to Critics* (Trenton, NJ: Africa World Press, 2000).

31. Stephen Howe, *Afrocentrism: Mythical Pasts and Imagined Homes* (London: Verso, 1998).

32. Kambon, *The African Personality in America*.

33. See Molefi Kete Asante, *Malcolm X as Cultural Hero and Other Afrocentric Essays* (Trenton, NJ: Africa World Press, 1993).

PART II

Community Service, Social Activism and the Academy

CHAPTER 4

Town and Gown: Reaffirming Social Responsibility in Africana Studies

Charles E. Jones and Nafeesa Muhammad

Georgia State University

Since the formal establishment of Africana Studies at San Francisco State College in 1968, scholars have grappled with the essential features of the once academic interloper. As a discipline born of the twin principles of academic inclusion and community outreach, its very origins were wrought in controversy. Heated debates ensued over its legitimacy, subject matter, structure, personnel, and intended audience. Conflict continued over its geographical domain, inclusion of gender, and its relationship to the broader black community. During the past four decades, scholars advanced the discipline of Africana Studies by addressing many of these salient issues. New theoretical formulations, paradigmatic construction, and innovative research, among other developments, contributed to the maturation of the discipline. Two examples include Afrocentricity's theoretical refinement of the "Black perspective" and groundbreaking research enhancing our understanding of the richness and complexities of women of African descent. As Robert Harris, historian and early advocate of Black Studies, proclaimed, "Africana Studies has achieved legitimacy and has become institutionalized within higher education."[1] This newfound stature is perhaps best underscored by the presence of Black Studies doctoral graduate programs in institutions of higher learning where most administrators and faculty once vigorously opposed its *entrée* to the academy.

While the discipline currently enjoys unprecedented standing in academe, particularly when compared to the once pariah status of its formative period (1968–72), we argue that the second principle—community outreach—suffers from uneven attention in the advancement of the discipline. At its onset, Black Studies was an enterprise committed to the twofold mission of academic inclusion and community outreach. In 1969, Michael Thelwell, a founding faculty member of the W. E. B. Du Bois Department of Afro-American Studies at the University of Massachusetts-Amherst, wrote:

> It is important that we emphasize the two equally important considerations which are basic to the concept of black studies. The first requires an autonomous interdisciplinary entity, capable of coordinating its curriculum in traditional disciplines, to ensure an historical, substantive progression and organic coherence in its offerings. The second function, which is no less crucial, requires this entity be sufficiently flexible to innovate programs which involve students in field study and social action projects in black communities.[2]

In 1975, the founders of the National Council for Black Studies (NCBS), the discipline's primary professional organization, recognized the importance of this dual thrust when they adopted the organizational objectives of *academic excellence* and *social responsibility*.[3]

This chapter begins with a discussion of the social responsibility imperative of Africana Studies by drawing on the writings of early architects and advocates of the discipline. Next, it investigates the extent to which Africana Studies graduate programs incorporate the social responsibility exemplar. We then survey the disciplinary landscape to identify concrete, practical examples of social responsibility initiatives. The chapter concludes with a call for Africana Studies scholars to commit themselves once more to the empowerment mission of the discipline.

SOCIAL RESPONSIBILITY: AN ORGANIC MISSION

During the nascent years of the discipline (1968–72), most Black Studies advocates stressed the importance of community outreach. Early architects of the discipline envisioned a cross-fertilization relationship between their academic units and the broader black community. Black Studies programs would provide expertise and resources to empower the black community; in turn, the community offered a laboratory setting for students to apply theoretical concepts taught in the classroom. In the 1970 inaugural issue of the *Journal of Black Studies*, Boniface Obichere noted that "the long-term goal of Black Studies would be the creation of viable links between universities and the black community."[4] Students trained in Black Studies would utilize their academic knowledge on behalf of the black community. DeVere Pentony, Dean of Behavioral and Social Sciences at San Francisco State College, explained, "out of the black studies experience are to come black students, committed, socially aware, ambitious, devoted to the welfare of black people, and equipped for helping the black community assume its rightful place in American society."[5]

The community service precept undergirding the discipline of Africana Studies is steeped in the long intellectual-activist tradition reflected in the writings and legacy of such stalwarts as W. E. B. Du Bois, Anna Julia Cooper, Carter G. Woodson, and Mary McLeod Bethune. These precursors to Black Studies' formal entry to the academy represented a black intelligentsia committed to social activism in order to empower the black community. In her response to a 1930 survey authored by Charles S. Johnson, sociologist and president of Fisk University Anna Julia Cooper explained "my 'racial philosophy' is not far removed from my general philosophy of life: that the greatest happiness comes from altruistic service and this is in reach of all of whatever race and condition."[6] In one of the first comprehensive assessments of the discipline, *Black Studies: Threat or Challenge*, Nick Ford found that the "vast majority" of the 200 Black Studies programs devoted more attention to "the need to promote sympathetic interest and the dedicated involvement in the improvement of the black community (local, national, and worldwide) than to any other single concern."[7] Manifestation of this "dedicated involvement" included field study research seminars and internships, as well as programmatic collaborations between Black Studies academic units and community organizations.

Nathan Hare addressed the issue of community involvement in his 1968 conceptual proposal for the Black Studies Department of San Francisco State. Hare explained, "[t]o develop the key component of community involvement, it is necessary to inspire and sustain a sense of collective destiny as a people and a consciousness of the value of education in a technological society."[8] He proposed innovative pedagogical strategies and curricular programs to foster departmental participation in the black community. Among his suggestions were Black Cultural Councils to sponsor activities in the arts; Black Information Centers to collect data, conduct research, and provide governmental relations advice to community residents (e.g., security benefits); as well as Bureaus of Black Education which would organize community liberation schools. Hare also recommended student apprenticeships with community organizations, businesses, and educational institutions that "would tend to increase the commitment of black students to the community while simultaneously permitting them 'to learn to do by doing' and comprising a flow of volunteer assistance to cooperating functionaries in the community."[9]

During the historic "Black Studies in the University: A Symposium" conference at Yale University in May 1968, Professor Hale further elaborated on the dual mission of Black Studies. With support from the Ford Foundation, the school's Black Student Alliance sponsored one of the nation's first major scholarly conferences on the emerging academic discipline of Black Studies. William Sims, author of *Black Studies: Pitfalls and Potential*, argued that the landmark symposium provided a major catalyst to the development of Black Studies by legitimating the academic field of inquiry during its embryonic stage.[10] Conference co-organizers Armstead Robinson, Craig Foster, and Donald Ogilvie edited the symposium proceedings which Yale University Press published. Robinson et al.'s collaboration is among the influential Black Studies texts of the discipline's early development.[11] Perry Hall, author of the insightful *In the Vineyard: Working in African American Studies*, explained that "the debates and discussions codified in this document [Robinson et al.] are fairly representative of the manner in which these issues were engaged in academic settings across the country during that period."[12] Other invited symposium speakers, including Maulana Karenga, Harold Cruse, and Abdul Alkalimat, joined Hare in articulating the saliency of community outreach to Black Studies.

Black Studies academic units established after the inaugural department at San Francisco State tended to incorporate the empowerment mission proposed by Hare and other early Black Studies advocates. Indeed, in 1973, Nick Ford found that "almost all organized Black Studies programs have in their objectives some reference to community service and campus relations."[13] Greater adherence to the community outreach component of the discipline's twofold mission characterized the formative era of Black Studies. Darlene Clark Hines, one of the nation's leading authorities on Black Women's history, explained,

> many Black Studies scholars agree that the field is distinguished
> from other academic endeavors because of the tension between
> theory and practice and that they must always respond to the

needs of two masters, the academy on the one hand, and the Black community on the other.[14]

Beginning in the 1990s various scholars lamented that the discipline of Africana Studies was drifting away from its outreach mission. Edmund T. Gordon, director of the Center for African-American Studies at the University of Texas at Austin, warned, "We've moved dangerously away from our origins," while Charles P. Henry, chair of African American Studies at the University of California, Berkeley, remarked that the "firm community link most departments started [with] have been disappearing."[15] In the following section, we assess the extent to which the discipline addresses "the needs of two masters—the academy and the community" by examining the role of the social responsibility mission in Africana Studies graduate education.

MISSION IMBALANCE?

Because graduate programs are critical to transmitting the discipline's core values, paradigmatic assumptions, and ethos, they represent an appropriate gauge of the primacy of the social responsibility imperative in the discipline. Post-baccalaureate training, particularly at the doctoral level, is arguably the highest measure of academic respectability and legitimacy since it permits a discipline to sustain itself by producing scholars who give shape and direction to the study of the relevant subject matter. This watershed development in Africana Studies occurred in 1988 when the Department of African American Studies at Temple University under the leadership of Molefi Asante, editor of the *Journal of Black Studies* and leading theoretician of Afrocentricity, launched the discipline's first PhD program. Since then, nine institutions of higher education have followed Temple by adding PhD programs in Africana Studies to their graduate degree offerings (see Table 4.1). The most recent newcomers include the Department of African American and African Diaspora Studies at Indiana University (2009–10), the Center for Africana Studies at the University of Pennsylvania (2009–10), and the Department of Africology of the University of Wisconsin at Milwaukee (2010–11).

Graduate training in Africana Studies at the MA level has a longer history in higher education. In 1971, the Africana Studies and Research Center at Cornell University established the first MA degree in Black Studies, which

Table 4.1   Africana Studies PhD programs

School	Academic Unit*	Inception Year
Harvard University	African and African American Studies	2001–2
Indiana University, Bloomington	African American and African Diaspora Studies	2009–10
Michigan State University	African American and African Studies Program	2004–5
Northwestern University	African American Studies	2006–7
Temple University	African American Studies	1988–89
University of California, Berkeley	African American Studies	1997–98
University of Massachusetts, Amherst	W. E. B. Du Bois Department of Afro-American Studies	1996–97
University of Pennsylvania	Center for Africana Studies	2009–10
University of Wisconsin, Milwaukee	Africology	2010–11
Yale University	African American Studies	1993–94

All academic units are departments unless otherwise stated.

was soon followed in 1972 by the Department of Africana Studies at the State University of New York, Albany. Currently, sixteen universities offer an MA in African American Studies (see Table 4.2). Recent additions to the opportunity to pursue an MA degree in Africana Studies include the Department of African American Studies at Syracuse University (2006); the Department of African-American Studies at Georgia State University (2008); the Department of Africana Studies at the State University of New York at Stony Brook (2009); and the Department of African and African-American Studies at the University of Kansas (2009). By all indications, one can expect the continued proliferation of Africana Studies graduate programs.

At least four universities—Cornell, Ohio State, Virginia Tech, and Cincinnati—are presently developing Africana Studies PhD programs.

To assess the significance of the empowerment mission among the Africana Studies graduate programs, we gleaned data from the websites of those programs and supplemented those findings with a three-item questionnaire. During the 2008 fall semester, the chair and/or graduate director of the Africana Studies units currently offering an advanced degree were requested to respond to the following questions:

Table 4.2 African Studies MA Graduate Programs

School	Academic Unit*
Clark Atlanta University	African and African American Studies and Africana Women's Studies
Columbia University	Institute for Research in African American Studies
Cornell University	Africana Studies and Research Center
Florida International University	African and African Diaspora Studies (Program)
Georgia State University	African-American Studies
Indiana University, Bloomington	African American and African Diaspora Studies
Michigan State University	African American and African Studies (Program)
Morgan State University	History (M.A. in African American Studies with a Concentration in African Diaspora History)
New York University	Africana Studies
Ohio State University	African American and African Studies
State University of New York, Albany	Africana Studies
Syracuse University	African American Studies
University of California, Los Angeles	Ralph J. Bunche Center for African American Studies
University of Louisville	Pan-African Studies
University of Wisconsin, Madison	Afro-American Studies
Yale University	African American Studies

All academic units are departments unless otherwise stated.

1. What are students in your department doing to empower the black community or communities in general?
2. Is there a community service component requirement for your students?
3. What future plans, if any, are there to incorporate the community empowerment component?

Representatives from the seven existing doctoral programs and sixteen MA degree programs in Africana Studies were first telephoned. To increase the response rate, we then emailed the designated officials of the graduate programs. In total, eleven individuals from twenty-three current Africana Studies graduate programs responded to our questionnaire. We operationalize the primacy of the social responsibility imperative among the Africana Studies graduate programs along three dimensions: (1) the formal degree requirements, (2) the mission statements, as well as (3) the sponsorship of community outreach projects.

Our findings suggest that the doctoral programs' impact on actualizing the community service mission of Africana Studies has been overstated. Professor Jennings, author of *The Politics of Black Empowerment: The Transformation of Black Activism in Urban American* and former director of the William Monroe Trotter Institute at the University of Massachusetts at Boston, previously suggested that:

> Revisiting this traditional role of community service in the field
> of black studies is a timely topic in that several doctoral programs
> offering courses of study in black studies have been established
> recently. There are now doctoral programs in black studies at
> Temple University, the Ohio State University, the University of
> Massachusetts, and the University of California at Berkeley. The call
> for the linkage of praxis with theory, and the pedagogy of community
> service, is an important component of these doctoral programs.[16]

In fact, only one of the PhD programs, the African American and African Studies program (AAAS) at Michigan State University, incorporates a community outreach component among its formal degree require-ments. Students enrolled in this doctoral program must complete AL 893A Internship in African American and African Studies in an African American community (1–2 credit hours), as well as AL 893b, an interna-tional internship with an entity in a black community outside of the United States. The internship requirement operationalizes the AAAS program's mission statement, which states that "the objective of the program is to develop scholars committed to academic excellence and social responsibil-ity in the Black world and the broader community."[17] PhD candidates in the AAAS doctoral program have completed internships at such sites as the Malcolm X Academy of the Detroit Public Schools, the "Sister to Sister" mentoring program at Otto Middle School in Lansing, Michigan, local schools in Jamaica, as well as the Presbyterian Secondary School—Osu in Accra, Ghana.[18]

Three of the seven PhD Africana Studies programs' mission state-ments reflected the discipline's dual mission. Those units include the AAAS program at Michigan State University, African American Studies at the University of California, Berkeley and the W. E. B. Du Bois Department of Afro-American Studies at the University of

Massachusetts-Amherst, whose mission statement contains a strong "social justice" component:

> the objective of the Doctoral Program in Afro-American Studies is to produce scholars and teachers in the tradition of the Department's namesake, W. E. B. Du Bois, a native son of Massachusetts who throughout his long life insisted that a commitment to social justice must be rooted in scholarship of the highest order.[19]

Similarly, approximately half of the Africana Studies PhD programs sponsored community service projects. For example, the Department of African American Studies at Berkeley's "Poetry for People" program operationalizes the community outreach element of its mission statement. Initially launched in 1991 by the late June Jordan, the "Poetry for People" program exposes "high school students and community residents to the world of poetry writing and appreciation while at the same time introducing them to the world of academia."[20] Evelyn Higginbotham, chair of African American Studies at Harvard University, reported that her department has a social engagement pedagogical initiative in which students are putting a freshwater well in a Ghanaian village as a part of the academic curriculum. Professor Martha Biondi noted that the Department of African American Studies at Northwestern University has "an internship in African American studies which places students with Chicago area non-profits working in the Black communities."[21] However, unlike the AAAS program at Michigan State, the internship is not a formal degree requirement of the PhD candidacy.

Our findings show that the social responsibility imperative among the MA Africana Studies graduate programs is equally mixed. The paucity of MA programs (16 percent) which incorporated the empowerment mission among its formal degree requirements closely resembled the PhD (14 percent) programs. Clark Atlanta University's African and African American Studies department, the first Black Studies graduate program in the South, requires students to complete an internship with an organization that positively affects the Black community. Students seeking the African-New World Studies MA degree from the African and African Diaspora Studies program at Florida International University must complete the AFA 6940 Community Project/Internship Research in African-New World Studies course. Nearly half of the mission statements of the MA graduate programs referenced the dual mission of Black Studies, while a slight majority (55 percent) of the MA cohort sponsored community projects. Examples of the outreach efforts undertaken by the MA degree programs include the Community Extension Center in Columbus, Ohio, sponsored by the Department of African American and African Studies at Ohio State University; the Africana Criminal Justice Project led by Manning Marable at Columbia University; the Saturday School organized by the Department of Pan African Studies at the University of Louisville; and the service-learning curriculum project of the Department of African-American Studies at Georgia State University.

In sum, our investigation indicates that the primacy of social responsibility has dissipated since the discipline's formative era. We found uneven attention to the empowerment mission among the Africana Studies graduate programs. Few of the programs formally incorporated the social responsibility precept among the degree requirement while approximately half of the units sponsored community outreach projects. Consequently, it appears that the empowerment mission is of minimal import in the graduate training of future Africana Studies scholars. In light of the discipline's institutionalization and stature, how does one account for the underdevelopment of the social responsibility component of the dual mission of Africana Studies?

First and foremost, disciplinary vigilance to the twofold mission of Africana Studies suffers from the absence of external forces which undergirded the saliency of community outreach. In his *Introduction to Black Studies*, Maulana Karenga explained that Black Studies "began as both a political and academic demand with grounding in both the general student movement and the social struggles of the 60's out of which the Student Movement evolved."[22] Beginning in the late 1970s, these "extra-academic forces" waned. As a result, less external pressure and ideological commitment to the importance of educational relevance existed in academe. In the midst of this vacuum, the position of an intellectually detached academic enterprise gained currency within the discipline of Africana Studies. Notwithstanding the broad consensus on the primacy of Black Studies' dual mission, a dissenting view asserts that Black Studies should follow the path of traditional disciplines that stresses a strict demarcation between the academy and the community and that this has always existed. It further purported that Black Studies could best achieve academic legitimacy via rigorous, critical, and intellectually detached scholarship. Community outreach was not viewed as the proper purview of a scholar. In a 1969 essay, Martin Kilson, a political scientist at Harvard University, declared,

I frankly doubt the intellectual and practical value of black studies programs seeking to make "relevant contributions" to the Negro community. Such contributions would be better made through technical or quasi-professional two-year colleges which would train nurses and other sundry technical workers. A black studies curriculum should in the main be organized and operated like other disciplines in a liberal arts college.[23]

Beginning in the late 1970s, the position of an exclusive academic focus acquired ascendancy during the discipline's maturation phase. Martin Kilson proposed a classificatory delineation of the evolution of the discipline in which he suggested Black Studies achieved maturation as an academic enterprise when stellar scholars/administrators "*disciplinized* black studies." According to Kilson, this discliplinizing process occurred as "they slowly interlocked the structuring of the academic regime of black studies with the established academic disciplines in the social sciences and the humanities."[24] Kilson identified two curriculum outcomes as manifestations of the maturation of Black Studies evident by the expansion and broadening of the traditional disciplines. Courses on the black experience, such as African American Literature, African American Politics, African American Philosophy, expanded the curriculum offerings of the traditional fields while innovative interdisciplinary theoretical interpretive constructs (i.e., Black cultural studies) broadened the explanatory richness of the mainstream academic disciplines. Suffice to say that Black Studies' quest for legitimacy in higher education, via linkages to and impact on the traditional disciplines, is an academic endeavor which undoubtedly minimizes outreach efforts to the black community. The reward system of academe—promotion and tenure—largely rests on scholarly publications that reinforce an exclusive academic focus.

Secondly, the funding strategy of the Ford Foundation has been a contributing factor in the diminishing significance of the community outreach goal. In her controversial book *White Money/Black Power: The Surprising History of African American Studies and the Crisis of Race in Higher Education*, Noliwe Rooks, assistant director of the African American Studies program at Princeton University, put forth the provocative argument that attributes Black Studies' growth and institutionalization to the funding efforts of the Ford Foundation. She contends that "the Ford Foundation began to craft and then fund a strategy aimed at ensuring a complication-free birth and life for African-American Studies on college campuses."[25] Rooks maintains that targeted funding of specific Black Studies units ensured the development and acceptance of Black Studies in higher education. While disagreement exists among Black Studies scholars over the centrality of the Ford Foundation's role in institutionalizing the discipline, no one can discount the substantial monies awarded to developing Africana Studies as an academic enterprise. Between 1982 and 2007, the Ford Foundation, under the auspice of its "Knowledge, Creativity and Freedom" program area, allocated approximately $31 million in grant monies to develop and institutionalize Black Studies as an academic enterprise.[26]

Farah Jasmine Griffin, director of the Institute of African American Studies at Columbia University and author of the Ford Foundation's *Inclusive Scholarship: Developing Black Studies in the United States*, explained that the Foundation awarded Black Studies grants based on a model recommended by Sir Arthur Lewis, Caribbean Noble Prize economist who held a faculty position at Princeton University. According to Jasmine Griffin, Lewis urged the Ford Foundation to focus its attention on helping to build a strong academic field by supporting scholarly and pedagogical initiatives that adhere to the standards of traditional disciplines.[27] Consequently, proposals seeking funding for projects such as the Community Extension Center of the African American and African Studies department at Ohio State University rarely receive grant monies. Rather, the Foundation favored funding academic endeavors such as fellowships (pre- and postdoctoral), course development, and the creation of degree programs (undergraduate and graduate). Since 1968, a relatively small (eleven) cohort of prestigious research universities have been the primary recipients of Ford Foundation funding in the area of Black Studies. The exclusive academic focus dictated by the Ford Foundation grant awards undoubtedly diverted systematic attention from the social responsibility mission of the discipline.

As Rooks poignantly observes, "we cannot know how much more successful Black Studies might have been in its transformational impulses if allowed the funding and given the encouragement to go even further."[28]

RE-ESTABLISHING THE SOCIAL RESPONSIBILITY EXEMPLAR

While our findings suggest that the disciplinary landscape is not completely barren of community outreach efforts, the social responsibility exemplar, nonetheless, remains underdeveloped in Africana Studies graduate education. We seek to initiate the process of restoring balance between the two core missions of the discipline by providing examples of community outreach initiatives to serve as models for replication by other Black Studies units. We primarily draw our examples from the recipients of civic and community engagement grants sponsored by the National Council for Black Studies (NCBS). With funding from the National Black United Fund Federation of Charities, NCBS awards civic and community engagement grants "to support projects in which Africana Studies knowledge and skills are made available to local communities."[29] Black Studies units which have an NCBS institutional membership are eligible to receive between $2,500 and $5,000 to sponsor community outreach endeavors. In light of the nation's broad array of Africana Studies units, a social responsibility initiative continuum was constructed to encompass the diverse circumstances (personnel, resources, and location) of the various Black Studies academic entities. The parameters of the social responsibility initiative continuum range from minimum to maximum community involvement determined by the longevity, resource allocation, and impact of the outreach activity.

Not surprisingly, the vast majority of the community outreach initiatives we identified fall within the minimum community involvement category. These activities usually require nominal resources and are implemented on an occasional basis. Initiatives in this category range from community lecture and film series internships, student enrichment symposia, tutorial programs, non-credit community courses, and K-12 teacher workshops. The Africana Studies program at Richard Stockton College of New Jersey sponsorship of "The Black Essentials: African American Films for the Community" program is representative of an outreach initiative reflecting minimal community involvement. The Africana Studies program and its co-sponsor 101 Women Plus, screened twelve black films on consecutive Thursday evenings from April 6 to June 29, 2006. A faculty representative of the Africana Studies program led a post-film panel discussion.[30]

K-12 teacher infusion workshop is another typical initiative which reflects minimal community involvement. Its goal is to provide information, strategies, and tactics for incorporating knowledge of people of African descent into the K-12 curriculum to enhance teaching effectiveness in urban settings. The Department of African American Studies of Temple University and the Imhotep Charter School in Philadelphia sponsored the "Black Studies/Public School Initiative: Rescuing our

Youth with Factual Information: Toward Pragmatic Solutions," a one-day workshop which thirty public school educators attended. Similarly, the Department of Africana Studies and the National Center for Urban School Transformation (San Diego) sponsored a one-day workshop entitled "Infusion of Africana Studies in K-12 curriculum in San Diego, California." The teacher workshop initiative has great utility as a community outreach project since it is not dependent on the presence of an identifiable black community. Both white teachers and students can benefit from an effective multicultural education.[31]

Tutorial programs, such as the "Builders of a New Generation-Rites of Passage," were sponsored by the African American Studies and Research Center at Purdue University. College mentors were paired with approximately forty-five students (grades 3–5) during bi-weekly mentoring sessions which targeted such issues as self-esteem, health, and African American history during the 2007–8 academic year. The Septima P. Clark Afterschool Program at Dekalb High School (Dekalb, IL), sponsored by the Center for African-American Studies at Northern Illinois University, a bi-monthly program with tutorial assistance in Black history, is another example of the tutoring programs sponsored by Africana Studies academic units. While the activities of the minimal involvement category are laudatory in their own right, since they represent attention to the empowerment mission, the lack of continuity minimizes the overall impact of these initiatives.

Community outreach projects carried out annually constitute examples of initiatives which reflect moderate community involvement.[32] The "Pottery for the People" program, sponsored by the Department of African American Studies at the University of California at Berkeley and the "Saturday Academy" at the Department of Pan African Studies at the University of Louisville are examples of social responsibility initiatives which reflect the requisite longevity indicative of moderate community involvement. Both community outreach initiatives have existed for nearly two decades. As noted earlier, the "Pottery for the People" program was first initiated in 1991, the same year that J. Blaine Hudson, member of the Pan African Studies faculty, launched the "Saturday Academy" in Louisville. Under Hudson's leadership, faculty members of the Pan African Studies department taught African American history to community residents and presided over forums which discussed local policy issues as well as pertinent current events. The "Alternative Spring Break" study abroad program is another illustration of a moderate community involvement initiative. The Department of Africana Studies at San Diego State

University (SDSU), chaired by Shirley Weber, past president of NCBS, offers a prototype of this relatively new international outreach endeavor. Since 2000, Weber and her Africana Studies colleagues, in conjunction with the school's service learning office, operate an "Alternative Spring Break" in Pretoria, South Africa with a significant community service component. In the past, students volunteered with Love Life (an AIDS prevention organization), orphanages, and youth centers. The SDSU department formed a partnership in 2004 with the Ithuteng Trust Youth Center. The SDSU delegation provided mentoring assistance, African American history and literature books for the library, shoes for the students, and the sponsorship of an educational video conference.[33]

The Community Extension Center (CES) of the Department of African American and African Studies of Ohio State University exemplifies maximum community involvement via a Black Studies social responsibility initiative. The CES seeks "to serve as the link between academic study and practical application" of knowledge to empower the Black community in Columbus, Ohio. Founded in 1985 under the leadership of William E. Nelson, then chair of Black Studies, the CES is located in the historic Mt. Vernon area, a predominately African American community in Columbus. Initially housed in the basement of St John's Baptist Church, the CES now operates out of a thirteen-room complex located on Mt. Vernon Avenue. The CES mission is:

> to promote and coordinate research, teaching, and service projects
> that support The Ohio State University's land grant mission as
> well as address the concerns of the city's Diasporic Communities
> by: (1) serving as a liaison between The Ohio State University and
> Columbus' urban communities; (2) fostering greater interaction
> between members of the community and university; and (3)
> partnering with university, faculty, staff, and students to provide
> opportunities for learning, discovery and engagement.[34]

CES offers a host of programs, among them computer literacy courses for senior citizens, a math and science program for school children (grades 4–12), an African American history summer residential program for high school students, and a monthly lecture series. In addition, the CES conducts research, host conferences, offers classes (credit and non-credit), and sponsors the Ray Miller Institute for Change and Leadership. The Center has ongoing partnerships with the OSU Medical Center, the OSU Frank

W. Hale Jr. Black Cultural Center, and the Center for Urban Progress. While commonplace during the formative era of the discipline, the CEC is one of the lone contemporary instances of an off-campus physical facility operated by a Black Studies academic unit.[35]

The service-learning curriculum project of the Department of African American Studies at Georgia State University (GSU) represents a second initiative which meets the criteria of maximum community involvement. The GSU service-learning initiative integrates instruction and community service to enhance academic outcomes, stimulate civic participation, and benefit the Atlanta metropolitan community. Since 1995, all students enrolled in AAS 2010 Introduction to African American Studies are required to fulfill fifteen hours working with an instructor approved non-profit organization. AAS 2010 satisfies the university's social science requirements of the core curriculum and is a required course for all students who either major or minor in African American Studies. The Department of African American Studies at GSU has offered a minimum of four sections of AAS 2010 per semester since the 2005–6 academic years. These sections averaged fifty students per class who worked with a wide range of advocacy and non-profit organizations, including the Atlanta Urban Ministry, which serves homeless women and children; Cool Girls, Inc., a mentoring and tutorial organization; Forever Family, which assists children of incarcerated parents; as well as the Federation of Southern Cooperative and the Center for Black Women's Wellness. Service-learning offers critical support to community organization often beset with meager resources. Indeed, the impact of the GSU service-learning project is evident by the sheer volume of volunteer hours generated by the outreach initiative. During the ten-year period 1995–2005 students enrolled in AAS 2010 provided over 30,000 volunteer hours to non-profit organizations in the Atlanta metropolitan area.[36]

The Africana Criminal Justice Project (ACJP) directed by Manning Marable, editor of *Souls: A Critical Journal of Black Politics and Society* and Black Studies scholar at Columbia University, serves as another curriculum-related social responsibility initiative that denotes maximum community involvement. ACJP is a multi-pronged research and education initiative that utilizes the notion of "living history" as a conceptual thrust to interrogate the contemporary crisis of the racialized criminal injustice. According to Marable, "behind the idea of 'living history' is the core belief that powerful narratives we construct about the past have the potential capacity to reshape contemporary civic outcomes." He further notes that "the goal is not just to educate and inform, but to transform the objective material and cultural conditions and subordinate status of marginalized groups, through informed civic engagement, and by strengthening civil society."[37] Launched in 2003, the ACJP incorporates a litany of pedagogical strategies and programmatic activities which include oral history projects, conferences, public education forums, partnerships, and academic courses. In conjunction with the ACJP initiative, the Institute for Research in African-American Studies at Columbia University offered such classes as Juvenile Justice in the African American Experience, Africana Criminal Justice, Oral History Research Seminar, and Cultural Resistance: The Role of the Arts in Social Justice Movements. Examples of ACJP public education forums include "Chanting Down the Walls: Using the Arts to Combat America's Prison Crisis" (November 2003) and "Final Count of the Collision between US and Them: Hip-Hop Prison and New Democracy" (October 2004). Among the sponsored conferences are "Africana Studies Against Criminal Injustice" (April 2003) and "Criminally Unjust: Young People and the Crisis of Mass Incarceration" (April 2005).[38] In short, ACJP at Columbia University represents an exemplary model of excellence by integrating theory and praxis as envisioned by the early Black Studies architects.

CONCLUSION

Forty years after its controversial entry into higher education, the discipline of Africana Studies presently enjoys unprecedented status in academe. During the past four decades, curricular expansion, groundbreaking research, innovative pedagogical strategies, effective administrators, and the proliferation of scholarly outlets are all among the major academic developments leading to the institutionalization of Africana Studies. While Black Studies scholars have devoted requisite attention to the academic concerns of the discipline, the community outreach goal of the discipline's twofold mission largely remains underdeveloped. Beginning in 1984, James Turner, founding director of the Africana Studies and Research Center at Cornell University, warned,

> many of the first faculty in the field are gradually de-emphasizing
> involvement in community activities as they have succumbed
> to (or have been seduced by) the orthodox norms of academic
> traditionalism in their pursuit of careerist aspirations for legitimacy
> and acceptability for purposes of job stability.

He furthered lamented that "younger faculty have not been quite as engaged by commitment to community outreach and the wedding of intellectual and social activism on behalf of the liberation of the Black community."[39]

Our findings support Turner's poignant observation concerning the increasing lack of systemic attention to the discipline's community outreach mission. Our investigation found that the social responsibility exemplar assumes a minimal role in Africana Studies graduate programs, particularly at the doctoral level. Only one of the seven existing PhD programs incorporated the empowerment goal among its formal degree requirements. The African American and African Studies program at Michigan State University requires students to complete a domestic and international internship to satisfy PhD candidacy requirements. While three of the doctoral programs did include the community outreach program goal within their respective mission statements, the Department of African American Studies at the University of California, Berkeley sponsors the sole community outreach initiative—"Poetry for People" program—which reflects moderate community involvement. Few of the MA degree programs included the empowerment mission among their respective formal degree requirements. Both the Department of African American Studies at Clark Atlanta University and the African Diaspora Studies program at Florida International University are exceptions to this finding. However, Africana Studies units offering MA degrees at Ohio State University, Georgia State University, and Columbia University do, in fact, sponsor model community outreach programs. Nevertheless, half of their MA counterparts failed to offer any community empowerment initiative.

Needless to say, this paucity of attention to the discipline's community outreach goal does not comport with the vision of the early architects of the discipline. We acknowledge that our findings and conclusions are qualified by two identifiable limitations. First, our examination of the primacy of the social responsibility goal among the Africana Studies graduate programs did not include the production of knowledge via student theses and dissertations, which may indeed reflect the integration of theory and praxis in addressing salient public policy problem of the black community. Secondly, we did not conduct an exhaustive survey of the discipline since we focused solely on the Africana Studies graduate programs. An appropriate and worthwhile future research project would be to update Ford's earlier comprehensive study, *Black Studies: Threat or Challenge*, to ascertain the continuity of the commitment to community outreach by contemporary Africana Studies units. Notwithstanding these limitations, the sobering reality is that too few Africana Studies graduate programs are properly attentive to the social responsibility imperative of the discipline. We seek to stimulate discourse and to refine the community outreach mission of the discipline by offering a wide range of empowerment initiatives, which reflect varying degrees of commitment that may serve as models for replication by other Africana Studies units.

As Bruce Hare, James Stewart, Alfred Young, and Delores Aldridge remind us,

> given the traditional focus on community outreach in Africana
> Studies, properly situated the field can play a leading role in
> assisting colleges and universities in designing and implementing
> outreach activities, particularly to traditionally ignored,
> underserved populations not only locally, regionally, nationally, and
> internationally.[40]

President Obama's advocacy of volunteerism offers an opportunity for Africana Studies units to serve as forerunners in this endeavor. The Obama administration launched its "United We Serve" community service initiative in June 2009 in which the President urged citizens to volunteer to help solve a myriad of community needs. The Corporation for National and Community Service directed the initiative, which began with cabinet members as well as the First Lady participating in a host of community service projects across the nation and culminated with a National Day of Service and Remembrance on September 11. President Obama remarked, "And I hope you will continue the service work you begin this summer for the rest of your life. Because American's new foundation will be built one community at a time—and it starts with you."[41] By returning to the organic roots of the discipline, we can restore the balance between the twofold mission of Africana Studies which will undoubtedly poise Africana Studies to spearhead President Obama's commitment and challenge to community service and volunteerism.

NOTES

1. Robert L. Harris, "The Intellectual and Institutional Development of Africana Studies," in Jacqueline Bobo, Cynthia Hudley, and Claudine Michel, eds., *The Black Studies Reader* (New York: Routledge, 2004), 18.

2. Michael Thelwell, *Massachusetts Review of Black Studies*, vol. 1, 1969.
3. William M. King, "The Early Years of Three Major Professional Black Studies Organizations," in Delores P. Aldridge and Carlene Young, eds., *Out of the Revolution: The Development of Africana Studies* (Lanham, MD: Lexington Books, 2009), 115–22; Deborah F. Atwater, "A Woman of Vision: Dr. Bertha Maxwell Roddy," *International Journal of Africana Studies*, vol. 10, no. 1 (2004), 117–30.
4. Bonifact I. Obichere, "Challenge of African American Studies," *Journal of Black Studies*, vol. 1 (1970), 169.
5. DeVere E. Pentony, "The Case for Black Studies," in John W. Blassingame, ed., *New Perspectives on Black Studies* (Urbana, IL: University of Illinois Press, 1971), 67.
6. Anna Julia Cooper, "My Racial Philosophy (1930)," *The Voice of Anna Julia Cooper: Including a Voice from the South and Other Important Essay, Papers, and Letters*, ed. Charles Lemert and Esma Bhan (Lanham, MD: Rowman & Littlefield, 1998), 236.
7. Nick Aaron Ford, *Black Studies: Threat or Challenge: Threat or Challenge* (Port Washington, NY: Kennikat Press, 1973), 57.
8. Nathan Hare, "A Conceptual Proposal for a Department of Black Studies," in William H. Orrick, Jr., ed., *Shut it Down: A College in Crisis* (San Francisco: San Francisco State College Study Team, 1969), 163.
9. Hare, "A Conceptual Proposal for a Department of Black Studies."
10. Willlian E. Sims, *Black Studies: Pitfalls and Potential* (Washington: University Press of America Inc., 1979)
11. Armstead L. Robinson, Craig C. Foster, and Donald H. Ogilvie, eds., *Black Studies in the University: A Symposium* (New Haven, CT: Yale University Press, 1969).
12. Perry A. Hall, *In the Vineyard: Working in African American Studies* (Knoxville, TN: University of Tennessee Press, 1999), 18.
13. Ford, *Black Studies*, 156.
14. Darlene Clark Hines, "The Black Studies Movement: Afrocentric-Traditionalist-Feminist Paradigms for the Next Stage," *The Black Scholar*, vol. 22, no. 3 (1992), 12.
15. Marjorie Coeyman and Black Studies on the Move, "For Scholars on the Move: For Scholars of the African American Experience. It is a Debate that Has No Easy Answers," *Christian Science Monitor* (February 12, 2002).
16. James Jennings, "Theorizing Black Studies: The Continuing Role of Community Service in the Study of Race and Class," *Dispatches from the Ebony Tower: Intellectuals Confront the African American Experience*, ed. Manning Marable (New York: Columbia University Press, 2000), 178.
17. www.msu.edu/~aaas/phd.html. Accessed July 8, 2009.
18. The authors wishes to thank Kefense Chike for providing this information.
19. www.umass.edu/afroam/department.html. Accessed July 14, 2009.
20. africam.berkeley.edu/p4p.html. Accessed July 8, 2009; June Jordan, *Some of Us Did Not Die* (New York: Basic Civitas Books, 2002).
21. Evelyn Higginbotham, "Re: African American Studies Community Empowerment," email to Nafeesa Muhammad, November 21, 2008; Martha Biondi, "Re: African American Studies Community Empowerment," email to Nafeesa Muhammad, January 1, 2009.

22. Maulana Karenga, *Introduction to Black Studies*, 3rd edn. (Los Angeles, CA: University of Sankore Press, 2002), 9.

23. Martin Kilson, *Massachusetts Review of Black Studies*, vol. 1, 1969.

24. Martin Kilson, "Black Studies Revisited," in Manning Marable, ed., *Dispatches from the Ebony Tower: Intellectuals Confront the African American Experience* (New York: Columbia University Press, 2000), 174.

25. Noliwe M. Rooks, *White Money/ Black Power* (Boston, MA: Beacon Press, 2006).

26. Farah Jasmine Griffin, "Introduction," in Farah Jasmine Griffin, ed., *Inclusive Scholarship: Developing Black Studies in the United States* (New York: Ford Foundation, 2007), xxii.

27. Griffin, *Inclusive Scholarship*, xiv.

28. Rooks, *White Money/ Black Power*, 119.

29. National Council for Black Studies Organization Handbook, 21.

30. National Council for Black Studies 2008. Combined Federal Campaign application of the National/International Independent Organizations and Numbers of Federation, Office of Personnel Management, United States Government, Washington, DC.

31. Combined Federal Campaign application.

32. Combined Federal Campaign application.

33. National Council for Black Studies, 2006. Combined Federal Campaign Application of the National/International Independent organizations and Numbers of Federation, Office of Personnel Management, United States Government, Washington, DC.

34. African American and African Studies: Community Extension, *Your Partner in Education*, Ohio State University; See also AAASCES About Us Five Year Plan, aas. osu.edu/resources/aaasces/aboutus/fiveyearplan.ltm. Accessed March 13, 2009.

35. African American and African Studies: Community Extension.

36. Charles E. Jones, Patricia Dixon, and Akinyele O. Umoja, "Return to the Source: The Role of Service-Learning in Recapturing the 'Empowerment' Mission of African-America Studies," *The Black Scholar*, vol. 35, no. 2 (2005), 25–36.

37. Manning Marable, African American and African Studies: Community Extension, www.columbia.edu/cu/ccbh/acjp/about/intro.html. Accessed March 13, 2009.

38. African American and African Studies: Community Extension.

39. James E. Turner, "Foreword: Africana Studies and Epistemology, A Discourse in the Sociology of Knowledge," in James E. Turner, ed., *The Next Decade: Theoretical and Research Issues in Africana Studies* (Ithaca, NY: Africana Studies and Research Center, 1984), xx.

40. Bruce R. Hare, James B. Stewart, Alfred Young, and Delores P. Aldridge, "Africana Studies: Past, Present, and Future," in Robert Diamond and B. Adams, eds., *The Disciplines Speak*, vol. II (Washington, DC: American Association of Higher Education, 2000), 144–5.

41. *Remarks of President Barack Obama*, www.serve.gov/remarks.asp. Accessed June 20, 2009; Cheri Cabot, *United We Serve—A Challenge to Volunteer by President Obama*, www.gather.com/viewArticle.action?articleId=281474977717844. Accessed June 20, 2009.

CHAPTER 5

Reflections on the Journey: Interview with Danny Glover (May 2008)

Jeanette R. Davidson

University of Oklahoma

ON STUDENT DAYS

JRD I'd like to begin our interview by asking you about back in the 1960s so that we can cover your experience of the history of the student movement at San Francisco State College.[1] I know you were involved in the efforts for Black Studies so I want you to recall the genesis of the student action and your collective motivations and goals and your hopes. You've talked before to me about the "collective vision."

DG I think there are very unique circumstances which bring people together at any moment and, without a doubt, for an historic moment. It was not only what happened with the students at San Francisco State, but what was happening in the community surrounding the area. And that's the moment at the center. Most of my activity took place within and around specific communities. We had a distinct Hispanic community, a distinct Asian community, and two distinct African American communities. One was Hunter's Point and the other Fillmore, now called Western Addition. All of those communities intersect in some way. San Francisco State was unique also because, being a teachers' college, in order to provide opportunities for work-study for students, they had tutorial programs.

What I think happened, and was important, was that the BSU [Black Student Union] was able to recognize, even though we were a small minority on the campus, the inherent power that lies within the structure that existed. That was the first thing. Also, because San Francisco is strategically located . . . the whole space [was] created for organizing and, because of its history, people came to San Francisco to return to school. Men and women from SNCC [Student Nonviolent Coordinating Committee][2] came there. Men and women from other places around the country came at that particular time. We were there where all these forces met—the disintegration of the Civil Right Movement, the new activism around Black Empowerment, and the Black Power Movement. All these things seemed to intersect historically at that particular moment in time.

And then there was San Francisco's uniqueness as a bastion for culture as well. So here you have in the midst of San Francisco this alternative culture, often referred to in so many books in the 1960s. One, you have an enormous political framework. It starts back with people like Harry Bridges.[3] Harry Bridges was a socialist, and leader of one of the most radical unions, ILWU [International Longshore and Warehouse Workers Union]. You have a progressive outlook in terms of the union. Harry Bridges, in 1934, in the midst of a strike, went to Black churches in the Bay area and said, "If you don't become 'scabs' in the strike, if you help us and win this strike with us, I will make sure that Black people, Black men, will be on the jobs when we win the strike." That's the kind of forward thinking that helped. All these kinds of things happening in San Francisco and is the historic legacy for all of this. You know that Paul Robeson, Martin Luther King, all of them, spent a great deal of time in San Francisco. There's a legacy . . . that's an incubator of ideas and thoughts that were generated in San Francisco, and the Bay Area. The Free Speech Movement with Mario Savio and Berkeley.[4] So that's the kind of thing, that's the kind of energy that I was part of, that Wayne [Thompson][5] came into, John Bowman[6] was part of, and all the other people who came here. That was the place where all these things were happening. And San Francisco State, because it was a working-class college, and because of the history, and because, I think, we were arrogant—arrogant and everything else—was a unique breeding ground for us. That's how we had the overlay for the activities that were happening—what we read, what we did, how we tried to insert ourselves in community activities, how we became a part of that. Our motto was that, whatever we were learning in college, our responsibility was to take it back to the community. The disintegration of the Black community because of gentrification and redevelopment, all those things played roles in the battles being waged. Battles around education were being waged, battles around housing were being waged, and battles around job creation were being waged and inserted into this mixture.

I also think about San Francisco as unique—geographically. It's a very small space. Within a space of forty-nine square miles, seven miles one way, seven miles the other way, all of this was happening, so there were unique elements to this particular process. If you're in a city like New York, it doesn't happen the same way. If you're in a place that has at the most 700,000 people—then you have another place. Oakland has 400,000 people. So, in the midst of all this, there are just over a million people in this defined area. A third of the population of Oakland is Black. Only about ten percent, at the most twelve percent, of the population of San Francisco was, is, African American. So, all these things were happening at the same time. Going on were the counter-culture, the Civil Rights Movement, the Movement of Black Power, as it resonated in San Francisco. What I'm saying, considering all the other places, whether Detroit, Chicago, and what was happening, it was a pretty liberal place. So all those things gave rise to the ideas and the expression of those ideas. That was a changing point in time in 1967. After basically taking over the associated student budget, we did two things. In the spring of 1967 we brought out Amiri Baraka[7] to start what he called a Community Communication Program. All of a sudden San Francisco became the center point, the apex of all these things, all activities happening culturally around the earth, around the country, because what we'd done was pulled a coup. We'd brought the most influential voice in Black culture at that time to *our* school, in the spring of 1967 and housed him there for six months. Whatever we said, what we wanted to do in the community, we took to another level. Other poets came, and people like Ed Bullins[8] the playwright, "wannabe" poets, and Huey P. Newton.[9] I heard Huey P. Newton read at the Black House[10] in 1967. All of them gravitated to this spot near here. In the fall of that year, we brought out Nathan Hare.[11] We made the agreement with Summerskill,[12] the university president, a liberal president, to bring out Nathan Hare. So all of a sudden, he began the Black Studies program. Mind you, only the Black Studies program. There was a quantum leap when we had to begin to talk about an Ethnic Studies[13] program too. It was not a process that initially was a part of our vision of ourselves, but a process we found ourselves growing into. There were internal struggles that happened—an internal struggle changed the Negro Associated Student Union to the Black Student Union. The internal struggles and the absolute taking of power in a sense, through ways of organizing, through ways of manipulation, and everything else. All those things helped.

JRD Can you talk a little bit about the organization? I mean how did you organize?

DG Well, if you were to look at the functional part of the BSU, the true part of the BSU, outside of the twelve members of the central committee, its core may have been at its initiation, another two dozen people. And there were people who were loosely associated with it and others who were not as associated. There were people who were fancied with the idea. They had all the paraphernalia and all the looks, and everything else, but at the beginning that was the kind of core we had. We did two things: first of all, we began to expand in terms of the activities that we did, what we brought about, the activities around the BSU, the activities of bringing people there. We brought Baraka out there and we'd brought all these things together. We brought musicians out there too. We brought Huey P. We brought Hugh Masekela.[14] We had this place we would use and there were times a lot of money was circulating. We had guys who were emerging as filmmakers around there. All these things were happening. It was a very rich moment for being young, and having that rich and diverse [an environment] was incredible. So that became the foundation that we began to build on. I think that, on the one hand, the strike was a bold move. The strike came about mainly because Nathan Hare's contract was not renewed. Once that came about, that started a chain of events which essentially made the strike inevitable. Also, with all due respect, we got carried away with the idea of it all. I mean we can look back on this in retrospect and see some of the good ideas that we had. But let's just say in our naivety as young men and young women, there was a certain degree of arrogance and pompousness as well. You know, what happens with all youth. That's what happens, that's what makes being young and everything so exciting. You believe you're invincible and that you can change the world.

JRD Right, and you were challenging people who were in the academy . . . and often people in the academy are very arrogant and elitist. I mean it took a lot of courage as well as arrogance.

DG We all exist within a framework, a social framework. If you were going to be at San Francisco State, you had an anti-war movement happening. You had a counter-culture happening right there. You can imagine that we were still under that climate. Remember, we were only a decade after the McCarthy era,[15] which was a very repressive era. You had people coming back and, as a student teacher, you didn't choose San Francisco State unless you wanted to be bold to some extent. I think what contributed to what we felt and what we tried to do, were, like I said, all kinds of movements that were happening. That's what we walked into. Of course, we didn't know the breadth of that. I think that the administration was also poised to respond to this particular potential expression, you know. Before we'd had Watts,[16] we'd had urban riots too. That was the kind of landscape that we inherited and we tried to exploit.

JRD Did some students end up having to pay a price for doing what they did?

DG Well, I imagine that several students paid a price, whether that was spending time incarcerated. Some students' lives were altered. For some students, their actions caused friction and created a distance between their parents and their family. Remember, you are dealing with also a number of Black students who represented the first generation to go to college. Of course, a lot of that stuff we don't know, but some of them may have acquired records which influenced their employment life, what was happening in their life. I think those things did happen. I remember one brother, a student from Nigeria, was deported. His father was a general in the Nigerian army. I'm sure that caused a scandal for the family and everything. I know the long-range effects of the strike on people's personal relationships, romantic relationships perhaps, were made even more difficult because of the strike.

JRD Can you talk a little bit about the relationship between the students and the Black Panthers?[17]

DG One of the more interesting dynamics that came out of this was particularly that relationship. The Black Panther Party had emerged as the key voice in the Black community. Initially, I think people were attracted often to the romanticism attached to the Party, the idea of one's struggle. I knew the Black Panther Party in California. I attended some of their meetings in the spring and in the summer of 1966. I can't remember now how I may have been approached. Part of me, part of us, were dealing with the loss of Malcolm in some way, and the anger with that loss, and finally were finding some sort of expressive response to that. So I think two things happened, particularly when they came in with guns to the California State Assembly and posted themselves while the State Assembly was in session. Young people saw that. People were impressed by that. For those who were impressionable, it was just so symbolic at that particular point in time. So we all were attracted to the idea of the Black Panther Party. And then, of course, when you have such a dynamic force, there's always an attempt to figure out how you're going to contend for space. There is only so much space, so how are you going to contend for the space? The bold, courageous position that they took inspired and influenced a lot of people. Certainly, in our space, we had created something which was just as bold on the campus. Two things happened with the Black Panther Party in how the relationship emerged between the Black Panther Party and the BSU. A number of the leaders in BSU had been involved in the Civil Rights Movement. They had been a part of SNCC and had come back and migrated to San Francisco after five years of engagement with SNCC. Some of the brothers had very close ties with the leadership of SNCC. It had had its own break-up, where it was based on tactics. There's a very long article, on a very long conversation that Dr King has, explaining the second march to Selma where he was battling with James Forman[18] and also Stokely Carmichael[19] over the use of Black Power. The split-up with SNCC happened over whether there were going to be White people or not in leadership roles and whether White people were going to be involved as members of SNCC in the struggle. All these things were precursors to this particular moment. So when SNCC was now taking another avenue, of course it was certainly attracted to the relationship possible with the Black Panther Party. Our relationship with SNCC, by virtue of members in the BSU who had come back to San Francisco State, put us directly in line, and eventually the relationship that was formed— pre-strike, during the strike, and post-strike—would be with the Black Panther Party. Of course, there were many roles the students could play, like helping to proofread the newspaper. Many of us played some role in that, like maybe contributing an article to the Black Panther Party paper. The Black Panther Party began to incorporate its programs. I was involved in the Free Breakfast for Children program in 1968. There was a Catholic Church where we provided free breakfast to young kids in the community. So those were the kinds of relationships that began to evolve. The strike itself was another case because the community was always out at the campus. Those are the kinds of relationships, the kinds of things I think you don't often see. I think it was a very strategic relationship. We often had political education classes. Part of that was the fact we all had been reading Fanon,[20] Marx, Chairman Mao. We read books; we had political education classes together. After the Bobby Hutton[21] murder, the arrest of Huey P. Newton, we often participated in protests, marching outside the courthouse. Now, we're talking about only a short period of time. And when we talk about the BSU, we're only talking about a short period of time. Students come to school; they don't have a lifetime on this campus. We're talking about that period of 1967, I think the spring of 1967, both inviting Baraka then securing Nathan Hare, through the strike, and through the spring of 1970. So we're talking about three years. Yeah, but it was an intense three years. You know, a bunch of us had been on trial all the summer of 1969 on charges around the strike. So it was an intense three years. But in that three-year period so many things were happening. From the relationships that we developed to the strike itself and the formation and the evolution of the Ethnic Studies program.

JRD I saw you a few months ago at the National Council for Black Studies [NCBS][22] and you were with some of your fellow students from SFSU. From what you know about contemporary Black Studies departments and programs, do you think we've reached some of the goals, some of the hopes that you had back in the 1960s?

DG It's hard to say because my involvement specifically with the Black Studies department has been one of an indirect involvement from the time that I left SFSU. It's very interesting, because I was talking to a politician who comes out of this very progressive atmosphere as well. She said, "One of the problems I'm having now, I get a lot of students who come out of college and come in here, but they don't know anything about organizing." In a sense she says some students from Black Studies programs have a lot of the names down and they know all the history and everything and that programs may have become more of a seat for understanding. I think from what I understand and feel that Black Studies should be a place that not only is able to reconstruct our social political past, and all its warts and everything else, but also understand the critical, political, social dynamics that play out today, the relationship between the past and the present with some sort of inference and emphasis placed upon the future as well, so that the program itself is a dynamic process, not a stagnant process. And I think it's not the [Black Studies] department itself, it's the clampdown of the university itself. The university should be a space, a place in which empire or power is challenged whatever that power is . . . If a power is challenged, the question then comes, where does the Black Studies program stand within that? I don't believe it can be a place that is without a position in the struggle. When I'm saying position, I don't mean a rhetorical position. I mean that it has to be a position in which it challenges and questions. And a lot of that challenge is going to be in service of movement building. It should be building movements . . . movement of ideas.

JRD When we last saw each other, you said you wanted to talk about some revisionist history occurring. Could you clarify what you meant by that, please?

DG Well, I think, certainly, there's a history that always forms, places itself as a part of a revisionist history. It's the history that diminishes people's contribution. That's the first part. They either deny that contribution or have amnesia about the contributions or talk about its relevance, or consider it to be irrelevant. Then there's the other kind of history. Ourselves. We're removed forty years from the strike and none of our memories are that great. I think we have the capability of over-embellishing what we actually did. What we actually did and what we could have done, perhaps are two different things. What we actually did, I think it is remarkable. The theory was quite extraordinary. I think we were quite extraordinary in that sense. Whether we were remarkable in its application is a whole other thing. But the idea, I think, was pretty spectacular. I know that in some sense, I think about how I've grown and I often reflect on what I might have done . . . if I had done something else, how I might have grown differently. But, yeah, we have to give ourselves credit. And there's plenty of credit. But we have to be truthful about that as well. I think we have to distinguish between the work we think we did and the work we actually did. But that's a whole other discussion too. And it's a discussion that we all fall into. We are all repositories of these stories, and within the stories, we tend to overlap reality with fantasy . . . It's like everybody's going to tell you they were scared when they went to jail [*laughter*]. The role we can be most beneficial in is to be able to dismantle our own thoughts about what happened and in doing so have an opportunity to use that as a platform of envisioning, to complete the work. If we knew what this was, even if it's a sketchy framework or even though they're half-baked ideas, we can have the opportunity now, with what we've learned and how we've grown, to add some new dynamic. We can tell our story. And we can say, "these are the things that we could have done." Imagine if there hadn't been an active Asian American Student Union or an active La Raza Hispanic group . . . Imagine what would have happened to us. We wouldn't have had the allies to build the coalition that we built had that not been the case. We did have the foresight, even though we were pulled dragging and screaming into it, to realize that in order to make this strike more effective, and as it became more effective, as it became a head-line, to be able to embrace these other ideas and embrace these coalitions. We did have the foresight to do that, and that's to our credit too because it began, certainly, not as a battle for Ethnic Studies, but it began solely, in a very narrow way, as a battle for Black Studies.

ON ACTIVISM

JRD You mentioned the relationship between the community and the students. As you know, one of the hallmarks of Black Studies is that we should be involved with the community. I think now, when we talk about the community, we're talking about not just the local community, but we're thinking globally. So we can be talking about activism and working politically in the local community, but we can also be talking about further afield. What are your thoughts about that? And also would you talk a little bit about your activism. We have a lot of students who come into Black Studies and they say, "I want to serve, I want to give back to the community" and that might be the local or the larger community.

DG I think my activism is not particularly singular, in some sense. What I believe and what is the strong core of my belief is the fact that I remain engaged with people who are trying to envision and construct relationships, and that's what's important to me. I remain engaged in that process and that process is deliberate, and that process is strong, and that process is what energizes me. I think more than anything else that maybe what I say is a collective effort. I've been able to sustain some sort of idea of myself and some sort of relationship with this because of the way in which I've been brought into various struggles. My involvement in the Anti-Apartheid Movement deepened and enriched my career, my work, as an artist. So, that brought me right into work I did as an artist, right into this intersect with the Anti-Apartheid Movement. You can't separate those two things. I could have made choices like some people did, just done the play, gotten the benefit of the play and gone home. But the choices, because of my own political development, brought me into another place. This allowed me to feel comfortable, because sometimes actors don't feel comfortable in having a space. They may have that space as a character in a play. That doesn't necessarily mean they want to have that space in real life. And because they feel uncomfortable, because they have not had the kind of political nurturing . . . they may have read about it . . . but not understood the passion. So they are able to take whatever information they do have and translate it into a performance within what they are doing. But I think it's important to understand that when I began to search for people that I wanted to align myself with, people that I think were supportive of my ideas, I wanted to identify with people like Harry Belafonte.[23] I wanted to identify with people like Ossie Davis[24] and Ruby Dee.[25] I wanted to identify with Paul Robeson[26] . . . which meant that I was not only an artist, but I wanted to be able to articulate and understand the other dynamics, political dynamics, the dynamics that are part of the journey. And I don't think that I would have ever been sustained as an actor if the other part was not part of it. I couldn't sustain myself as an actor. I couldn't sustain myself in some sort of way of delineating and deconstructing these two relationships.

JRD Listening to what you are saying makes sense. I guess you got into activism even before you were an artist.

DG You know, I think we're born into it. For all of us who were children of the Civil Rights Movement, all of us who were born into it, I think our early sensibilities and consciousness began to evolve at that particular point in time. And so as children we made choices in terms of deciding: this is what we wanted to hear, this is who we wanted to hear, and this is what we wanted to believe. There was a seriousness with which we applied ourselves as we began to read Fanon and others. Of course, we always thought that we had new tools. And we were expanding our own intellect and our own reference point by talking about these people, understanding what they had to say, making the connection and applying what they had to say to our own experience. I think that was a very important part of our collective understanding of what we were doing . . . the idea of coming out of something, believing that you are doing something important, believing that you're not singular in this effort, in this movement, in this journey and were trying to find a different understanding of your own discontent. You're young and you have all this stuff in you. Some people were able to express that in some kind of antisocial behavior. We chose to express that in some sort of behavior that was productive. I think more than anything else that I was fortunate that I was able to move from that and be able to take that sensibility and that understanding and translate it into my work.

JRD I mentioned earlier that our students often want to serve the community. What if a Black Studies student were to come up and say to you, "How would you recommend I get started being an activist?" How might you respond?

DG Well, the first thing is to explore what ways you can be active on the campus itself. Even though I think what has happened on campuses now is the stifling of dissent, it can be a very fertile place to begin that process. What kind of dialogue do you find? It's going to depend. Now there's been a lot of talk about a "green" economy, communities becoming "green." How can you search out those kinds of things in the community? Service means engaging in the community and getting yourself out of your comfort zone in order to explore, understand, learn, and by doing so, having empathy for people's struggles. You cannot serve unless you have empathy for people's struggles. What I see in the community is not a bunch of victims, but people finding ways in which they can access power for power within the self. If you see them from that vantage point and support that evolution that's another part of it. It's supporting people's own sense of themselves, the sense of their own power. That's an integral part of activism. But, it's something that has to be a part of your consciousness because it's not something that you do and walk away from and pin a plaque on your wall to say, "I did this, on this date." I remember I spent a lot of time in New Orleans after the hurricane[27] and I saw students who came down there in groups, volunteers from various colleges, or students who were protesting in relationship to the Jena Six.[28] How do you now take that and run with that in some other way? How do we mentor, elicit the kind of response that gets them thinking proactively about what they are doing, what they've seen? It's very interesting; I've been playing with this thing around vision, seeing. I did a film, *Blindness*.[29] As I thought about it and talked about it, what are the challenges of seeing something, bearing witness to something and then responding to what you've seen? Responding in a humane way to what you see. Now, you can walk away and pretend that you didn't see it, or you can walk away and allow that to be erased from your memory. But how does that memory in some sense activate something in you to do something about it? Often, associated with seeing something is a whole other level of fear because now you have to respond to what you see. One of the questions early in the movie is, after seeing torture, one of the young women responds. Actually she was a lawyer, I believe, and she talked about the mechanics of the case. The mechanics of the case may work in your favor within a structurally flawed system, but that does not in any way now validate the system. It may validate that you found a loophole to get through the system. But how do we find the system, how do we define the system and re-imagine the system itself and then work toward a new kind of way of looking at the system or a new system itself? So that's the kind of substantive work that I think has to be connected to service. In some sense, we have to question; we have to address the moment, the immediacy of it, the urgency at hand; and then we have to begin to find ways in which we can change the paradigm. Not only change the paradigm in the expression and discourse involved—we have to find ways in which we change the discourse. That's part of what I mean when I think about service. I have a guy who says, "Man, I dig you, and the causes you finance." I said, "I'm not into causes." I don't collect causes. There's a connection. When I think about things we need to do and the things that we need to service, the issues on economic and social justice, they're not causes, they're movements. They are movements for equality and change. So, on the one hand, I think service has to be tied to that. Just as much as King's words about "I have a dream" are misused and abused, I think his words about service are misused. It's important to serve meals to hungry people, but if I'm serving meals, I have to find out and understand the root of hunger, the root of joblessness, the root of homelessness, and put that in the framework as I move toward changing it. Not to add any Band-aids to the situation, but disrupt the whole situation and change the situation.

JRD What has been the most challenging fight in which you've been involved, in terms of seeking social justice?

DG Without a doubt, the death penalty . . . the abolition of it. When you live in a culture that is so vengeful, a culture where there's no love or redemption or reconciliation, that's grounded in a violent response to almost every single thing, never looking at the kind of underlying social dynamics, and the response is reaction to what has happened somewhere down the line—it's the hardest thing. You know, I worked on Gary Graham's case for seven years. I think it was 2000 that they finally executed him. You know, giving money, doing all the things, going down there. Always down to Austin, Texas, Houston, Texas. I thought for sure the combined effort of all of us, me and my visibility, the people who were mobilized, would at least give us some sort of redress of the situation. It's the most frustrating fight of all. Mike Farrell,[30] God bless him, has been so steadfast as an opponent of the death penalty. It was Mike Farrell who called me in '93 and said, "Man, they're scheduled to execute this kid." I got on a plane and went down to Houston, Texas. I remember saying to a newscaster that I didn't know what else to do. If I was going to be in pain about this I might as well be down there. That's been the most difficult. It eats you up because you're dealing with one case, and even if you win one case, does it dramatically change the kind of systemic structural application of the death penalty? Not at all. Just that single case.

JRD And Texas is the capital of the death penalty.

DG It is the capital, you know. I carry a pin in my bag. I've been carrying it about a young kid. He's eighteen years old. He's marrying this girl. He's been on death row. His mother and father, God bless them. His father is a minister. And I hold on to the memory, but you're almost scared to call, because it's endless. I keep looking for some light at the end of the tunnel, someplace where people will say that it's unethical, it's immoral, to execute your own citizens. An eye for an eye, as Gandhi said, leaves us all blind. It's been very hard for me after Gary Graham[31] to get involved too deeply. I've been opposed to the death penalty since I was a kid, and marched in the demonstrations before an execution in San Quentin in the early 1960s.

JRD What keeps you keeping on with all of this?

DG Well, you know, Jeanette, what keeps me more than anything else is that I will not allow power to relegate us to irrelevancy. And that's what it is. I will not allow them to do that. And if it just becomes a handful of us, still like that, I will not allow us to be relegated to irrelevancy. And that's what they attempt to do every day, to diminish us and to make us feel irrelevant. So, in that sense . . . it's self-serving, because I want to wake up in the morning and feel that what we, what I have to say, what I feel, matters and is relevant. Some may not like me for saying it, but I sleep at night and know I said it. And it's about the fact that I'm not afraid. In a sense we're all afraid. I'm afraid. I fear. I say "Hey, I'm afraid." Sometimes I walk down the street and sometimes that fear is physical, for physical danger. I don't know who's walking behind me. I don't carry an entourage or bodyguards. But most of the time, I'm not afraid. I feel like I've learned and grown and experienced things with people and that gives me the right to dissent.

JRD Who has been your inspiration?

DG Without a doubt, my initial inspiration is from my mom and dad. Not that they did something that was a landmark in terms of the work that they did. But the climate that they provided . . . I don't know how to describe it. Maybe it's indescribable, but there was a climate, a presence, a smile, a feeling of being loved. You didn't have any question about that, or that I loved them. There never was a question about that. Without a doubt they're my strongest inspiration.

JRD I always like to hear you talk about your mom and your dad because it shines out of you what was going on in that relationship. It's like me with my mom and dad.

DG Yeah . . . Yeah . . . Yeah . . . I miss my parents every day. And with my mother, because of my dreams, there's always been a presence . . . the present, not the past. And I'm so grateful that I have them. Nothing spectacular. No great panache or audacious expressive, demonstrative whatever . . . Just . . .

JRD Just always there . . .

DG Just there . . . Yeah . . . very simple, you know. I remember my mom. She was just so beautiful and she had so much pride, you know. And my dad . . . "Hey man, what's happening? What's going on dude?" . . . My man . . . yeah.

JRD And they're smiling down on you right now . . .

DG Yeah . . .

ON TELLING STORIES

JRD I'd like to ask you about the links between education, advocacy, and creative production and how these are integrated for you. What are some of the ways that you want to educate with your films? And then also, what stories of the community do you want to tell through your films? You talk a lot about telling stories . . .

DG One of the best ways of storytelling is to tell a story which we don't often see, tell a story of a major event or change . . . through the eyes of those people we wouldn't necessarily think about on that day, like when King is assassinated in Memphis. What happens in Memphis and how did that change their lives? You can tell life-affirming stories and transformation. The key part of that is transformation, from ordinary to extraordinary. Those are the kinds of stories that most move me. And what is the emotional danger that one has to overcome in order to go through that path and follow that track? That really is the kind of story to tell.

JRD What would be a good example? How might you illustrate that?

DG Let's take a film about a guy who is haunted by something that happened to him thirty years ago. I don't mean haunted like in a scary sense. Something happens in his life that brings all the forces from thirty years back and he has to contend with it and deal with it. And he doesn't know exactly all the elements of it. He knows that something is happening . . . he's putting the pieces together. That would be an interesting story. Even though it was contrived in a lot of ways, I liked *Marathon Man*[32] with Dustin Hoffman and Sir Laurence Olivier. From the first moment you see these explosions, you don't know what happened. I like those kinds of stories. How do we now invest it with some real other kinds of cultural and political stuff that happens in it? Who said what? Who did what? That's one example of a story.

JRD What about a film that you've acted in or produced? Which ones can you imagine being used in Black Studies in this way that you are discussing?

DG When I think about the idea of Black Studies, I think about it as an artist, in images, and how images are presented, and how stories are told, and what choices are made in terms of the storyteller, and how information is disseminated and what choices are made about what information you get, that are accessible to you. All of those are framed within the very simple way of what I do in some way, and the nuances of all the projection of images, nuances in relationship to the application of images. With *Buffalo Soldiers*[33] the purpose was to explore racial reconciliation and healing. Film can be a process of reasserting our own sense of our own history, and documenting our own story. We understand who people are and how they see themselves through the way in which they express themselves through their fiction. I gave a fictionalized account based upon the values that I wanted to uphold, the values that I wanted to embrace within a relationship between Native Americans and African Americans. The moment after I finished the film, the film was aired; I got a call from the great-great-granddaughter of an Apache chief and she told me all through her experience, her experience as a child in the storytelling and their communicating about the past, they heard of such an incident that I just dramatized, that I fictionalized, because that's the relationship that I wanted to explore. What a validation. What a reaffirmation about what we have the capacity to do. Imagine what kind of bridges we could build. As an artist I can begin to view my vision of the world through my art. I became a conduit. I feel fortunate.

JRD That's wonderful, and it's a great example.

DG I suspect this whole odyssey, this journey I've been on to do the story [about Toussaint L'Ouverture][34] of the Haitian Revolution will also reveal something else in that sense. There's some value in this for people who understand the human struggle for social justice. I suppose because it had a certain value to a certain people, to a certain group, the Haitian Revolution is a part of the people's history. It may not be a part of the empire's history, you know. Our empire's own take or its expression of its early history is *its* invention. But it's certainly part of the people's history. Those are the kinds of things that keep me, my spirit, alive and help me navigate through this whole thing.

JRD Could you talk about *Beloved?*

DG Yes. *Beloved.* I don't really think we understand the importance of such a film. We walk down the street, and we move through life, and we contend with what we have to deal with. We contend with our past, our past memory, our historic memory of our life. But *Beloved.* What does it feel like? You're at this place where some people who have been institutionalized by a brutal system for so long are now free. I always find that Watch Night[35] is very interesting. Watch Night is from December 31st through to the first [of January], that period of time after midnight. What that must have been like? You know, all this collected pain all of a sudden is released. But not released. You could make an argument that it hasn't stopped now. It's another form. What does it feel like when you come out of that, that moment with all your fears and all your anger and all your guilt? They're all part of that. *Beloved* was about the discovery of self. What is self like and everything imposed upon the self? Everything imposed upon you as a human being has relegated you to be less than human, without any comprehension of a self. What is it like to slowly, meticulously, and often in a collective way learn about that? And *Beloved* was about that. It was all of the darkness, all of the darkness. I love Psalm 139, verses 6 through 12.[36] The last verse is "The darkness *and* the light are the light to you." On this thought that's come to me, what is it like, what is that like? Ex-slaves referred to Abe Lincoln as "the coming of the Lord . . . The coming of the Lord! The coming of the Lord!" Freedom from their bondage! You know there is something so heroic and humbling at the same time to come out of that experience. And I think all the glimpses that you see of us Black people, the way they do what they do, that's so incredible, you know, to come out of all of that pain. *Beloved* was about all of that—to celebrate, a collective celebration, discovery of a self. That's what I think *Beloved* was about.

JRD Yes. It is incredible.

DG Yeah.

JRD What words of encouragement would you have for students reading this text, who want to become agents of change? And what other words might you have for students who are looking at you as a role model?

DG I don't know about the role model part of it. But certainly I want them to believe that they, while ordinary, can become extraordinary. I just want them to believe that they're loved. That loving and caring are the two most important things you can do. I think that's what I want them to believe every day.

JRD That's a great note to end on. Thank you, Danny, for all the time you have given me in a day that was already very busy for you. Please know I really appreciate you.

We give special thanks and appreciation for our dear friend Wayne C. Thompson (1946–2008) who first introduced us and made this, and another, interview possible. (See Jeanette R. Carlisle Davidson, "A Conversation with Danny Glover and Joslyn Barnes," *World Literature Today*, vol. 82, no. 2 (2008), 24–9.) Wayne had a passionate love of Africa and the people of the African Diaspora, an intense commitment to social justice, and was a tireless advocate for all people in need. He was integral to the fight for the freedom of members of the San Francisco 8 (see this volume, Chapter 9) and was a staunch supporter of the University of Oklahoma's African & African American Studies program, which now honors his legacy of service with the Wayne C. Thompson Memorial Scholarship.

JRD and DG

NOTES

1. The first Black Student Union (BSU) was formed on the campus of the San Francisco State College. BSU, along with Third World Liberation Front, formed a student-led strike along with faculty and community activists.
2. The Student Nonviolent Coordinating Committee was established in 1960.
3. Harry Bridges (1901–90) was an Australian American leader of the International Longshore and Warehouse Union. He was prosecuted during the 1930s, 1940s, and 1950s by the US government and was convicted by a federal jury when accused of lying about Communist Party membership. The conviction was later set aside. The Harry Bridges Center for Labor Studies was established in his honor in 1992 at the University of Washington, Seattle.
4. Mario Savio (1942–96), born in New York. Political activist and key member of the Berkeley Free Speech Movement.
5. Wayne C. Thompson (1946–2008), born in Oklahoma. Community activist for social justice throughout the US, Mozambique, Haiti, and elsewhere. Friend of Danny Glover from the 1960s.
6. John Bowman of Oklahoma. Community activist. One of the San Francisco 8. Long-time close friend of Danny Glover and Wayne C. Thompson.
7. Amiri Baraka (1934–) from Newark, NJ, is an acclaimed author of over forty books of essays, drama, poetry, music history and criticism; political activist; Professor Emeritus, State University of New York, Stony Brook and Poet Laureate of New Jersey.
8. Ed Bullins (1935–), playwright, educator, and activist.
9. Huey P. Newton (1942–89), born in Louisiana. Co-founder of the Black Panther Party.
10. Black House, cultural and political organization. Active participants included Ed Bullins, Eldridge Cleaver, Huey Newton, Bobby Seale, and others.
11. Nathan Hare (1933–), born in Oklahoma. First person to coordinate a Black Studies program at San Francisco State College in 1968.
12. John Summerskill, president of San Francisco State College 1966–68.
13. The establishment of Asian American Studies, Black Studies, La Raza Studies, Native American Studies-in Ethnic Studies began in 1968–69 when students of the Black Student Union and Third World Liberation Front, staff, and faculty, as well as members from the larger Bay Area community, organized and led a series of actions to protest systematic discrimination, lack of access, neglect, and misrepresentation of histories, cultures, and knowledge of indigenous peoples and communities of color within the university's curricula and programs.
14. Hugh Masekela (1939–) born Witbank, South Africa. Trumpeter, singer, composer, bandleader. Jazz; Afrobeat.
15. McCarthy era. McCarthyism, named after Senator Joseph McCarthy, was a period of intense anti-communism, which occurred in the United States from 1948 to about 1956, when the government actively persecuted the Communist Party USA, its leadership, and others suspected of being communists.
16. The Watts Riots of 1965 was a large-scale riot, which lasted six days in the Watts neighborhood of Los Angeles, California, in August 1965. The riots started after the

arrest of a young African American motorist pulled over by a White patrolman, for suspicion of driving while intoxicated. A crowd of onlookers watched as he was being arrested and tensions rose between the police and the crowd. The community of Watts rioted in protest at poor living conditions, bad schools, and unemployment.

17. See texts on the Black Panther Party by two authors in this volume: Curtis J. Austin, *Up Against the Wall: Violence in the Making and Unmaking of the Black Panther Party* (Little Rock, AR: University of Arkansas Press, 2006); and Charles Jones, *The Black Panther Party [Reconsidered]* (Baltimore, MD: Black Classic Press, 1998).

18. James Forman (1928–2004) was an American Civil Rights leader active in the Student Nonviolent Coordinating Committee, the Black Party, and the International Black Workers Congress.

19. Stokely Churchill Carmichael (1941–98) was a Black activist in the Civil Rights Movement in the 1960s. He was the first leader of the Student Nonviolent Coordinating Committee (SNCC) and later served as leader of the Black Panther Party. He later became affiliated with the Black Nationalist and Pan-Africanist movements.

20. Frantz Fanon. See *Black Skins White Masks* (New York: Grove Press, 1967). Originally published in French, *Peau noire, masques blancs* (Paris: Editions Du Seuil, 1952).

21. Bobby Hutton, at age sixteen, was the youngest member of the Black Panther Party. The Oakland police killed him after he had surrendered and stripped down to his underwear to prove that he was unarmed.

22. African American scholars who wanted to formalize the study of the African World experience and to meet the need of the developing discipline of Africana/Black Studies established NCBS in 1975. Today it is the leading organization of Black Studies professionals headed by Charles Jones, an author in this volume.

23. Harry Belafonte (1927–). Actor, composer, author, producer, singer, and activist who grew up in Jamaica, British West Indies. Belafonte was an early supporter of the Civil Rights Movement in the 1950s. Like many civil rights activists, Belafonte was treated badly during the McCarthy era. He raised thousands of dollars to release imprisoned civil rights protesters; helped finance the Freedom Rides; supported voter registration drives; and helped to organize the March on Washington in 1963.

24. Ossie Davis (1917–2005) was an actor and an unwavering social activist who came under an anti-communist attack for his support of the powerful African American actor, singer, and social activist Paul Robeson. An avid supporter of the US Civil Rights Movement and close friend of Martin Luther King, Jr. Davis helped to facilitate the rally at the historic 1963 March on Washington, along with his wife, Ruby Dee. During that rebellious period of the 1960s, Davis became a good friend of Malcolm X and later delivered a moving eulogy at his funeral in 1965.

25. Ruby Dee (1924–), actor, author, and activist, is a member of the Congress of Racial Equality (CORE), NAACP, the Student Nonviolent Coordinating Committee (SNCC), and the Southern Christian Leadership Conference (SCLC). Dee and husband Ossie Davis were personal friends of both Martin Luther King, Jr. and Malcolm X. See also Ossie Davis and Ruby Dee, *With Ossie and Ruby: In This Life Together* (New York: William Morrow, 1998).

26. Paul Robeson (1898–1976). Internationally renowned bass-baritone concert singer, scholar, actor of film and stage, professional athlete, writer, multilingual orator, and lawyer, who was also noted for his wide-ranging social justice activism. Robeson was the first major concert star to popularize the performance of Negro Spirituals and was the first Black actor of the twentieth century to portray Shakespeare's Othello on Broadway. Robeson's political views and activism for civil rights for African-American and oppressed peoples worldwide caused him to suffer public condemnation in the United States.

27. Hurricane Katrina. See *Trouble the Water* (Zeitgeist Films, 2009). Academy award nominee for best documentary feature on the story of Hurricane Katrina of 2005, directed and produced by Tia Lessin and Carl Deal. Executive produced by Joslyn Barnes and Danny Glover of Louverture Films.

28. The Jena Six are a group of six African-American teenagers convicted in the beating of a White student at Jena High School in Jena, Louisiana in December 2006, due to racial tensions between Black and White youth. The original charge of attempted second-degree murder was seen as excessive and racially discriminatory.

29. See *Blindness* (Miramax Films (USA) and Focus Features (International), 2008), starring and narrated by Danny Glover.

30. Mike Farrell, actor and life-long opponent of the death penalty.

31. Gary Graham was a juvenile at the time of his arrest. His case received much attention, in part because of substantial evidence indicating that he was innocent of the murder charge and because his court-appointed lawyer failed to mount a serious legal defense. Anti-death penalty advocates, including actor Danny Glover, Reverend Jesse Jackson, Reverend Al Sharpton, and Amnesty International's Bianca Jagger, became involved with Graham's case in 1993, releasing public statements in support of his claim of innocence and arguing that the Texas justice system discriminated on the basis of race and class. Protests intensified after the NAACP Legal Defense Fund filed a complaint with the US Department of Justice contending that Graham was on death row as a direct result of widespread racial discrimination within the Texas criminal justice system.

32. Oscar-nominated movie *Marathon Man* (Paramount Studios, 1976).

33. See *Buffalo Soldiers* (Warner Home Video, 1997), starring Danny Glover.

34. Toussaint L'Ouverture (1743–1803) was a leader of the Haitian Revolution. Toussaint led enslaved Africans in a long struggle for independence from French colonizers, abolished slavery, and secured control over the colony of Haiti. Currently (i.e., 2008), Danny Glover is in the process of bringing this story to film.

35. Watch Night is a service celebrated on New Year's Eve in Black churches throughout the world. It can be traced back to December 31, 1862, known as "Freedom's Eve." On that night, Blacks gathered in churches and private homes awaiting the news that the Emancipation Proclamation had been made law. At the stroke of midnight, January 1, 1863 all the slaves in the Confederate states were declared legally free. There were shouts of praise and prayers given to God for this. Black churches still gather on New Year's Eve to thank God for another year.

36. Psalm 139: 6–12. New International Version. "6 Such knowledge is too wonderful for me, too lofty for me to attain.7 where can I go from your Spirit? Where can I flee

from your presence 8 If I go up to the heavens, you are there; if I make my bed in the depths, you are there. 9 If I rise on the wings of the dawn, if I settle on the far side of the sea 10 even there your hand will guide me, your right hand will hold me fast. 11 If I say, "Surely the darkness will hide me and the light become night around me,"12 even the darkness will not be dark to you; the night will shine like the day, for darkness is as light to you."

CHAPTER 6

Black Studies for the Public: Interview with Manning Marable (September 2008)

Jeanette R. Davidson

University of Oklahoma

ON THE COMMITMENT TO THE PUBLIC

JRD You have intimated that you believe Black Studies should be for the public. I wanted to ask first, what exactly do you mean by that and why is it important?

MM For me, Black Studies is the African American intellectual tradition. It is grounded in, and an analysis of, the lived experience of Black folk through their history and the consciousness derived from that experience. African American Studies is the interdisciplinary interrogation of that experience. As a body of critical texts, it has over the years acquired certain characteristics. African American Studies is, first and perhaps foremost, "descriptive." It provides, if we use Geertz's expression, "thick description."[1] It provides a thick description, a nuanced approach to the realities of Black life, of love, of work, of faith, of activism, of triumph and tragedy. It is a thick description of Black life as Black people understand it to be. It is "corrective" in that much of Black Studies literature is a defense of the humanity of Black people. So much of the Social Sciences, and especially the Natural Science literature about people of African descent, is a running "dis" of Black people. So someone has to defend us as human beings and our innate capacities like other human beings to think, to reason, and to be worthy of civil and human rights. And so Black Studies defends Black people and it is "prescriptive." Black Studies seeks not only to interpret but to transform the world in ways that empower Black people. So there is an element of advocacy in Black Studies that some scholars feel taints the field because it links it to various social justice or political projects.

There are very dedicated practitioners of African American Studies and very prominent scholars who feel that Black Studies should not, in any way, be political. I had a debate with my good friend Henry Louis Gates[2] about this in the *New York Times* back in April 1998, I believe, about this very issue. My feeling on this is pretty straightforward. If you are Black in America, given the history of this country, everything is political. We would, at our peril, feel any other way. We have to contest, vigorously, the processes of racialization and stigmatization that are imposed upon us, and so consequently Black Studies must be prescriptive. It must be in the forefront of providing solutions to real problems that Black people have in their daily lives. If Black Studies does not go into prisons, where over a million Black men and women are, what good is it? If Black Studies is not going to the community to focus on voter education and registration and mobilize people around issues such as police brutality, or environmental racism, or of the devastating absence of public healthcare, then what good is it? Black Studies must shed light on the lived experiences of Black folk and the problems we encounter, and provide meaningful solutions to those problems, if we can. So, the intellectual body of the work of Black Studies has tended to be descriptive, corrective, and prescriptive,[3] all of which serve the public. That is, for whom is Black Studies? Who does it exist for? It exists foremost and firstly for Black folk. That is not to racialize the audience of Black Studies. That is to say that, through intellectual inquiry, the stories we preserve, the culture we celebrate, the heritage that we document, serve to reinforce and underscore memory and tradition and a vision and possibility for young Black people who are only entering school now, and for those not yet born . . . that there is a heritage and tradition worth defending and not apologizing for. That doesn't mean that scholarship can't be produced by Euro-Americans. Extraordinary works of great clarity and intellectual rigor have been written by colleagues who are Euro-American. Black Studies is for everyone. It's for White students, Asian students, African-Americans. But it does have a special meaning and purpose for Black people. It goes to the heart of their culture and their tradition and heritage, and that we cannot deny. So yes, it is for the public. It must be accessible to people and something that they can use. It must be grounded in the lived experience of Black people in all its rich diversity; therefore it cannot be uniform. It has to reflect that rich diversity. And that's what makes Black Studies so exciting.

JRD Yes, it is. Can you tie this in, historically, with the development of Black Studies, please?

MM Yes. There are different points of view about this. I'm thinking about my good friend Maulana Karenga,[4] who tends to think of Black Studies as evolving out of the 1960s. I take a different point of view. I see it as the African-American and Afro-Caribbean intellectual tradition that evolved in the beginning in the early nineteenth century in the United States and the Caribbean as Black scholars, outside of the "ivory tower." Working with very few resources and limited institutional support, they fought to develop a body of work that would preserve the heritage of the people of African descent and would interpret the meaning of Black culture and Black life. I point to people like Edward Wilmot Blyden[5] in the Caribbean and in the United States and a number of people that I can think of. The first person who comes to mind is Du Bois.[6] Also in the nineteenth century there were a variety of people, educators, abolitionists, lecturers, like Frederick Douglass[7] and Anna Julia Cooper,[8] who helped lay the foundations for what would become Black Studies. Martin R. Delany,[9] in his powerful, immigrationist critique of White Supremacy in 1851, helped to set up the foundations for a Malcolm X a century later. Without the scholarship and the writings of Black women and men in the nineteenth century, we would not have produced a Garvey,[10] or a Malcolm, or the Black Panther Party in the twentieth century.[11] It simply would not have happened. So the scholarship and the writing go back to that period and come all the way forward. During the period from roughly the 1880s until the early 1960s—nearly a century—the vast majority of Black scholarship was produced at Historically Black Colleges. The simple reason for that was Jim Crow. White people simply did not hire Black people, generally until World War II. When I arrived at Columbia in 1993, the total number of Black tenured faculty in the College of Arts and Sciences was five, counting myself. Today, it's a little over thirty. We've had a big change in the last fifteen years and I'm glad to have been a part of that change, all because for ten years I was the director of the Institute for Research in African American Studies[12] and I helped to initiate, directly or indirectly, a number of those hires. But White Supremacy is so deeply ingrained in American academe that scholars like Ralph Bunche[13] would never be hired at White institutions, so he pursued a career path that took him to the United Nations. Horace Clayton[14] or say a St. Clair Drake,[15] who came to intellectual maturity after World War II, was able to have access to a place like Roosevelt University and then Stanford University, during and after the Black Power period. But prior to that, oh no! Du Bois, with his PhD from Harvard and advanced studies at the University of Berlin, could never be hired at a White institution. So it was the Black Colleges that sustained Black Studies. Most of the classic texts that we teach in African American Studies come from that period. So, unlike some who say Black Studies started in the 1960s, I disagree. It didn't start then. That's ridiculous. You know, the literatures that we teach emanate from that period of Jim Crow and racial segregation, and historically Black Colleges were sites of intellectual production. We are legatees of that, we are connected to that and build from it.

JRD Can you describe Columbia University's Center for Contemporary Black History?[16] And if you would, please talk, first, about its general function and then the kinds of projects that are developed at the Center.

MM The Center for Contemporary Black History is probably what I would have created had someone given me *carte blanche*—or perhaps I should say *carte noire*—when I first arrived here more than fifteen years ago. Instead, I was offered the opportunity to create a permanent African American Studies program. Here, one did not exist prior to 1993. There was something in the catalog that said African American Studies, but it really didn't exist. The Institute for Research in African American Studies, where we're sitting now, and the offices around us and other places, are a part of what was constructed since 1993. In 2002, I was preparing for my own liquidation as the director. I didn't have what I call the Black College Presidents' syndrome, where you want to hang around forever and be an impediment to younger scholars. I wanted to complement their work. I feel a great deal of pride and joy in the fact that everybody I hired was significantly younger than me. And, at fifty-eight, I still don't feel anachronistic. I knew that I was going to leave being the director of the Institute but I wanted a structure which would allow me to pursue intellectual projects of the public nature that would impact people's lives. Many of these projects would be digitally based—all of them, actually—would be grounded in multi-media where we would use film, and we would develop innovative websites. We'd develop documentary films, things like that. And so we created the Center. The provost approved the existence of it. The Institute—I'm going to use the acronym, we call it IRAAS—provides base funding, but I am obligated to go out and raise money for it. I've been very fortunate in that the Soros Foundation,[17] the Open Society Institute,[18] and the Ford Foundation[19] have funded part of our work over the years, as well as IRAAS, and I also contribute, especially to *Souls*,[20] personally to underwrite the journal. Journals never make money, but *Souls* is like my child and it's an investment in the intellectual future. But I've done that for some time. Of the projects that we pursue, *Souls* is the first. We started *Souls* in January 1999. It has now celebrated its tenth year. Volume 11 begins in January 2009. It is a quarterly journal that is published by Columbia University's Center for Contemporary Black History in partnership with Taylor & Francis Publishers of the UK, based in London and also Philadelphia. It goes throughout the world. They're very happy with us. We're expanding the size of it. We have an editorial board of contributing editors of over seventy-five. Some of the most prominent scholars who write on the issue of race in the Americas and the Caribbean are on our board. We have an editorial working group of about a dozen people who really do the work of setting up the journal. At least once a year, we do an issue that focuses outside of the United States, so we've done issues on Jamaica, South Africa, Latin America. We have a double issue this year on Black social protest movements and we're looking comparatively at people of African descent in the Indian Ocean, to Latin America, to Asia, to Europe, with Clarence Lusane[21] writing a brilliant piece. We try to look at the total Black experience transnationally. Our focus is the United States, but not exclusively, so that's one project. The second project is the Malcolm X Project. It's my major biography of Malcolm. The website is www.malcolmxproject.net. We're going to make it much more robust. But right now we get about 3,500 hits a week to 5,000 hits a week. Many people have used the site for research papers and things like that. The biography is coming along well. We should be done—I say "we" because the grad students that work with me are MXP'ers, Malcolm X Project grad students. We should be done with the book in about a year or less. It should be out in 2010. The third project is the Africana Criminal Justice project. Soros started us out with that back in 2002. We have done several things in the project. We taught a course for four years in Rikers [Island],[22] working with young Black men and Hispanic men in arts education, to get young men to write about their experience being incarcerated through spoken word. We used poetry as a vehicle for them to interrogate race, crime, and justice. We also have developed a reader on *Racializing Justice, Disenfranchising Lives*[23] with Palgrave Macmillan. Keesha Middlemass, who is a brilliant professor of Political Science and Criminology at Rutgers University at Newark, and I co-edited, so that's a project. Another project that we are actively involved in has been funded for several years by the Ford Foundation, called amastadresource.org.[24] This is a website where we are teaching teachers how to teach Black history in Junior and Senior high schools, developing PDFs for them to drop into the classroom setting that are eminently teachable. They can teach and they have maps and video clips and newsreel footage, as well as the narrative text I provide. And it's free. The whole idea of it is to make these resources free to public school teachers. Ford is underwriting it, but we are going after, hopefully, a seven-figure support on the outside so we can make these resources free to people. Not based on market economics, but based on the need our people have to know their own history and to teach it effectively. So these are the kinds of projects our Center does, with very few resources and a very small staff. It's me and Courtney Teague, who's a great secretary, and my grad students. That's our shop.

JRD It's amazing. I wanted to ask about your audience. You talked about how many hits you have, and I was going to ask you about—and I know it's one of your areas that you care very deeply about—the number of African American men and women who are incarcerated. I wanted to know about your work's impact on them.

MM In fact, I left out the most recent project. Just before you came today, I was invited to speak at Omaha, Nebraska, which is the birthplace of Malcolm X, in January 2008. I met a group of Black folk from the city who have set up a non-profit corporation to celebrate Malcolm's life. Some of these brothers and sisters had been incarcerated. And they celebrate Malcolm, in part, because of the triumph of his life in overcoming criminalization in the "Detroit Red" phase of his life and because they had left prison and were leading productive lives which were transformative to the Black community. I thought it was a great idea. Over the last couple of months, about once a week, they have had meetings and they call me and we talk about how you can incorporate Malcolm X's life into a curriculum that can go into the prison to be transformative for prisoners . . . for them to have successful re-entry into civil society. How do you do that? And what lessons can we learn from Malcolm's life that will empower them? This is what Malcolm would respect. This is what Black Studies must do. To me this is a Black Studies project. There are a million Black people in prison, and if Black Studies scholars aren't in prisons, then there is no defense for their intellectual work. There has to be an interrogation of significant sites that reproduce racialized inequality. The prison industrial complex is the major site in the twenty-first century that reproduces racism, without a shred of doubt. Those kinds of places are where Black scholars must be. That's what I see as the function of our Center. To be places, to defend our humanity, and to document who we are as Black folk, and to try to find ways of empowering our people to lead productive and healthy lives.

I feel very good about those notions of advocacy being central to my intellectual project.

JRD I can see the link throughout what you are saying, with the Black intellectual tradition being descriptive, corrective, and prescriptive.

MM Right, exactly.

ON INTERDISCIPLINARITY AND PEDAGOGY

JRD In your projects, how do you tap into the interdisciplinary nature of Black Studies? Also, how are you inclusive of the particular as well as the universal? I'm using these words as you use them in your writing about the particular, looking at the racial variable, but also looking at the universal of which we have to be inclusive.

MM All right, let's think about, first, interdisciplinarity. There are a number of intellectual debates about this. Actually, both pedagogical discussions or debates and methodological debates about "What should Black Studies be?" in terms of a field or a discipline—or is it an interdisciplinary kind of field? My own sense of it is that Black Studies is best described as an intellectual tradition that has certain characteristics. Interdisciplinarity is one. It's central. The best example of that is the life of Du Bois. Here's a guy who acquires a PhD at Harvard when he's in his twenties. His PhD is on the transatlantic slave trade, so it's a classic kind of history. But he gets hired at Wilberforce University in Ohio, teaching Latin and the Classics, and Greek. After a short stay at the University of Pennsylvania, he goes to Atlanta University, where he develops, in effect, the foundations of modern Black Studies through the annual conferences he holds from 1898, through about 1913. When he's rehired at Atlanta University in 1934, he's hired as a professor of Sociology. So he's in Political Science, Sociology, History, the Classics. I've had something of a similar career in that my PhD is in History, which I received from the University of Maryland in 1976. I've been tenured in Political Science, in the Departments of Political Science, Economics, Public Affairs, the School of International Public Affairs, as well as in History and African American Studies. So, I think of myself as a renegade historian, in that history should be used to empower the oppressed and to challenge and to speak truth to power . . . to those "in power" . . . and that history is the foundation for any possible empowerment project on the part of the oppressed because, if you don't have a sense of where you've been . . . you can't possibly know where you want to go.

That history, the historical knowledge, grounds us to processes that transcend generations and push us forward. And so I found history, especially the methodology of oral history which I use, which is really central in the Malcolm X Project . . . has been a very powerful tool in telling the story that has always been suppressed. I see Black Studies, by definition, as an intellectual field that utilizes tools that draw upon various disciplines. Several years ago I wrote a book called *Living Black History*[25] and I basically argued that to reconstruct Black life, you need a 360-degree approach that must be interdisciplinary. Using tools from different disciplines to reconstruct a moment, a life, an event . . . that is central to the telling of Black truths, about who we are as a people. It could be a biography, it could be a novel, it could be any kind of narrative that is anchored to an event, a person, a place that is central to the telling of our truth as a people, so [it] must be interdisciplinary. So I draw upon music and folklore and art and religion. You have to take the tools that are hammered out in those disciplines and apply them in creative ways to the telling of that story.

JRD So you do that, for example, with the telling of the story of Malcolm.

MM That's right. You could do it no other way. I'll give you a good example. Malcolm comes to maturity at a time when bebop emerges in New York City, during the war. If you listen to Malcolm, what you hear, what musicians heard in Malcolm when they listened to him, was a bebop artist. His voice and his intonation and the way he used syncopation and the way he used his voice was like a jazz musician—how a jazz musician uses his instrument. That's why musicians followed him around; that's why they loved him. A brother came in off the street a couple years ago and he said, "I'm a jazz musician. I loved Malcolm." This was a brother who was in his late sixties, early seventies. He said, "I was there that day at the Audubon, and I put my tape recorder on the stage, and I was taping Malcolm and then the murder occurred. The assassination happened." He said, "So here's the tape." [He] gave me a tape-recording of Brother Benjamin Kareem, who was the assistant minister, giving his lecture, leading into Malcolm coming up on the stage. And it's an audiotape of the assassination. So why did musicians love Malcolm? Because Malcolm's voice was like an instrument. He was like "Bird."[26] He was like Dizzy Gillespie.[27] He was like this creative and talented genius, who could make people feel and see and desire things and see themselves in new ways. And that's what great art does. The reason the art is powerful is because it transforms us and makes us see new possibilities. That is what Malcolm did, right? It's what Edward Said[28] said, "The true revolutionary intellectual creates new souls." Said was right. That's what Malcolm did. So that's why it must be interdisciplinary. You draw upon all of those tools.

JRD So when you go on your website, your Malcolm website, you can pull up some of the music so that you are not just saying "this is the case," you're showing how it actually played out.

MM We tried to, although with limited resources that we have I'm happy that we're even able to have the website. We have a lot of material that we've put on. One of my big problems has been that in the evolution of the internet, so much material is proprietary, so that, for example, we have built, between 2001 and 2004, a multimedia version of the autobiography of Malcolm X. But you have to be at Columbia to see it. Because we use copyright material, it's embargoed. I checked recently on how much would it cost for me to get the rights to make this available to people. It's something like three-quarters of a million dollars. Since we don't have $750,000 in our budget, to utilize that resource you've got to be here at Columbia. However, our MalcolmXproject.net website provides a great number of things, especially things that we've drawn from the public domain.

Going back to this question, though, about the particular and the universal, you mentioned—I hadn't forgotten it—I think there are a lot of ways to answer that question. But I'd like to push you and ask you, how should this be taken? In other words, is this a philosophical question, or is it something that relates to how African American Studies is developed or constructed? Or is it a pedagogical question about how we go about teaching things?

JRD Actually, that's where I was coming from, as I was thinking about the Malcolm X Project for example. I tried to get on the website for Amistad, but I realized it was down. So really I was thinking pedagogically. I was looking at what you have written about focusing on the particular and the racial, but also having to be inclusive in order to speak globally.

MM I understand. In African American Studies, in the late 1960s and the early 1970s, when I was an undergraduate student, there was a big debate: "Should White people teach Black Studies?" Was there something that was uniquely drawing upon the Black experience by the individual instructor that gave her or him the capacity to reveal truths that White people couldn't reveal? Well, after seeing Clarence Thomas[29] and Condoleezza Rice,[30] I think we should be very clear that truths do not necessarily come in racialized packages. In other words, just because you are a Black person and you've lived a life as an African American in the United States, doesn't mean that you're going to come up with any kind of analysis that will benefit Black people generally. Perhaps this is the way that it should be, that once and for all we bury the notion of symbolic representation. When I was a kid, when we were asked, "What do Black people want?" We would say, "A Black face in a high place." We wanted somebody who looked like us in a position of authority because we believed that Black people, regardless of ideology, would have a sense of kinship and connectedness to Black people's problems and that, regardless of political party, they would fight for our interests. We were wrong. History has proved that wrong. There are many times in history where some of the greatest contributions, intellectually, were made by people who were not a part of a particular ethnic group, but who came to it from a different angle and who dedicated their lives to the integrity of telling that story with rigor and with courage. I think immediately of Herbert Aptheker[31] who was a great Black historian, but he happened to be White. I think of Condoleezza Rice, who is the face of US imperialism to much of the non-White and the Third World. This is not to play politics or to say something that is unfair, but is to describe the fundamental political truths that are occurring in the twenty-first century throughout this world and how the US is perceived as a militaristic Leviathan that crushes self-determination and the right of people to define for themselves what their collective political futures may be. We've drifted far away from the notion of life, liberty, and the pursuit of happiness or the democratic institutions that were a proud part of the country for many years, existing—as flawed as they were on questions of gender and race and class—to the point where there is a suppression of thought and, in the post-9/11 world, levels of surveillance and incarceration that shame us before the world. So there is a link between the particular and the universal. In telling the story of a Malcolm X, that is truthful story. I'm not in the business of building Saint Malcolm. His greatness is found in his humanity. He made mistakes. There were errors of judgment. There are things he shouldn't have done. But what's remarkable about him is that he's so richly and deeply human. The reason people love him is that they make a connection with him as a human being and so we honor him as an African American. I can tell this story. I teach a seminar on Malcolm X. I asked my class, "What was the fundamental difference between Dr King and Malcolm?" One of my students raised his hand and said, "Dr Marable, that's easy. Dr King belonged to the entire world, but Malcolm X belongs to us." There is a truth in this, which is not to discredit in any way Dr King, but it is to say that there is something that Malcolm spoke to that is deeply organic in Black life and the Black experience in ways that transcend nearly any other person. You could think of several other people who were very much like that . . . say, Paul Robeson.[32] You know, they could disagree with the Nation of Islam, but they really dug Malcolm. What's great about it is that the lessons in his life and the events that occurred and the manner of his death—all these have lessons that are universal, that speak to greater universal truths than anyone, regardless of their familiarity or lack of knowledge about African American culture, can learn from. Black Studies must seek to do both. It must begin with the particular but speak to the universal. It must draw upon a body which is very rich, but speak in a language that is accessible to everyone and make our literatures and our social science inquiries and our political analysis and our historical narratives, framing them so that we have the maximum exposure to interaction with people across this planet. The stories of African American people have extraordinary power and resonance with people of all countries and who speak different languages. We should never limit the boundaries of our field. I'm sorry to be so wordy.

ON THE USE OF ELECTRONIC MEDIA AND TECHNOLOGY

JRD No, this is great. I just want to say, "Yes, you're right, all the way through!" I wanted to go back to one point too, when we were talking about your audience. I think you really alluded to this, but I wanted you to articulate about the populations that you're reaching. Are you reaching populations overseas with your website? Are you reaching people, say, in Africa, in Cuba, elsewhere in the Diaspora? Then I'm going to move on to questions about the use of technology because that's opened up all these avenues for you. Then also we'll move on to talking about globalization. These questions are all interconnected.

MM That's fine. I'll give you a good example. I try, as a public intellectual, to utilize electronic media to impact political and public discourse. I have a number of friends, from Michael Eric Dyson[33] to Cornel West[34] and bell hooks[35] and Patricia Williams[36] and Kimberle Crenshaw,[37] who, far better than I, know how to do that. One nice thing about being in New York City, however, is that the media is very accessible. There is hardly a week goes by when I don't do something on Brazilian television or on Obama for example. Just in the last month I did Romanian television, Brazil, German television, the French version of public television that we have here. I've done Channel Four in the UK many times. They used to have a show where they would go to a city and they would have somebody from that country, or that city, be the moderator. I do BBC radio frequently. I see that as part of Black Studies. That's a part of it because you're reaching millions of people in terms of interpreting social and political issues. Documentary films, I do either as a consultant, but now more frequently, since I'm so dedicated to the Malcolm biography, just as a commentator, I'll be in the film. Most recently I was in a film that was released on Mohammad Ali, in Miami.[38] I haven't seen it yet myself. Everybody else has seen it and they stop me on the street and say, "I love you in that film." I say, "I've got to see it." I'm in a number of films on Reparations,[39] all kinds of political issues, documentaries. That should also be a part of Black Studies, where we frame issues for the public through film, especially documentary film. The website and web resources allow us to be accessed by the world. We get a remarkable number of letters from all over the world every week asking for all kinds of things that, if we were ten times larger, we might be able to provide. Students who want to study here, people who want help with their homework, graduate students who want to do research, people who drop in on their way into the United States who just want an hour to talk with you. That happens to me every week. I'm fortunate to have an infrastructure, unlike most scholars, that allows me to be responsive to individuals. I'm an historian. In fact, my mother decided I would become an historian before I was born. This is a true story. She was enrolled at Wilberforce University in the fall of 1944. She worked as a housekeeper for Dr Charles H. Wesley,[40] the president of Wilberforce University, and then later Central State University. When the split occurred at Wilberforce between the State side and the Church side, Dr Wesley went with the State of Ohio and he became the president of Central State in 1948. My mother graduated from Central. She was second in the class. She promised that if she had a child . . . she was just getting married to my father . . . that one of her children would become an historian. That was me. And I came along in 1950, so I had no choice. No choice in doing what I do, and I love it. That's part of the intellectual legacy, the link between Wesley and then going back to Du Bois. So I come by it honestly! Now where were we?

JRD We've been talking about technology . . .

MM Oh yes, different modes of presenting African American Studies content and documentary films . . . and sites of racial injustice and sites of justice making. In African American Studies this is a very big thing with me, although I haven't been able to do it very often. In 1982 Columbia

University had bought up the Audubon Ballroom, the site where Malcolm was murdered. They wanted to destroy the building and put a bio-tech building on the site. By the mid- and late 1980s there was community opposition to it, even though the building was decrepit and a number of homeless people lived in the building, a number of the people used the building for crack, it was dangerous, etc. It's right across the street from Columbia Presbyterian Hospital Health Sciences campus. Students got involved. There were demonstrations. A deal was struck with the city and Betty Shabazz, Malcolm's widow, where part of the building would be preserved and a bio-tech building would be built around the old building. It's there today. In 1995 it was opened. But the question was, what happens with the assassination site? After five years of agitation, I convinced Columbia basically to give me $50,000 and I would build three kiosks so that when you go to the site there's a hand-touch screen—the story of Malcolm X and Dr Betty Shabazz comes alive. I interpret their lives for visitors, and you can see film clips and photos, letters and material. I said, ". . . and make it free. Give it to them. Place it in the site so you contribute to public education." Columbia said, "OK." So sometimes big institutions do the right thing! For me, again, that's what I mean by renegade historians. We intervene to do the right thing, to preserve our history, and to allow others to share in it. And you make it available for people for free. Now, unlike most people in the United States, I don't mind calling myself a socialist. I do not have a market model in mind. I believe knowledge should be free. I'm a democratic-socialist, I have been all of my adult life. I believe that knowledge should be accessible to people, just like healthcare should be free. You know education, health, all of these things should be free, for human beings, and made accessible. In the United States, this is a truly radical idea.

JRD And it shouldn't be a radical idea.

MM It shouldn't be radical at all.

JRD You're just calling it like it should be.

MM Exactly. This is the way it should be. But that's what a committed scholar should try to do, I think: to make our knowledge accessible, especially to our own people, and at a site where a great crime was committed. I think about, say, the site of Amadou Diallo's[41] death in a vestibule in the Bronx, and you compare that to the Kennedy assassination site in Dallas. Americans, overwhelmingly, would consider Kennedy's site hallowed ground. Do Black people have the capacity to create hallowed ground? Are our deaths socially meaningful? Do the crimes committed against us matter, such as the assassination of Medgar Evers?[42] At the site, at the home, there's no physical monument that tells anybody what happened there. There finally is now a statute of Medgar in Jackson, Mississippi. There was a fight and great resistance to renaming the airport for him. Until his widow Myrlie Evers Williams and I sat down and put together the biography of Medgar Evers, back in 2005, there was not a single book that documented his thought or life. I said, "We owe the brother a book." There were more books on Byron De La Beckwith, the man who murdered him, than on Medgar. Something's wrong with that, right? So I collected eight of his speeches, his letters, and his memoranda to the NAACP and reconstructed his life, then made that available to people. That's what public history is. We keep faith with sisters and brothers, Fannie Lou Hamer[43] and Ella Baker,[44] and Rosa Parks[45] and Medgar Evers. These people died for us, and we don't honor them by preserving their thought. We, the intellectuals, should be at the front lines of that. That's what I see public Black Studies is. That is, a vigorous defense for our memory and our legacy, because if we don't do it, it won't exist. If we don't do it, it won't happen, especially at those sites of contestations, sites of justice making. There should be a site in Tulsa, Oklahoma,[46] of the bombing and the destruction of an entire Black community. You know, first time in US history that an aerial bombardment of an urban center, of any population, occurred against us.

JRD I think the kids nowadays in Tulsa learn about the Tulsa Race Riots, but even just a few years ago they did not. It was ignored in the history texts. When I've taught at the OU-Tulsa campus, or would train social workers in Tulsa, people usually did not know about the Tulsa Race Riots—even social workers who were dealing with the reality, the repercussions. And it's all there . . . the history is just breathing down on all of it. I would teach them about it. I would say, "This has implications for your social work and for why things are the way they are and why there's all this tension in the city" because you can feel it. People always talk about how wonderful Tulsa is, and yet you go there and there is this tension . . . That's the living history.

MM That's what I mean by living history, because there is all of this that is underneath, that informs. That's the deep structure of the society that helps us to explain the racial chasm that still exists today. It's not simply because of the O.J. trial of the mid-1990s.[47] It's not simply because of Kobe Bryant.[48] It's because there were profound racial atrocities against African Americans that were not only not recognized, that were deliberately suppressed. There were crimes against humanity. This is not hyperbole.

This is fact: crimes against humanity, destructions of entire communities, wiping them off the face of the planet. There were thousands of lynchings. And until August 2005, the US Senate had never apologized for lynching. But get this, when it went through in the Senate, there were still fifteen Republican White male senators who didn't vote for it. Now, seven of them changed their minds, when they learned that an oversized copy of the Bill was going to be hung in the Capitol Rotunda, but eight others still refused. This is essentially denouncing the Senate for its failure to pass anti-lynching legislation, and they still refused to sign it—which means if you're White, you never have to say you're sorry . . . if you're on the side of White Supremacy, from their point of view. This is why a vigorous defense of Black history is absolutely essential to Black political empowerment and the two are deeply linked. There can't be an honest dialogue in this country about what the future of this country will be unless there is a deep recognition, and a reckoning on the part of the majority of the population in this country, with the racialized crimes that have existed in this country, that undergird the structure of power and privilege of American society. That's just an uncomfortable fact, but it's one that I deeply believe to be the case. This is a society that is grounded in what Jean-Paul Sartre refers to as "mauvaise foi," bad faith. A deep, deep dishonesty about what the nature of the society is—how the wealth was accumulated, and the structural disadvantages that were borne on the backs of people of African descent. It resounds in so many ways. I'll just cite one thing, the fact that Black home-ownership is less than 50 percent (it's about 46, 47, maybe 47 percent). White homeownership is nearly 75 percent. How did that happen? Well, in part, the GI Bill, which was racialized in its application, but also because of redlining[49] by banks. Why is it that, despite growing parity . . . not parity . . . but the reduction of the wage gap between Blacks and Whites in terms of take-home pay, especially for workers who have at least a college education, there is a wealth gap that is profound? That Blacks, on average, only have about one-tenth the wealth that Whites have in terms of household wealth, counting everything? It is a product of history. You can earn the same salaries, but if you don't have the same net wealth, then your children's and grandchildren's lives are restricted in so many profound ways. There is no fairness, even when there is affirmative action. Affirmative action was never designed to be an anti-poverty program. It was never designed to redistribute wealth. We've never had that deep conversation in this country about the restructuring of resources that allows for genuine opportunity and equality based on material conditions. That has never happened. Black Studies is one way to broach that discussion, as I have in my own writing.

JRD Yes, I know you have. I did want to go back to one issue. While you are able to use this wonderful technology to reach people, we still have obstacles for some in terms of the "digital divide." I think that's a call to action, of course, for us in Black Studies and we do try to address it in our program because certainly we have students who face these kinds of obstacles. Of course, if we're going to look at the global picture, certainly there are "digital divide" obstacles that some of the people whom we want to reach are going to encounter. For example, some time ago I was in Ethiopia and we established links with a university there . . . but their system was always "down"—you know the kind of story. There are many places where we still can't reach people because we have issues of a "digital divide" even with so much wonderful technology that we can use. I'm wondering if you have some thoughts about how we can address some of these challenges.

MM I think through, in part, the development of partnerships and even articulation agreements institution to institution throughout the African Diaspora that allow us to share information and resources in meaningful ways. One example is Columbia University [which] recently acquired, through its rare book and manuscript library, the papers of the brilliant Trinidadian intellectual, C. L. R. James.[50] Part of that agreement is that we are going to reproduce every sheet of paper in the James archives and make that available in whatever format the University of the West Indies at St. Augustine desires, whether it's Xeroxing or digital, or whatever. Part of that partnership I would like to see is scholarly exchanges and the development of partnerships in other capacities. I personally have been involved in different kinds of partnerships with institutions throughout the Black world. This is especially true in the country of Jamaica, in part because my wife is Jamaican and part because I was a friend of Michael Manley[51] and a political supporter of the People's National Party for about a quarter-century. I think the first time I spoke at the People's National Party Convention was in 1983 as their international speaker. I'm a kind of adopted Jamaican, so that much of my political work has always been transnational. In the Black world you try to find practical ways of providing resources and information and sharing those with partners, institutional partners, throughout the Black world. I especially feel this strongly about South Africa. It's a country I deeply love. My dissertation was a biography of John Dube,[52] who is the founder of the ANC [African National Congress]. Last November, one event that I take great pride in was I gave the commencement address at the University of Witwatersrand Business School. And, it's a marvelous feeling. You know SNCC used to use the expression that you had to put your body on the line, and that part of the way that we make that connection is the way that you did by going to Ethiopia. It's the way I did by going to University of Witwatersrand and giving the commencement address . . . you put your body on the line. You actually physically do it to make that connection. There's no substitute for that. You get to meet people, you talk to them, you travel, you see sights. I went to the sites of student resistance in '76, '77 in Soweto, during that most recent trip. It just had a profound impact on me. And the Apartheid Museum[53] is just an incredible experience. That is also transformative for us. Just as I'm sure the things that you saw in Ethiopia, when you travel throughout the world, experiences have a profound impact on you and your scholarship, your pedagogical approaches, your methodological approaches, how you write. All of that helps to shape and bring a sense of greater clarity, but also urgency to the work we do.

JRD Exactly. Transformative is the word that comes to mind.

ON PROGRAM INITIATIVES IN BLACK STUDIES

JRD As we think about the Center and the kind of projects you are involved in, are there similar projects coming out of other Black Studies departments, or programs, or centers, that you know of? You know, many of us are in smaller institutions with fewer resources. How can we emulate some of what you're doing if we are in a smaller institution, or one that doesn't have the Columbia "name"?

MM Well, there's bad news and good news. The bad news is, on the criminal justice front, we as a field are not doing what we should do. Back in 2005, our shop did a survey of Black Studies programs and departments. We asked, "Are you teaching any courses on criminal justice, or dealing with race, crime, and justice?" We tracked down about 118 responses, either people contacted us or we contacted them. Out of those 118 programs or departments, only five offered courses. Only five! That really is a tragedy to me, and it's inexplicable. It's indefensible because this is such a central issue. Small programs I understand, but any program that has at least a dozen people ought to have something, even on an adjunct basis. It doesn't have to be in Sociology or Criminology or Political Science. It can be in Literature, about prison narratives by Black people. Think of the great literature that our people have produced while in prison and start with that—for example, the Letter from the Birmingham Jail[54]—then go through Malcolm, go through other people and go to Garvey . . . Just think of the magnificent literature that Black folk have written while incarcerated—George Jackson[55] and others. So that's the bad news. The good news is—and it doesn't get a lot of press—a number of Black Studies departments have for many years done public Black Studies. What comes to mind immediately are several of the larger Afrocentricity-oriented programs—I'm thinking of Temple, for example—that for many, many years have done educational programming, public outreach of very high quality in the Philadelphia community. I'm thinking, for example, of some of the work around Hip Hop that Marcyliena Morgan[56] has done when she was at Harvard. When she was at Harvard, she had a project that was really great, doing spoken word and working in youth development in the city of Baltimore. My daughter Sojourner was working in that project. The use of spoken word, as a way of empowering young people, was used by a linguist, but developing a program that was for the public. And, it's brilliant. There are scholars with deep commitments to public Black Studies who cut across the range of thought within our field. That's one of the great joys that we have about this field. To keep faith with people like Du Bois, we can't do anything but what we do. When I first arrived here, for the very first conference we did, in the fall of 1994, we rented out a hall on 126th Street. Some brothers from the Malcolm X Mosque, El-Hajj Malik El-Shabazz Mosque, came by and said, "Who's doing this program?" Angela Davis[57] was the keynote speaker and they had other people speaking. "Who's bringing Angela Davis to Harlem?" We said, "Columbia University." And they were stunned. This was like a surreal experience. Usually when we did a conference it was a two-day event and one of those two days was either at the Schomburg[58] or a venue in the community. There's this fictive notion that Columbia is not in Harlem, but when you can walk to the Apollo Theater in about twelve minutes you're in Harlem. Morningside Heights is a little hill that's in Harlem. I wanted to erase the barrier between the community and the campus. That kind of thing is happening in all kinds of programs throughout the country, Not as much as I would want, but in ways that aren't always publicized, but do occur. Clay Carson[59] at Stanford has done extraordinary work with Martin Luther King Projects working with educators and school systems in Oakland and East Palo Alto. He has for years [done] just extraordinary activities, utilizing the resources, in the image and the words of Dr King, but in dynamic ways for young people. Again, this is a public Black Studies approach.

ON THE CURRENT STATE OF BLACK STUDIES

JRD How do you evaluate the current state of Black Studies? And what have you seen change over the past decade? What changes have you seen? Changes for the better, changes for the worse. And how would you evaluate where we are right now?

MM Well, there's good news and bad news. The good news is I feel tremendously heartened by the brilliant young women and men who identify themselves with the Black intellectual tradition coming into our field, and the flowering of new sub-fields in Black Studies. For example, Black Power Studies as a sub-field in African American contemporary history is fantastic. Great works have been produced. Great young scholars are doing exciting things. I have a partnership, a working relationship, with Peniel Joseph,[60] who did a brilliant book, *Waiting 'Til the Midnight Hour*, on the foundations of Black Power in the period from the late 1950s to about the mid-1960s. And now he's working on a biography of Stokely Carmichael,[61] a study that we have long needed. He's doing the serious work, and many other scholars of his generation are producing the kind of quality work that we have long needed in our field. So I feel very positive about that. Now for the bad news. The bad news is that the dismantling of public education in the United States and the under-funding of public universities has made it extremely hard to develop the resources that are necessary for intellectual production. I can cite about a thousand examples. One that comes to mind is what I just read in the *Chronicle of Higher Ed*, where the University of Georgia has basically rescinded sabbatical leaves promised to faculty for research for this coming year. Teaching a full load and never having the opportunity to engage in critical scholarship on a sabbatical leave means that you'll never be a productive scholar. You're chained to the classroom, and ultimately your classroom work suffers because there is a dialectical relationship between research and the quality of what you bring to the classroom. It's just true pedagogically and you're crippling students by this. I see this all over the country because of the kind of fiscal crisis that exists in public universities. There's a kind of two-tiered educational hierarchy that is really coming into existence in the United States. The elite private institutions that are heavily and fully endowed operate in a different way from most, with only a few exceptions, say like the University of Texas or University of Michigan or some of the University of California schools like Berkeley and UCLA. They're exceptional. But most public institutions just don't have the resources. I understand the difficulties that being an elite institution—described by themselves as an elite institution, I don't give that title to them—there are resources that you have that allow for the acceleration of work and scholarship. I have a secretary and she works for me, and that would never happen at a public university. I have the resources to develop multi-media websites because there is a structure called the Center for New Media Teaching and Learning at Columbia, and also DKV [Digital Knowledge Ventures], which is a for-profit corporation, owned by Columbia, which I have partnered with over the period of ten years. So I have "techies." If I have a concept and content, then I have technical partners who can produce the resource. That accelerates our ability to intervene that at a smaller institution you cannot do. That deeply troubles me.

JRD Often that impacts Black Studies even more than it impacts other disciplines, I would say. I'm inviting you to reflect on that, because there have been institutionalized inequities in the discipline all along. We still deal with it. So, while the English, History or Modern Languages departments are under-funded, the Black Studies department is being downsized or can barely get a teacher hired, never mind get a sabbatical. I'm interested to hear how you think that we can empower ourselves.

MM Right. I have thought a great deal about this. The nice thing about being older and having a long history of working with such programs is that I have many experiences upon which I can draw. Over twenty years ago I was hired as the chair of Black Studies at Ohio State. And OSU is in Columbus. The state capital, the state legislature, is right down the street. I developed a course called the Black Experience in Columbus, Ohio, where the curriculum would be a combination of scholarly works about Blacks in Columbus, combined with newspaper articles about Black people in Columbus. In a Kinko's reader, back in the days when you could copy anything you wanted, I put together a book. Then I taught the class in the community center that the Black Studies department, prior to my coming, had established in East Columbus. We had community people as well as students and extension students, students who were not full-time students, but who were taking class for credit. Then we would have a break, then we'd roll in the television cameras, and we had cable access, and we had a discussion about an issue, and I'd bring in . . . say, it was on police brutality or police relations with the Black community of Columbus . . . you'd have a captain or lieutenant from the police department. You'd have an anti-police brutality person activist, you'd have a sociologist, and they'd be on a panel. I would play the role of Oprah where I would interview them and then people would ask them questions. Since the students in the class had just heard a lecture from me for the past hour on that topic, they were up to speed on asking very sharp and pointed questions on that issue. We aired it on television. See, this is public Black Studies, and it didn't cost anything. It's just organizing the course and getting cable television to show it. And that was in 1988, it was twenty years ago . . . so, there should not be impediments with cost to do creative projects, whether they're in prison or on cable access television, or whether we develop websites. Now part of the good news is that with digital technology the price has dropped sharply. You can do really quality products and make them very accessible. This is an exciting time technologically for us. But it isn't, regarding political economy. It may be, depending upon what happens in November [2008, i.e., the presidential election] . . .

ON THE POLITICAL ENVIRONMENT

JRD I was going to ask you, how do you think the current political environment might impact Black Studies?

MM In a profound way.

JRD And, of course, that could be very different depending on what the result is in November.

MM That's right. It greatly concerns me . . . The only thing I'm going to take a break from on Malcolm is on this [presidential] election, which is so critical. I'm speaking this weekend and throughout the country in different places. It's not really a test of [Barack] Obama. This election is a test of White America. Is it possible, is it conceivable, that the majority of White people, by voting for their own material interests, will do so even at the cost of having to vote for a Black person? Or will they vote against their best interests and therefore vote against Obama? That's simply put, but that's true . . . for working people, lower income people, people on fixed incomes, those who are unemployed who don't have health insurance, the fifty million who lack health insurance. Knowing that McCain will never deliver on it, has no intention of it, and knowing that Barack would make the difference in their children's lives. Yet, will White racism be so powerful a force, so strong, that they will deliberately vote against their children's interests? Is that possible? Yes it is, if you live in this country. But, you know, we always as Black folk have a deep abiding faith. Martin said the moral arc of the universe is long, but it bends toward justice. I like to think that's true, but history has told me repeatedly that it only happens if we make it so. This is a real test of America's capacity, not to transcend the racial divide but to learn from it, and by embracing their own best interests they can also redress racial injustice. By voting for Obama, they vote not to erase the past, but to learn from it and to create a new future, a possible future. Not a new one, but a possible one, of a multiracial, multi-ethnic, democratic society. It has never existed. It will take some courage from many of them. It is not an easy decision for millions of our fellow White citizens. I'm aware of that. Because of all of the indoctrination to which they have been subjected it will be hard. For people who are under the age of thirty-five, who have been socialized in a very different way, then the future is very bright. Now, of course, I'm impatient. These older folk eventually will disappear from the scene, so we have great optimism for the future, but I'm concerned about what happens in 2009, not what's happening in 2099.

ON SUGGESTIONS

JRD I hear you! I think about it all the time . . . I have two more quick questions. To go back to the issue of chronic under-funding and inequities . . . how do you think university administrators can make a difference? How can they be proactive in supporting Black Studies?

MM That's a great question, and actually, the success internally at Columbia has been on a partnership I developed with the Office of the Provost, Jonathan Cole. When I arrived here, Provost Cole hired me basically. I think the key was that in the 1980s and early 1990s, Columbia's standing, its rankings, especially in the Social Sciences other than History, had fallen. He was concerned about enhancing the quality of the Social Sciences. I knew that. So when I went in to talk with him during the hire, I said, "You know what would be unique about a Black Studies program here?" I said, "Almost nowhere in the United States is there a Black Studies department that is primarily anchored to the Social Sciences." Not that we would not teach Humanities—far from that. We would have courses that would cover everything. But with our core faculty there would be a strategic notion of what is the intellectual project of Black Studies. Our project is Black America since the Civil War, primarily during the twentieth century, in urban areas that focus on social problems and struggles for empowerment. Jonathan Cole basically bought that concept, so

I recruited faculty, most of whom I was able to hire, but some I wasn't, whose work falls into that domain. You can go through and look at some of the people who are here. Sudhir Venkatesh,[62] whom I hired, is a star in the Sociology Department. He has written brilliant books on racism and housing. Stephen Gregory,[63] who until just a few months ago was the director of the Institute, wrote a brilliant book, *The Devil behind the Mirror*, which is on sex work and prostitution and the political economy of sex work in the Dominican Republic. Robin Kelley,[64] whom I hired as director, and Michael Eric Dyson, who was here for several years, are scholars who have done work that falls within that domain. So that's one of the ways you do it. If I had to be critical of Black Studies programs and departments throughout the country, probably the sharpest criticism I would have is that no one, not even Harvard, can be great at everything. Nobody has the resources to do that, so you have to decide what you are going to be good at. Here's another clue. You have to think about building an intellectual community, that is, people whose work dovetails and reinforces each other, so that there are intellectual conversations. I can teach the transatlantic slave trade and the Black experience in colonial America. The question is, what is your primary area of work that you do your research in, your scholarship? Knowing that Farah Griffin,[65] a brilliant scholar in African American literature, is focusing on women writers in Harlem in the 1940s and 1950s complements what I do on Malcolm in Harlem in the 1940s and the 1950s and 1960s. So we can share information. She taught a course called "Harlem's Heritage" last semester that is a history of Harlem's memory of itself from the point of view of Harlemites. You draw upon the resources of the community. That's another area where Black Studies needs to be strengthened. I believe that you teach what is in your environment. You teach what's in your environment and that's not possible in many places, in lonely outposts. I won't name them, but there are many schools where there are virtually no Black people and they are not adjacent to a Black community. Wherever there is a Black community, or wherever there is the memory of a community, we can teach it. We can construct a curriculum and involve people who live in the community because people are empowered through the memory of themselves, because what White racism seeks to do is to destroy our history and our memory of ourselves. People who are not critically self-conscious cannot act in their own interests. I see it as the reclamation of not just memory and tradition, but the fight for justice and empowering people. So you have a site like the Audubon. Of course, we put kiosks there for educating young people about the historical significance of the site. Of course, we reach out to prisoners, whether they're in Omaha, Nebraska, or they're in Rikers Island. Of course, we develop programs that make things available on the web for free and our students learn those technologies, and they're better teachers because of it. We have a different mission and model of pedagogy. We don't do things like that in the History Department, but then we're not the History Department . . . We just do different things.

ON STRATEGIES

JRD The last question I want to ask you is, do you conceptualize Black Studies as always operating from the margins?

MM That's an interesting question, and there's been an evolution of my thought about this over the last thirty years. When I first started teaching African American Studies, I saw it as a kind of insurgent body of work, because we had scaled the ivory tower and we were on terrain that had never been developed for us. We were members of the household, but not members of the family. We were clearly not wanted, and so there was an insurgency and a kind of problematic status we had. Perhaps, in coming to Columbia, I approached it differently and the strategy that worked here may not work well at other institutions, but will work well at large research universities, I believe. That is, what are the strategic goals of that institution, or even tactical goals, over, say, a ten- or twenty-year period? Like a provost that wants to strengthen the Social Sciences. Find out what those are and how can those be used to benefit Black Studies. Approach problems of capacity building in ways that enhance the achievement of [the] strategic goals of that institution. Instead of being at the margin, you actually operate right at the center. Then you make demands for resources that are in the strategic interests of the university. For example, between 1998 to about 2003, Columbia spent over $50,000,000 on digital knowledge. It's no coincidence that since 1999 I've built all of these things. For the multi-media version of the autobiography of Malcolm X . . . we did it in three years . . . it cost us $750,000 and it was internally funded. That wasn't because the administration was just captivated by my brilliant rhetoric; it was because that was within their strategic objectives! We laid claim to resources based on *their* priorities. Then the second strategy that has worked is to have strategic alliances with departments and centers, so that we can enhance our own capacity, build it collectively. We have a strategic alliance with

Women and Gender Studies that has existed since I came here. Our very first meeting was held in the Women and Gender's seminar room. We share resources and space. I gave them one of the offices that was built for us that's right next door . . . We've been partners, and it has worked out well for both of us. The Center for Ethnic Studies, which was formed after our creation, which focuses on Latino Studies and Asian-Pacific American Studies, is a partner to us. I'm on the board of that. I help pick out tenured faculty for it, so that we work together. We have partnerships with six or seven different centers and programs like that. We have strategic partnerships with particular departments with whom we work. For example, in Political Science, we have Fred Harris,[66] whom we recruited away from the University of Rochester, from the Fredrick Douglass Institute. He's started a Center of Race and Politics. Dorian Warren[67] of the University of Chicago is here. He does great work on labor and race, Black workers and labor, and the politics of Black labor. We've been very successful in partnering and that's what you have to do in order to build capacity in an interdisciplinary program. The weakness of the model that I developed here, which has continued to be a problem, is that because we are interdisciplinary and there is a strong tradition of disciplinarity at Columbia, all tenured hires have to be vetted through a traditional department. Now that means scholars who are deeply committed to interdisciplinarity find themselves frequently under heavy scrutiny. Very much like in the West Indies, they use the expression "heavy manners." They're under heavy scrutiny by tradition-bound scholars who question the legitimacy of their work simply because they don't understand it, and that can cripple any program.

JRD Would they be joint appointees?

MM The agreement that I struck with the administration in 1993 is a little unusual. We make a distinction between roster and tenure. Core faculty in the Institute are rostered here. That is, the revenue stream that is attached to them flows through us and we control the money. The tenure process is controlled primarily, but not exclusively, by the department. So the hire is made. They have to leap the hurdle of the department. For junior faculty I retain the right, not only to write a statement on promotion and tenure, but also to testify before the P & T [Promotion and Tenure] committee, so I've done that. It's unique, but . . . by the time I got here I'd been running departments for nearly twenty years, so I knew what to ask for. It has worked generally well. Sometimes you also lose very, very good people that way, but we have, to our credit, recruited successfully very, very strong scholars of whom I'm very proud. Some of the younger people, whom I first recruited, have gone on. One person who comes to mind immediately is Lee Baker,[68] who is really now central as a main figure in Black Studies at Duke University. I'm proud to say he was, as he would say, largely trained here as the assistant director working with me. He helped to initiate and conceive our highly successful Master's degree program. And Lee was just an extraordinarily gifted teacher and effective organizer and ran our Conversations in African American Studies for several years. Conversations is a series I started in '93, which is based on bringing in scholars who are involved in the actual writing of something, where they talk about their work so that you get a sense of the architecture of the intellectual work, or they talk about a book they just finished, or they're working on, or they talk about a problem they're working on. And we called it Conversations because we didn't want them to read a fixed text so much, but to talk about what scholarship is. We have had, I think, nearly 200 of those events over the last fifteen, sixteen years. But Lee Baker was a critical figure in helping make that series successful and so was Curtis Stokes,[69] for example, who was my assistant director for nearly three years, who is now like the central figure in African American Studies at Michigan State University. So, we've also helped develop other programs.

JRD Thank you, Professor Marable. I really appreciate this. Are there any final comments that you want to make about what you're doing here or about Black Studies in general?

MM Well, I feel very optimistic about the field and its future, given the quality of the young scholars I see emerging now. Also, from a technological standpoint, the innovative resources, the innovative technologies that now exist, allow us to reach the public in very dynamic and low cost ways that were unimaginable even a decade ago. Technologies have now accelerated our scholarly production so that, just in the Malcolm X Project in the past several years, digitizing most of the *Amsterdam News* allows us to do great searches that we could only dream about just two years ago, very exciting things that accelerate scholarly production . . . that's what I'm about. In the course of my life so far, the main works that I've done have focused on Black intellectuals, Black leadership, and social justice movements in the Black world, primarily in the twentieth century. I'm very excited about the works that I'm planning over the next two decades. The most exciting part of that is working with young people and encouraging their own innovative scholarship. The young scholars, the young PhDs with whom I'm working now . . . I'll just cite two. Russell Rickford[70] is a brilliant young man, son of John Rickford, who for many years was a key figure, director of African American Studies at Stanford. Russell's doing a great PhD on Black Power education, looking at independent Black schools that were formed in the Black Power period of the 1970s. Very few people have ever thought about the institutional development of independent Black institutes, of schools, and how they were shaped by Black Power and Pan-Africanist ideology. It's very exciting work. Then Zahir Ali has been a doctoral student of mine. For the last few years he's been doing a dissertation on a building, Mosque 7. It's a brilliant concept—a history of Mosque 7, from 1955 to 1975. There were only two ministers of Mosque 7 during that twenty-year period: Malcolm X and Louis Farrakhan. Great dissertation topic, and wonderful for oral history, in interviewing people in the mosque or who were in the NOI [Nation of Islam], and what they gained from that experience. So we can preserve our history and we can present in very dynamic ways that history, in unimaginable ways, creative ways, with documentary films, through educational kiosks, through websites, through blogs. The resources to do those kinds of things cost much less than they did just a few years ago. So that's why it's a great time to do the scholarship . . . I'm very optimistic about the future of public Black Studies, and more generally about the future of the Black intellectual tradition which we continue to expand and build upon.

JRD Thank you very much. I really appreciate your time for this interview.

NOTES

1. Clifford Geertz, *The Interpretation of Cultures* (New York: Basic Books, 1973).
2. Henry Louis Gates is a scholar, educator, literary critic, and public intellectual. He is Alphonse Fletcher University Professor at Harvard University and director of the W. E. B. Du Bois Institute for African and African American Studies.
3. Manning Marable, ed., *Dispatches from the Ebony Tower* (New York: Columbia University Press, 2000).
4. See Maulana Karenga's classic edited text, *Introduction to Black Studies*, 3rd edn. (Los Angeles: University of Sankore Press, 2000).
5. Edward Wilmot Blyden (1832–1912), born in St Thomas, Virgin Islands, emigrated to Liberia where he was an educator and statesman. His publications include: *A Voice from Bleeding Africa* (1856); *Liberia's Offering* (1862); *The Negro in Ancient History* (1869); *Christianity, Islam and the Negro Race* (1887); *West Africa before Europe* (1905); and *Africa Life and Customs* (1908). See also Edith Holden, *Blyden of Liberia: An Account of the Life and Labors of Edward Wilmot Blyden* (1966); and Hollis R. Lynch, ed., *Black Spokesman: Selected Published Writings of Edward Wilmot Blyden* (1971).

6. See the classic text of W. E. B. Du Bois, *The Souls of Black Folk*, first published in 1903.
7. Frederick Douglass (1818–95) was foremost an abolitionist and civil rights activist. He fought against his own slavery and continued the fight against the institution of slavery, until its abolition, through lectures, publications, and activities with the Underground Railroad. His autobiography, *The Narrative of the Life of Frederick Douglass, An American Slave, Written by Himself* was published in 1845 (reprinted from the revised edition of 1892, New York: Collier Books, 1962). Douglass was also an ardent supporter of women's rights.
8. Anna J. Cooper (1858–1964) was an author and prominent African American scholar. Her first book, *A Voice from the South: By a Woman from the South* (1892), is considered to be one of the first Black feminist publications with its focus on self-determination through education, and social uplift.
9. Martin Robison Delany (1812–85) was an African American abolitionist and proponent of Black Nationalism.
10. Marcus Mosiah Garvey (1887–1940) founded the Universal Negro Improvement Association and African Communities League (UNIA-ACL). He was a publisher, journalist, and entrepreneur. As a Pan-Africanist he sought to inspire a global mass movement which focused on Africa.
11. See Curtis J. Austin, *Up Against the Wall: Violence in the Making and Unmaking of the Black Panther Party* (Fayetteville, AR: University of Arkansas Press, 2006).
12. Manning Marable is current director of the Institute for Research in African American Studies (IRAAS) at Columbia University.
13. Ralph Bunche (1903–71), an African American political scientist and diplomat, received the Nobel Peace Prize for his mediation in Palestine in the late 1940s.
14. Horace Roscoe Clayton (1859–1940) was a journalist and politician, born on a Mississippi plantation to a slave and a White plantation owner's daughter. See Horace Clayton, *Long Old Road: An Autobiography* (New York: Trident Press, 1965).
15. St. Clair Drake (1911–90), an African American sociologist, created one of the first African American Studies programs in the US, at Roosevelt University. Later he chaired the African American Studies Department at Stanford University. See his work (in collaboration with Horace R. Clayton, Jr.), *Black Metropolis*. See also, *Black Folk Here and There* (1987).
16. Manning Marable was founding director of the Center, in 2002.
17. Created by George Soros.
18. Management team coordinating Soros Foundation.
19. The Ford Foundation is a private foundation, incorporated in Michigan and based in New York City, to fund programs chartered in 1936 by Edsel Ford and Henry Ford.
20. *Souls: A Critical Journal of Black Politics, Culture, and Society.*
21. Clarence Lusane, *Regionalism against Racism: The Trans-Europe Struggle for Racial Equality*, vol. 6, no. 2 (2004), 51–63.
22. Rikers Island, New York City's jail facility.
23. Manning Marable, Keesha Middlemass, and Ian Steinberg, eds., *Racializing Justice, Disenfranchising Lives: The Racism, Criminal Justice, and Law Reader* (New York: Palgrave Macmillan, 2007).

24. See the history of rebellion by Africans on the ship *La Amistad*, off the shores of Cuba. Following capture by the US Navy and transportation of the Africans to Connecticut, the US Supreme Court ruled their importation was illegal and they were ordered free.

25. Manning Marable, *Living Black History: How Reimagining the African-American Past Can Remake America's Racial Future* (New York: Basic Civitas Books, 2006).

26. Charlie Parker, nicknamed "Bird," was an influential jazz musician who was central to the development of bop in the 1940s.

27. John Birks Gillespie, nicknamed "Dizzy," was born in 1917 in South Carolina. He was a brilliant trumpet player and helped establish bebop. See Raymond Horricks, *Dizzy Gillespie and the Bebop Revolution* (New York: Hippocrene, 1984); Gene Lees, *You Can't Steal a Gift: Dizzy, Clark, Milt, and Nat* (New Haven, CT: Yale University Press, 2001); and Alyn Shipton, *Groovin' High: The Life of Dizzy Gillespie* (New York: Oxford University Press, 1999).

28. Edward Said (1935–2003) was longtime Professor of English and Comparative Literature and University Professor, Columbia University.

29. Associate Justice of the United States Supreme Court.

30. Condoleezza Rice, former Secretary of State in the George W. Bush administration.

31. Herbert Aptheker (1915–2003), American Marxist historian and political activist, authored over fifty volumes, including *American Negro Slave Revolts* (1943) and *Documentary History of the Negro People in the United States* (1998).

32. Paul LeRoy Bustill Robeson (1898–1976) was an internationally renowned concert singer, actor, and social justice activist.

33. See books by Michael Eric Dyson, including: *Come Hell or High Water: Hurricane Katrina and the Color of Disaster* (New York: Basic Civitas Books, 2006); *Is Bill Cosby Right? Or Has the Black Middle Class Lost Its Mind?* (New York: Basic Civitas Books, 2005); *The Michael Eric Dyson Reader* (New York: Basic Civitas Books, 2004); and *Know What I Mean? Reflections on Hip-Hop* (New York: Basic Civitas Books, 2007).

34. See Cornel West, including *Race Matters* (Reading, MA: Beacon Press, 1993, 2001); *The Cornel West Reader* (New York: Basic Civitas Books, 1999); also *Cornel West: A Critical Reader*, ed. George Yancy (Malden, MA: Blackwell, 2001).

35. See texts by bell hooks, including: *Black Looks: Race and Representation* (Boston, MA: South End Press, 1992); *Feminist Theory from Margin to Center* (Boston, MA: South End Press, 1984); *Killing Rage: Ending Racism* (New York: Henry Holt, 1995); and *Remembered Rapture: The Writer at Work* (New York: Henry Holt, 1999).

36. See *The Alchemy of Race and Rights: A Diary of a Law Professor* (1991); *The Rooster's Egg* (1995); *Seeing a Color-blind Future: The Paradox of Race* (1997); and *Open House: Of Family, Friends, Food, Piano Lessons, and the Search for a Room of My Own* (2004).

37. See *Critical Race Theory*, ed. Crenshaw et al. (New York: New Press, 1995); *Words that Wound: Critical Race Theory, Assaultive Speech and the First Amendment* (with Mari. J. Matsuda et al.) (Boulder, CO: Westview Press, 1993).

38. *Muhammad Ali: Made in Miami*. Alan Tomlinson, Garpar Gonzalez, and WLRN Public Television (2007).

39. Reparations refer to the legal precedence that, when a society knowingly and willingly commits crimes or moral wrongdoings against another, compensation is due from the institutes representing the offending society or group.

40. Charles Harris Wesley, noted African American historian, educator, and author. See *Negro Labor in the United States, 1850–1925* (1927); *The Negro in our History with Carter G. Woodson* (1962); *Neglected History: Essays in Negro History* (1965); *The Quest For Equality: From Civil War to Civil Rights* (1968).

41. Amadou Bailo Diallo (1975–99), an unarmed Guinean immigrant, was shot and killed by four New York plain-clothed police officers. Forty-one shots were fired, nineteen hitting Diallo. In 2000 the officers were acquitted of all charges.

42. Medgar Evers (1925–63) civil rights activist, murdered in Jackson, Mississippi.

43. Fannie Lou Hamer (1917–77), American voting rights activist and civil rights leader.

44. Ella Josphine Baker (1903–86), leading African American civil rights and human rights activist.

45. Rosa Parks (1913–2005), civil rights pioneer.

46. 1921 Tulsa Race Riots.

47. Trial (1995) of O. J. Simpson, accused of murdering Nicole Brown Simpson and Ronald Goldman, and found not guilty in criminal trial.

48. Trial of Kobe Bryant (2004) for alleged sexual assault, with charges dropped when the plaintiff refused to testify.

49. Redlining is the practice of arbitrarily denying or limiting financial services to specific neighborhoods, generally because its residents are people of color or poor, by banks and insurance companies.

50. C. L. R. James (1901–89), born in Trinidad and Tobago, was an historian, journalist, socialist theorist, and essayist.

51. Michael Manley (1924–97), fourth Prime Minister of Jamaica and leader of the Jamaican People's National Party.

52. John Dube (1871–1946), first President of the African National Congress (ANC), which led the struggle against apartheid in South Africa.

53. Soweto & Apartheid Museum, Johannesburg.

54. Martin Luther King, Jr. wrote this letter to fellow clergymen on April 16, 1963, while in a jail in Birmingham, Alabama.

55. George Jackson (1941–71), Black Panther. See *Soledad Brothers: The Prison Letters of George Jackson* (New York: Coward-McCann, 1970); and *Blood in My Eye* (Baltimore, MD: Black Classic Press, 1990).

56. Marcyliena Morgan, Executive Director of Hiphop Archive, Harvard University and author of *Language, Discourse and Power in African American Culture* (Cambridge: Cambridge University Press, 2002).

57. Angela Yvonne Davis, History of Consciousness Department, University of California, Santa Cruz. Publications include: *Angela Davis: An Autobiography* (1974); *Global Critical Race Feminism: An International Reader* (1999); and *Are Prisons Obsolete?* (2003).

58. Schomburg Center for Research in Black Culture, of the New York Public Library, a national library for resources documenting the history and experiences of peoples of African descent throughout the world, located at 515 Malcolm X Boulevard.

59. Clayborne Carson, Director, Martin Luther King, Jr., Research and Education Institute, Stanford University.

60. Peniel E. Joseph, author, historian, and activist. *Waiting 'Til the Midnight Hour: A Narrative History of Black Power in America* (2006).

61. Stokely Carmichael was a Black activist, active in the 1960s American Civil Rights Movement. He rose to prominence first as a leader of the Student Nonviolent Coordinating Committee (SNCC) and later as the head of the Black Panther Party. He popularized the term 'Black Power'.

62. Sudhir Venkatesh is William B. Ransford Professor of Sociology at Columbia University. His publications include: *Gang Leader for a Day* (2008); *Off the Books: The Underground Economy of the Urban Poor* (2006); and *American Project: The Rise and Fall of a Modern Ghetto* (2000).

63. Steven Gregory, *The Devil Behind the Mirror* (Berkeley, CA: University of California Press, 2006).

64. Robin D. G. Kelley, Professor of American Studies and Ethnicity, University of Southern California. Publications include: *Yo' Mama's DisFunktional: Fighting the Culture Wars in Urban America* (1997); and *Freedom Dreams: The Black Radical Imagination* (2002).

65. Farah Griffin, Yale University. Publications include: *Who Set you Flowin'? The African American Migration Narrative* (1995); and *If You Can't Be Free, Be a Mystery: In Search of Billie Holliday* (2001).

66. Fredrick Harris. Publications include: *Something Within: Religion in African American Political Activism* (1999).

67. Dorian T. Warren's publications include: "Wal-Mart Surrounded: Community Alliances and Labor Politics in Chicago," *New Labor Forum*, vol. 14, no. 3 (nd), 8–15.

68. Lee D. Baker, Duke University. Publications include: *From Savage to Negro: Anthropology and the Construction of Race, 1896–1954* (1998); and *Life in America: Identity and Everyday Experience* (2003).

69. Curtis Stokes, Michigan State University. Publications include: *Racial Liberalism and the Politics of Urban America*, ed. with Theresa A. Melendez (2003); and *Race and Human Rights* (2009).

70. Russell Rickford, New York University. Publications include: *Betty Shabazz: A Life Before and After Malcolm X* (2003); and (with John Rickford) *Spoken Soul: The Study of Black English* (2000).

PART III

International Perspectives

CHAPTER 7

Africa and its Importance to African American Studies

Tibor P. Nagy, Jr.

Texas Tech University

A frica is to African American Studies much as oxygen is to the study of life on earth; the second would not exist without the first. This chapter does not examine the history of that link—that would have to be a much longer work. Instead, I will focus on the importance of contemporary Africa and how African American Studies should be a catalyst—not only for making known Africa's reality beyond its grossly distorted image, but also for helping Africa assume its proper role in today's global system. One hopes this will challenge readers to make involvement in Africa part of their life's work. We will examine the current state of Africa, both its negatives and positives, with data as well as non-quantifiable factors. I will then discuss the importance of exchanges. Finally, I will present some opportunities for getting involved.

Although this chapter relates to "Africa"—much of my discussion will be specific to Sub-Saharan Africa (SSA)—the forty-eight countries south of the Sahara Desert. While the African Union and United Nations agencies are organized along continental lines, many international organizations and US government agencies, such as the US Department of State, treat SSA as a distinct grouping, and include the nations along Africa's Mediterranean coast as part of the Mid-East group.

BYPASSED AGAIN

The first time I met the Reverend Jesse Jackson was in 1992 when he was in Cameroon attempting to mediate between the authoritarian government and a radicalizing opposition which was seeking democratic change. He spoke one Sunday in one of Yaoundé's larger Protestant churches and focused on the issue that the recently liberated nations of Eastern Europe (Hungary, Poland, etc.) were suddenly receiving billions of dollars in development assistance and direct foreign investment, while Africa was yet again being bypassed. His complaint was that the world was redirecting resources from helping Africa in favor of a region inhabited by other ethnic groups (in this case the Caucasians of Eastern Europe).

Afterwards, when we met and I introduced myself as the Deputy US Ambassador, he asked where I was from. When I replied "Hungary," I could see he was steeling himself for my strong objection to his opposing the financial assistance my former country was receiving. Instead, I told him that I fully supported his position. Africa has been the perennially neglected Continent and needed development assistance much more than any of the former Soviet bloc nations. Furthermore, I expressed my strong belief that just as Hungarian Americans, Polish Americans, etc. had mobilized to pressure the US government to be very generous to their ethnic homelands, it is vitally important for African Americans to mobilize in support of Africa—not just for increased development assistance, but even more importantly for political and economic liberalization.

Almost two decades later, this is still just a dream which will remain unfulfilled until African Americans gain a deeper understanding of the Continent and can see beyond the negative headlines that promote and maintain a false image of Africa as the place which produces only bad news. I have found Americans in general to be woefully ignorant about Africa's history, culture, geography, politics, development, etc., and I'm not sure that African Americans as a group have any greater insight. This is most unfortunate, since both African Americans and the Continent stand to benefit greatly from enhanced mutual understanding and strengthened communications. For this to happen, not only must African Americans undertake more in-depth studies of African issues, but also recognize the need to establish exchange opportunities to enable significantly more African American students, scholars, researchers, and professionals to visit the Continent.

GEOPOLITICAL PRIORITIES

In pursuing diplomacy, the US Department of State divides the world into regions and is organized into geographic bureaus which focus on each region's issues. The US is a global power, and all regions have some strategic importance. Although never voiced officially, by definition one region is less important than the others—and unfortunately Sub-Saharan Africa has traditionally occupied that role. Several factors have contributed to this reality. One is historical: until the 1960s, the US viewed Africa as the domain of colonial powers, and even after independence, viewed the Continent through the simplistic lens of US-Soviet global rivalry. Economics is another factor. Until recently, Sub-Saharan Africa, aside from providing some key commodities (titanium, chrome, diamonds, gold, etc.), played an insignificant role in the global trading system. Another factor is political; from the time of independence Africa has suffered from chronic coups, political instability, civil wars, and every imagined form of human-induced misery. Development issues are another factor. Sub-Saharan Africa has been in constant need of the international community's help to respond to humanitarian emergencies resulting from natural and man-made disasters, as well as huge sums of money to promote development.

Many Africans, on the other hand, say that Sub-Saharan Africa's lower priority is due to the developed world's enduring racist view of Africa, which results in a policy of paternalism, lower expectations, and insufficient attention to African issues. For example, Africans point out that if the enduring crisis in Somalia—which has left that nation without a *de facto* government for almost two decades—had taken place anywhere besides Africa, the international community would have responded forcefully long ago to end the anarchy.

However, part of the reason for Sub-Saharan Africa receiving less attention is also that its natural US constituency (i.e., African Americans) has not been as effective in lobbying for their "homeland" as most other hyphenated Americans. Compare, for example, the tepid US response to genocide in Rwanda with America's hyperactive policy toward resolving turmoil in the Balkans. It is perhaps here that Africa may be of greatest significance to African American Studies: by broadening and deepening understanding about Africa among greater numbers of Americans, Africa's natural US constituency may finally become energized, empowered—and perhaps even enlarged to the larger US population. Then it can demand that the US government give Africa the priority (diplomatic attention and resources) it deserves. This is critically important, since the geographic region considered a lower priority also receives less financial and human resources within our government to deal with issues which may arise.

To be fair, our government does respond effectively and generously to human catastrophes which demand immediate action, but performs less well on simmering, or long-running crises, or to crisis prevention. For example, when I alerted Washington as Ambassador to Ethiopia that famine was threatening the Ethiopian lowlands in 2000, we were the first donor to put several hundred thousand tons of relief grain on the ocean within weeks; famine was averted. On the other hand, in 1999 when Guinea was threatened along its border with Sierra Leone by attacks from the Revolutionary United Front rebels, Washington did not have the resources to bolster the Guineans, leading to serious loss of life and the destruction of several major Guinean border towns.

While the well-staffed and resourced European Bureau can focus effectively on a number of simultaneous crises, the US State Department's African Bureau must continuously juggle boiling pots from the front of the stove to the back, having only enough hands to keep one or two from spilling over. This is one of the reasons why a long-running crisis such as Somalia has never been adequately addressed; the Department of State simply doesn't have the resources to give proper attention to all major African issues. For example, while most African Bureau professionals care greatly about Somalia, other, more urgent and deadly crises keep erupting and pushing Somalia to the "back burner." Rwanda, Liberia, Sierra Leone, Eastern Congo, South Sudan, Ethiopia-Eritrea, Darfur, and other issues all required immediate attention given the magnitude of the disasters; so Somalia still remains largely neglected.

Thankfully, this is all changing. However, the driving force is economic/commercial and geostrategic, rather than an appreciation of Africa's human and cultural resources. As valuable as those "left brain" reasons are, from my experience the "right brain" ones are even more significant for humanity in the twenty-first century. We'll examine some of these factors later in the chapter.

AN AFRICAN AMERICAN'S UNIQUE SKILLS

Reverend Jackson's presence in Yaoundé in 1992 is a good illustration of the nexus between Africa and the African American experience. His long-term leadership role in the US Civil Rights Movement gave him instant credibility with the Cameroonian opposition leaders. They viewed themselves as facing some of the same challenges in trying to gain fundamental freedoms for Cameroonians as African Americans had during the civil rights struggle. In turn, Reverend Jackson's skills in dealing with leaders and elites made the Cameroonian leadership feel equally comfortable in using him as an interlocutor. Very few people of other nationalities, if any, could possess the unique combination of skills which an American civil rights leader was able to bring to the table as a mediator for inter-African issues.

I had an opportunity to see this nexus again at first-hand in 1998 when Reverend Jackson came to Guinea as a special presidential envoy to participate in a very small, very private meeting between three heads of state—President Conte of Guinea, President Kabbah of Sierra Leone, and President Taylor of Liberia. Aside from the three heads of state and Reverend Jackson, only our State Department Director for West African Affairs, an Embassy note-taker, my secretary acting as interpreter, and I participated. Relations between the three countries were extremely sensitive. Both Guinea and Sierra Leone felt threatened by Taylor, while Taylor accused Guinea of supporting rebels intent on toppling him. Watching Reverend Jackson's interpersonal dynamics with the three heads of state reminded me again how only a US civil rights leader could possess the combination of traits necessary to be able to say the things he did and have the kind of gravitas to be effective with these African presidents. It was obvious that the three men greatly respected Reverend Jackson's background, experiences, and struggles. No French, British, Russian, or Chinese diplomat could have brought those same qualities to bear.

The examples above illustrate one way the shared African American experience is greatly relevant to Africa. At the same time, just the fact that about forty million Americans trace their origins to Africa makes the Continent greatly relevant to African American Studies. According to a December 2007 Census Bureau press release commemorating Black History Month, in July 2006 there were an estimated 40.2 million black residents in the US, including persons of more than one race (14.6 percent of the US population).[1] However, African American scholarship is greatly needed to perceive and appreciate Africa beyond the dismal numbers which is as far as most Americans get, if they think about Africa at all.

THE BAD NEWS

Unfortunately, the data alone do not present an encouraging picture. Africa is the poorest Continent and the only one which has become poorer over the last twenty-five years. The average per capita income was $530 in 1992,[2] and in some countries, such as Ethiopia, it was about $150.[3] I often ask my students to imagine trying to live on $0.50 a day! Sub-Saharan Africa's combined Gross Domestic Product (GDP) equals that of a mid-sized European country (e.g., Belgium), with most SSA countries' GDP averaging between $2 billion and $3 billion, or about the same size as that of a mid-sized US city. During my years as Ambassador to Guinea, that nation's annual budget was about $600 million— the weekend turnover at a major US shopping center. Only about a third of Africans have access to clean water, with millions of women walking hours each day to collect whatever water they can find.[4] I found a stark example of this when I visited the Borena zone of southern Ethiopia, where women walk six hours in each direction at the height of the dry season to find water!

The bad news goes on. There are about thirty-three million Sub-Saharan Africans living with HIV/AIDS, or two-thirds of all infected persons in the world;[5] about three million of them will die this year (about the same number as die from malaria). Eight out of every ten women infected with HIV are in SSA, and there are about 18 million AIDS orphans.[6] At the same time, there are more Ethiopian doctors practicing in Chicago—who immigrated to the US, mostly by overstaying their visitor's visa—than in Ethiopia's capital. (This statistic was used by both the Ethiopian government and the various US government agencies in Ethiopia in reports and speeches.) Conflicts also take their toll. There have been at least twenty-five major conflicts since 1998, killing hundreds of thousands, displacing millions, and leaving hundreds of thousands of landmines. And as old conflicts are settled (e.g., North vs. South Sudan), new ones arise (Darfur).

Sub-Saharan Africa comes at the bottom of development indices on such key factors as levels of education, especially for women, life expectancy, and access to healthcare. Infrastructure in much of SSA is abysmal. During my twenty-plus years I traveled tens of thousands of miles on unimaginably bad roads, including one stretch of seven miles in Guinea which took two hours to navigate. Even in most SSA capitals (South Africa being an exception) electricity is sporadic, trash pickup erratic or nonexistent, piped water (when available) undrinkable, and sewage systems (where they exist) limited. SSA also features at the top of corruption indices and at the bottom of global economic activity and political stability. In 2005, SSA represented just 1 percent of world economic activity and just over 1 percent of global trade.[7] Decades of bad government, represented by tyranny, human rights violations, non-democratic elections, and bad economic policies, negated whatever positive effects the billions of dollars of development assistance might have produced.

BUT IMPROVING

Yet in my farewell speech in Guinea in 1999, during a ceremony at which I received a knighthood from President Conte, I was very sincere in stating that when outsiders look at Africa, it is similar to when most people hold up a glass with water; they tend to see it as half-empty, when in fact the glass is decidedly half-full and the water is rising. As I noted above, there are "left brain" and "right brain" factors about Africa which are key in looking at the Continent. We'll examine each set.

As pessimistic as the data seem, they are just a snapshot, which can only be interpreted in view of the overall trends; these are much more positive:

Politics

The Continent is the freest it has been since before colonization. Despite the 2008 electoral disasters in Kenya and Zimbabwe, since 1990 more than thirty SSA nations (out of forty-eight) have evolved from single-party rule to some type of multi-party system.[8] According to "Freedom House," an organization which rates individual countries on the amount of political freedoms and civil liberties they grant their citizens, the number of SSA nations that are rated "free" or "partly free" grew from nineteen to thirty-four between 1990 and 2006. In addition, between 2003 and 2007 there were fifty democratic elections at all levels in SSA.[9]

Conflicts

One by one Africa's major conflicts have been ending, although for every two steps forward there seems to be one step back. For example, just as southern Sudan signed the Comprehensive Peace Agreement with the northern, "Arab"-dominated government in 2005, the crisis in Darfur was erupting in the western part of that country. Nevertheless, of the more than dozen SSA conflicts which were raging in 2000, that number is down to a handful, with a parallel reduction in casualties. Of the remainder, there is movement toward peace in each, and they could all be ended quickly with more involvement and resources from the international community. As an unfortunate illustration, while adequate peacekeeping forces have been authorized for both the Darfur and Somalia conflicts, the international community has been unable or unwilling to contribute the necessary troops and logistical support.

OF SHORT SLEEVES AND LONG SLEEVES

Stalin was alleged to have said, "a single death is a tragedy, a million a statistic." The horror of Africa's conflicts was made very personal to me in 1998 while I was serving as US Ambassador to Guinea. I accompanied our Ambassador for War Crimes to Guinea's border with Sierra Leone to interview victims of that country's civil war. I met sweet, soft-spoken men and women who, within the last few days, had had their hands or arms chopped off by Revolutionary United Front rebels, but had subsequently been fortunate enough to make it across the Guinean border. We listened to their tales of unspeakable cruelty, told with bandaged stumps still seeping blood—all of their accounts with one common theme: they did not understand why this had happened to them or how anyone could have been so cruel. The only choice they had been given was whether to have their arms chopped off above the elbow (short sleeve) or at the wrist (long sleeve). The Revolutionary Front was defeated in 2001 and Sierra Leone is at peace today, but thousands of these victims remain. So while Africa's conflicts grow fewer, even one is too many.

Economic Situation

Africa's economic performance has improved considerably in recent years, with African countries recording average growth of 5.4 percent over the last decade, an enviable rate for any "developed" economy. While the increase in commodity prices has no doubt been a factor, the World Bank found that even eighteen resource-poor African countries, home to 34.5 percent of Africa's population, recorded growth of more than 4 percent.[10] As far as natural resources go, Africa is the world's treasure house. Indeed, Africa has a huge potential for adding to the world's supply of food and energy with its unexploited hydro-power, petroleum reserves, and even bio-fuel capacity. In 2006 Africa supplied about 22 percent of US crude oil imports, which exceeded our imports from the Middle East and represented double the amount of our 2002 African oil imports.[11] Africa's reserves are expected to increase dramatically since it is the only Continent with large areas still unexplored.

MANGOES IN KANKAN

During my many trips through the African countryside I often experienced the paradox of Africa's failures within sight of tremendous unrealized potential. I visited the northern Guinean city of Kankan in 1996 in late autumn, just as the mangoes were ripening. Every inch of ground—including the roads—was covered with thousands upon thousands of fallen mangoes, while the tree limbs were hanging with the weight of the fruit which had not yet ripened. Of course, such a large supply in the vicinity of relatively little demand meant all of this freshly ripened fruit had no value—almost all just rotted where they fell. If these mangoes could have been transported to the port of Conakry for onward shipment to Europe, or even turned into pulp, the people of the region would have realized a tremendous economic benefit. Unfortunately, the region's roads were so abysmal that any mangoes shipped by truck would have turned into mush, and the canning factory which had been sold by Italy was totally unsuitable for producing mango pulp. I saw a similar situation in another part of Guinea with potatoes—except this was even more inexcusable because the growing area was only 30 miles from a town in Senegal which connected to Senegal's much superior road network and the port of Dakar.

Health Issues

The partnership between African nations and donor countries is finally starting to succeed in confronting Africa's monumental health crises. Overall, HIV rates for new infections appeared to peak in Africa in the late 1990s and some countries are finally showing declines.[12] The combination of education, prevention, and treatment is showing positive results, and the availability of antiretroviral drugs has greatly expanded over the last few years. While malaria continues to be a major killer and has so far defied a preventable vaccine, many African countries are making treated malaria nets available, thus dramatically reducing infection rates. Just as donors have become more generous in recent years, African nations have faced the responsibility of improving their overall health systems for delivering basic health services. There is still a long way to go, and as long as many African health professionals choose emigration over staying and working in their own countries, progress will be limited.

A GENERAL'S UNEXPECTED TAKE ON A WAR

In 1999 the Ethiopian-Eritrean war over their undefined border had settled into a World War I-like stage of hundreds of thousands of troops—most of the forces available to the two nations—facing each other from trenches, with no actual combat taking place, just a wary stalemate. Our Embassy in Addis Ababa maintained contacts with high-ranking Ethiopian military officers to gauge their views of the war, and one time our military attaché had a long conversation with the Ethiopian force commander. When our attaché told the Ethiopian general that we all hoped the war would end soon, the general enthusiastically agreed, but said that his reasons were different from ours. According to him, each weekend high school-age girls by the hundreds would take public transport from their communities close to the border to visit the troops and engage in commercial sex. The general feared that the longer the stalemate continued, the more of his forces would become infected with HIV, leading to a serious degradation of the entire Ethiopian army. Within weeks of this conversation, the Ethiopians did launch a major offensive and won the war, and the Ethiopian armed forces instituted an imaginative and effective campaign of using returning HIV-positive soldiers to work with their home villages to alert people to the dangers of HIV/AIDS.

AFRICA IN TRANSITION

As the preceding paragraphs indicate, Africa is undergoing tremendous change—almost all of it positive. After several false starts and decades of unrealized optimism, Africa's renaissance may finally be happening as most of its nations cast off the debilitating legacy of colonialism, kleptocratic tyrants, poverty, and underdevelopment. African American scholarship can make a significant contribution. Every aspect of Africa's politics, economics, development, infrastructure, agriculture, environment, educational system, health delivery system, etc. is open to, and in need of, fresh views and creative ideas. A few examples:

How to Design the African State

A structural problem for most African countries is that they have within their colonially imposed, artificial borders a number of ethnic groups with historical animosity toward each other. If African states could have developed naturally, the borders would be totally different and these ethnic groups would have ended up in different countries. Since the borders are the way they are (and the Africa Union has agreed to maintain them), there has been tremendous ethnic conflict and fighting across the Continent (witness the 2008 post-electoral violence in historically stable Kenya). African states are trying a variety of approaches to reduce these tensions through creative power-sharing measures (such as the post-election compromise in Kenya, which gives one major ethnic group the presidency and the other the prime minister post). Ethiopia has gone a step further by redrawing the country's internal governmental units to align with the territories of its major ethnic groups and decentralizing most political power to localities. More creative ideas are needed to help reduce or eliminate one of the major causes of Africa's misery.

Micro-enterprise Development

As Ambassador to Ethiopia I attended a monthly donor's group meeting, composed of my colleagues from "rich" nations, which together gave Ethiopia hundreds of millions of dollars annually in the form of grants and aid. Although my colleagues were well intentioned, I found the discussions consistently patronizing, along the lines of: this or that European expert was coming to do a study to help the Ethiopians grow crops, or develop irrigation, etc., as if people who had been farming in an area for thousands of years didn't know what they were doing! Once, tiring of this type of discussion, I told my colleagues that what we should do instead of hiring consultants and experts to do studies and write reports was to take all our aid money and throw it out of an airplane over the most needy areas since the local people were rational economists and would know better what to do with our aid than anyone else. They thought I was joking; I wasn't! Another strong conviction I've had since early in my African experience is that donors can accomplish more with a grant of several hundred dollars to an individual or group than millions to, or through, a government. Recent development theory has caught up as "experts" have come to the same conclusion; donors are establishing institutions which give very small grants or loans to enterprising individuals or small groups (most of whom happen to be dynamic women), who then have phenomenal success in bettering their own and their families' lives, and their local economies. There is still so much to be done as development theory is undergoing radical revision and evolution, and African American scholars could make a tremendous contribution.

The two examples above barely scratch the surface of potential opportunities available in all fields of study—they literally are unlimited as Africans search for new models of success appropriate to their systems, history, traditions, and cultures. Unfortunately, in my experience most non-African scholars and experts I have encountered on the Continent tended to be from the former European colonial power or other parts of Europe with (not always unselfish) interests in Africa, who bring their own cultural biases and attitudes immaterial of their individual altruistic motives. In my view, African American scholars would bring a much more positive outlook, higher expectations, and no national bias in developing new models for Africa.

THE HEART OF THE MATTER

When speaking about Africa, after reflecting on the various statistics regarding Africa's negative and positives, I like to say that while Africa may not be the world's wallet, it is undoubtedly its heart and soul. In my twenty-plus years on the Continent, I have developed the greatest respect for, and appreciation of, Africa's cultural riches, which transcend ethnic groups, regions, religions, and languages. The face of the Continent which comes to my mind when I hear the word "Africa" is not that of conflict, famine, disease and poverty. Instead, I think of:

- The villages where people may not have a watch, but they have all the time in the world for their families and friends (and visitors).
- African families who will open their house to a relative, no matter how distant (in our Western minds), and share their meager resources for extended periods of time.
- An inherent human dignity, strength, and optimism, despite indescribably difficult life challenges and losses.
- Tireless work to survive and even thrive in environments which are at best marginal for life. (Most African crops are rain-fed and soils

extremely poor, so even a minimal variance in rainfall can mean total crop failure—and starvation.)

- Parents' fervent belief in getting the best education possible for their children, and the children's dedication to going to school—even when it means walking dozens of miles with an empty stomach and then returning to a full day's chores in the village.
- Keen intellects, even when uneducated. I never met an African who did not speak at least two or three languages: that of their own ethnic group; that of a neighboring ethnic group; and usually that of the former colonial power—the "official" language of the country.
- Music, art, and dance which are among the best in the world—even if the least known internationally!

THE "RICHES" OF IROB

When the Ethiopian-Eritrean war ended in 2000, our Embassy wanted to make a maximum impact with our relief efforts, so we selected the most war-devastated part of Ethiopia and financed the rebuilding of the infra-structure—wells, schools, and some housing; we even replaced the cattle. The Irob region had been totally laid waste—the Eritrean army had occupied the region and destroyed or damaged almost everything (including some churches), and the people of Irob had suffered greatly and had been forced to live in caves for over two years. After the fighting stopped, they had no material possessions, no shelter, no water, and no means of resuming their former lives.

By 2001 the rebuilding was well on the way and I scheduled a trip to Irob in late September—no small undertaking given the miserable roads and long distance—to ceremonially cut the ribbon on some newly built projects. Then the September 11 tragedy happened, which required me to stay in Addis Ababa for several weeks, but I went on to Irob at the end of the month. The official "ribbon cutting" was enthusiastic, with grate-ful speeches, dancing, and very spicy Ethiopian food. After the ceremony, my interpreter told me the community elders wanted to speak to me about something. I accepted with hesitation, thinking of other occasions when, after the official ceremony, I would be given long lists of additional needs of the community. Instead, the elders—representing a community which had suffered war, killings, rape, pillage, and the total destruction of their area—expressed their sympathies and great regret over what had happened to the World Trade Center, told me the people of Irob were with the people of the US, and said that if they could help us in any way, or give us anything they had, they would gladly do so. The magnitude of such a generous and selfless gesture brought tears to my eyes; it was very difficult for me to remain the professional diplomat and respond with my mind instead of my heart. This gesture was not only from Irob or from Ethiopia, it is the response of Africa in such circumstances and represents the greatest wealth of the Continent. To me, it is a wealth far beyond Africa's diamonds, oil, and gold.

BACK TO AFRICA

I had prepared intellectually for my diplomatic service by studying Africa's history, politics, geography, culture, economy, etc., but I really had no sense of Africa until that first landing in Lusaka, Zambia in 1979. And what a landing it was—because Zambia had been helping the Rhodesian rebels in their fight against that country's white minority regime, the plane had to make a corkscrew landing to avoid anti-aircraft fire from rebels camped near the airport. They often mistook civilian aircraft for Rhodesian fighter jets! Only by being on the Continent and experiencing its vastness, complexities, treasures, problems, and people can a non-African truly form some semblance of understanding of Africa's essence. One can read everything written about the slave forts along the West African coast, but only when one sets foot on the haunted grounds of El Mina castle is there true comprehension of the horrors which occurred there.

Getting there is still not easy, but it's getting much easier. Although Africa still offers the most limited number of exchange opportunities among the world's regions, the programs and potential sites are expanding rapidly. Following are some considerations:

Looking beyond the Obvious Destination

Most Americans, when considering exchange programs in Africa, think of South Africa, Ghana, Kenya, and perhaps a more developed Francophone country such as Senegal. In fact, there are exchange possibilities in almost every SSA country, as long as the participant has realistic expectations and understands the limitations involved. Texas Tech University recently inaugurated a program with Mekelle University in northern Ethiopia—one of the world's poorest countries—whereby a group of our medical students spend six weeks in Mekelle and in some outlying villages. The first group returned wildly enthusiastic about their experiences and service learning opportunities. While the infrastructure and facilities in less developed countries will most certainly be more Spartan, the benefits can be tremendous.

Limitations

As noted above, aside from a few universities in the more developed SSA countries, facilities and local infrastructure will verge from the disappointing to the shocking for first-time visiting American students and scholars. Overcrowded dormitories and classes, sporadic and slow (when working) internet service, severely limited libraries and research facilities, dilapidated buildings, ethnic diets, frequent power and water outages, autocratic university hierarchies—these are just some of the factors which can demoralize American participants. (In most SSA countries universities are all governmental, with free tuition, but they are also severely under-funded and under-resourced.) However, even with such limitations, I consistently encountered dedicated Americans at the many SSA universities I visited, absolutely delighted with their experiences and what they were able to accomplish and learn. For example, as noted previously, Guinea has some of Africa's most challenging infrastructure, and the University of Kankan in northern Guinea shares many of the hardships I noted above. But there I met one of the most enthusiastic scholars I've ever come across, absolutely delighted with studying the Kora in the region where the musical instrument was developed and learning from local players in villages surrounding Kankan. These are the types of opportunities which are unavailable anywhere else.

The Good News

Month by month, Africa's infrastructure is improving—as are its universities. African governments are also finally allowing the creation of private universities. While in those countries which have not had a tradition of private education some of these new institutions are fragile and weak, the sector as a whole is thriving and will force public universities to improve. African universities are also eager for partnerships with US institutions and collaboration on exchange programs. I found most African universities to be flexible, supportive, and willing to go to great lengths to accommodate American students and scholars. Mekelle University, for example, knowing that our students were used to much higher standards (higher than even their European exchange students), did everything possible to provide accommodation and support which our students found quite acceptable. On our side, some US university organizations (e.g., the Association of Public and Land Grant Universities) are eagerly embracing Africa and providing inducements for their members to develop African partnerships.

US Government Support

US foreign policy priorities change, due either to geopolitical factors, such as the dramatic need for Islamic Studies after 9/11, or in response to US domestic politics. Both factors are raising Africa's importance—whether for its natural resources or its role in international security, humanitarian and development needs, economic/commercial potential, agricultural potential, etc. Both the Clinton and Bush administrations were tremendously supportive of Africa, and indications are that President Obama will move even further. (The Kenyans joke that it is the height of irony for the US to have a Luo president before Kenya does, the Luo being one of Kenya's major ethnic groups which has been kept out of the presidency through political manipulation.) This should mean that more resources will be available for US institutions and individuals to pursue interests in Africa.

The US Department of State-sponsored Fulbright program (www. iie.org/Template.cfm?section=Fulbright1) offers a number of wonderful opportunities for students and scholars to study, research, and teach in Africa in almost any field. Since Fulbright proposals are reviewed by the US Embassy in the country of the project, interested persons should consider smaller African countries which do not receive as many proposals. Some of the most interesting projects I encountered were in places such as Togo or Zambia—not the most popular, but certainly among the most interesting destinations!

The two US government development agencies—the US Agency for International Development (USAID) and the Millennium Challenge Corporation (MCC)—also have a strong focus on Africa and make available millions of dollars for development projects. While such projects are limited to institutions or partnerships, both organizations offer internships for interested students or opportunities for faculty on sabbatical to work in their areas of interest.

Africa for Students

Interested students can study in Africa a number of ways. Many colleges and universities run their own programs with partner institutions, and many others are in the process of developing these. In addition, several major "Education Abroad" institutions have long-established programs in Africa, including: Consortium for International Education Exchange; American Institute for Foreign Study; School for International Training; School for Field Studies; and International Student Exchange Programs. Given Africa's challenging environment, the best method for students to visit may be the faculty-led model, whereby faculty members from the students' home institution accompany a group of students and serve as the instructors (often in conjunction with a local colleague) on site. Ideally, the US institution will have a partnership with a local university for using its teaching facilities, sharing faculty, etc. for the program. Many parents prefer this model, since they believe it provides greater safety and security.

Unfortunately, student exchange programs with African institutions are not easy; it is financially difficult for most African students to afford to travel to the US, unless they receive major scholarship assistance. Some African countries even limit the amount of currency a citizen can take with them. "Joint Degree" and "Dual Degree" programs do offer possibilities whereby parts of the program are completed at each institution. However, here again, the US partner would have to offer financial help when the African participants come to the US site.

Distance learning offers tremendous potential and the environment for this is improving rapidly. This would be one way to resolve the problem of the great financial difficulty for African students to travel to the US. Unfortunately, in most African countries internet connectivity is still sporadic and slow (Mekelle, for example, still only has semi-reliable dial-up connection), which severely limits the amount of content which can be transmitted and its timeliness. This area will, however, grow tremendously in the next few years as Africa's internet infrastructure catches up, as has its cell phone technology and coverage.

Africa for Faculty

Of the many US faculty members I have met either in Africa, or after their African experience, all have been uniformly laudatory about the incredible intellectual satisfaction and personal enrichment they gained from their experience. African universities are all eager to have visiting US faculty to teach or do research for any period of time. The welcome will be overwhelming, and the university will eagerly provide whatever support it can. The frustrations US faculty face are usually related to the African institution's rigid bureaucracy and limited resources. Also, some US faculty get discouraged in trying to make arrangements when correspondence is not answered in a timely manner. However, perseverance will usually be rewarded and US participants should not hesitate to contact the local US Embassy (Public Diplomacy Officer) for help in making contact.

As I noted above, every possible academic field is open for further research in Africa, and more and more funding will become available from the US government, international development agencies, and major US foundations with a focus on Africa. Getting African faculty to the US is less difficult than is the case with students. A number of organizations (e.g., USAID, ACE, Fulbright) and individual US Embassies sponsor such programs of varying duration. These are highly useful for both sides and African American studies programs should seize such opportunities.

Internships

Many internship opportunities in Africa, or working on African issues in the US, exist in the public and non-governmental sectors; others are being developed in the private sector as American companies expand into Africa. The US Department of State (www.careers.state.gov) offers internships at many of its embassies in Africa during fall, spring, and summer. For anyone considering diplomacy as a career, the internships provide a fantastic opportunity to gauge the work. In addition, by interning at a smaller African embassy, the intern is usually assigned the same level of work as US diplomats—and gains valuable experience. Another way a student can decide if they would be interested in a career in Africa is through the Peace Corps' Masters International program (www.peacecorps.gov/index.cfm?shell=learn.whyvol.eduben. mastersint). This excellent program combines a Master's degree in a number of fields (from over seventy-five participating US universities) with a twenty-four month Peace Corps tour. Those participants I met have overwhelmingly called it a life-changing experience. Other internships are available in Africa with major NGOs, religious organizations, and even UN agencies. As more and more US companies expand into Africa, they are also offering student internships (check companies listed with the Corporate Council for Africa: www.africacncl.org/Default.aspx).

Professional development is another category in which Africa is both professionally and personally enriching. I have worked with groups of visiting dentists providing dental care to people who had never in their lives visited a dentist (and they encountered medical conditions they had never seen). I've met teams of physicians spending their summer vacations establishing a makeshift clinic in a part of Addis Ababa where thousands of people do not have a neighborhood doctor, and treating hundreds of people each day. I've also worked with a management team from Exxon who were building a bridge to take visitors into Korup national forest in Cameroon, one of the world's last large reserves where no tree has ever been felled. I've had the privilege of meeting with US farmers who were exchanging information with Ethiopian cultivators about crops, soils, fertilizer, and irrigation. All said they learned so much more than they imparted, and all were eager to return.

AFRICA RISING

While not everyone will want to make Africa their life's work, I hope I have persuaded you to learn more about the Continent, to find a way to study, research, or at least visit there, and—most importantly—to become an advocate for Africa. Once enough Americans, especially African Americans, gain an appreciation of Africa's tremendous riches and potential, our government will no longer be able to treat Africa as last among our global strategic interests. And the Reverend Jackson will never again have to complain about Africa being left behind yet again!

NOTES

1. US Census Bureau, *Black History Month: February 2008* (December 2007). See www.census.gov/Press-Release/www/releases/archives/facts_for_features_special_editions/010969.html.
2. N. J. Colletta, J. Balachander, and X. Liang, *The Condition of Young Children in Sub-Saharan Africa* (1996). books.google.com/books?id=U3QtTPMIr7sC&pg=PA4&lpg=PA4&dq=Sub-Saharan+Africa+avg+per-capita+%24530&source=web&ots=ebFQEksnoo&sig=W_q7i65A1kzoqlqtaovCl692c70&hl=en&sa=X&oi=book_result&resnum=3&ct=result.
3. Foreign & Commonwealth Office, *Sub Saharan Africa: Eritrea* (October 8, 2007). www.fco.gov.uk/en/about-the-fco/country-profiles/sub-saharan-africa/eritrea?profile=all.

4. Development Assistance, *Data on the Web* (October 2006). www.data.org/issues/development_2006_waterBriefing.

5. Sub-Saharan Africa, Report on the global AIDS epidemic, *UNAIDS* (2008). www.unaids.org/en/CountryResponses/Regions/SubSaharanAfrica.asp.

6. HIV/AIDS facts and figures. Statistics from *UNAIDS 2007 Report on Global Aids Epidemic and UNICEF* (2007). www.starfishcharity.org/general-content.aspx?id_Content=193.

7. "Statistics in Africa: 50 Factoids about Sub-Saharan African," *The World Bank on the Web* (2007). web.worldbank.org/WBSITE/EXTERNAL/COUNTRIES/AFRICAEXT/EXTPUB.REP/EXTSTATINAFR/0,,contentMDK:21106218~menuPK:3094759~pagePK:64168445~piPK:64168309~theSitePK:824043,00.html.

8. P. Smith, "Africa's Year of Democratic Reverses," *BBC News on the Web* (December 29, 2005). news.bbc.co.uk/2/hi/africa/4552930.stm.

9. D. Bennett, "Africa Rising," *The Boston Globe on the Web* (December 9, 2007). www.boston.com/bostonglobe/ideas/articles/2007/12/09/africa_rising?mode=PF.

10. "Africa Achieving Healthy and Steady Growth Rate," *The World Bank on the Web* (November 14, 2007). go.worldbank.org/1C8ALNNFZ0.

11. D. Shinn, "Africa, China, the United States, and Oil," *Center for Strategic and International Studies—Africa Policy Forum on the Web* (May 8, 2007). forums.csis.org/africa/?p=34.

12. "HIV and AIDS in Africa," *AVERT* (July 30, 2008). www.avert.org/aafrica.htm.

CHAPTER 8

Black Studies in the UK and US: A Comparative Analysis

Mark Christian

Miami University, Ohio

Although my association with the field of Black Studies[1] now spans some sixteen years, in the formal sense of teaching the subject matter in the UK and US, my connection goes back at least twenty years in terms of fighting for its existence in the British education system. Thus, this chapter must be part-autobiographical due to the deep connection I have with the themes and perspectives of this book. That stated, the essence of this chapter will be to highlight some of the key factors in the development of Black Studies in the UK context compared to the US. I therefore examine the origins and development of Black Studies from the perspective of both nations. Within the British context, the city of Liverpool will be a focus as it is a key example of the struggle to develop a Black Studies curriculum via grassroots Black community educational advocates. However, because the US is qualitatively different in terms of its Black Studies experience, this chapter will make reference to both the historical and contemporary development in the North American academy.

Before we start though, it is important to give the reader an insight into my background and qualifications to write this chapter. As already touched on, when I reflect on my experience in education in the UK and US, the notion and practice of Black Studies has been at the heart of my social background, activism, and scholarship. The fact that I was born in the 1960s—literally a child of the '60s—when Black students, with some progressive White students, were fighting for Black Studies on US campuses during the Civil Rights Movement, makes the intersection of my biography and history that more relevant, as we shall see.

My father arrived in Liverpool from Jamaica during World War II to work in the munitions factories. Britain drew labor from its colonies when times were bad; and when times were good would want 'these' people, particularly those of color, to return to the colony from which they had come. My father was a dark-skinned Jamaican technician from a middle-class background. His parents and siblings moved between Kingston, Jamaica, and Columbus, Ohio in Midwest USA. My grandparents had eight children and I believe my father was the third oldest. My grandfather, George Rupert Christian, was a follower and advocate for the Black Nationalist leader Marcus Garvey and the Universal Negro Improvement Association (UNIA).

My mother was born in Liverpool of Spanish origin. Her father was a merchant sea captain. She was also one of eight children. Both my grandmothers were essentially housewives. In the British context my mother's family would be considered upper working class (in the US context they would be deemed middle class). My parents met and fell in love in a Liverpool munitions factory and had thirteen children between 1945 and 1962. We were by all social measures regarded as a "Black Liverpool family" and lived our lives as the "other" in British society.

I was the twelfth of the thirteen children. My older siblings were influenced by the sounds of rhythm and blues coming from the African American experience. Liverpool in the 1960s and 1970s had a vibrant Black culture via the club scene. The Black community could be depicted as a creolized population with its mixture of African seaman, African Caribbean migrants, African American GIs based at the US air force base in Burtonwood, and local women, both Black and White.

This is the social backdrop to my life in Liverpool and its Black experience. The point for the reader is that this is an African Diaspora experience based in Europe, with ancestral links to the African Caribbean and African American worlds. Moreover, Black settlement in the city goes back to the eighteenth century when Liverpool was a major port for the transatlantic slave trade in African humanity.[2] The legacy of this era leads to a history of racism in Liverpool that is well documented in the contemporary sense.[3] Hence the notion of Black Studies in the UK is as relevant and necessary to the social history of the Black British communities as it is to the US and the African American experience. Although the focus here is limited to the UK and US, it is important to note that the study of the African Diaspora is a global reality. In fact, there are literally hundreds of African Diaspora experiences. Too often Black Studies is confined to African American phenomena, when in fact this is only true in regard to its contested presence in US society and its higher education system.

THE BLACK BRITISH PERSPECTIVE ON BLACK STUDIES

Unlike the US, the UK has yet to have Black Studies institutionalized within the British education system. However, taking the lead from the African American experience, during the 1960s and 1970s there was a concerted effort to provide supplementary schooling for British Black children to offset "cultural depersonalization" taking place in primary (5–11 years age group) and secondary (11–18 years age group) schools. In other words, progressive educationalists in the 1960s-1970s were adopting an anti-racist approach to combat the lack of Black perspectives in the curriculum and broader British society.[4] The British education system, it was argued, was failing its Black students in terms of their social development and self-esteem. Yet the best that could be done to combat this was to set up supplementary schooling that came from grassroots, often voluntary, support.

It should also be noted that in this period the term "Black" in Britain often politically defined all peoples of color experiencing institutionalized racism, and their struggle for a unified front against it.[5] Therefore, indigenous Black British and migrant African Caribbeans, African continentals, Asians from India, Pakistan, Sri Lanka, and Bangladesh could all be deemed "Black" in the political sense. This would later be contested, and by the 1990s each cultural group would be examined for its unique British experiences.[6]

Although there could be political unity under the term "Black," when it came to teaching Black history and culture, British school children of African heritage would be taught most often from a Pan-Africanist perspective via supplementary schooling in the larger conurbations, where Black communities had educational grassroots resources. Writing at this time to promote the need to combat the effects of White racism on Black children, Bernard Coard argued, in a powerfully written pamphlet entitled *How the West Indian Child is Made Educationally Sub-Normal in the British School System*:

> We need to open Black nursery schools and supplementary schools
> throughout the areas we live in, in Britain. Our nursery schools
> should have Black dolls and toys and pictures, and story-books about
> great Black men and women, and their achievements and inventions.
> Our children need to have a sense of identity, pride, and belonging,
> as well as mental stimulation, so that they do not end up hating

themselves and their race, and being dumped in ESN [educationally sub-normal] Schools. Pride and self-confidence are the best armour against the prejudice and humiliating experiences which they will certainly face in school and in society.[7]

The message Coard sent Black parents and educationalists was simple: we need to take care of our children's education, as they are being miseducated into becoming subnormal, self-hating misfits. Coard goes on:

> These classes can be held on evenings and Saturday mornings. We should recruit all our Black students and teachers for the task of instructing our children. Through these schools we hope to make up for the inadequacies of the British school system, and for its refusal to teach our children our history and culture. We must never sit idly by while they make ignoramuses of our children, but must see to it that by hook or crook our children get the best education they are capable of . . .[8]

Here, then, are the beginnings of the systematic struggle for Black Studies in Britain. Unlike the US, the UK's Black communities fought for Black history and culture to be taught at the grassroots level and primarily to younger age groups (11–18-year-olds). We now know that in the US it was higher education, via student protest, that witnessed most of the struggle for Black Studies. This is important when we consider Black Studies in a comparative framework.

Overall, the origin of Black Studies in Britain was a grassroots community activity, not one that emerged out of elite higher education. One could find Black Studies classes taking place in dilapidated and under-resourced buildings throughout inner cities. For example, in Liverpool a number of community venues taught Black history and culture, but arguably the most prominent was based at the Charles Wootton Centre,[9] which was established as an adult education provider, mainly for young Black adults who had been failed by the mainstream school system. The "Charlie," as it was known locally, provided a safe environment not only for Black students and working-class Whites, but also for Black educators who had faced employment discrimination in the British education system.

As a student of Charles Wootton (class of '81), I had my first Black history lessons, and gained greater self-awareness and a social consciousness in terms of comprehending the historical oppression and inequality meted out to peoples of color and other powerless groups. Ron "Babatunde" Phillips, an educator and community activist, was my first Black Studies teacher and he opened my mind to many aspects of the global Black experience, including: Marcus Garvey, Malcolm X, Martin Luther King, Jr., Mary Seacole, Sojourner Truth, Angela Davis, and many other Black personalities. He also recognized my academic potential, which I did not see at the time, nor had been made aware of during my primary and secondary schooling. Without his contribution to my scholarly development at a relatively young age, this chapter might not have been written. On reflection, the Charles Wootton Centre gave me and so many other young Black Liverpudlians the spirit to survive and fight against the odds in an environment that was hostile to Black development. The "Charlie" gave one confidence that was not generally received from the mainstream British education system as a person of color.[10] At the heart of this was the teaching of Black history and culture, and an atmosphere of togetherness and empowerment in the classroom.

THE WHITE LIBERAL BACKLASH TO BLACK STUDIES IN BRITAIN

Too often anything related to Black education offered in the mainstream sphere had a "White face" on it. Put another way, anything to do with "race" and education had a "White expert" (usually male) articulating what Blacks in Britain were experiencing. It could be deemed as "White liberal paternalism" which had little to do with the actual empowerment of Black youth and more to do with the White liberal's own career as a sociologist, political scientist or journalist, for example.

Paradoxically—or maybe not if we consider careerism—the major attacks on Black Studies in the 1970s and 1980s in Britain came from the White liberal fraternity. Two such academics who made a name and career for themselves in "race studies" were Ernest Cashmore and Barry Troyna, who contested the efficacy of Black Studies.

> Whilst not being totally dismissive of black studies propagators and their aims, we cannot be enthusiastic about the futures of the projects themselves [in Britain]. The real issues remain untouched by their efforts and those very efforts may well prove destructive to relationships between young blacks and the rest of society in the long

term. The black studies are, in our opinion, cosmetic in function and their masters myopic.[11]

These two leading White liberal "experts" on "race relations" professed to comprehend the Black British experience more profoundly than those who had both lived and taught it. They insulted "masters of black studies" as being "myopic," but failed to recognize the social reality of their own paternalism. It was in fact the staple attack on those community education activists who endeavored to do something about the glaring discrimination meted out to Black youth in the British mainstream education system. It is intensely annoying to have White privileged "outsiders" "explain" what is best for Black people in terms of the social experience of living, learning, and surviving in White Britain. Again Cashmore and Troyna contended:

> Black or Afro-studies portray the black man as a courageous, skillful, intelligent creator of his own culture, a worshipper of his own gods, and politician of acuity and unremitting independence. His continent was one of prosperity and one which, if left alone by whites, would surely have flourished. This is not falsification but is more a satisfying picture, an exaggerated representation highlighting certain, selected characteristics while neglecting others, than a graphic reminder that this was reality, it is no longer reality and has no necessary connection with life in England in the late twentieth century- not even for blacks.[12]

Cashmore and Troyna's analysis is highly selective in relation to the struggle for Black Studies in Britain. Indeed, it is difficult to think of them as sociologists or "race" experts at all in this context. They are completely off-base in terms of comprehending the social significance of Black Studies. It is true that Black Studies courses did offer a perspective in not viewing peoples of African heritage merely as victims of the European enslavement and colonialism eras, and there was an effort to examine the classical African civilizations that emerged on the continent long before Europe even existed.[13] If in this examination of historical facts it is discovered that Africans were "skillful and intelligent creators" of their own culture, the truth should be known and widely disseminated. For centuries the truth about African civilizations had been whitewashed in European world history books, which give no indication that Africans contributed positively to human evolution and development.[14] Yet concrete evidence can be found by visiting the British Museum, London, which houses many examples of ancient African artifacts and relics produced by African humanity and culture, dating back hundreds to thousands of years.

The fact that Europeans disrupted the natural progress of African civilizations is also an historical reality, and again is well documented.[15] Therefore, given the history of Africans on the continent and its Diaspora over the last 500-plus years, it is imperative for Black Studies scholars, wherever they are located, to examine and note this important history as it is fundamental in the deconstruction of historical myth concerning African inferiority.

The great African civilizations may well be consigned to the history of a golden age and not be particularly relevant to the present, but this does not mean we should forget that they ever existed. Further, the notion that Africans were uncivilized heathens without a history is patently untrue. Cashmore and Troyna[16] did not fully comprehend the fact that European culture and British history had largely not been kind to the history of African peoples. One of the key aims of Black Studies is to deconstruct the false history perpetuated by European racists during and beyond the time of enslavement and colonialism. To suggest that this history has nothing to do with the contemporary conditions of Black experiences is folly. The legacy of racism has tentacles that go back as far as the development of eighteenth- and nineteenth-century pseudo-scientific racial theories which deemed White Europeans superior to all other racial groups.[17]

In essence, Cashmore and Troyna[18] exemplify the hegemony of the White liberal in British academia who has steadily controlled Black thought and intellectual practice for decades via the British education system. Even as I write today, the situation in Britain remains largely unchanged. Very few Black British academics can be found who are offering an alternative to the type of perspective Cashmore and Troyna[19] offer. This White liberal academic perspective proved to be a major obstacle to the development of a coherent and stable Black Studies curriculum in the British education system, from the 1970s to the present day. Very few scholars have emerged from the British higher education system to teach Black Studies in the fullest sense; that is, to approach knowledge from the vantage point of African peoples that makes them central, not marginal, to the subject matter.[20]

It is ironic that ancient African history is viewed as meaningless to contemporary Black youth, yet ancient Roman history is not questioned as being futile to the lives of working-class White youth in Britain. When one considers Cashmore and Troyna[21] in this sense, one can gauge best their subliminal effort to hold on to the right to interpret the Black British experience and to assert what is best for Black British people. One can witness the "Whiteness" of many White liberal educators when a Black intellectual teaches from the viewpoint and empowerment of African peoples. This is not to suggest an essentialist or static assessment of all White liberal educators. There are some wonderful, honest White thinkers—among them Basil Davidson, Joe Feagin, Tim Wise, and Andrew Hacker, to name just a few—who comprehend the reality of White paternalism referred to here.

One of the major criticisms of Black Studies that has come from White educationalists in Britain, as evidenced in Cashmore and Troyna,[22] is the notion that Black Studies is merely a "feel-good" exercise. Well, let me be bold and brief. It is only a fool that would argue against the fact that the past is connected to the present. Of course, Black youth will "feel good" if they learn that their ancestors had a key role in building monuments like the pyramids of ancient Egypt/Kemet or the Great Zimbabwe empire, or that they contributed to medicine, art, philosophy, and so on. What is wrong with giving Black youth concrete examples of past achievements in African heritage? Indeed, teaching this can only help inspire current and future generations to aim for greatness themselves. However, teaching both positive and negative historical facts is even more important. After all, not everything that has come from African civilizations has been positive and not everything from European civilization has been negative. Black Studies offers a crucial corrective to false knowledge if it is taught properly. That is what the best scholars in the field seek to do—teach properly and professionally to all students, regardless of their ethnicity or social background.

Overall, the fight for Black Studies in Britain was fought for and won at the grassroots community level, but lost, or was never established systematically, in the mainstream British education system.[23] As pointed out, Cashmore and Troyna[24] are part and parcel of the White-dominated education system in Britain. They had the audacity to argue that masters in Black Studies are "myopic" and, ultimately, misguided in teaching Black history and culture to Black youth. They stated also that the idea and practice of Black Studies is a "cosmetic" exercise that obscures the social reality of Black deprivation, exclusion, and disenfranchisement. They represent the White liberal, colorblind mentality that promotes, directly or indirectly, an historical amnesia whereby peoples of African heritage ought to think only of the here-and-now, or if they look back, start with the abolition of slavery in the nineteenth century and work forward from there. Indeed, for generations this has been the "normal" schooling for Black youth in Britain. Their collective historical and contemporary achievements are rarely taught outside of a Black Studies class. Hence, ignorance of Black history and culture continues to plague Black youth and communities in Britain.

Brian Richardson's edited *Tell It Like It Is: How Our Schools Fail Black Children*[25] confirms that the present situation for Black children in British schools has not improved much in the almost forty years since Bernard Coard published *How the West Indian Child is Made Educationally Sub-Normal in the British School System*. The contributors, many of whom are Black British community education activists, reflect on the British system and the continued lack of Black perspectives or Black Studies. Sally Tomlinson pays tribute to Coard's legacy, and with pessimism writes:

> Despite rhetoric of inclusion, new ways have developed of excluding many Black children from full participation in mainstream education. The school curriculum continues to be Anglocentric, and teachers are even less likely to be trained to teach in a multiracial society than in the 1970s.[26]

When one considers the dire state of the British higher education system when it comes to promoting diversity, there is little surprise when one learns that contemporary teachers are not being educated to teach multicultural perspectives. Teachers need to be taught too, but if there is nothing offered to them from Black Studies and other minority cultures when they learn how to become teachers, how can we blame them? The culpability lies with those who hold the power in British universities.

Finally, in comprehending the complexity of the White liberal perspective, it is important to point out in comparing the UK and US that there is a growing critical school of thought among White liberals in the US, a school of thought that the UK could benefit from. This critical look at "Whites on Whites" is exemplified by Barbara Trepagnier's *Silent Racism: How Well-Meaning White People Perpetuate the Racial Divide*.[27] Trepagnier takes to task White liberals who consider themselves "non-racist" and it would be most useful if a book like this were written for the UK context of racialized relations, especially in regard to the discussion of White liberal resentment of Black Studies.

BLACK STUDIES, BLACK BRITISH INTELLECTUALS, AND MAINSTREAM BRITAIN IN THE 2000S

In March 2005 the *Times Higher Education Supplement* (THES) published a series of articles looking at Black Studies in Britain, or its absence, and why it is that so many Black British intellects were leaving, primarily for the US, to develop their careers. I was asked to write an article[28] on why Black British academics were leaving in such "large" numbers, given how few we are! My argument was simple: Black British academics, those specifically wanting to express a Black perspective, were leaving to take up opportunities that were not generally available in the UK. Nothing new really; the same exclusion that had been historically meted out to Black citizens was also a part of the British education system. The problem though, for the British, was that many Black British academics were achieving great success in "racist America"—ironically, according to many British academics.[29]

The March 2005 THES series headline read: "The doors to the mainstream are shut to pioneers [Black British academics]." Mandy Garner, the series editor's argument was that the UK academy was still reluctant to give recognition to Black academics and Black Studies. As editor she brought together a group of Black British and progressive White academics to discuss the problems faced by Black academics in contemporary Britain. Heidi Mirza, an expert in Black British feminist theory, argued that Black academics in Britain would not gain the momentum required to effect change until the "gatekeepers" opened the doors to opportunities to develop in the area of Black British Studies. Overall, the panel was pessimistic about British higher education funding a Black British Studies effort as it was not a profitable project. The moral aspect in providing a broader multicultural perspective in education was given little weight.

In my THES article I concluded that it is those who have power to make change that must take responsibility for the lack of opportunity in allowing the growth of Black British Studies curricula:

> Those with the authority to make positive changes cannot hide from the fact that Britain has many Black experiences that need to be researched and studied by college and university students. From the responses of those Black British scholars who have left to teach in the US, it appears that many would have stayed in Britain if there had been opportunities for them to do so.[30]

For the British education system to lose such an array of talent is unpardonable. However, given the historical struggle against racialized discrimination that Black people have faced in Britain, is anyone really surprised? More to the point, does anyone really care?

The responses to the THES feature were largely supportive. A number of published letters confirmed this support, but one letter accused the "tone" of my article of being "worryingly racist and segregationist."[31] Again, this is often the response from White liberals when a Black perspective on the social world is expressed. Another letter in the same THES edition adequately addressed Timothy Insoll's preposterous accusation. It came from William Ackah, a fellow Black British scholar and colleague, who wrote:

> When will [British] universities and the white liberal intelligentsia recognise that they cannot continually talk about ethnic minorities in the media and conduct research on us yet deny us the opportunity to write and teach about our own experiences? That is exclusion of the worst kind.[32]

He continued:

> Something is wrong when two British scholars (Mark Christian and Paul Gilroy) debate the nature of black British studies from the US. Such debates should be a central feature of British academic life. Ethnic minorities should be seen and heard at all levels of higher education . . .

As Ackah pointed out, there is something odd about two Black British scholars discussing the state of Black Studies in the UK from the distant shores of the US. Although Gilroy has since returned to the UK from Yale University's Department of African American Studies, he has not come back to develop Black Studies in Britain. On the contrary, he will be focusing primarily within mainstream sociological discourse, emphasizing social theory, via an Anthony Giddens professorship.

Black Studies as a discipline has most often been on the periphery in British higher education. Without a concerted effort to improve the situation there is unlikely to be institutional support for this field of knowledge. That means Black communities in Britain will continue to have no voice within higher education that speaks to their collective and varied history and culture. Even raising the topic can mean being confronted by the White liberal hegemony that controls cultural studies in the UK. One can do many things as a social theorist, but not talk too loudly about "Black perspectives." These are moribund viewpoints in the British system of higher education, a system that rarely allowed them to breathe or come to life in the first place.

THE CONTEMPORARY US BLACK STUDIES SCENE

It would be naïve to suggest that all is rosy in the US when it comes to the role of Black Studies in the academy. I have dealt with some of the contemporary key concerns facing the field elsewhere.[33] However, one could argue with relative ease that Black Studies as an institutionalized body of knowledge in US higher education is, conservatively stated, at least fifty years ahead compared to the UK. Indeed, whereas Black Studies in the UK is largely supported and projected at the grassroots level,[34] in the US context we could argue that it is more established in higher education than it is in the grassroots communities. Ideally, the best Black Studies situation would be to marry the grassroots enthusiasm of the British scene to that of the higher education experience in the US. Currently, some commentators in the US are arguing that that there should be more focus on the original call for Black Studies in the 1960s, which was to link the community to the campus and the campus to the community.[35]

A recently published study by an African American literature professor speaks to his experience of Black Studies/African American Studies at the University of California, Berkeley, one of the elite Ivy League schools. In a rather contentious book, *Dude, Where's My Black Studies Department? The Disappearance of Black Americans from Our Universities*, Cecil Brown claims in particular that African Caribbean scholars have "taken over" as overseers and effectively stunted the growth of the original mission of Black Studies in the US. Moreover, he contends that, on an intellectual level, there has been a shift from a focus on African American to a more African Diaspora-based curriculum. As he puts it:

> The 1960s project to create Black Studies departments at
> universities across the country has now been totally co-opted.
> Although Black Studies was initially a way for African American
> students to engage with their community outside the university,

most Black Studies departments are now largely refocused on the
African Diaspora and the concerns of Black immigrants . . .[36]

Earlier, in relation to his Berkeley experience, he had stated:

Under the leadership of [Percy] Hintzen and other imported
Caribbean professors, the African American Studies department
UC Berkeley—and other Black Studies departments across
the country—have used a modernity-fabricated rubric, that of
diaspora ideology, to steer away from the basic ideology of Black
Studies, which was to bridge a gap between the university and the
community, between the abstraction of literary book-learning and
the oral reality of culture . . .[37]

What Brown argues has some truth to it, though in part he is incorrect in
his analysis. I cannot speak directly to his experience at UC Berkeley, but
it is obvious he has had a negative interaction with those he deems African
Caribbean scholars based there. To suggest, however, that all US Black
Studies departments and programs have been "taken over" by African
Caribbean people is wrong. He fails to mention the influx of Africans
from the continent who have also had, and continue to have, an important
impact on broadening the notion and practice of Black Studies in the US.
One should not dismiss the fact that Euro-Americans are now found in
many Black Studies departments and programs.

In terms of the validity of his argument, it could be contended that many
Black Studies departments have deviated from the original mission of Black
Studies. However, I would not place this at the feet of African Caribbean
scholars. This is a philosophical issue, one that can transcend ethnicity. For
example, there are African Americans, African Caribbeans, Africans, and
others of African heritage who come from Europe or elsewhere who hold
strongly to a postmodernist perspective, which largely denies the notion
of cultural solidarity. Instead, it argues for an "anything goes" intellectual
discourse. Phrases such as "intersectionality" of "race," class and gender,
"queer studies" or "multiple oppressions" are commonplace in contemporary output of Black Studies. It must be highly frustrating for a scholar like
Brown, who lived in the era of the US struggle for Black Studies and, from
what he implies, was an originator of the field.

However, if he is to be considered a well-read practitioner of Black
Studies, it is equally odd that Brown does not refer to or cite Molefi K.

Asante, the African American and internationally renowned intellectual, who originated the first PhD in African American Studies. He fails also to make reference to Maulana Karenga, a prominent philosophy professor in Black Studies, again of African American heritage, and the creator of the now global Pan-African and largely African American holiday, Kwanzaa. These two intellectuals alone refute the idea that the African American perspective and original message of Black Studies have been "totally co-opted."

Also, when reading Brown, I was struck by inaccuracies—some minor, some serious. One minor error is in stating that Malcolm X's death was in April 1965, when in fact it was February 21, 1965.[38] Also, he situates Paul Gilroy's *The Black Atlantic* as both a "West Indian" and an "African text," thereby taking away the importance of African American texts.[39] Gilroy's book may have been lauded in some Black Studies circles, but as a Black Studies graduate from the Black British experience, based at Ohio State University in 1992–93, I can state that *The Black Atlantic* was criticized profoundly for being more Eurocentric in tone than Africa-centered. Gilroy, among other things, failed even to locate Africa in the text!

Lastly, Brown makes reference to Stephen Small being akin to the other "African Caribbean overseers" at UC Berkeley (from 2002 onwards).[40] The problem here is that Brown cannot distinguish the patois of the African Caribbean from that of the Black British (here a Liverpudlian), for Stephen Small has a very strong Liverpool accent (although his father was of Jamaican heritage, Stephen and his siblings were born and raised in Liverpool). Like Brown, Small gained his PhD at UC Berkeley (1989) and, after teaching "race" and ethnic studies in the British higher education system, he returned to Berkeley to become a professor of African American Studies. Small has not "sold out." He may not be an Afrocentric scholar, but neither is he an uncritical admirer of postmodernist discourse.

These errors should not deter one from accepting some of Brown's points. There are many contemporary problems with Black Studies/ African American Studies departments that fail to empower the African American experience first and foremost, and *then* take note of the African continent and its broader Diaspora. Indeed, one cannot teach Black Studies/African American Studies properly without discussing Africa and its Diaspora. However, like Brown, I agree that African American experiences should take precedence over any other African and African Diaspora location when taught in the US. Similarly, I would argue that it is logical that the Black British experience should take precedence if it were taught in the UK.

It is very dangerous to single out, say, African Caribbean scholars for the "demise" of African American intellectuals and the original promise of Black Studies. Instead, there ought to be a focus on the philosophical orientation of the departments and programs. I have argued elsewhere that only qualified scholars should be hired in Black Studies, those with a BA, MA or PhD in Black Studies. Ideally, every faculty candidate should have a PhD in Black Studies/Africana Studies. However, if this cannot be achieved, then candidates ought to have at least a BA or MA in the discipline. This would mean, at the very least, that opportunists would not be able to infiltrate Black Studies departments and programs. I recognize Brown's concerns, but his argument is parochial and off-base.

Rightly or wrongly, we are a Pan-African experience. This holds true from Wilmot Blyden's day up to Marcus Garvey's; it traversed the 1960s too. Why was Frantz Fanon's *The Wretched of the Earth*[41] so important for the likes of Bobby Seale, Fred Hampton, H. Rap Brown, and Kwame Ture in the 1960s? Why did a book written by an African Caribbean (Martinique-born) resonate so strongly with young African Americans? I suggest it was because it spoke to a Pan-African struggle for African humanity and freedom from Eurocentric oppression. This is something we should not forget as we consider Black Studies in the twenty-first century and beyond. Whether in the UK, the US or anywhere else in the world, there will be issues facing people of African heritage that deserve intellectual attention from a Pan-Africanist perspective, as well as a specific local examination.

The contemporary US Black Studies/Africana Studies field is far from perfect. However, after forty years it is now a standard feature in most North American universities. In the UK we cannot boast of a single department or program catering for Black Studies within a British African and African Diaspora context. Given its history of Black presence, this is an unpardonable omission.

CONCLUSION

This chapter has discussed Black Studies in the UK and US context via aspects of my biography and experience in the field, having studied, researched, and taught the subject in both the UK and US in both the grassroots community and universities. The primary focus has been on the British context as the UK "grassroots origin" of Black Studies experience is still largely unknown in the US. Moreover, I am aware that other chapters in this volume speak in-depth to the US context of Black Studies.

Liverpool does not represent the entire understanding of Black British Studies, but it does provide an excellent case study. My experience of being Black *and* British, as well as a Black Studies advocate and scholar, has contributed to this chapter in a way that I did not initially envisage. However, the more I considered the topic, the more it was impossible to divorce myself from its content. It is hoped that the reader comprehends my being "organically interwoven" into Black Studies through my life, student, and scholar experience.

The lack of support for Black Studies in Britain reveals more than mere neglect on the part of the British education system; it demonstrates contempt for Black presence and humanity. Indeed, given the history of the British Empire, it is unpardonable that Black Studies as a discipline is not an integral aspect of British school children's and the college and university sectors' curricula. After all, the UK is regarded as a multicultural nation, and if the education system fails to include the histories of its cultural minorities, there is little wonder that institutional and everyday racism continues.

The role of the White liberal has been touched upon here, but it needs further attention as it has had a tremendous impact on the lack of genuine empowerment of Black communities in relation to an education that speaks to their lives and culture. There should be no place for paternalism in the twenty-first century when it comes to understanding human agency and cultural diversity. It is acknowledged too that Black communities need support from progressive White allies in securing an education that speaks to their histories and culture. However, this should not mean any form of control and knowing what is "best" for disempowered Black communities. In regard to Black Studies, it is the sense of empowerment that comes from learning that leads to further achievements in society. It is an important element in one's education as a person of color to know that one's history is not entirely encased in subordination. The White liberal ought to be concerned with genuine empowerment of Black communities via Black Studies curricula. This will mean adopting a deeper insight into what empowerment means. It certainly is not about knowing what is best for powerless groups from a privileged vantage point.

Overall, the UK and US have followed different paths to development in Black Studies. As argued, the US is by far the more advanced society in terms of the establishment and development of Black Studies in college and university curricula. This does not mean that the US faces no problems in this regard. There are many issues to confront and, by and large, support for Black Studies/Africana Studies/African American Studies appears to be waning in college and university administrations when it should be increasing. Only time will tell if there will be a greater appreciation of Black Studies in the UK, and whether it will increase in the US or remain contested. One thing is certain: Black Studies will continue in one form or another. History has testified to this.

NOTES

1. The term "Black" here relates to persons/groups who claim African heritage, and the term "Black Studies" is used for clarity to acknowledge the era when Black Studies was established in the US higher education mainstream from the mid-1960s onwards. However, I am aware that many Black Studies departments and programs in the US during the 1990s and 2000s have adopted the nomenclature "Africana Studies." Other departments have been renamed African American Studies, African American and African Studies, African and African Diaspora Studies, and Pan-African Studies. Regardless of the names they are all related to the field of Black Studies.

2. See Mark Christian, "Black Struggle for Historical Recognition in Liverpool," *North West Labour History*, vol. 20 (1995), 58–60; "An African Centered Approach to the Black British Experience: With Special Reference to Liverpool," *Journal of Black Studies*, vol. 28, no. 3 (1998), 291–308; ed., *Black Identity in the Twentieth Century: Expressions of the US and UK African Diaspora* (London: Hansib, 2002); also R. Costello, *Black Liverpool: The Early History of Britain's Oldest Black Community, 1730–1918* (Birkenhead: Picton Press, 2001).

3. See Mark Christian, "An African Centered Perspective on White Supremacy," *Journal of Black Studies*, vol. 33, no. 2 (2002): 179–98; and "The Politics of Black Presence in Britain and Black Male Exclusion in the British Education System," *Journal of Black Studies*, vol. 35, no. 3 (2005): 327–46; also L. Gifford, W. Brown and R. Bundey, *Loosen the Shackles: First Report of the Liverpool 8 Inquiry into Race Relations in Liverpool* (London: Karia Press, 1989).

4. F. Dhondy, B. Beese, and L. Hassan, *The Black Explosion in British Schools* (London: Race Today, 1982).

5. A. Sivanandan, *A Different Hunger: Writings on Black Resistance* (London: Pluto Press, 1982), 62–3.

6. Tariq Modood, Sharon Beishon, and Satnam Virdee, *Changing Ethnic Identities* (London: Policy Studies Institute, 1994).

7. B. Coard, *How the West Indian Child Is Made Educationally Sub-Normal in the British School System* (London: Karia Press, 1991; first published 1971), 41.

8. Coard, *The West Indian Child*, 44.
9. The Charles Wootton Centre was established in 1974 for adult education classes in the predominately Black community area of Liverpool (Liverpool 8, or Toxteth). It provided English, Math, Black History, Music, Nursing, and Business classes. Once qualified, students could go back into the mainstream education system and take up technical or academic courses in nearby colleges and universities. Hundreds of local Blacks benefited from the Centre during its existence (1974–2000). In 1992 it gained the status of "College" and developed courses in media and information technology. At the height of its development it played host to Black educationalists from the Africa and African Diaspora, particularly scholars and activists from the US. Closer to home, one of the strongest supporters of Black communities in Britain, the Slavery Reparations Movement, and the Charles Wootton was the late Black Member of Parliament, Bernie Grant (1944–2000). He was a frequent visitor to Liverpool from his base in London, and he became a patron of the college.
10. The story of the Charles Wootton College deserves far more attention than can be given here. In a forthcoming publication I shall elaborate on my experience in Liverpool and this famous institution which was at the heart of Liverpool's Black experience for a quarter of a century.
11. E. Cashmore and B. Troyna, eds., *Black Youth in Crisis* (London: George Allen & Unwin, 1982), 24.
12. Cashmore and Troyna, *Black Youth in Crisis*, 24.
13. See Molefi K. Asante, *Classical Africa* (Palo Alto, CA: National Press Books, 1994); J. G. Jackson, *Introduction to African Civilizations* (New York: Citadel, 1990); and, "Treasures of Egypt," *National Geographic*, vol. 5 (July 28, 2003).
14. B. Davidson, *The Lost Cities of Africa*, revised edn. (London: Little, Brown, 1987).
15. W. E. B. Du Bois, *The World and Africa: An Inquiry into the Part which Africa has Played in World History* (New York: International Publishers, 1990; first published 1946), 44–80; also K. Nkrumah, *Africa Must Unite* (London: Panaf, 1985; first published 1963), 1–8. See also W. Rodney, *A History of the Upper Guinea Coast, 1545–1800* (New York: Oxford University Press, 1970); and *How Europe Underdeveloped Africa*, revised edn. (Washington, DC: Howard University Press, 1982).
16. Cashmore and Troyna, *Black Youth in Crisis*.
17. P. Fryer, *Staying Power: The History of Black People in Britain* (London: Pluto Press, 1984).
18. Cashmore and Troyna, *Black Youth in Crisis*.
19. Cashmore and Troyna, *Black Youth in Crisis*.
20. Mark Christian, "African Centered Knowledge: A British Perspective," *The Western Journal of Black Studies*, vol. 25, no. 1 (2001), 12–20; see also Molefi K. Asante, *The Afrocentric Idea*, 2nd edn. (Philadelphia: Temple University, 1998).
21. Cashmore and Troyna, *Black Youth in Crisis*.
22. Cashmore and Troyna, *Black Youth in Crisis*.
23. Often universities would hire adjunct Black Studies scholars to teach a module or a course, but rarely in the British education system has there been a permanently

established Black Studies curriculum like those that can be found in the US with departments and programs.

24. Cashmore and Troyna, *Black Youth in Crisis.*

25. Brian Richardson, ed., *Tell It Like It Is: How Our Schools Fail Black Children* (London: Trentham Books, 2005).

26. Sally Tomlinson, "A Tribute to Bernard Coard," in Richardson, *Tell It Like It Is,* 84.

27. Barbara Trepagnier, *Silent Racism: How Well-Meaning White People Perpetuate the Racial Divide* (Boulder, CO: Paradigm Books, 2006).

28. Mark Christian, "Why We Go Abroad," *Times Higher Educational Supplement* (March 4, 2005), 20–1.

29. It is important to point out that I do not have a naïve understanding of the historical reality of racism in North America. I am after all a student of the Civil Rights Movement and the 1960s. It is in the fact that I studied at Ohio State University for my Master's degree in Black Studies (1992–93); and later was a senior Fulbright Scholar at Kent State University's Department of Pan-African Studies (1997–98), that I was probably an attractive prospect to any Black Studies department or program in the US. The fact that I have now made my life in the US for the past decade, that my wife is African American, and our daughter was born in the US makes North America my adopted home.

30. Christian, "Why We Go Abroad," 21.

31. See Letters and Opinion, Timothy Insoll, Manchester University, *Times Higher Education Supplement,* vol. 17 (March, 11, 2005).

32. *Times Higher Education Supplement,* vol. 17 (March 11, 2005).

33. Christian, "African Centered Knowledge"; also Mark Christian, "Unmasking Miseducation and Other Impediments to the Progressive Black Studies Scholar," *Africalogical Perspectives,* vol. 1, no. 1 (2004), 49–75; ed., *The State of Black Studies in the Academy,* special issue. *Journal of Black Studies,* vol. 36, no. 5 (2006); "Philosophy and Practice for Black Studies: The Case of Researching White Supremacy," in M. K. Asante and M. Karenga, eds., *Handbook of Black Studies* (Thousand Oaks, CA: Sage, 2006), 76–88; and "Notes on Black Studies: Its Continuing Necessity in the Academy and Beyond," *Journal of Black Studies,* vol. 37, no. 3 (2007), 348–64.

34. Christian, "African Centered Knowledge."

35. See Christian, "Notes on Black Studies"; Maulana Karenga, *Introduction to Black Studies,* 3rd edn. (Los Angeles, CA: Sankore Press, 2002); and Manning Marable, *Dispatches from the Ebony Tower: Intellectuals Confront the African American Experience* (New York: Columbia University Press, 2000).

36. Cecil Brown, *Dude, Where's My Black Studies Department? The Disappearance of Black Americans from Our Universities* (Berkeley, CA: North Atlantic Books, 2007), 34.

37. Brown, *Dude, Where's My Black Studies Department?,* 33.

38. Brown, *Dude, Where's My Black Studies Department?,* 67.

39. Brown, *Dude, Where's My Black Studies Department?,* 39–40.

40. Brown, *Dude, Where's My Black Studies Department?,* 38–9.

41. Frantz Fanon, *The Wretched of the Earth* (New York: Grove Press, 1963).

PART IV

Selected Areas of Scholarship

CHAPTER 9

Africana Studies and Oral History: A Critical Assessment

Leslie M. Alexander

Ohio State University

and Curtis J. Austin

University of Southern Mississippi

ORAL TRADITION AND AFRICAN PEOPLES

In 1989, renowned historian Amadou Hampâté Bâ wrote, "Oral tradition is the only path that can lead us right into the history and spirit of the African peoples." For Bâ, the oral tradition, the process by which people transmit testimony about the past from one person to another, is the only true way for the history of African people to be fully understood and appreciated.[1] Such a contention would not seem surprising to most scholars of African and African American history, particularly those who examine pre-colonial Africa or African Americans during enslavement. Since these civilizations and communities were largely pre-literate, the transmission of culture and history within these societies was almost exclusively dependent upon a strong oral tradition. This chapter argues that oral history and the oral tradition are central to the fields of African American history and Africana Studies, regardless of the period or topic under examination. As Bâ suggests, the oral tradition not only has a long and revered history in African and African American society, but it is fundamental to understanding the essence of the African American experience. Indeed, we maintain that no exploration of African American life or political consciousness is complete without an analysis and discussion of oral culture and history, or without giving voice to the people themselves. Thus, this chapter seeks to provide a brief overview of the function of the oral tradition in African American culture and demonstrates, through an analysis of contemporary oral interviews, the importance of oral history in Africana Studies.

The oral tradition has an ancient and illustrious history among African peoples; in fact, evidence of oral culture among West African people dates back more than 700 years.[2] Since most African societies prior to European contact were pre-literate, oral culture became a foundational component of many West African civilizations. The telling of stories—sharing experiences, both triumphant and tragic—is fundamentally rooted in our African heritage and manifested in a variety of ways, including storytelling, art, music, and dance. As Harold Courlander, one of the first scholars to investigate African oral culture, maintained:

> The range of African oral literary forms is seemingly endless. It includes creation myths, myth-legends, half-legendary chronicles and historical narratives either in song or prose; tales that explain natural phenomena, tribal practices and taboos, and cultural or political institutions; stories and fables that reflect on the nature of man and his strengths and weaknesses; tales of adventure, courage, disaster, and love; epics with legendary heroes or fictitious heroes, and tales of confrontation with the supernatural and unseen forces of nature; moralizing stories and stories that define man's place and role in the universe; riddles that amuse and teach, and proverbs that stress social values; and a virtually inexhaustible reservoir of animal tales, many of which, at bottom, are morality plays, while others are pure humor.[3]

In short, oral culture is the process by which African peoples have expressed themselves and given shape to their social, cultural, and political realities.

Despite the obvious significance of the oral tradition among African peoples, scholars have historically tended to doubt or challenge the legitimacy of oral sources—and, by extension, oral history—on the grounds that it is somehow less reliable. According to Bâ, African and African American oral sources have often been unfairly dismissed within the intellectual community. "In the modern nations, where what is written has precedence over what is spoken, where the book is the principle vehicle of the cultural heritage, there has been a long-standing notion that peoples without writing are peoples without culture." Fortunately, however, Bâ also noted that due to the diligence of historians and ethnologists, the African oral tradition has finally gained credibility within scholarly circles.[4] As many historians have noted, this was an important step for the field of Africana Studies because oral history is crucial to the study of African peoples. As historian Jan Vansina explains, "For all its wealth of written documents . . . history would be dry and forbidding without the contributions of informants who, through [oral] tradition, add the priceless African view of things."[5]

Even more importantly, however, African-centered scholars have recognized that it is virtually impossible to grasp the essence of the African American experience without utilizing and acknowledging the centrality of oral history and oral culture. Since African American culture remains deeply rooted in its African past, the oral tradition persisted during enslavement and continues to be an influential aspect of Black culture and society in the contemporary era. As Courlander explained, "The oral literature and traditions of African peoples communicate to us the scope and nature of our common identity."[6] Historian Jan Vansina concurred, noting that oral culture is not simply about communication, but also serves as a method of "preserving the wisdom of the ancestors . . . the oral approach is an attitude to reality and not the absence of a skill."[7] It was, in fact, these two factors—a desire to forge a common identity and a passion for honoring the ancestors—that caused African oral culture to survive and thrive among African peoples in the Americas.

Perhaps the most obvious examples of the persistence of African oral culture among African Americans can be found in studies examining slave culture during the antebellum era. Scholars have extensively documented the multifaceted role of oral culture among people of African descent throughout the Diaspora, particularly among African Americans in the southern United States.[8] Courlander notes, for example, that African oral culture was evident among enslaved African Americans in various forms, such as music, dance, religious expression, storytelling, folktales, and "recollections of historical happenings."[9] Moreover, linguist Geneva Smitherman argues that the influence of African oral culture in Black America lasted far beyond slavery in both the sacred and secular realms. As Smitherman proves, the oral tradition "preserves the Afro-American heritage and reflects the collective spirit of the race."[10]

Our point here is not to offer a detailed analysis of the influence and varied manifestations of African oral culture within the African American community. Such a monumental task is beyond the scope of this chapter and such research has already been performed by a generation of previous scholars. Rather, our purpose is to demonstrate that at the center of the African oral tradition is an essential component that has survived well into the twenty-first century, one that Smitherman identified when she described how "everyday people" transmit "lessons and precepts about life and survival" between generations.[11] This core principle manifested in most pre-colonial West African cultures in the form of a single person, a community genealogist, historian, and storyteller often referred to as a griot. Although such a figure had different names—and even sometimes slightly different roles—in various societies, the central function of the griot in most West African cultures remained consistent: to provide the genealogy of their community, for the purpose of educating current and future generations about the history of their people. More specifically, griots were considered to be "dynamic and interactive" historians who (unlike the Western conception of an historian) were responsible for linking the past, present, and future. As scholar Thomas Hale explains, "the griot as historian emerges as a 'time-binder,' a person who links past to present and serves as a witness to events in the present, which he or she may convey to persons in the future."[12]

It is these core components of the African oral tradition embodied in the griot—using the power of one's voice to bear witness to the present, and using the lessons of the past and present to educate future generations— that remain vitally important to the African American freedom struggle, and should therefore play a central role in the field of Africana Studies. Admittedly, there has been significant debate among scholars over the legitimacy of oral history and how oral testimony ought to be incorporated into scholarly writing.[13] We argue not only for the legitimacy of oral history, but for its *centrality* in Africana Studies. And we are not alone. Even Aimé Césaire, distinguished leader of the Negritude movement, declared that his role as a scholar and poet was "'to be . . . one of those 'griots' who link the people to its history."[14] We believe that the evidence speaks for itself. For, as the upsurge in recent scholarship on the Black freedom struggle reveals, no one can effectively articulate or grasp the passion, depth or humanity of the African American battle for liberation without hearing the voices of the people themselves.

ORAL HISTORY AS METHODOLOGY

Given this reality, it is not surprising that oral history has been paired with African American history from its inception. In fact, the two lead articles of the very first issue of the *Oral History Review* (journal of the Oral History

Association) were examinations of the importance of oral history to African American history.[15] In recent years, oral history has become an essential focal point of research on the modern Black freedom struggle. Oral history is a valuable resource for civil rights and social movement scholars for two key reasons. First, oral history—as opposed to written history—is often the domain of those who choose to give voice to people who would be mere footnotes in many types of traditional historical documents.[16] Because of its documentation of "the folk," oral history offers rich investigation for researching widespread social movements, which tend to be complex, multilayered, and seldom the intellectual property of one individual or group. Secondly, oral history is the domain of recent history, focused on events in people's memories.[17] This is especially salient when it comes to the Black freedom movement.

The civil rights struggle has proven to be highly salient in the public memory, and in the United States is inescapable. Even beyond the gripping drama of the movement itself, racial asymmetry was such an all-encompassing cultural milieu in the nation that, when interviewed, almost all Americans with southern roots—whatever their race, whatever the original topic—end up talking about civil rights and race relations. To discuss American history is, at least in part, to discuss civil rights. The pervasiveness of the topic makes for an incredibly rich pairing of medium and research subject.[18]

In recent years, the Civil Rights Movement has emerged as a major research focus for American historians and social scientists. In addition, this movement has increasingly become a topic of study for college courses or curriculum segments for high school students. As such, oral history has been a particularly important tool in documenting the Civil Rights Movement, and oral testimony is central to many of the major works produced about the Movement to date. A review article in the *Journal of American History* demonstrates the centrality of oral history to the growing body of literature by listing recent titles that rely significantly on oral history to tell the story of the Civil Rights Movement. A partial list of these works includes: John Egerton, *Speak Now against the Day: The Generation before the Civil Rights Movement in the South*; Charles M. Payne, *I've Got the Light of Freedom: The Organizing Tradition and the Mississippi Freedom Struggle*; Gerald Horne, *The Fire This Time: The Watts Uprising and the Civil Rights Movement*; John Dittmer, *Local People: The Struggle for Civil Rights in Mississippi*; James R. Ralph, Jr., *Northern Protest: Martin Luther King Jr., Chicago, and the Civil Rights Movement*; Kay Mills, *This Little*

Light of Mine: The Life of Fannie Lou Hamer; and Adam Fairclough, *Race and Democracy: The Civil Rights Struggle in Louisiana*.[19] More recent additions include: Stokely Carmichael (with Ekwueme Michael Thelwell), *Ready for Revolution: The Life and Struggles of Stokely Carmichael [Kwame Ture]*; and Diana Block, *Arm the Spirit: A Woman's Journey Underground and Back*. Perhaps Duke University professor William Chafe put it best when he noted in his groundbreaking history of Greensboro, North Carolina that the story of the Civil Rights Movement:

> could neither be told nor researched on the basis of written sources
> alone. Traditionally, historians have used newspapers, diaries,
> manuscript collections, and government documents as a basis
> for their investigations. But until recently, almost all of these
> sources have represented a white perspective. Whites have run
> the newspapers, held the public offices, deposited the manuscript
> collections, and preserved the diaries. Whether consciously or
> unconsciously the record has therefore transmitted a white point of
> view. Simply stated, the perspective cannot do justice to a past that
> has been multiracial throughout, with blacks as primary actors as
> well as objects of actions undertaken by others.

He concludes that "only through extensive use of oral history interviewing, grounded in the written sources, has it been possible to gain even a glimpse of the rich multiracial fabric," which made the Movement possible, and without this combination of sources, "there would be no possibility of discovering what happened" during the Movement.[20] Chafe's assessment of the role of oral history in documenting the history of the Black freedom struggle is critical to our understanding the historical legacy of the Black Panther Party, a popular though much maligned Black Power organization that captured the hearts and minds of millions of Black Americans in the late 1960s.

THE BLACK PANTHER PARTY AND THE SAN FRANCISCO 8

The Black Panther Party (BPP), founded in Oakland, California in 1966, by Huey Newton and Bobby Seale, emerged to fight widespread police brutality and murders of Black people. Expanding its goals to include calls for fair housing, Black self-determination, exemption from the military draft, fair trials by a jury of peers, justice, land, bread, and peace, the BPP organized local communities all over the United States and throughout the world to struggle for liberty and justice for all. The BPP's efforts to equalize the social, political, and economic interests of all people both inside and outside the US were increasingly viewed as a danger to the status quo. As a result it became the best known and most widely demonized of the Civil Rights/Black Power era organizations. Labeled in 1968 by FBI Director J. Edgar Hoover, "the greatest single threat to the internal security of the Unites States," the BPP's legacy nevertheless includes the creation of nationwide free breakfasts for school children programs, free health clinics, sickle cell anemia research and testing, and a plethora of other social services. It is this varied, tragic history that has in the past made studying the organization so difficult. Today, however, its members are beginning to speak out about this hitherto hidden history and are making it plain that participating in the struggle for freedom and justice is neither for the faint hearted nor for those who seek instant, immediate change.[21]

Though the BPP ceased to exist as a national organization by 1982, some of its former members, forty years-plus later, continue to experience harassment, arrest, and imprisonment by local, state, and federal authorities. Accused of crimes that date back to the late 1960s and early 1970s, these former Panthers and their associates, having endured the wrath of the FBI's Counter Intelligence Program (COINTELPRO), have been subjected to new methods of harassment brought about after the September 11, 2001 attack on the World Trade Center. Originally created in 1956 to thwart what the federal government viewed as a growing communist menace, this program eventually evolved into a tool that could be used to intimidate, imprison, harass, and assassinate activists seeking to alter the status quo. It did so via the use of wiretaps, infiltration, frame-ups, and outright violence directed toward those who insisted on supporting the move toward social, political, and economic change for Blacks.[22] Although Congress labeled COINTELPRO unconstitutional and demanded its closure in the early 1970s, the newly enacted Patriot Act has been instituted in its stead and engages in many of the activities once declared illegal.[23] The story of what followed this new round of legislation is jolting.

In 2005, California and federal authorities brought five men, four whom were former members of the Black Panther Party, before a California State Grand Jury. Though the men were not advised of any specific charges at the time, the authorities wanted to question them about their knowledge of a 1971 San Francisco police killing. Denied the right to legal counsel during the proceedings, John Bowman (now deceased), Ray Boudreaux, Richard Brown, Hank Jones, and Harold Taylor exercised their Fifth Amendment right not to testify against themselves. Offers of immunity notwithstanding, the men held fast to their decision and were subsequently jailed for refusing to cooperate with the Grand Jury. They were released on October 31, 2005, once the Grand Jury term expired. As scholar Dan Berger noted,

> The men stated their moral and ethical opposition to the proceedings, arguing that attempting to reinstate old charges based on tortured confessions was an attempt to use post-9/11 legal shifts to legitimize barbarous investigatory practices. The grand jury did not pass down any indictments, and the men were left alone until their arrest.[24]

At approximately 6:30 on the morning of February 23, 2007, federal agents and local police officials arrested Harold Taylor, Ray Boudreaux, Richard Brown, Richard O'Neal, Hank Jones, and Francisco Torres. Two other men, Herman Bell and Jalil Muntaqim, who had already spent thirty-seven years in New York state prisons and who remained imprisoned at the time, were also arrested. The authorities charged the men, almost all of whom either had past associations with or who had been members of the Black Panther Party, with the murder of San Francisco police officer John Young in 1971. Police officials said the men entered the Ingleside police station and shot Officer Young. The authorities also charged the group with conspiracy to commit murder against police officers between 1968 and 1973. The eight, rounded up in coordinated sweeps in Florida, California, and New York, spent nearly a year in jail and, before their lawyers successfully argued its unconstitutionality, had bail set as high as $5 million.[25] Accused of being members of the Black Liberation Army, a radical group of revolutionaries who fought pitched battles with law enforcement all over the country and who reportedly maintained close ties to the Black Panther Party, these sixty to seventy-something year olds engaged in the fight of their lives as their lawyers scrambled to organize an adequate defense.[26]

Even though a San Francisco judge dismissed identical charges against the men in 1975, the authorities saddled several of the arrestees with the same charges in 2003 and 2005. When federal and state Grand Juries expired without indicting them, they had to be released and allowed to go free—or so they thought. In 2007, federal and state agents renewed the charges based on what they called new evidence and arrested the activists again. These arrests created the environment that gave birth to the San Francisco 8, which quickly became known throughout the US and internationally as elders who had contributed mightily to the 1960s era freedom struggle.[27]

Below, Black Panther Harold Taylor, one of the members of the San Francisco 8, tells his story of sacrifice, torture, and incarceration. Reliving a train of events that started in 1969 and ended in 1973, Taylor's harrowing tale exposes an aspect of the Black freedom struggle only obtainable through the method of oral history. Arrested in New Orleans in 1973 along with his associates, Taylor's odyssey provides a glimpse into the life of one of the few survivors of government-sanctioned torture, imprisonment, and harassment. Without oral testimonies like this, our understanding of the past, and by extension of how and why things came to be today, would be greatly diminished.

ORAL HISTORY OF HAROLD TAYLOR

This [story] is a perfect example of what can happen to you if you dare to struggle, if you dare to fight or confront the enemy. These stories about the Black Panther Party are from stories that are very true. My near-death experiences, my being tortured in New Orleans and beaten by the New Orleans police department, being a victim of COINTELPRO, being the victim of numerous investigations, being the victim of numerous arrests, watching the Black Panther Party being destroyed from within by infiltrators, provocateurs, FBI agents, and some of the members themselves. I'm not going to name names and start talking bad about anybody because it's not my place to do that. But my place is to tell you the story of how I came to be a member of the Black Panther Party. I became a member of the Black Panther Party because I saw injustice as a young child. I saw injustice when I used to go to Louisiana when I was a kid back in the fifties. I saw [the] injustice [of] how Black people were treated, how my grandmother would tell me while walking down the street in Shreveport, Louisiana, not to look a White man in the eyes and how to step off the sidewalk so they can pass and how to say "yes, sir" and "no, sir." And how I watched my uncles, grown men, "yes sir-ing" young White dudes, young White boys, and how it was a humbling factor.

But back in '63 I think is when I first saw Malcolm X, when I was just a kid. I think maybe I was twelve, thirteen years old. And my uncle, Big Boy, took me to the Nation of Islam on Broadway. Temple number, number twenty-seven I think it was. And I heard what Malcolm said, and I noticed that my uncle grew a goatee after that, you know, because Malcolm had a goatee. We'd listen to those things, and then I never really thought how much it would affect me until after Malcolm was killed in '65. When the Watts Riots broke out, I kind of put them two together. It was because of people like Malcolm that brought that awareness to the Black community. We were tired of being attacked by the police department and the racism that existed in those days. First time I ever seen the power of unity in a neighborhood.

. . . so when I got in this struggle I didn't want accolades. All I wanted to do was the work. That's what mattered to me most. And one of the greatest things in my lifetime was joining the Black Panther Party and meeting [Los Angeles BPP leader] Bunchy Carter. He challenged me in a way that nobody else ever challenged me. I always liked the last phrase of his poem. And it was the greatest phrase I ever heard in my life and it stays with me today because I memorized it. He said, "For a slave of natural death who dies / cannot balance out the death of two dead flies. / I'd rather be without the shame. / A bullet lodged within my brain. / If I were not to reach our goal, / a bleeding cancer torment my soul." That spoke volumes to me. That gives me chills today. And that's how I come by being a member of the Black Panther Party. We were seeing the leadership and the strength of a Black man, a *short* Black man. He wasn't tall and big in stature, but he had presence and charisma, and he was a man. And I envied that. [Along the way,] I met Roland Freeman; we all became comrades and we started this fight, this long battle in the Black Panther Party. And I met a lot of great comrades all across this country. I talked to Bruce Richards the other day and we reflected upon things. I remember sitting in the county jail in Los Angeles after being shot up by the police, being shot six times, still having nightmares. As a matter of fact, I had one this morning, trapped in that car again. But you know, torture and terrorism is a life sentence. And the true terrorists have been the United States government and they terrorized and brutalized Black people for hundreds of years. So it's really funny that they labeled me as a modern-day terrorist, me and my comrades and associates. We're the terrorists now. So, you know, this country is known for its torture and terrorism and murder of oppressed people. They took the land from the American Indians and stole shiploads of Black people to come here and work this land. Those things are very simple to me. I don't have to read a long drawn-out book to look at it very simple and understand that oppression means you have something I want and, if you don't give it up, I will take it. And not only will I take it, but I will enslave you to work it for me.

I wanted to say a few things about what took place that day when we was set up by COINTELPRO. Me and Ray [Boudreaux] and J. B. [John Bowman] were in the car and we were trapped in that car when the police officer came up to the car and told everybody to put their hands up on the seat. We complied to that, we did all of that. We did everything they asked us to do. Then he stuck his gun in the car and he shot me in my leg. I felt he was going to shoot me in the head, so I turned my head and threw my leg up to try to get to my gun and he fired and shot me in the top of my thigh. And I come back with my gun to defend myself and I shot him, maybe once or twice, maybe three times. I don't know, not sure how many times I shot him. But the shooting started and there was shooting everywhere. There was something like eight police officers behind us. And the shooting continued for maybe two minutes where they fired over 200 something rounds into the car, shooting Ray, shooting J. B., shooting me. [They] shot me in the side of the head. And we were there trying to survive. It was an assassination attempt. And from there we went to the hospital. After they drug us out of the car, [they] tried to smother us and tried to beat us. They beat us. They didn't *try to*, they did all of these things. But they beat us, tried to drown me in gutter water. And the people come out of the houses and they was screaming and hollering at the police to stop it. That happened about 9:00 in the evening and we never reached our hospital. Matter of fact, we went to a major hospital there in Los Angeles, where the doctors wouldn't treat us because the police wouldn't take the handcuffs off. So we had to go to general hospital, which is in east LA, another fifteen to twenty miles away, and I think we ended up in the hospital about 11:00 that night. FBI agents and police officers were trying to question me during the time that we were laying in the hospital, and they tried to question Ray, they tried to question J. B. Ray's arms were broken from gunshot wounds. They dragged him out of the car and shot him after he was out of the car. J. B. was shot in the back. And we stayed in the hospital, I think J. B. stayed about four days and they took him over to the county jail and then I stayed there for maybe a week or two where I stayed chained to a bed. And Ray stayed there maybe a month. And we were transported to LA county jail where we were put in a high security unit and kept in solitary confinement for months until we got court orders to be together so that we can prepare for our defense in our case. We stayed at the old county jail up until '72, I think it was. And we got bailed out of jail, and we went different directions, and we met up in New Orleans, myself, J. B., Ray, we're talking about organizing and rebuilding the structure of an organization that's going to continue to do the people's work. While I was there, that's when it [the torture] happened. Ruben Scott was arrested for some miscellaneous crime. And when they found out who Ruben was, we were all arrested in New Orleans. And that's when the torture began. On day one, it was beating and torture. The moment me and John Bowman was arrested, we were in the car together, there was a car pulled behind us, a red LTD, Ford, one of the favorite cars that the FBI were using at that time. And they pulled us over. And I knew right away that it was a bust, it wasn't just a pull-over because they had shotguns and rifles. Myself, John Bowman, Cathy Berkowitz, and her daughter were in the car.

We were taken to the New Orleans City Police Department. We were stripped of all clothes, down to our underwear. I was thrown in a holding cell. Inside that holding cell, there was Ruben Scott. He was really afraid. He was scared and I can tell he'd been beaten on. I was in there for maybe five minutes and the door opened. Three police officers from New Orleans came and dragged me up by my heels, took me to a chair where they hand-cuffed me to the chair, handcuffed my ankles, my feet to the bottom part of the chair. Without asking me any questions, they commenced to beat me. They beat me, they punched me, they kicked me, they spit on me. They called me a lot of vile names. And then they told me that they was gonna kill me if I didn't cooperate with them. They came out with a plastic bag and put it over my head. Then they started beating me with the bag over my head. By the time I was about to lose consciousness, about to pass out, they snatched the bag off. And while I'm trying to catch my breath, they started beating me again. So I asked them, "What do you want?" And they just continued on with it. They didn't ask me any more questions. They didn't ask any questions really. Then he came out with this cattle prod. I knew what it was because being off of a farm when I was a kid my family used to go to Louisiana every year to work the family farm and my uncles and I had some cows and we used cattle prods to move those cows up the chutes and stuff like that. So I seen that and I knew what it was. [They shocked me with the electric cattle prod] down on my private parts, under my neck, behind my ears, down my back, around my anus. I think I passed out one time and they woke me back up. They were taking me to another room. Two detectives had me by each arm and a detective came out of nowhere and knocked me straight out. I was unconscious. They took me to a holding cell. They put water on me. I was soaking wet. It was cold. [Then they] pulled me out of there at maybe about six or seven in the morning and told me they had somebody they wanted me to talk to and I better cooperate and if I didn't, I was going to get more of the same. So they put me in there with two detectives from San Francisco. I later found out that it was [Frank] McCoy and [Ed] Erdelatz. They started asking me questions. They told me they had a script. I'm sure I saw a recorder too and they was reading to me about what took place in San Francisco and I told them I had no knowledge of it.

All during the time this is taking place, I can hear John Bowman in another room where he was hollering. You can hear the licks being passed. They took what you call a slap-jack, it's like a little short black-jack and they started working the back of my neck, my shoulders, then one would get down and he'd work my shins and between my knees. They would beat me like that. They did that, I don't know [*pause*] it seemed like it was an hour. It could have been thirty minutes, it could have been an hour, it could have been two hours. I don't know. [Then they came] back again with the plastic bag. This time they had a blanket. I don't know what they soaked it in but it was really, really hot and they just covered me with that blanket and put that plastic bag over my head and I couldn't scream, I couldn't holler, I couldn't get my hands up to poke a hole in the bag because my hands were handcuffed to the chair and my legs were tied to the chair and they kicked the chair over and let me just suffocate. I was just about to pass out; they snatched it off, spit in my face, and left me sitting there for a little while. [After this,] McCoy and Erdelatz started asking me questions. I had no idea of the things they were asking me so I couldn't answer them. So they turned off the recorder and they said, "We'll tell you what happened and after we tell you, that's what we want you to say." [When I failed to cooperate,] one guy got behind me and he took his hands and he slapped them over my ears. I couldn't hear nothing. My ears were just ringing so bad. I could feel fluid running down the side of my face and they were talking to me, but I couldn't hear them. All I could hear was just the ringing. Whenever they stood me up to make me walk, I couldn't walk. They kind of just carried me back to the room and when they got me back in there they'd start again.

[From there,] they beat, and they beat, and they beat, and then Erdelatz and McCoy would come back in and they would kind of grin and laugh.

They were all laughing. They thought it was funny. They thought it was a big joke. They started asking me questions so I started talking to them. I followed their whole script. Everything they told me to say I said it. Just like whatever Ruben told them, I repeated it, what Ruben said. So they said, "Well, we got what we want."

[After that, a] federal magistrate in New Orleans ordered me out of the custody of the New Orleans Police Department. That's the only way I got away from them. They put me in the custody of the sheriff's department and they had pictures of me and had doctors that said I had bruised eardrums. And they ordered us over there, in Parish Prison under the sheriff's department where they kept us in a cage. After all that happened, years passed by. Because of harassment by the FBI and other police agencies in Los Angeles, I could no longer live there. I had to relocate. So in 1980, I moved to Florida, found a job, got married, had three kids, everything was going smooth.

Just out of the blue I get a visit from [pause] the FBI. The District Attorney from here [Bay County, Florida] and McCoy, of all people, he comes with him. I walked into the room and I looked at him and I said, "What is this about?" They said, "We want to have a conversation with you, we want to talk to you about something in San Francisco." And McCoy said, "You know what I mean." And I said, "Well, you know I think I need a lawyer, I don't have anything to say to you guys." He said, "Harold, we want to talk to you." I said, "No, because you know what you did in New Orleans and you recognize the fact that what took place in New Orleans [pause], that what you guys did to me and John Bowman, how you beat us and tortured us.' And I wouldn't talk to him, [so they had no choice but to leave]. [On another night in 2006,] just out of the blue, the sheriff's department knocked at my door, I think it was about six police altogether. It's three deputy sheriffs; you got two FBI agents and two people from the state of California. They came to ask, tell me that they were serving me a subpoena for me to appear in front of the Grand Jury. I said, "You know what, I need to contact a lawyer before I acknowledge any of this stuff because I don't understand what's going on." So they said, "Well you got to appear in court at eight-thirty in the morning."

I refused to testify, I stood on my constitutional rights. Fourteenth, Fifteenth, and Fifth Amendment and they told me that the judge ordered me to testify, asked me did I understand, I told him yes, I understand. They took me back to the Grand Jury. I still decided [to exercise] my right, so he held me in contempt [and put me] in jail. They put me in a cell by myself, wouldn't let me have no pencil, pen, wouldn't let me make a phone call, wouldn't let me contact my lawyer. I thought in my mind, this is like New Orleans; next, it's gonna start all over again, but it didn't take place and I stayed there for a month and a half.

I still try to serve the community, do different functions in my community. And what happened with this experience is that it just reminded me that it never goes away, that they maintain the same status quo, that power, people in power are gonna exploit what they want and they'll continue to brutalize, kill, anywhere on the planet; they choose to do that and they feel justified because they have that power. And I'm willing to go anywhere to tell people about this experience and let them know that this still happens every day. Not only here, but the same thing has happened in Guantánamo Bay, the same thing has happened in Iraq, Iran, all over the world. The same thing has happened in Africa. Everywhere that he's been, [he's been] able to spread misery and to exploit and take advantage of the world resources; [Anybody or any country] that has something that the power structure wants, he does what he has to do to get it.[28]

*

In 1971, William Sullivan, J. Edgar Hoover's second in charge, confirmed Taylor's assertion when he told a congressional investigating committee:

> During the ten years that I was on the U.S. Intelligence Board, a
> Board that receives the cream of intelligence for this country from
> all over the world and inside the United States, never once did I
> hear of anybody, including myself, raise the question: "is this course
> of action which we have agreed upon lawful, is it legal, is it ethical
> or moral?" We never gave any thought to this realm of reasoning,
> because we were just naturally pragmatists. The one thing we were
> concerned about was this: will this course of action work, will it get us
> what we want, will we reach the objective that we desire to reach?[29]

Taylor's treatment at the hands of the FBI and other law enforcement officials has gone unprosecuted and unacknowledged. Despite the beatings, false imprisonment, harassment, and physical aggression against activists like Taylor, and despite the payment of millions in damages to a few former activists, no one in authority has been prosecuted or otherwise taken to task for their illegal activities. These tactics do not seem to have been permanently shelved. Even though the Church and McClellan committees eventually outlawed the actions and activities of the FBI's COINTELPRO operations, the past several years have seen a resurgence in identical activity. Now called the Patriot Act and Patriot Act II, which includes the government's right to engage in no knock warrants, warrantless wiretaps, and other surveillance not explicitly authorized by a court, these activities are eerily familiar to those who suffered under COINTELPRO.[30]

THE AFTERMATH

In January 2007, some thirty-seven years after his arrest and torture in New Orleans, local, state, and federal authorities arrested Taylor again on charges of murder and conspiracy to murder. For two years, he and his seven co-defendants endured imprisonment, the loss of their jobs, family breakups, and the loss of their homes. Demonized in the press and ridiculed by the courts, they finally overcame these obstacles. In July 2009, District Attorney David Druliner dropped all charges against six of the San Francisco 8. The prosecution then struck a deal with Jalil Muntaqim and Herman Bell, allowing them to plead no contest to conspiracy to attempt manslaughter and guilty to manslaughter respectively. Already imprisoned, the court gave them both sentences of time served and short stints of probation.[31] It is important to note that the prosecution's claims of new evidence in this case proved untrue. No new evidence ever emerged during any of the several discovery hearings and, to date, the prosecution has failed to introduce any of the witnesses it insisted it had when the men were arrested in 2007. In hindsight, it is difficult to understand why authorities leveled such baseless charges at the eight and why, in these times of economic crisis, they were willing to spend millions of dollars defending such charges. Perhaps those who claim that the case was meant to help rewrite civil rights history and stifle present-day dissent are correct. Scholar Dan Berger addressed this issue when he wrote, "These prosecutions, like all invocations of collective memory, speak more to the political landscape in which they emerge than to the historic one about which they comment. The trials are symbolic rituals organized by and through the state to intervene in the contemporary politics of black citizenship and political mobilization."[32] Whatever the reasons are, the economic hardship, the loss of family, and the constant mental strain on the part of those subjected to the whims of law enforcement have succeeded in spreading the terror beyond those who experienced the physical torture.

Reminiscing about the effects the torture had on him, Taylor remarked:

I read something today that Nelson Mandela said about invisible wounds. Torture is an invisible wound. You live with that the rest of your life. Even though these charges have been dismissed against me, Ray, Hank, Richard Brown and Richard O'Neal, I still suffer from what happened in New Orleans. That's an invisible wound and it never goes away. It'll always be there. It'll be there the rest of my life. We all were young men at that time and we just saw something that was wrong and we wanted to change it. So being in the Black Panther Party was the greatest experience of my life. And I would take not one minute back from there. But going back to being arrested in my living room and taken to a cage in 2007. I think it was 23rd January 2007, taken to a cage and shipped back to San Francisco; it was like being a slave being shipped from Africa into this country. Nor did the methods really change. Everything was basically the same. And to sit in chains in isolation was a reflection for me of when I was arrested in New Orleans and me and J. B. was tortured and beaten and ironically we were taken to the same place where slaves were sold from slave ships at Orleans Parish Prison. And we were put in chains, as young Black men. We still had that desire and will to fight. I find all these things that took place to be something that really molded me as a person and a man and gave me fortitude. We were men, and we were trying to do what we thought was right. And we wanted to let Black folks know that there was a group of us out there that was willing to defend ourselves, and defend our community, and defend our people. That we were willing to put our lives on the line to fight on behalf of Black people. I was just a humble Black man, but I understand one thing, that, many were called but few were chosen. And I feel real proud about being one of the chosen few. And I want to do whatever I have to do to enhance the situation of Black people. And I continue to fight on those basic principles. I fight because I am who I am and I am a man. I am a Black man. And I am a humanitarian. And I am a people's soldier.[33]

To date, no amount of counseling or therapy has succeeded in preventing the sleepless nights, nightmares, and constant pain that Taylor experiences as a result of his torture. Despite this, Taylor continues to lecture nationally about his experiences in the Black Panther Party and to work with students, his former Panther associates, and a myriad of school and community organizations in his attempt to make the world a better place.

One would be hard pressed to find these kinds of experiences in sources outside of oral testimonies. Because these incidents take place beyond the watchful eyes of newspaper reporters, magazine editors, and television hosts, few people are aware of the depth to which the establishment went to maintain the status quo. The aggressors generally do not share this kind of information, and most scholars and researchers do not have the time and resources required to build the rapport necessary to uncover what essentially amounts to a complicated maze of repressed thoughts and memories. It is for this reason that oral history is so vital to uncovering and telling the story of African descended people in the United States.

In effect, oral history as a methodology is essential to the field of Black Studies because it provides an authentic window on the past. From the voices of those enslaved Africans who lived to tell about the horrors of their bondage and those African American leaders who attended the first White universities to the Black American icons who made the music and culture of the jazz age and the Depression come alive, one can see that the oral tradition has maintained its vitality and importance. Despite arguments to the contrary, this methodology has increased in importance as time has passed. This can be clearly seen when looking at the life and times of those Blacks who lived and struggled through the tumultuous post-World War II period. This watershed moment in US and world history reshaped American politics and society in ways that are still being felt. Despite the fact that thousands of African Americans fought and struggled for justice and equality and contributed to changing the status quo, many of their more lasting contributions have gone unnoticed. Indeed, the modern era has demonstrated an even greater need for oral testimony since the mainstream media, in the guise of newspapers, magazines, television, and films, has either distorted, misinterpreted or, in too many cases, omitted the important work carried out by those individuals most responsible for pushing the United States further along the road toward real racial and social equality.

CONCLUSION

While numerous books have been written to delineate the unfolding of the Civil Rights Movement, few scholars, using newspapers, government documents, police reports, FBI files, and the many other traditional "sources" that help illuminate our past, can capture its essence as Taylor's words above do. Even fewer are able to translate the fears, insecurities, and motivations of those who joined and stayed in the movement for any significant amount of time. For example, the following quote from Bea Jenkins, a little known Mississippi native who simply grew tired of her and her people's mistreatment in the Magnolia State's closed society, made it clear that joining the movement was a deliberate act of conscience when she told one interviewer about the impact of the 1955 murder of fifteen-year-old Emmett Till. She recalled that she:

> heard that he passed by this store, him and some more boys. They passed by a White store. And they accused him, the owner of the store accused [him] of whistling at his wife. And that night, they went in, to take him from his grandparents. And they was screaming and hollering and asking, begging them not to take him. And they just took him by force, and carried him out and [brutally] murdered him. Just every part they could cut off of him, they did that. And I was just so filled up with that and other things that they had been so brutal to our Black people. And when that evening came, I went back to the field. I was picking cotton, and I just fell down on my sack, and I asked the Lord, "Why? Why it have to happen to us all the time? We have to take this brutality. We haven't did anything. Why?"[34]

Soon after her reflection in this Mississippi cotton field, Jenkins joined SNCC and later became active in the Mississippi Freedom Democratic Party, which succeeded in 1968 in forcing the regular Democratic Party to allow Black participation in state and national political conventions. This participation led eventually to the election of Barack Obama, the nation's first African American president.[35]

It is clear that students can learn a great deal about life in mid-twentieth-century United States by employing the techniques of the oral historian. Not only does engaging in this process help to create new knowledge, it also aids in community building by creating relationships between the young and the old and by allowing the elders to pass down stories about organizing strategies, problem-solving, critical thinking, and movement culture. By creating a link between the Black Studies classroom and the oral histories of people from the community, we find that not only can learning be fun, but also a process that ensures the creation of a better tomorrow. At the very least it guarantees that one more generation of scholars and laypeople will be exposed to the histories of those people and movements that are often bypassed in many mainstream publications. By looking at what transpired through the eyes of those who lived through these times, one can acquire a comprehensive view of what it means to live and struggle under a government for the people, of the people, and by the people. The outcome will not only be a more informed citizenry, but a population that understands its role in the making of a system that is responsive to the needs of all Americans. Only by engaging this methodology will we be sure that people like the Black Panther Party's John Bowman, who was tortured in New Orleans along with Harold Taylor, acted selflessly on behalf of more than himself. In what turned out to be the last recorded words of his life, Bowman explained:

> The organizing that took place, as a member of the Black Panther Party for Self-Defense, what I did, it was motivated by love of my people. I was motivated by a desire to serve a greater cause other than myself. I, myself, was harshly punished. I, myself, present time, 2005, am being harshly punished for being a member of the Black Panther Party for Self-Defense, but I accept the challenge. I accept the challenge, so that my children's, children's children will have some dignity. My nieces and nephews will have dignity and have purpose and understand the history of struggling in this country for basic human rights, and that's all we were trying to do. Basic human rights.[36]

As Taylor and Bowman's testimonies reveal, the power of the oral tradition has remained strong within African-descended communities in the Diaspora. Indeed, after experiencing their words, there can be little doubt about oral history's function in African American culture as a crucial link in the chain that binds Africans in the Diaspora to both their forebears and their contemporaries in the Motherland. Most obviously, these activists powerfully assumed the role of griot referenced at the outset—they used their own stories, and the tales of those they struggled with to bear witness to their experiences and to use the lessons of the past and present to educate future generations. As such, they have proven that the oral tradition in African and African American history is not only a vital component in disseminating knowledge and culture, but this cultural tool can also be used to harness the healing and rehabilitative power of history. Fortunately, this realization has slowly been making inroads into academia. Increasingly

seeing the methodology of oral history as an extension of the ancient traditions of Africa, many scholars are coming to see that authenticity can best
be found in the perspectives of those whose lived experiences corroborate,
complement, and contextualize the more traditional written record. As
Africana Studies celebrates its fortieth anniversary in the academy, we urge
our colleagues to embrace oral history as a vital and crucial methodology in
the noble endeavor of investigating, articulating, and analyzing the history
and culture of the African Diaspora.

NOTES

1. Amadou Hampâté Bâ, "The Living Tradition," in *General History of Africa:
    Methodology and African Prehistory*, ed. J. Ki-Zerbo, abridged edn. (Paris and
    London: UNESCO, 1990), 62; Jan Vansina, *Oral Tradition: A Study in Historical
    Methodology* (Chicago: Aldine, 1965), xi.
2. Thomas A. Hale, *Griots and Griottes: Masters of Words and Music* (Bloomington and
    Indianapolis, IN: Indiana University Press, 1998), 1.
3. Harold Courlander, *A Treasury of African Folklore: The Oral Literature, Traditions,
    Myths, Legends, Epics, Tale, Recollections, Wisdom, Sayings, and Humor of Africa* (New
    York: Crown Publishers, 1975), 3.
4. Bâ, "The Living Tradition," 166.
5. Jan Vansina, "Oral Tradition and its Methodology," in *General History of Africa*, 61.
6. Courlander, *A Treasury of African Folklore*, 1–2.
7. Vansina, "Oral Tradition and its Methodology," 142.
8. Vansina, "Oral Tradition and its Methodology," 142; Courlander, *A Treasury of
    Afro-American Folklore*; Harold Scheub, *African Oral Narratives, Proverbs, Riddles,
    Poetry and Song* (Boston, MA: G. K. Hall, 1977); Joseph C. Miller, ed., *The African
    Past Speaks: Essays on Oral Tradition and History* (Hamden, CT: Archon Books,
    1980); Robert D. Pelton, *The Trickster in West Africa: A Study of Mythic Irony and
    Sacred Delight* (Berkeley and Los Angeles, CA: University of California Press, 1980);
    Roger Abrahams, *African American Folktales: Stories from Black Traditions in the New
    World* (New York: Pantheon, 1999); Daryl Cumber Dance, ed., *From My People: 400
    Years of African American Folklore: An Anthology* (New York: W. W. Norton, 2003);
    Darryl T. Mallard, *African American and African Folklore* (New York: Author House,
    2009).
9. Courlander, *A Treasury of Afro-American Folklore*, 2–7.
10. Geneva Smitherman, *Talkin' and Testifyin': The Language of Black America* (Detroit,
    MI: Wayne State University Press, 1977), 73.
11. Smitherman, *Talkin' and Testifyin'*, 73.
12. Hale, *Griot and Griottes*, 23.
13. One example of an insightful volume that illuminates the scholarly debate over the
    use of oral sources in African history is Bogumil Jewsiewicki and David Newbury,

eds., *African Historiographies: What History for Which Africa?* (Beverly Hills, CA and London: Sage, 1986).

14. Hale, *Griots and Griottes*, 322.

15. See Alex Haley, "Black History, Oral History and Genealogy," *Oral History Review*, vol. 1, (1973), 1–25; and Courtney Brown, "Oral History and the Oral Tradition of Black America: The Kinte Foundation," *Oral History Review*, vol. 1 (1973), 26–8.

16. Two excellent examples of the importance of oral history as a methodology are David K. Dunaway and Willa K. Baum, eds., *Oral History: An Interdisciplinary Anthology*, 2nd edn. (New York: Alta Mira Press, 1996); and Paul Thompson, *The Voice of the Past: Oral History*, 3rd edn. (New York: Oxford University Press, 2000).

17. See Robert Perks and Alistair Thompson, eds., *The Oral History Reader* (New York: Routledge, 1998); and Valerie Raleigh Yow, *Recording Oral History: A Guide for the Humanities and Social Sciences* (New York: Alta Mira Press, 2005).

18. To see how oral history can be useful in bringing alive the Civil Rights Movement through video, see Constance Curry, producer, *The Intolerable Burden*, DVD (New York: First Run/Icarus Films, 2003); and Roz Payne, *What We Want: What We Believe: The Black Panther Party Library*, DVD (Oakland, CA: AK Press, 2006).

19. Kathy L. Nasstrom, "Beginnings and Endings: Life Stories and the Periodization of the Civil Rights Movement," *Journal of American History*, vol. 86, no. 2 (September 1999), 700–11.

20. William Chafe, *Civilities and Civil Rights: Greensboro, North Carolina and the Black Struggle for Freedom* (New York: Oxford University Press, 1981), 10.

21. Hoover quote in Holland Kotter, "Art/Architecture; The Black Panthers' Beauty Moment," *New York Times*, May 25, 2003. For a history of the Black Panther Party, see Curtis Austin, *Up Against the Wall: Violence in the Making and Unmaking of the Black Panther Party* (Fayetteville, AR: University of Arkansas Press, 2006).

22. See US Senate, *Final Report of the Select Committee to Study Governmental Operations with Respect to intelligence Activities*, Books I–III (Washington, DC: US Government Printing Office, 1976), 187. See also Austin, *Up Against the Wall*, chapter 6.

23. For information regarding the Uniting and Strengthening America by Providing Appropriate Tools Required to Intercept and Obstruct Terrorism (USA PATRIOT ACT) Act of 2001, see epic.org/privacy/terrorism/hr3162.html. Accessed February 28, 2010.

24. Dan Berger, "Rescuing Civil Rights from Black Power: Collective Memory and Saving the State in Twenty-First-Century Prosecutions of 1960s-era Cases," *Journal for the Study of Radicalism*, vol. 3, no. 1 (Spring 2009), 5–6. See also freethesf8. org. Accessed March 23, 2010. These men were also arrested in 2006 on a DNA warrant where they had bodily fluids and fingerprints taken to be used to prove the prosecution's allegations. In the final analysis, the DNA evidence proved beyond doubt that none of the men were involved in the crime of which they had been accused.

25. John Koopman, "Hearing in '71 Cop Killing is Delayed a Month," *San Francisco Chronicle*, June 9, 2009; see also Herb Boyd, "Drop Charges against San Francisco 8," *New York Amsterdam News*, November 29, 2007; and "San Francisco 8

Supporters Attend Court Dates, Hold Screenings of 'Legacy of Torture.'" www. indybay.org/newsitems/2007/02/19/18365745.php. Accessed February 28, 2010.

26. See Wanda Sabir, "San Francisco 8 Case Takes Critical Turn," *San Francisco Bay View*, www.sfbayview.com/2009/san-francisco-8-case-takes-a-critical-turn. Accessed February 28, 2010.

27. See Bob Boyle, "The San Francisco 8 and the Legacy of COINTELPRO," *Guild Notes*, vol. 33, no. 4 (Winter 2007), 6–7. *Academic Search Premier*, EBSCO*host*. Accessed February 28, 2010.

28. The earlier part of this dialogue before the discussion of the arrest in New Orleans is taken from Harold Taylor, interviewed by Curtis Austin, August 1, 2009, Panama City, FL. Cassette recording in possession of author. The remaining can be found in Taylor's oral testimony in *Legacy of Torture: The War Against the Black Liberation Movement*, directed and produced by Andres Alegria, Claude Marks, DVD (San Francisco: Freedom Archives, 2006).

29. US Congress, House Committee on Internal Security, Hearings on the Black Panther Party, *Gun Barrel Politics: The Black Panther Party, 1966–1971*, 92nd Cong., 1st sess. (Washington, DC: US Government Printing Office, 1971), 117.

30. See epic.org/privacy/terrorism/hr3162.html. Accessed February 28, 2010.

31. "Free the San Francisco 8!" freethesf8.org. Accessed February 28, 2010. See also freedomarchives.org. Accessed February 28, 2010.

32. Berger, "Rescuing Civil Rights from Black Power," 11.

33. Taylor interview. The New Orleans Parish Prison, which remains in use today, served as the location where imported Africans were auctioned for sale to slave traders and plantation owners.

34. Bea Jenkins, quoted in Curtis Austin, *Ordinary People Living Extraordinary Lives: The Civil Rights Movement in Mississippi* (Hattiesburg, MS: University of Southern Mississippi Center for Oral History, 2000).

35. Jenkins, quoted in Austin, *Ordinary People Living Extraordinary Lives*.

36. John Bowman, oral testimony in *Legacy of Torture*.

CHAPTER 10

African American Philosophy: Through the Lens of Struggle

George Yancy

Duquesne University

INTRODUCTION

In this chapter, I provide a general characterization of African American philosophy which presupposes the continuous encounter by persons of African descent with the absurd in the form of white racism. While by no means exhaustive, I provide a broadly contextual approach to African American philosophy, emphasizing meta-philosophical themes and assumptions that I take to be salient. I then provide a sketch of a few early African American philosophers who earned their PhDs in the field of philosophy, focusing especially on two of those pioneer figures who have been historically neglected. Thematizing the neglect of early credentialed African American philosophers by those engaged in the project of explicating the meaning, structure, and various historical trajectories of African American philosophy functions as a form of critique. I then conclude, briefly, with African American philosophers' efforts to create sites that nurture a sense of critical community and self-determination. Such efforts are dialectically linked to ideological and material anti-Black racist contexts out of which African American philosophy struggled and continues to struggle. Lastly, I make no claims to provide *the* last word on the subject of African American philosophy—as if there were such a thing. My approach to African American philosophy, and the assumptions that inform that approach, as with every hermeneutic framework, both discloses and yet conceals. One always begins an inquiry *in medias res*. There is no hermeneutic perspective from nowhere. Every perspective (etymologically, "to look") is a partial, *unfinished* look, a beckoning for one to look again.

THE INTERPRETIVE MATRIX OF STRUGGLE

By foregrounding the social and historical *struggle* of Black people, African American philosophy reconfigures certain perennial assumptions about the nature of philosophy and the philosopher as conceived within the context of mainstream Western philosophy. Theorizing African American philosophy within the social matrix of anti-Black racism situates philosophical reflective thought within the concrete muck and mire of *raced* embodied existence, thus deconstructing the myth of philosophy and the philosopher as Olympian. Within the context of discussing the preponderance of African American philosophers who deal with issues in the area of value theory and political and social philosophy, Robert Birt argues that "the leisure and liberty to dwell on metaphysical concerns with Olympian composure . . . isn't so easy for an outcast and denigrated people."[1] Bodies that suffer, bodies in pain, lynched bodies, and mutilated bodies constitute the existentially *lived* reality of Black people in America. I argue that it is within the context of such pervasive suffering that African American philosophy articulates its normative concerns. In stream with Cornel West, any really serious philosophy that grapples with life must make sense of what he calls the "guttural cry."[2] For my purposes, African American philosophy is a critical process of rendering that cry, that scream, and that struggle visible and intelligible. Charles Mills is also cognizant of the "rage . . . of those invisible native sons and daughters who, since nobody knows their name, have to be the men who *cry* 'I am!' and women who demand 'And ain't I a woman?'"[3] Within this context, Mills explicitly emphasizes the importance of this rage in terms of its meaning for persons of African descent who have been deemed sub-persons. In stream with Mills, I theorize the meaning of African American philosophy within the context of Black sub-personhood. After all, Black people have had to struggle to redefine themselves against longstanding historical racist acts of dehumanization.

My discussion of African American philosophy is defined in relation to its explicitly non-Cartesian or anti-Cartesian assumptions. This is not a novel approach, but it transcends the familiar *and* familial "Oedipal conflict" subtext that is often associated with so many thinkers who eagerly unseat the patriarch of modern philosophy. To think of the history of Western philosophy as constituting a family with cross-generational (monochromatic) ties, it is important to note that Black people were never even part of the family; they were always already outsiders, deemed permanently unfit to participate in the normative philosophical community.[4] A non-Cartesian approach to African American philosophy is conceptually fruitful given the oppression of persons of African descent during European modernity. Blacks are those who occupy the underside of modernity. Because various Cartesian epistemological assumptions and moves are crucial to modernity, the Cartesian predicament becomes, as Mills demonstrates, "a kind of pivotal scene for a whole way of doing philosophy and one that involves a whole program of assumptions about the world and (taken-for-granted) normative claims about what is philosophically important."[5] Given the materially and ideologically reinforced sub-personhood status of Black people in America, African American philosophy is referentially *this*-worldly; it is a site of conceptualizing the world that looks suspiciously upon and rejects the *a-historical* nature of the epistemic subject. African American philosophy's point of critical embarkation is not preoccupied with "the danger of degeneration into solipsism, the idea of being enclosed in our own possibly unreliable perceptions, the question of whether we can be certain other minds exist, the scenario of brains in a vat, and so forth."[6] To get a sense of the non-Cartesian, *this*-worldly constitution of African American philosophy, consider a few philosophical assumptions by René Descartes.

In his *Meditations on First Philosophy*, Descartes assumes the posture of a skeptic. After describing what he depicts metaphorically as having fallen into a whirlpool, a vortex that has tossed him around and thrown him off his epistemological footing, he reaches his Archimedean point, the indubitable insight that "'I am, I exist' is necessarily true every time I utter it or conceive it in my mind."[7] Knowing incontrovertibly *that* he exists, Descartes will shut his eyes, stop up his ears, and withdraw all of his senses in order to uncover the nature of the self. As he says, "I will attempt to render myself gradually better known and more familiar to myself."[8] This approach has embedded within it the assumption that the self can be better known through withdrawing from (or radically doubting) the social world, thus challenging the notion that the self is fundamentally socially transversal, constituted dialectically, and thereby inextricably linked to the reality of the social world, its dynamism, and its force of interpellation.

The Cartesian approach also presumes that the predicament of the Cartesian self is a universal (decontextualized) predicament,[9] one unaffected by the exigencies and contingencies of concrete history. In short, Cartesian epistemic subjects (denuded, as it were, of historical and corporeal *particularity*) are substitutable pure and simple, and faced with the same epistemic global problems. This substitutability assumption places under erasure important markers of African American philosophy, how African American philosophy, with its questions, problems, and dilemmas, evolves out of a context where *raced* embodied subjects undergo shared existential crises of struggle within the context of anti-Black racism. This does not mean that African American philosophy does not share philosophical concerns with other philosophical traditions and paradigms. However, to understand African American philosophy one must reject the substitutability assumption in favor of a perspective that focuses on and highlights the relationship between social ontology and particular aspects of Black *Erlebnis*, that is, the range of ways in which Black people make meaning within the context of various occurrences or experiences where, in this case, anti-Black racism is salient. In this way, African American philosophy, with its specific philosophical concerns and articulations, does not aspire to forms of universalism that obfuscate modes of particularity. Moreover, African American philosophy does not presume to speak for all epistemic subjects *simpliciter*. Its point of philosophical embarkation does not rest upon the assumption of a fixed set of abstract and universal problems or solutions. Leonard Harris alludes to this when he argues that "as a genre, it [African-American philosophy] is dominated by issues of practicality and struggle, which means that it is not committed to a metaphysics in the sense of having a singular proposition out of which all other propositions arise."[10] And describing his important first anthology, published in 1983, a text which was and still is historically pivotal in terms of gathering together important Black philosophical themes and figures, Harris writes, "*Philosophy Born of Struggle* is predicated on the assumption that a good deal of philosophy from the African-American heritage is a function of the history of the struggle to overcome adversity and to create."[11] It is important to note that the publication of Harris's text grew out of struggle. Within a context where "important" philosophical texts are determined by white consumption and white norms of canon formation, Harris notes, "There wasn't anybody who was willing to publish it. Not a single publisher in philosophy."[12] Even Howard University Press, the publisher of an important HBCU, would not publish Harris's text because of its narrowly defined "Negro genre."[13]

While the complexity of African American philosophy should not be reduced to struggle, its historical genesis as a professional field of inquiry, its salient themes, and its forms of praxes, presuppose a world of White Supremacy, a world that is fundamentally anti-Black. Unlike Descartes, Black self-understanding grows out of a social matrix of pain and suffering;

a site where the Black body is a site of marked inferiority, difference, and deviance. To withdraw from the senses as Descartes does, which is a form of negating embodiment as a necessary condition for self-understanding, is to presume an abstract subject from nowhere. As such, this move renders the self incapable of knowing itself, as self-understanding is always already from a *here*, a place of lived embodied knowledge, a *here* that presupposes a community of intelligibility. Hence, to understand Black *lived* experience, and to understand African American philosophy, it is important to begin with embodiment, history, and *lived* social context, a context within which Black people were and are reduced to an epidermal logic that signifies pure externality, thus denying any subjective interiority to the Black body. The Black self, then, is not enclosed within a solipsistic bubble, free of inter-pellation and oppression. The Black self has struggled to understand and define itself within a context where whiteness functions as a transcendental norm, where white embodied others' ego-genesis is parasitic upon the ontological distortion and nullification of Black bodies. Hence, whiteness as synonymous with humanity is purchased not only through opposition, but through *negation*. The Black is raced and so rendered non-normative (i.e., not white). On this score, whiteness is deemed normative and un-raced. As James Cone notes, "Whites can move beyond particular human beings to the universal human being because they have not experienced the reality of *color*."[14]

To understand Black being-in-the-world, and the historical context of African American philosophy, the self/Other dialectic is crucial. Not only is it a fundamental assumption of African American philosophy, but the self/Other dialectic captures the concrete reality of racism. While racism is not a necessary feature of the self/Other dialectic, the former presupposes the latter. Hence,

1. the self is dynamically plastic;
2. the self does not exist anterior to the existence of Others, or, the self is not pre-given or the result of auto-genesis; and
3. the self is always already ensconced within a larger historical context of prejudices and value-laden assumptions that mediate and shape self-understanding and the understanding of the world and Others.

In their effort to delineate various generative themes that give rise to the views of Black philosophers within their text, *I Am Because We Are: Readings in Black Philosophy*, Fred Lee Hord and Jonathan Scott Lee emphasize the self/Other dialectic as one important theme. They argue that "constitutive of the black philosophical tradition . . . is the idea that identity of the individual is never separable from the sociocultural environment. Identity is not some Cartesian abstraction grounded in a solipsistic self-consciousness."[15] The *sum* (I am) of the self is not self-constituted; rather, "I am" presupposes "they are." The Cartesian self in its self-certainty has no need for the category of sociality. African American philosophy, however, does not begin with an ego-logically fixed self for "the experience of the self with other selves is the meaning of 'sociality.'"[16] And while the we-relationship that constitutes any particular self might be taken for granted, the we-relationship's dynamism nevertheless *exists* and precedes the performative "I am." As Maurice Natanson notes, "We are before I am."[17]

Read through the lens of racism, the point here is that African American philosophy presupposes a social ontology where the self—in this case the Black self—is positioned by anti-Black racist forces in terms of which the Black self must contend. In its racially configured form, the self/Other dialectic is captured implicitly by Cornel West where he asks, "What does it mean to be a philosopher of African descent in the American empire?"[18] West's question raises the issue of philosophical identity beyond the sphere of pure contemplation and *thinking substances*. His question presupposes an identity in context, a situated self, one that is anti-essentialist in its constitution. Hence, within the context of racist hegemony, the centrality of the American empire becomes an important axis around which African American philosophical identity must be defined. Lucius Outlaw even sees the very attempt by Black people to address important meta-philosophical concerns around the issue of whether or not there can be a Black philosophy as an outgrowth of struggle. He notes that confronting "this issue of 'Black philosophy' is the expansion of the continuing history-making struggles of African and African-descended peoples in this country (and elsewhere) to achieve progressively liberated existence as conceived in various ways."[19] Indeed, while African Americans received PhDs in the field of philosophy prior to the activism and liberating struggles to establish Black Studies programs in the 1960s and 1970s, it is important to note that the overall raising of consciousness during this period functioned as a catalyst for African Americans who entered advanced degree programs in the area of philosophy. It is also important to note, however, that African American philosophy and African American philosophers have been neglected topics not only in mainstream philosophy, but also in Black Studies. After examining two early pivotal Black Studies reference books published in the early

1970s, John McClendon found both to be wanting. In *Black American Writers, 1773–1949*, he found that the section on philosophy only included theologians and psychologists; and in *A Bibliography of Doctoral Research on the Negro, 1933–1966*, there was a subsection on the humanities, but not any reference to philosophy.[20]

The question regarding philosophers of African descent within the context of the American empire bespeaks the role of power and oppression as important foci of African American philosophical engagement. The philosophical selves that are implicated in West's question are selves that take seriously "the worldliness of one's philosophical project."[21] West also rejects the Cartesian presumption regarding "the absolute autonomy of philosophy."[22] For West, Cartesians assume that "philosophy stands outside the various conventions on which people base their social practices and transcends the cultural heritages and political struggles of people."[23] He concludes, "If the Cartesian viewpoint is the only valid philosophical stance, then the idea of an Afro-American philosophy would be ludicrous."[24] Indeed, any philosophy that takes seriously the importance of struggle against oppression through the exercise of human agency rejects philosophy as a practice that transcends the horror, messiness, and joy of human existence.[25] Within the context of this chapter, existential struggle not only denotes the historical matrix out of which African American philosophy evolved and continues to evolve, but the motif of struggle also functions as a source for meta-philosophical insight. Hence, struggle, as used here, is not only descriptive,[26] it is also heuristic.

Out of his successful effort to teach an introductory course in African American philosophy for the first time, Mills shares that he effectively deployed the unifying theme of "the struggles of people of African descent in the Americas against the different manifestations of white racism"[27] as an important point of critical and insightful inquiry. Mills especially emphasized how Black people were and are defined as sub-persons and how this sub-personhood is an example of what he terms *non*-Cartesian *sums*. Mills' approach helps to flesh out in insightful ways West's point regarding the non-Cartesian sensibilities of African American philosophy. Mills argues that if we take seriously the conception of sub-personhood, and how such a status presupposes a certain social ontology, then the morphology of philosophical questions asked, and which philosophical issues and themes are deemed serious and relevant, will be different. He contrasts a Cartesian *sum* with a non-Cartesian *sum* or the kind of *sum* that is portrayed in Ralph Ellison's *Invisible Man*. Descartes was pained with questions about solipsism, whether or not he could know with certainty that the external world exists, and whether or not he could distinguish between when he was dreaming as opposed to being awake. These sorts of questions presuppose a range of implicit assumptions about the self, the world, and one's *lived* experiences. Ellison's invisible man does not doubt his existence in the privacy of a stove-heated room; rather, he is made to feel invisible, insignificant, within a public transactional space where whites refuse to see him, refuse to respect him. The drama of his invisibility takes place *between* selves. Of course, the Black self is not deemed a Thou, but an ontologically truncated self, and in other cases not a self at all. As Descartes *doubts* his own existence, Ellison's invisible man is constantly *reminded* of the denial and diminishment of his self/existence. According to Ellison's invisible man, "I am invisible, understand, simply because people [in this case white people] refuse to see me."[28] Think here of Pecola Breedlove, the young Black female protagonist in Toni Morrison's *The Bluest Eye*. Like Ellison's invisible man, she finds herself in a white racist world that refuses to see her, so that while buying some candy from a store owned by Mr Yacobowski, a European immigrant, he does not see her, "because for him there is nothing to see."[29] She does not live in a world in which she is philosophically incredulous about her existence. On the contrary, she *desires* to disappear in a world that has stereotyped her as "ugly" and "distasteful." Because of white gazes[30] that refuse to see her, Pecola begins to desire her own invisibility, her own non-existence as Black. Her internalized self-hatred already presupposes an external world that refuses her the privilege of hyperbolically *thinking* that world away.

Lynch mobs make a mockery of Cartesian hyperbolic doubt. The vitriol of white racism forces one to be ever cognizant of the existence of other minds, not in vats, but as embodied and raced. Solipsism has no place in a world where Black bodies are mutilated and burned for the pleasure of others.[31] Hence, for Black people, the philosophical problem is not whether one exists or not, but how to collectively resist a white supremacist world of absurdity where one is degraded, marginalized, humiliated, oppressed, and brutalized. On this score, taking flight into the sphere of a private subjectivity is overwhelmed and mocked by the sheer weight of racial violence. Within the context of colonization, Fanon suggests that this hermetic turn inward is an idol that the colonized will abolish. He writes, "The colonialist bourgeoisie had hammered into the native's mind the idea of a society of individuals where each person shuts himself up in his own subjectivity, and whose only wealth is individual thought."[32] For Fanon, the very concept of friend within the colonial context belies subjective withdrawal. Friendship presupposes an always already preexisting social matrix and signifies a centrifugal process of mutual recognition. Fanon notes, "Brother, sister, friend—these are words outlawed by the colonialist bourgeoisie, because for them my brother is my purse, my friend is part of my scheme for getting on."[33]

Sociality is the matrix within which racist action takes place. It is within the mundane everyday world that Black people struggle *to be* and *attempt to make sense of their existence*. Existence in Black, then, which is a fluid site of identity formation and the articulation and re-articulation of meaning within the matrix of sociality, presupposes a set of social ills that are conspicuously absent *vis-à-vis* an ego that takes itself to exist as an island unto itself. As socially embedded and embodied, existence in Black speaks critically to the narrowness of the field of philosophy. To do philosophy in Black within a social context of white racism, where one's very existence is at stake, where one is reduced to a sub-person, even by those white philosophers who have been canonized within the Western philosophical tradition (Hume, Kant, Hegel, to name a few), one must critically engage and overthrow Western philosophy's misanthropy. Moreover, to do philosophy in Black, one must critique Western philosophy's thanatonic normative assumptions. Indeed, one must be suspicious and critical of *dead* philosophical idols and metaphors, fossilized and existentially inconsequential, that fail to speak to the lives of Black people. Within this context, West emphasizes the importance of de-disciplining modes of knowledge. He writes, "To dedisciplinize means that you go to wherever you find sources that can help you in constituting your intellectual weaponry."[34] Disrupting the disciplinary "purity" and marshalling discursive material that speaks to the lives of Black people is what Angela Davis did as early as 1969. When she began to teach philosophy at UCLA, she discovered that "there was not a single course that had anything to do with African-American ideas."[35] She decided to design a course where she got students to compare Frederick Douglass's understanding of the slave-master relationship with particular passages in Hegel's *Phenomenology of Spirit*. She notes, "I found that it was extremely important to legitimate the production of philosophical knowledge in sites that are not normally considered *the* philosophical sites."[36]

Drawing on the work of William Barrett, Outlaw argues that professional philosophy is a site of deformation "evidenced by the degree to which the 'problems' of philosophy continue to be, even in these very problematic times, discipline immanent, thus without foundation beyond the boundaries of the discipline itself. *They have not emerged from the practices of life.*[37] The fact that some philosophers of African descent leave "philosophy" or are unwanted in various philosophy departments is linked to the disciplinary hegemony, philosophical narrowness, and racist practices of so many Anglo-American departments of philosophy. Not only does Lewis Gordon point out that he was denied a position in a philosophy department because it was said that he might attract "'too many Black people,'"[38] but he argues that even those Black philosophers who primarily do logic and epistemology are at risk of not being hired by particular philosophy departments if they raise serious questions about what it means to live in a racist culture as Black people; that is, questions that counter the legitimating practices of mainstream philosophy. Gordon argues that if the universities found this out, "then that person is automatically not going to be considered at that institution in the department of philosophy."[39] Commenting on the need to have African American philosophers well placed in departments of philosophy, Laurence Thomas notes, "I believe that no philosophy department in America would hire a Black who would trouble the waters."[40] What becomes obvious is that philosophy's disciplinary myopia and its prevalent monochromatic membership have militated against the presence of Black people. Harris describes the case of Broadus N. Butler, who received his PhD in philosophy as early as 1952 from the University of Michigan, to illustrate an important point about racism and the profession. After he received his doctorate, Butler applied to teach in a mostly white university. According to Harris, Butler found out that his letter of reference stated, "'a good philosopher, but of course, a Negro,' and the one-line response, 'Why don't you go where you will be among your own kind?'"[41]

Gordon insists upon "raising the question of whether philosophy has been responsible to itself in terms if what it is."[42] Anita Allen asks, "With all due respect, what does philosophy have to offer to Black women? It's not obvious to me that philosophy has anything special to offer Black women today."[43] Given this, what becomes especially relevant is West's observation that "a relativizing of the discipline's traditional hierarchies of importance and centrality thus becomes necessary."[44] The logic and significance of West's observation is captured in an example provided by Allen, where she talks about studying analytic metaphysics at the University of Michigan. She notes:

Yet as a Black person it felt odd to sit around asking such questions like "How do you know when two nonexistent objects are the same?"

There you are in the middle of the era of affirmative action, civil rights, women's movements, etc., and you're sitting around thinking about nonexistent objects and how to tell when they are the same.[45]

Albert Mosley also experienced this tension after he was invited by prominent philosopher of science Rom Harré to study with him at Oxford. Mosley was passionate about issues in the philosophy of science. He applied for a Fulbright scholarship and received it. "But," as he says, "1966–1967 found me torn again between scholarship and activism. I almost refused the Fulbright scholarship because I felt guilty that I was not actively involved in the civil rights struggle."[46] And while Bernard Boxill was steeped in Bertrand Russell and Alfred North Whitehead's *Principia Mathematica* and works by Alonzo Church and W. V. O. Quine, he was passionately attracted to all of the discussions and political upheavals around 1965. Boxill eventually wrote his dissertation on the Black Power debate through the lens of Fanon's work. It is important to note, though, that Boxill did not abandon the tools of analytic philosophy; rather, conceptual analysis was used to address significant issues such as social justice and affirmation action *vis-à-vis* the lives of Black people.[47]

The insights of Mills, West, Outlaw, Davis, Gordon, Allen, Mosley, and Boxill raise the issue of critically rethinking and transgressing the narrowness of philosophy's self-image. Concerning the paucity of Blacks in the field of philosophy, West maintains that philosophy has not been made attractive enough. The image of the philosopher that we have is "the analytic philosopher who is clever, who is sharp, who is good at drawing distinctions, but who doesn't really relate it to history, struggle, engagement with suffering, how we cope with suffering, how we overcome social misery, etc."[48] Linda Selzer is correct where she observes, "Not surprisingly, many blacks in philosophy found themselves drawn to Marxism, existentialism, phenomenology, and pragmatism, philosophies whose insights seemed directly applicable to the economic, historical, and psychological status of marginalized groups."[49] And even as these philosophical paradigms are still dominated by white philosophers, they raise important questions— inter-subjectivity, freedom, responsibility, history, embodiment, agency, oppression, *lived* meaning—that are germane to Black people and their experiences of being defined and treated as sub-persons. "The *sum* here, then—the *sum* of those seen as sub-persons—will be quite different."[50]

African American philosophy's point of embarkation, then, will begin with a different set of existential problematics. W. E. B. Du Bois points out that, for whites, Black people don't simply have problems; rather, they are a problem people, ontologically. The very wish "to make it possible for a man to be both a Negro and an American, without being cursed and spit upon by his fellows, without having the doors of Opportunity closed roughly in his face"[51] already raises significant issues around the struggle for self-definition, political power, and survival. The existential weight of this struggle, which again speaks to the reality and importance of sociality, presupposes the capacity of white Others who have the political and material power to make non-whites suffer. When one shouts a greeting to the world and the white world slashes away that joy, and one is told "to stay within bounds, to go back where [you] belong,"[52] one must begin with opposition; one must take a stand, one must rethink and critically evaluate one's status within the polity, one must engage in forms of critical thought that enable one best to navigate the terrain of anti-Black racism. Indeed, one must take to task the hidden philosophical anthropological assumptions upon which the polity was/is founded. One must raise the question of philosophy's duty to *this* world, the world of the "cave," where white, ghostly appearances have killed and brutalized Black bodies in the night. On this score, situated Black bodies within the context of white gazes generate questions regarding the *here* of *embodied subjective* integrity in ways that are more urgent and immediate than traditional philosophical discussions regarding the mind/body distinction. Allen notes, "Two very prominent philosophers offered to look at my résumé (I was flattered) and then asked to sleep with me (I was disturbed)."[53]

Allen was reduced to her Black body; she became the object of their white sexual fantasies. Here is a context where armchair discussions around the conundrums of the mind/body distinction are transformed into serious matters of ethical and political urgency because of the reality of lived trauma. Through the white male gaze, *she is her body*. In their eyes, Allen is a Jezebel, the Black slut whose interiority is nullified through the racist mythology that Black women are, as it were, solely constituted as lustful and lascivious. Within the context of white racist myth-making regarding Black women, T. Denean Sharpley-Whiting notes, "Epitomizing hypersexuality, driven by some racially coded instinct, the black female renders herself available, even assailable, yet simultaneously unassailable, sexually invulnerable, in effect, unrapeable, because of her 'licentiousness.'"[54] Dorothy Roberts argues that, in 1736, the South Carolina *Gazette* depicted "African Ladies" primarily as women who had a "strong robust constitution," capable of long sexual endurance, and "able to serve their lovers 'by Night as well as Day.'"[55] There is something profoundly hollow about philosophers who sit around leisurely discussing Descartes' bifurcation between two substances (mental and physical) that are really distinct when Black women have been reduced to their bodies and raped, when Black people have been denied *Geist*. Adrian Piper, the first African American female philosopher to receive tenure, notes: "I think the primary problem [facing Black women entering the profession of philosophy] is that everybody assumes that Black women are basically maids or prostitutes and so you have a lot to get over when you go into a department."[56] To be hailed as a prostitute, to be defined as sexually insatiable, to be reduced to one's genitalia, and deemed a prisoner of a presumed "racial essence," points to a radically non-Cartesian *sum*. Such an experience has no pretensions to a form of decontextualized universality, where epistemic subjects are substitutable. In fact, such a false universality does an injustice to the intersectional, heterogeneous, *lived* reality of Black women and women of color. Out of the complexity of such experiences grow philosophical categories that render philosophical homogeneity deeply suspect.[57]

Contra Plato, the practice of African American philosophy is not one of death, but of life, of affirming life in the face of uncertain non-being. This is not the sort of uncertainty that all of us experience in the face of our inexorable death because of our finitude. The exclamation, "Look, a Negro!" has the power to objectify. It has the power, as Fanon says, to cause "a hemorrhage that spattered my whole body with black blood."[58] "A Black man did it!" has ignited forms of racist fanaticism that have resulted in unspeakable forms of bloodlust. Within such a context, the love of wisdom does not simply delight in immutable truths, but embodies modes of actively engaging in second-order critical reflection toward the end of making sense of one's *situational* reality and offering engaging critiques of systems of oppression that militate against freedom. From a Black *locus philosophicus*, the love of wisdom (*philo-sophia*) is a form of thought-*cum*-action. In other words, given the fact of pervasive and systemic anti-Black racism (and how this racism is non-additively linked to issues of class and gender), one way of thinking about African American philosophy is in terms of a discursive and praxis-oriented activity in which philosophers engage in second-order critical reflection on the lived experiences of Black people as they struggle against racist epistemic and normative orders that degrade, dehumanize, and militate against Black self-flourishing. In stream with Herbert Marcuse and Outlaw in terms of their characterization of critical thought, I would argue that African American philosophy is a species of *dialectical thought*, a mode of critical engagement that refuses to leave the world unchanged and static in its hubristic and procrustean ways.[59] In this regard, African American philosophy is *negative*. African American philosophy strives to destabilize the rigid conceptual terrain and normative landscape of Western philosophy's self-constituting and self-perpetuating narrative that presupposes whiteness as normative. Yet, understanding Black existence as a site of historically superimposed un-freedom, African American philosophy deploys its hermeneutic energies toward the *positive* aim of liberation struggle, of securing and asserting *lived* freedom, and telescoping the various ways in which Black people create frameworks of meaning that promote and sustain that freedom. On this score, African American philosophy inspires hope and engages in self-validating practices, thereby affirming one's agency and the restructuring of social structures of power in the quest for equality and the positive advancement of social transformation.[60]

Given the historical facticity out of which African American philosophy grew and grows, questions of identity, community, resistance, and survival become philosophically indispensable, themes that get configured and reconfigured within the context of a collective journey through the crucible of American racism. Mills notes, "African-American philosophy is thus inherently, definitionally *oppositional*, the philosophy produced by property that does not remain silent but insists on speaking and contesting its status."[61] In this way, African American philosophy asserts a philosophical anthropology that opposes misanthropy and calls into question many of the normative assumptions of modernity—the nature of rationality and who qualifies as human. Against the racist procrustean tendencies of modernity, Blacks have had to engage in "heroic efforts to preserve human dignity on the night side of modernity and the underside of modernity."[62] Such efforts are not carried out by monadic subjects, but within the context of a shared community, a shared sense of we-experiences that ground the sense of community, but should not stifle its augmentation and complexity. Harris is critical of thinking about African American philosophers as con-stituting a community through a specifically shared *philosophical* vocabu-lary. After all, there are philosophers of African descent who are Marxists, existentialists, phenomenologists, and pragmatists who conceptually dwell within different and conflicting discourse communities. Yet, Harris argues that there is an overriding aim which African American philosophers share that constitutes them as a community. It is the engagement "in the common project to defeat the heinous consequences of racism. That's the kind of community that it is . . . that binds them together regardless of their philosophy."[63]

There are some African American philosophers who do not see their philosophical reflections as primarily informed by the fact that they are African American philosophers or that their philosophizing is primarily informed by the concrete *lived* struggle of being Black in America. For example, when asked this question, Thomas was explicit: "My answer to that question is, I would say, no."[64] He does admit, however, that there are certain sensibilities that can give rise to various complex insights that are tied to being Black. He notes, "W. E. B. Du Bois talked about double consciousness and Ralph Ellison talked about invisibility, etc. I think that those are insights that come with the Black experience."[65] Michele M. Moody-Adams has written about moral psychology and moral responsibility without mentioning race. She does not see herself as starting with a set of fixed questions/problems that have been defined by Alain Locke or Du Bois. Yet she admits, "I may never mention race but I know that deep down that what is egging me on intellectually is a set of problems that come out of my experience."[66] Birt argues that even African American philosophers who are clearly interested in ontological and metaphysical questions "think and rethink such questions . . . in social terms."[67] And even African American philosophy done through an analytical philosophical lens, what Paget Henry calls "political logicism,"[68] constitutes a critical space that involves "the application of Anglo-analytical philosophy to the study of black problems, most significantly those that are a function of the impact of race and racism on the lives of black people."[69] African American philosophy, unlike Cartesian *sums*, takes seriously sociality. As a project that takes seriously human embodiment-*cum*-others,[70] and that thereby emphasizes the importance of social constitutionality with respect to the self, African American philosophy avoids abstract pretentiousness, de-contextual assumptions regarding what constitutes a philosophical problem, essentialist presuppositions regarding the self, and the bad faith of exclusive transcendence. Thus, the question of African American philosophy ought to be raised within a social and historical context of emergence. Not only at the heart of its discursive concerns is African American philosophy dialectically linked to struggle, but African American philosophers have also struggled against various efforts by communities of white philosophers who have refused to take Blacks seriously as philosophers, and who have characterized philosophical problems that evolve out of the Black experience as *ersatz* and sociological in nature. In other words, African American philosophers, and

Black people in America more generally, have been isolated and rendered invisible. Hence, it is important to give attention to early African American philosophers, which gives concrete historical illustrative testament to the preoccupations and strivings of "African American philosophy against all odds."[71] As I will show, from a contemporary perspective the existential motif of struggling against all odds speaks to the importance of building intellectual community. Such community efforts are not simply done to overcome alienation within the field, but such efforts function as a remedy to the kinds of philosophy undertaken by Descartes. Community building underscores the point that African American philosophers engage in endeavors that are inextricably linked to social spaces through the *mediation of the body* which, as I have argued, is precisely the site of white anti-Black hatred and vilification.

EARLY PIONEER AFRICAN AMERICAN PHILOSOPHERS

Philosophers and historians have not given due attention to African American philosophers who received PhDs in philosophy prior to the 1950s. In fact, in Bruce Kuklick's *A History of Philosophy in America: 1720–2000*, with the exception of Du Bois (who received his BA in philosophy from Harvard in 1890), there is no mention of a single credentialed African American philosopher.[72] One is left with the impression that Blacks did not receive advanced degrees in philosophy and did not produce any philosophy in America. One would think that Kuklick would have provided some space for Cornel West, especially given West's prominence and visibility as an American philosopher of African descent.

While there are very important and indispensable contemporary philosophical texts[73] that focus upon philosophical figures of African descent, there is still the need to do the important archival work necessary to ascertain the history and conceptual morphology of African American philosophy. "It is from here," according to McClendon, "that we can move to definition and interpretation, knowing full well that the limits of our inquiry into the history of African-American philosophy is empirical research."[74]

Some important early figures include Richard T. Greener, who became a professor of Mental and Moral Philosophy at the University of South Carolina as early as 1873.[75] He not only taught philosophy, but taught in the Departments of Mathematics, Greek, and Latin. Greener was also the first African American to graduate from Harvard with an AB degree. Albert Millard Dunham received his PhD in philosophy from the University of Chicago in 1933, William W. Fontaine from the University of Pennsylvania in 1936, Charles Leander Hill from Ohio State University in 1938, Forrest Oran Wiggins from the University of Wisconsin also in 1938, Cornelius Golightly from the University of Michigan in 1941, Eugene C. Holms from Columbia University in 1942, and Francis Monroe Hammond from the Université Laval in 1944.[76]

Within the context of delineating the historical origins of African American philosophy, many scholars and philosophers begin with Alain Locke who received his PhD in philosophy from Harvard University in 1918. However, at least three African Americans received PhDs in philosophy prior to Alain Locke. Remarkably, the first two African Americans to receive a PhD in philosophy were born under the legalized system of institutional slavery.[77] Marked as inferior, deemed chattel from birth, they struggled against racist mythopoetic constructions of the Black body and fashioned themselves as lovers of wisdom. Patrick Francis Healy (1830–1910) was the first African American to receive a PhD in philosophy, in 1865, from the University of Louvaine, Belgium (this was prior to the first PhD granted in philosophy by an American university).[78] He also received an undergraduate degree from Holy Cross in 1850. Healy's Irish father, Michael Morris Healy, was his slave owner. His father took Mary Eliza, an enslaved woman of light complexion, as his mistress. Healy taught philosophy at St Joseph's College and Georgetown. He eventually became President of Georgetown in 1874, the first African American philosopher to teach at a predominantly white institution of higher learning.

Thomas N. Baker (1860–1940) was the first African American to receive a PhD in philosophy from an American university. He completed the degree in 1903 from Yale with his dissertation "The Ethical Significance of the Connection between Mind and Body." Baker was born enslaved of enslaved parents, Thomas Chadwick Baker, a Civil War veteran, and Edith (Nottingham) Baker, on Robert Nottingham's plantation in Northampton County, Virginia. In 1881, Baker entered Hampton Institute in Virginia where he studied for the next four years (1885). Hampton, founded by General Samuel Armstrong, was designed to teach Blacks practical industrial education.[79] Many white philanthropists would have been doubtful of the benefits of teaching Black people an intellectually demanding subject such as philosophy. Critical of Hampton, Du Bois wrote, "The difficulty of Hampton is that its ideals are low. It is, as it seems to me, deliberately educating a servile class for a servile place."[80] Remarkably, Baker's philosophical spirit was not extinguished by his enslavement or because of his attendance at Hampton.

After Hampton, Baker attended Mount Hermon, which was founded by Dwight L. Moody. Struck by Baker's intelligence, John Denison, who was pastor of Williams College located in Massachusetts, offered to pay $100 annually toward Baker's tuition.[81] While Baker was certainly proud to have attended Mount Hermon, he may have been conflicted around its lack of concern regarding possible post-Yale academic career options for him. "Once Baker had earned his doctorate, Mount Hermon officials did nothing to recommend him to academic posts, even in southern institutions like Tuskegee."[82] This may have led Baker to wonder if the "Color Line" had influenced Mount Hermon. However, in 2002, Northfield Mount Hermon established a Thomas Nelson Baker Fellowship in Baker's honor.

Before his PhD, around 1890, Baker entered Boston University in the Liberal Arts School and was graduated in the class of 1893 (BA). He went on to attend Yale Divinity School where he took a three-year course (1893–96), graduating with a BD. He became the minister of the Dixwell Avenue Congregational Church in New Haven, Connecticut, and ordained there in 1897.

Baker published articles dealing with philosophical themes in the area of axiology *vis-à-vis* Black pride and aesthetics. His views concerning Black aesthetics and Black cultural identity constitute an early and significant philosophical precursor to the Harlem Renaissance and the Black Arts Movement of the 1960s. As early as 1906, before Alain Locke's *The New Negro*, which was published in 1925, Baker, in *Alexander's Magazine*, forged a philosophical critique of racism and advanced an aesthetic alternative to the reigning white aesthetic of beauty. He argued, "Not where we are, but what we are is the great and final question that should concern us."[83] For Baker, "It is the perversion of the aesthetical sense of physical beauty that the American Negro has struck his lowest depths of racial degradation."[84] And in the *Southern Workman*, suggestive of a critical pedagogy cognizant of creating representational and semiotic diversity, he argues that various "pictures of the boys and girls in school are just what the Negro child needs to see. If there is to be any real race love, the Negro child must be taught to see beauty in the Negro type."[85] Commenting on the pervasive hegemony of whiteness, Baker argued:

> Everywhere the colored man sees built into the steamboats, trains and waiting rooms the teachings of Nietzsche: "All that is best is

for my folk and for myself. If it is not given us, we take it. The best land, the purest sky, the best food, the most beautiful thoughts and the most beautiful women."[86]

Baker is concerned with the liberation of Black consciousness from a state of internalized self-hatred. He argued that the watchword of Black people should be, "Not Pity but Respect."[87] He launched a direct attack on the epistemic and aesthetic orders embedded within Jim Crowism. Along with his work on articulating race-specific ideals, there is also a concern for the *material* conditions under which Black people succeed or fail. In his dissertation, where he argues for the independence of the mind and body in terms of their origin, but emphasizes the interdependence of their development, Baker writes, "The well being of the body is the condition for the well being of the mind. Degradation of the body is always accompanied by the degradation of the mind."[88] Born enslaved, Baker's remark is laden with epistemic credibility. After all, how many Black bodies did he witness that were torn asunder, bowed by the sheer weight of white oppression and degradation? When one thinks about specific ways in which the Black body underwent physical trauma and the lack of material conditions supportive of the well-being of Black people, Baker's claim functions as a subtle critique of the view that Black people are "born" inferior to whites. Through his philosophical efforts to change the discourse of race pride and race identity, Baker is an important, though neglected, philosophical figure within the context of the history of African American philosophy.[89]

Gilbert Haven Jones (1883–1966) received his PhD in philosophy from the University of Jena, Germany in 1909, six years after Baker. Jones's dissertation was entitled "Lotze und Bowne: Eine Vergleichung ihrer philosophischen Arbeit" ("Lotze and Bowne: A Comparison of their Philosophical Work"). Earlier, he received his BSc. from Wilberforce, and a Bachelor of Philosophy degree at Dickinson College in Carlisle. Jones became Dean of the College of Liberal Arts at Wilberforce University (1914–24), and between 1924 and 1932 served as the fourth president of Wilberforce University. He also chaired the Philosophy Department at St Augustine Collegiate Institute, Raleigh, North Carolina.[90]

Jones authored *Education in Theory and Practice* (1919). He was the first African American philosopher to write a major treatise on education in which he theorized the self as a dynamic plasticity. Against the backdrop of racist theories that supported the "uneducable" nature of Black people,

Jones argued that the teleological function of education "is to create for mankind social advantages and opportunities in life by nurture which they could never hope to attain by nature."[91] Indeed, for Jones, "Great minds, 'men of genius,' are not so much born so (by nature) as they are made so (by nurture)."[92]

Education in Theory and Practice also embodies a conception of the mind[93] that rejects a form of philosophical idealism that might be deployed to undercut the efforts of Black people in their struggle. In other words, the view that the mind has no significant connection to the body/material conditions (given the belief that Blacks are *mentally* inferior) might be used to support the belief that Black people possess an inferior mental constitution. Whites, however, might be said to possess a superior mental constitution independent of nurture. Jones is doing more than traditional metaphysics in his discussion of mind and body in his educational treatise. Interrogating the belief that some of us have a spark of divinity that makes us greater than others, Jones writes, "If there is such a divinity there it certainly does not do much for us apart from opportunity and circumstance."[94] While Jones does not use race-sensitive discourse in his treatise, it is important to keep in mind that the text appeared in 1919. This was the year, known as the Red Summer, when at least twenty-five race riots erupted. Jones was aware that to equalize the opportunity toward an education was to prepare people to gain greater control over their lives and circumstances. He understood the importance of the utility function of knowledge in terms of its significance to empower. "Nothing," according to Jones, "has any value for its own sake, not even knowledge."[95]

Critiquing both race and class hegemony, Jones argues that the main reason for the discourse supporting the difference in the intelligence of individuals has to do with "a tacit knowledge that the equal opportunity which education gives will rob them [those in power] of their advantage and prevent the further exploitation of the ignorant by the intelligent, of the socially low by the socially high."[96] Within a *social* metaphysical framework that recognizes the reality of race as a powerful girder of social reality, where race is a *lived* reality, even if ontologically vacuous, Jones' philosophy of education stresses the importance of social critique's capacity to rethink/re-imagine the normative order, to change the world. Indeed, born within the crucible of struggle, African American philosophy valorizes the importance of critical reflection and engaged praxis toward the end of transforming the world or as Jones would say, "turn[ing] the world upside down."[97]

COMMUNITY BUILDING

Within an institutional context where white bodies numerically dominate the profession of philosophy, and where the image of the philosopher unconsciously signifies whiteness, African American philosophers have endured oppressive feelings of alienation, of drowning in a sea of white faces. The alienation is not simply felt at the level of numerical under-representation, but at the level of *normative* (white) philosophical hegemony, at the level of concepts, interests, and ways of looking at the world that do not speak to the Black experience. It might be argued that for many Black philosophers a feeling of philosophical homelessness, a form of disorientation, is experienced within classrooms, at conferences, on committees, editorial boards, and so on. Through collective praxes, philosophers of African descent have fought against marginalization and alienation within the profession. Indeed, despite the fact that Blacks constitute roughly one percent of the profession, they have forthrightly engaged in efforts to build community and institutional support for their philosophical efforts.

The Committee on Blacks in Philosophy was founded in the early 1970s by William R. Jones (the first chair) and others. Jones was aware of the *crisis* regarding the lack of Black philosophers in the profession of philosophy and fought to get the American Philosophical Association (APA) to finds ways of remedying this. Jones pointed to the "ominous gravity" of the situation. "Although blacks constitute more than 10% of the general population, they comprise less than 1/100 of the personnel in philosophy. Accordingly, to approximate their proportion in the general population black representation in philosophy must increase ten-fold."[98] When asked about the response of the APA to this crisis, Jones notes, "The APA did not see the oppression in their structures or in their policies because they were not looking at it from the angle of analysis that would reveal such things as oppression."[99] Howard McGary attests to the APA's lack of will to create infrastructural support for the advancement of Blacks in philosophy. He says, "I think that the APA has done very little as an organization. Very little."[100] The Committee on Blacks in Philosophy was the fruit of a collective effort on the part of Black philosophers to achieve self-determination within the context of a white association that was founded in 1900. Tommy Lott, who served as chair of the Committee from 1993 to 1996, observed that the Committee was "necessary to promote the interests of African-American philosophers by ensuring that they're included in the program and that the concerns of the African-American community . . . students in departments, professors going through tenure, get represented in the organization."[101] The *Newsletter on Philosophy and the Black Experience* (NPBE) was later sponsored by the Committee. The NPBE began in 1991 and was pivotal in terms of informing readers of the Committee's efforts, encouraging the examination of issues that grew out of the Black world, encouraging the end of racial discrimination, highlighting the various complex traditions and legacies within the context of the Black world, and providing critical reflection on current philosophical works that explored the subject of African American philosophy and philosophy of the Black experience.

Within a context where philosophical and (white) monochromatic inertia militates against the creative efforts of African American philosophers to engage issues that are pertinent to their *lived* experiences, issues that challenge the Western philosophical canon and its normative assumptions, *Kujichagulia* (or self-determination) functions as an indispensable axiological principle deployed against continued marginalization. J. Everet Green experienced firsthand this sense of marginalization at APA conferences. Green knew that persons of African descent needed their own forum. As a result, Philosophy Born of Struggle (PBS), an annual conference named after Harris's important text, was conceived by Green and founded in 1993. According to Green,[102] he wanted a space where people of African descent could come together and where students could find a voice and mentoring could take place. The choice of name for the forum was apropos given the struggle of persons of African descent within the normative (white hegemonic) context of European philosophy. He argues that it was believed that Black people did not have the intellectual capacity or tenacity that philosophy required. The presumption is that "real" philosophy grew out of Europe, but originated within Greek culture, which is believed to be the cradle of civilization and the origin of reason. Philosophy Born of Struggle is itself a site of struggle; it is a site of resistance to the longstanding and current assumption that to be a *Black* philosopher is an oxymoron, a bizarre creation like Frankenstein's monster.

For the last thirty years, the Society for the Study of Africana Philosophy (SSAP, previously known as the New York Society for the Study of Black Philosophy) has sustained a critical space for challenging the presumption that the activity of philosophizing is exclusively a Eurocentric phenomenon. The group has encouraged a diversity of Africana philosophical voices to engage ideas pertinent to the Black experience. Such a forum has been absolutely crucial not only in terms of nurturing philosophical ideas, but for creating a space for Black philosophical identity-formation and for creating a space for white philosophers who are deeply interested in the philosophical problematics that grow out of the Black experience. Seminal to its creation was Alfred E. Prettyman, who both founded SSAP and hosts its meetings out of his apartment. Asked about the importance of SSAP, West says, "Well, for me, it was crucial. It was monumental in terms of facilitating a context in which persons concerned with philosophical reflections of the Black experience could meet regularly at Al Prettyman's place there in New York."[103] During the meetings, papers were given and critically discussed. Also, encouragement was nurtured. There was a real sense of community building. For West, they "constituted an intellectual neighborhood, a real *community of inquirers* wrestling with the construct of race to philosophical traditions."[104] Howard McGary also remembers SSAP as a place "where people could come and give papers and many books and chapters of books were tried out in that forum."[105]

More recent critical spaces created for the purpose of examining the critical reflections of philosophers of African descent include the Caribbean Philosophical Association (CPA) and the Collegium of Black Women Philosophers (CBWP). CPA was founded in 2002 by a collective, which included George Belle, B. Anthony Bogues, Patrick Goodin, Lewis Gordon, Clevis Headley, Paget Henry, Nelson Maldonado-Torres, Charles Mills, and Supriya Nair. A central theme is to engage in shifting the geography of reason. This is an important move as it deconstructs the presumption that reason is the property of one group and one place. Indeed, it counters the hegemonic epistemic and axiological orders that privilege whites as the sole inheritors of reason. As a result, the organization debunks the myths supporting the racist philosophical anthropology that sees whites as those who stand at the apex of human history. The group is not limited to those with degrees in philosophy and encourages South-South critical dialogue. As such, CPA emphasizes a genuine interdisciplinary critical conversation, thus avoiding various forms of interdisciplinary hegemony. The Diaspora is treated as a rich confluence of ideas and epistemic practices that grow out of and speak to issues of colonialism, sexism, racism, global suffering, and questions of freedom and creative expression. CBWP was founded by Kathryn Gines in 2007 while she was at Vanderbilt University. This annual conference/organization is particularly important to community building among Black women in the field of philosophy, especially as there are currently fewer than thirty Black women in the profession. As a critical community, CBWP has a number of objectives that are designed to nurture Black woman at various stages in their development as philosophers. The organization provides an important space within which Black women are able to militate against the sense of dissonance felt within predominantly white and male philosophical spaces. In the spirit of Black women who have struggled mightily for their own voices, CBWP is designed to help burgeoning Black women philosophers find and cultivate their philosophical voices, to help with the often intimidating process of finding a teaching position, of moving up within academia, of completing the PhD, and of creating a critical space to share ideas that can lead to publication of articles and books. The organization also engages in proactive efforts to locate and nurture Black women at the undergraduate stage who might be interested in pursuing philosophy as a career.

CBWP is grounded in the bold spirit of the efforts of early African American women who received a PhD in philosophy. The following are some notable examples. Joyce M. Cook (1933-) was the first Black woman to receive a PhD in philosophy, which she received from Yale University in 1965. She was also the first Black woman to teach philosophy at Howard University (September 1970-June 1976). In the 1970s, within the context of various conferences and panel discussions, Cook was actively involved and instrumental in articulating the conceptual parameters of what constitutes the nature of Black philosophy. For example, in 1974, Cook presented "Prolegomena to a Black Philosophy," an address to Springhill College, Mobile, Alabama. She presented a paper entitled, "The Concept of Black Experience" to the American Philosophical Association (Western division meeting in Chicago, Illinois) in 1975. Additionally, in 1976, Cook, along with William R. Jones and Robert C. Williams, participated in a radio broadcast conversation regarding the meaning of Black philosophy.[106] Angela Davis (1944-) received an honorary doctorate in 1972 in philosophy from Lenin University. As mentioned earlier, she taught a philosophy course at UCLA as early as 1969, entitled "Recurring Philosophical Themes in Black Literature." At the time, this was unprecedented at UCLA.[107] Blanche Radford Curry (1949–) received her PhD in philosophy from Brown University in 1978. She was among a group of early Black philosophers[108] who worked together "to define a place for [themselves] within the philosophy profession, socially and intellectually, on terms that took into account and expressed [their] consciousness of being *black*."[109] She continues to address philosophical issues relevant to the lives of Black people. Adrian M. S. Piper (1948–) received her PhD in philosophy from Harvard University in 1981 and, as noted earlier, has the distinction of being the first tenured Black woman philosopher.[110] She is a

Kantian scholar and a leading contemporary artist. Her philosophical and artistic work explores issues of racism and sexism. Her work on Kant and xenophobia relates to the concrete problems of Black people. For example, while arguing that Kant's "conception of the self affords potent resources for understanding xenophobia as a special case of a more general cognitive phenomenon"[111] that has to do with resisting anomalous data to preserve a unified sense of self, Piper is aware that xenophobia "is of particular concern for African Americans. As unwelcome intruders in white America we are objects of xenophobia on a daily basis."[112] There is much work to be done detailing the lives, career journeys, and philosophical scholarship of Black women in the field of philosophy.

NOTES

1. George Yancy, "Robert E. Birt," in *African American Philosophers, 17 Conversations*, ed. George Yancy (New York: Routledge, 1998), 351.

2. George Yancy, "Cornel West," in *African American Philosophers*, 38.

3. Charles W. Mills, *Blackness Visible: Essays on Philosophy and Race* (Ithaca, NY: Cornell University Press, 1998), 10 (emphasis added).

4. And while it is true that white women were excluded from this normative philosophical community, they were nevertheless literally part of the monochromatic family.

5. Mills, *Blackness Visible*, 8.

6. Mills, *Blackness Visible*, 8.

7. René Descartes, *Discourse on Method and Meditations on First Philosophy*, transl. Donald A. Cress (Indianapolis: Hackett, 1637, 1641, 1998), *Meditations on First Philosophy*, sec. 25.

8. Descartes, *Meditations on First Philosophy*, sec. 34.

9. Mills, *Blackness Visible*, 8.

10. George Yancy, "Leonard Harris," in *African American Philosophers, 17 Conversations*, ed. George Yancy (New York: Routledge, 1998), 214.

11. Norm R. Allen, Jr., "Leonard Harris on the Life and Work of Alain Locke," in *African-American Humanism: An Anthology*, ed. Norm R. Allen, Jr. (Amherst, MA: Prometheus Books, 1991), 273.

12. Yancy, "Leonard Harris," 218–19.

13. Yancy, "Leonard Harris," 219.

14. James H. Cone, *A Black Theology of Liberation* (New York: Orbis Books, 1986, 1990), 86.

15. Fred Lee Hord (Mzee Lasana Okpara) and Jonathan Scott Lee, "'I Am Because We Are': An Introduction to Black Philosophy," in *I Am Because We Are: Reading in Black Philosophy* (Amherst, MA: University of Massachusetts Press, 1995), 7.

16. Maurice Natanson, *The Journeying Self: A Study in Philosophy and Social Role* (Reading, MA: Addison-Wesley, 1970), 47.

17. Natanson, *The Journeying Self*, 47.

18. Cornel West, "The Black Underclass and Black Philosophers," in *I Am Because We Are*, 356.

19. Lucis Outlaw, *On Philosophy and Race* (New York: Routledge, 1996), 23.

20. African American philosopher John McClendon's article "The Afro-American Philosopher and the Philosophy of the Black Experience: A Bibliographic Essay on a Neglected Topic in Both Philosophy and Black Studies," in *Sage Race Relations Abstracts*, vol. 7, no. 4 (November 1982), in my opinion, is the first serious and thorough research piece written on early professional African American philosophers and philosophy of the Black experience. It was published in 1982, a year before Harris's important text. McClendon holds a seminal place in the history of efforts to document and theorize African American philosophy and the philosophy of the Black experience.

21. West, "The Black Underclass and Black Philosophers," 357.

22. Cornel West, "Philosophy and the Afro-American Experience," in *A Companion to African-American Philosophy*, ed. Tommy L. Lott and John P. Pittman (Malden, MA; Blackwell, 2005), 8.

23. West, "Philosophy and the Afro-American Experience," 8.

24. West, "Philosophy and the Afro-American Experience," 8.

25. West's prophetic pragmatism shares this anti-Cartesian approach to philosophy. Not only does his prophetic pragmatism reject a form of epistemological foundationalism, but it highlights the importance of history, the tragic, and the hopeful; it "affirms the Niebuhrian strenuous mood, never giving up on new possibilities for human agency—both individual and collective." See *The American Evasion of Philosophy: A Genealogy of Pragmatism* (Madison, WI: The University of Wisconsin Press, 1989), 28.

26. There is no attempt to obfuscate the fact that there are many African American philosophers who, while they see themselves as doing African American philosophy, conceptualize the dynamics of struggle differently. Keeping abreast of this avoids eliding the political differences (Marxist-Leninist, liberal, conservative, etc.) that differentiate African American philosophers along significant ideological lines. Philosopher Stephen Ferguson is thanked for emphasizing this point in personal correspondence.

27. Mills, *Blackness Visible*, 6.

28. Ralph Ellison, *Invisible Man* (1947; reprint, New York: Vintage Books, 1995), 3.

29. Toni Morrison, *The Bluest Eye* (New York: Alfred A. Knopf, 1970), 48–50.

30. For a sustained philosophical analysis of the white gaze *vis-à-vis* the Black body, see George Yancy, *Black Bodies, White Gazes: The Continuing Significance of Race* (Lanham, MD: Rowman & Littlefield, 2008).

31. Outlaw has suggested that Black people were bombarded with such overwhelming racist absurdity that the issue for some Blacks became: "Should I continue or should I commit suicide." Under the weight of white racism, the disjunction became viable.

32. Frantz Fanon, *The Wretched of the Earth* (New York: Grove Press, 1963), 47.

33. Fanon, *The Wretched of the Earth*, 47.

34. West, "The Black Underclass and Black Philosophers," 357.

35. George Yancy, "Angela Y. Davis," in *African American Philosophers, 17 Conversations*, 23.
36. Yancy, "Angela Y. Davis," 23.
37. Outlaw, *On Philosophy and Race*, 25 (my emphasis).
38. George Yancy, "Lewis R. Gordon," in *African American Philosophers, 17 Conversations*, 112.
39. Yancy, "Lewis R. Gordon," 112.
40. George Yancy, "Laurence Thomas," in *African American Philosophers, 17 Conversations*, 293.
41. Leonard Harris, "Introduction," in *Philosophy Born of Struggle: Afro-American Philosophy from 1917*, ed. Leonard Harris (Dububue, IA: Kendall/Hunt, 1983), ix.
42. Yancy, "Lewis R. Gordon," 112.
43. George Yancy, "Anita L. Allen," in *African American Philosophers, 17 Conversations*, 172.
44. Mills, *Blackness Visible*, 10.
45. Yancy, "Anita L. Allen," 168.
46. George Yancy, "Albert Mosely," in *African American Philosophers, 17 Conversations*, 145–55.
47. See Bernard Boxill, *Blacks and Social Justice*, revised edn. (Lanham, MD: Rowman & Littlefield, 1992).
48. Yancy, "Cornel West," 38.
49. Linda Furgerson Selzer, *Charles Johnson in Context* (Amherst, MA: University of Massachusetts Press, 2009), 27.
50. Mills, *Blackness Visible*, 9.
51. W. E. B. Du Bois, *The Souls of Black Folk* (1903; reprint, New York: New American Library, 1982), 45–6.
52. Frantz Fanon, *Black Skin, White Masks*, trans. Charles Lam Markmann (New York: Grove Press, 1967), 115.
53. George Yancy, "Situated Black Women's Voices in/on the Profession of Philosophy," in *Hypatia: A Journal of Feminist Philosophy*, vol. 23, no. 2 (2008), 155.
54. T. Denean Sharpley-Whiting, "Thanatic Pornography, Interracial Rape, and the Ku Klux Klan," in *A Companion to African-American Philosophy*, ed. Tommy L. Lott and John P. Pittman (Malden, MA: Blackwell, 2005), 410.
55. Dorothy Roberts, *Killing the Black Body: Race, Reproduction, and the Meaning of Liberty* (New York: Vintage Books, 1997, 1999), 11.
56. George Yancy, "Adrian M. S. Piper," in *African American Philosophers, 17 Conversations*, 59.
57. See Alison Bailey's "On Intersectionality and the Whiteness of Feminist Philosophy," forthcoming in George Yancy, *The Center Must Not Hold* (Lanham, MD: Lexington Books).
58. Fanon, *Black Skin, White Masks*, 112.
59. Outlaw, *On Race and Philosophy*, 29–30.
60. I would like to thank philosopher Clarence S. Johnson for suggesting that the negative/positive distinction that I draw here be made more explicit.
61. Mills, *Blackness Visible*, 9.

62. Yancy, "Cornel West," 39.

63. Yancy, "Leonard Harris," 216.

64. Yancy, "Laurence Thomas," 291.

65. Yancy, "Laurence Thomas," 291, 292.

66. George Yancy, "Michelle M. Moody-Adams," in *African American Philosophers, 17 Conversations*, 126.

67. Yancy, "Robert E. Birt," 352.

68. Paget Henry, "Afro-American Studies and the Rise of African-American Philosophy," in *A Companion to African-American Studies*, ed. Lewis R. Gordon and Jane Anna Gordon (Malden, MA: Blackwell, 2006), 238.

69. Lewis R. Gordon, *An Introduction to Africana Philosophy* (Cambridge: Cambridge University Press, 2008), 111.

70. The reader will note that within the context of the history of African American philosophy, Charles Johnson and Tom Slaughter wrote seminal pieces deploying a phenomenological approach to Black body. These were two early and formative pieces in the tradition of what is now termed Africana philosophy of existence. Johnson's "A Phenomenology of the Black Body" was written as early as 1975, and was subsequently published in the Winter 1976 issue of *Ju-Ju: Research Papers in Afro-American Studies*. Johnson's article appeared prior to Thomas F. Slaughter Jr.'s "Epidermalizing the World: A Basic Mode of Being Black," which was included as a chapter in Leonard Harris's *Philosophy Born of Struggle*. For the first edited text to engage Africana philosophy of existence, see *Existence in Black: An Anthology of Black Existential Philosophy*, ed. Lewis R. Gordon (New York: Routledge 1997). Describing two features that run throughout the chapters within that text, Gordon notes, "The interesting thing about all of the essays is that all of them featured arguments (1) rejecting essence as a feature of human being and (2) supporting the importance of recognizing the sociohistorical context in which we theorize." See Yancy, *African American Philosophers 17 Conversations*, p. 105. It is important to note the meta-philosophical features that I have identified within this chapter regarding African American philosophy and the two salient lines of argument that Gordon identifies within his text.

71. Philosopher Clarence S. Johnson is thanked for this point.

72. Kuklick's reference to Du Bois appears to be limited to the former as a public intellectual.

73. See *I am Because We Are: Readings in Black Philosophy*, ed. Fred Lee Hord (Mzee Lasana Okpara) and Jonathan Scott Lee (Amherst, MA: University of Massachusetts, 1995); *Reflections: An Anthology of African American Philosophy*, ed. James A. Montmarquet and William H. Hardy (Belmont, CA: Wadsworth/Thomson Learning, 2000); and, *A Companion to African-American Philosophy*, ed. Tommy L. Lott and John P. Pittman (Malden, MA: Blackwell).

74. John H. McClendon, "The African American Philosopher and Academic Philosophy: On the Problem of Historical Interpretation," in *The APA Newsletter on Philosophy and the Black Experience*, vol. 4, no. 1 (Fall 2004), 8.

75. See McClendon, "The African American Philosopher and Academic Philosophy," 7; and www.essortment.com/all/richardgreener_pws.htm.

76. I would like to thank John McClendon for information about the work of Francis Monroe Hammond. See McClendon's "On the Politics of Professional Philosophy: The Plight of the African American Philosopher," in George Yancy, *Latin-American and African-American Philosophers on the Profession of Philosophy* (New York: SUNY Press, forthcoming).

77. The reader will note that Frederick Douglass, also born enslaved, is a pivotal figure within the context of African American philosophical thought and tradition, and wrestled with poignant philosophical issues such as the self-Other dialectic, religious hypocrisy, freedom, struggle, and social progress. See *Frederick Douglass: A Critical Reader*, ed. Bill E. Lawson and Frank M. Kirkland (Malden, MA: Blackwell, 1999).

78. Yale University was the first American university to grant the PhD in philosophy in 1866. See www.pragmatism.org/dmap.

79. It is important to note that Booker T. Washington also attended Hampton and came under the influence of Armstrong's pedagogical philosophy regarding the education of Blacks. In fact, it was Armstrong who made Washington head of Tuskegee Institute in Alabama.

80. William M. Banks, *Black Intellectuals: Race and Responsibility in American Life* (New York: W.W. Norton, 1996), 42.

81. www.nmhschool.org/magazine/2003_fall/no_slave.php. See Peter Weis, "No Slave to Fortune," 1978.

82. See Weis, "No Slave to Fortune."

83. Thomas Nelson Baker, "Not Pity but Respect," *Alexander's Magazine*, vol. 2 (May 1906), 111.

84. Thomas N. Baker, "Ideals" (Part 1), *Alexander's Magazine*, vol. 2 (September 1906), 28.

85. See Baker File at Hampton University Archives under "Items of Interest," *Southern Workman* (April 1908).

86. "Rev. Dr. T. Nelson Baker Says Hampton Institute Is Doing A Miraculous Work," *The Berkshire Eagle* (October 30, 1919). See Baker file at Hampton University Archives), n.p.

87. Baker, "Not Pity but Respect," 112.

88. Thomas N. Baker, "The Ethical Significance of the Connection Between Mind and Body" (unpublished dissertation, 1903).

89. For a more detailed treatment of the thought and life of Baker, see George Yancy, "On the Power of Black Aesthetic Ideals: Thomas Nelson Baker as Preacher and Philosopher," *The A.M.E. Church Review*, vol. CXVII, no. 384 (2001), 50–67.

90. www.jtamec.org/gilbertjones.htm.

91. Gilbert H. Jones, *Education in Theory and Practice* (Boston, MA: The Gorham Press, 1919), 14.

92. Jones, *Education in Theory and Practice*, 38.

93. For a more detailed treatment of Jones' life and work, see George Yancy, "In the Spirit of the A.M.E. Church: Gilbert Haven Jones as an Early Black Philosopher and Educator," *The A.M.E. Church Review*, vol. CXVIII, no. 388 (2002), 43–57.

94. Jones, *Education in Theory and Practice*, 38.

95. Jones, *Education in Theory and Practice*, 216.

96. Jones, *Education in Theory and Practice*, 39.
97. Jones, *Education in Theory and Practice*, 274.
98. William Jones, "Crisis in Philosophy: The Black Presence," in *Radical Philosophers' News Journal* (August 1974), 40.
99. From an unpublished interview with Jones, spring 1997.
100. George Yancy, "Howard McGary, Jr.," in *African American Philosophers, 17 Conversations*, 85.
101. George Yancy, "Tommy L. Lott," in *African American Philosophers, 17 Conversations*, 195.
102. This information was obtained through a personal correspondence. During this time, Green was influenced by Roy D. Morrison after taking his course on Søren Kierkegaard. Morrison taught at Wesley seminary in Washington, DC, where he explored issues around Black philosophy of culture and religion. At the time, Green was at Howard University where he was obtaining a Master's degree in religion and a doctorate in divinity.
103. Yancy, "Cornel West," 46.
104. Yancy, "Cornel West," 46 (emphasis added).
105. Yancy, "Howard McGary, Jr.," 84.
106. It was sponsored by the Johnson Foundation: Wingspread Conference Center in Racine, Wisconsin.
107. It was in this course that Davis got students to compare Douglass's understanding of the slave-master relationship with particular passages in Hegel's *Phenomenology*.
108. Within this historical context, Outlaw mentions Howard McGary, Jr., Leonard Harris, Joyce Mitchell Cook, Bernard Boxill, William Jones, the late Robert C. Williams, Ifeanyi Menkiti, Robert Chemooke, Albert Mosley, John Murungi, Tom Slaughter, Laurence Thomas, Cornel West, Bill Lawson, George Garrison, and Johnny Washington. See Outlaw, *On Race and Philosophy*, xxix. The reader will note that Charles Johnson, the prominent philosopher-literary figure, was a student of Tom Slaughter at Southern Illinois University. In her groundbreaking text *Charles Johnson in Context* (Amherst, MA: University of Massachusetts Press, 2009), Linda Selzer notes, "But in 1974 both Slaughter and Johnson entered the Ph.D. program in philosophy together at SUNY Stony Brook." Within this remarkable text, Selzer does an excellent and insightful job of situating Johnson within the historical context of African American philosophy.
109. Outlaw, *On Race and Philosophy*, xxix.
110. Yancy, "Adrian M. S. Piper," 61.
111. Adrian M. S. Piper, "Xenophobia and Kantian Rationalism," in *African-American Perspectives and Philosophical Traditions*, ed. John P. Pittman (New York: Routledge, 1997), 189.
112. Piper, "Xenophobia and Kantian Rationalism," 189.

CHAPTER 11

Song and Dance Nexus in the Africana Aesthetic: An Approach

Melanie Bratcher

University of Oklahoma

Kugusa Mtima (to touch the heart) is a Kiswahili term which has the advantage of helping us to understand our Africanness. It is the experience of being "touched," or "moved," "affected" by a self-consciously created form/phenomenon. These expressions are powerful energies which act on reality and act on us. They have the ability to change reality as we have. The concept of *Kugusa Mtima* takes "aesthetic" beyond "beauty" and "pleasure," expands it and places it into the context of the profound African understanding/ experience of the universe.[1]

Marimba Ani's definition of Africana Aesthetics cogently states the import of studies in African Aesthetics especially for African people.[2] Our conceptions of the universe come to the fore and provide maps with which the journey of our dramas can be traced. There is no history or culture or mythology without the facts of its art. Quite telling in her definition, which excludes the word "art," is the fact that our aesthetic goes beyond "fundamental issues in the philosophy of arts" for "art" is a term that is not without debate.[3]

The modes, patterns, percussiveness, rhythms, forms, and styles that form our existence are reflected in expressions of conditions that might be called artistic creation—authenticity becomes discovery, and discovery informs authenticity. When one examines the relationship of African artistry to the reality these creations represent, the world of compellingly liberating processes is eminent. Any such examination is a pointed source of spiritual and psychological uplift for Africans and can foster cross-cultural understanding and communication.

My modal approach to Kugusa Mtima—the Africana Aesthetic—privileges a focus on motion, the nexus of song and dance specifically, and ways it can be used to teach Africana Aesthetics. This discussion therefore moves through various scenes, exploring some of my practices in pedagogy, paradigm construction, and applied aesthetics. It must be noted that in aesthetic studies three confluent concepts prevail: science, perception, and beauty. Culturally-centered usage of these concepts is central to the formation of perspective in the evaluation of Africana art forms. Students learn to capture and report their intuition/logic process as a method (science); describe their visceral/analytical/metaphysical response (perception); and form their critique, using culturally-centered canons, rules, and theories to find elements of functionality (beauty).

From this perspective, I enter my classroom and begin to explain my approach by teaching students that *Kugusa Mtima* will best be understood if three questions accompany their epistemic journey: Why should I care about Africana Aesthetics and the aesthetic families that inform it? What will I learn from an introduction to this course of study that may inform my understanding of beauty—my own and in the world? What can I do with this knowledge, especially in terms of understanding Black, African, Caribbean–African Diaspora experiences?

A focus on motion—that is to say, an exploration or navigation that lends itself to assessing affect and effect in the flow of one sound to another sound, or the way a frame might be situated within a larger frame, or even why a step is placed behind a previous step and so on—is important for the students' understanding this process-oriented way of knowing. Moving students into a meaningful understanding of African culture, history, and mythology begins, literally and figuratively, by exposing them to the ancient, sacred, and complex conceptions of *Kugusa Mtima and Neferu* (that which is good and beautiful) in Africana "art" forms and experiences. This kind of exploration helps students understand Africaness[4] in the way Uya expresses its helical core,

The past ties the living community into the world of ancestors. The dead, or those who have left this present reality to the other, for they are not really dead, affects what goes on in the present community. In other words, laying a claim to authority becomes a correlation between pastness and sacredness. This is one of the reasons why the past in most African societies is conceived in mythological terms. It becomes mythical only because pastness, long enough, assures, the dimensions of sacredness.[5]

This fundamental dimension of the examination process enables students to better understand their own beauty in relation to their pastness. Like the nexus of pastness and sacredness, the nexus that song and dance share is central in African artistic creativity. Approaching the study of Africana Aesthetics through the nexus of song and dance initiates an approximation and embodiment of this "pastness" and "sacredness," and ultimately is a means of examination that transfers ancestral truths and sacred judgments into actual experiences.

SCENE ONE: PEDAGOGICAL TIDBITS

Imagine a professor entering a classroom, standing front and center, mentally noting that 30–45 seats are filled with eager, stoic, attentive, and even some text-messaging students. She then puts her left foot forward, mimicking the statuesque pose of the Ancient Egyptian (Kemetic) pharaohs. She asks, "If I proceed to walk, which foot will likely step forward?" They giggle and respond, "The right foot." The professor then asks, "Why am I asking you this?" They respond, baffled, with shrugging shoulders, "I don't know." So, she explains, "This is the way I proceed to walk well," and of course, there is no lack of confusion on the students' faces.

"To walk well," she adds, "begins when you first proceed to understand your environment based on the intuit. This is the wisdom of Ancient Egypt. To know a thing is to feel it, and feeling is a function of intuition—of the right brain. By standing with the left foot forward, one can commence an engagement with the world where all of its interrelated forces (*Ntu*) become accessible in a pre-perceptive mode that is intuitive—where an immediate knowledge of something is validated. This literal axiological Stance and its consequent worldview is one of the most important lessons the Ancient Egyptians taught the continent we know as Africa." At this point, the look on the students' faces is priceless. As the professor instructs the students on the culturally-centered location of their feet that will enable them to walk well, they do not yet realize they are being prepared for their walk into Africana Aesthetic experience.

[T]he very processes by which life is maintained tend to throw it out of gear with its surroundings. Therefore, when life continues, and if it expands, there is a triumph over factors of opposition and conflict. Disequilibrium becomes balanced. Hence, balance and harmony are attained through rhythm. Equilibrium is borne out of struggle and because of tension. Form or content is created during the process of reaching a stable equilibrium. This rhythmic movement between the loss and restoration of equilibrium is characteristic of all living creatures. But it is with human beings [Bantu] that this movement becomes conscious activity.[6]

Like Swindell's life-riddled description of African American music, their walks will be tempered by a focus on self-awareness of their potential or probable, if not pervasive, selective perception processes. This well-rooted selective perception process will be actively, asymmetrically countered with a keener application of Africa-centered perception processes. Dismantling and balancing of destructive bias are necessary. Consider Yhema Glendola Mills'[7] discussion of the ways in which conscious and unconscious "ethnocentric" bias has affected analyses of African dance and consequently the images to which many selectively resort when they think about African dance. The resulting images have tended to be negative, hinged on descriptions like primitive, wild, untamed, and, of course, lascivious.

While these kinds of biased descriptions are continually debunked as brutal and oppressive objectifications, they tend to remain at the core of the selective perceptions of those who observe or study African dance. Regardless of so-called "race," this ethnocentric bias sadly has been evidenced in my classes when I have asked students to describe African dance. How then can Beauty, with its numerous yet commonly oriented African modes and meanings, ever be perceived as intrinsic to African dance, or song, or visual art, or plastic art, or orature? In such a context, there is little chance that one could say the "art" walks well or touches the heart. For centuries, perceptions of African motion (phenomenon) have been dislocated, distorted, removed from the sacred pastness, the Pharaoh Stance—the ancestors.

At this point, the difficulty of explaining why anyone should care about Africana Aesthetics begins to decrease, hopefully. If only you, the students, could feel how Africana song dances from phrase to phrase, surely this confounded "Why?" would become less of a puzzle and more of a revelation. To help diminish the confusion, students are instructed to stand as the pharaohs stand. This time, however, a few vital values are to become evident to them.

The assignment I give to simplify the "Why" is as follows. Choose two pictures of people you think are beautiful and then describe in explicit detail why each is so. Oh! Upon return, they sing the words of description as colorfully as Pitchy Patchy's[8] costume in a Jonkunnu masquerade and as buoyantly as the motion of his dance-like cartwheels and percussiveness. From phrase to phrase, as they describe the tangible and intangible beauty of *their* people in the pictures, the Pharaoh Stance becomes more and more innate—many describe from the places where their hearts are touched, where they are walking well. A typical proclamation: "She is beautiful because of her big, round, light brown eyes and she is really beautiful because she is caring, loving, disciplined, giving, compassionate, calm, smart, and funny. She is my beautiful mom/sister/aunt/cousin."

We are still in the Pharaoh Stance, and the latter portion of this description provokes one of the most corporeal and spiritual definitions of beauty. Beauty is as beauty does—like Nefertiti, who was named such because of her deeds of beauty and goodness, of *Neferu*. It is a beautiful Stance, a righteous axis from which to proceed. From here one can perceive the world as infinitely interrelated forces and functions, where intuit and logic are in balance and harmony, in stride with the principles of *Maāt*.[9]

A sort of communal pastness is present; tangible and intangible perceptions of beauty are inextricably linked in the Pharaoh Stance—in the African worldview. *Their* people in the pictures become *our* people in the pictures. We are all interrelated forces! All things, words, thoughts, emotions, objects are interrelated forces! Beauty in Africana art forms may impact the ways that they perceive it in themselves. Keep on reflecting that Pharaoh Stance. The resounding question will be: Does it walk well?" This is the crux of evaluation.

SCENE TWO: PASTNESS AND PARADIGM ON PARADE

Key to my arrival at approaching Africana Aesthetics through the nexus of song and dance is my Afrocentric training at Temple University. Steeped in the Diopian[10] perspective that the culture of Africa will linger suspended in the air until Africa-centered scholars have the courage to unite it with the culture of Kemet (Ancient Egypt), I learned to look toward our ancient pastness as a source of correctness and epistemology. Such is the fodder for my pedagogical applications of the Pharaoh Stance—a principle taught by Cheikh Anta Diop's pupil and scholarly peer, Theophile Obenga.[11]

In Obenga's Ancient African Civilizations course, I studied the hieroglyphics known as *Mdw N<u>t</u>r* ("God's Words"/"Divine Speech") in Ancient Egypt, and the impetus of sound, even in a "dead" language, was penetrating. This coupled with inculcation in *African Aesthetics* and *African Dance* courses, specifically Kariamu Welsh's[12] Umfundalai technique of Contemporary African Dance, generated in me a learning style from which I now teach. Instinctively, I used/performed sound rhythms and song to commit Umfundalai movements to muscle memory, emotive memory, and cultural memory—a phenomenon that Molefi Asante would refer to as the "Circle of Memory", a place where "myths walk the syntax, and the soul is invested in the sentences."[13]

These performances of sound lent themselves to a unique conception of Sound Motion—that song and dance nexus—where philosophies and mytho-forms of African dance converge and become a matrix of canons against which I analyze songs and performances of sound. This is a traditional construction with a dynamic modal application. Bekerie deals with the oral traditions of Africa denoting that,

> According to an African proverb, "to say is to do," speech-centered knowledge is relevant in the construction of the ancient African past
> . . . To Africans, oral history is not only an article of the past but also a living "breathing" body of the present and future. Oral traditions cover virtually every aspect of life in society except that they may not provide quantifiable data or adequately mirror unconscious change. They are however, invaluable to reconstruct the socioeconomic-religious life of African communities.[14]

Like dance, song and sound, even when silent, are in motion. By continually focusing on motion, I began to record qualitative and quantitative patterning, modality, and stylization in the creative expressions of African experiences. Ever present, pastness shaped potentiality. Thus, the nexus of song and dance—the motion that lie at the core of our oral traditions—infused my approach to the Africana Aesthetic. This sense of Sound Motion begs the questions: What does the art form say to you? What does it say about the artists' experiences, about the experiences of their like-experienced people? Literally and figuratively, contained within this hearing sense or Oral Principle is motion sensibility.

Our communal creative expressions are well served through evaluations that employ this meta-sensibility.[15] Consider, for instance, Fiagbedzi's discussion on *African Musical Arts Aesthetics*. It reveals that an Ewe person's typical response to a musical/vocal event might be: "It walks well."[16] That there is an innate use of motion sensibility applied to sound moved me even closer to motion as a canonical means of establishing and understanding values in musical events and consequently in what our Western consciousness calls "art": sculpture, painting, literature, photography, film, etc. Additional questions leaped from my heart: How does the "art" move? How does it move you?

"When [culture, that is] daily activities, values, and behavioral preferences are concentrated in a conscious [and arguably subconscious or intuitive] process of creative expression, they become cultural forms of the highest order, what we call the arts—music, literature, sculpture, painting, dance, photography, etc."[17] "Black" culture and its arts act as a cornerstone in the discussion of Africana Studies. Africana Aesthetics grounds and highlights the intimate and intricate relationship between African cultural experiences and creative expressions. The former has always been the core from which the latter surfaced. Likewise, the latter has always contained mysteries that help to unlock the former.

As a student, I began to collect the tools with which to decipher and articulate varied and relevant nuances of African philosophy, culture, history, and heritage by studying motion in Africana art forms. As a teacher, I proffer the nexus of song and dance—Sound Motion—to my students. This nexus is omnipresent and persuades the valuation of Africana art in the questions: Does it walk well? Do I walk well? Do we walk well? Indeed, every question is a profound statement! And with students now situated in the Pharaoh Stance, definition, explanation, and examples of the Africana Aesthetic can commence.

SCENE THREE: APPLIED AESTHETICS THROUGH THE NEXUS

The way that singers employ nuances of sound shapes the words of their stories. Generally speaking, when such nuances of sound are examined using aesthetic rules, the science of perception is engaged. Taking it a step further, that is, when science and perceptions are examined in order to extract the function of those sound nuances, one is delving into a form of applied aesthetics. Robert Farris Thompson defines African Aesthetics in this kind of applied form as "a mode of intellectual energy that only exists when in operation, *i.e.* when standards are applied to actual cases and are reasoned."[18]

Consider the following from an African Aesthetic examination of African American female singers:

> Singers are not always aware that their stylization of sound is decidedly African . . . they may not be aware that those sound effects are connected to African cultural values. However, many African American singers use specific sound motions and sound qualities, such as slurs, guttural tones, bends, drops, moans, shouts, raspiness, and call-and-response to express something deeper than the lyrics alone can convey. [African singers'] compositions express traditions of survival—flexibility—and African motion is about flexibility and vitality[19] . . . their performances turn words into sound motion, and there is a source for every sound motion. That source is spirit.[20]

When the heart is touched—*Kugusa Mtima*—in the African context it is a matter of spirit. To explain this statement, the next example of African Aesthetics explores Sound Motion, employing a song and dance nexus.

NINA SIMONE'S *FOUR WOMEN*

Simone's[21] song explores four "types" of Black women who in terms of strength are prototypical and in terms of weaknesses are stereotypical. The stereotypes of the women form the crux of Simone's words. There is 1) black skin, wooly hair, long-armed Aunt Sarah; 2) yellow skin, long hair, mulatto-syndromed Saffronia 3) tan skin, fine hair, sexually prostituted Sweet Thang; and 4) brown skin, rough-and-"bitta", slave-heritage-crippled Peaches. Each had strengths and weaknesses that were forged in the fires of America's various types of enslavement—mental, physical, psychological, economic, and social.

However, the prototypes of the women form the crux of Simone's sound effects. It is the prototype of physical, spiritual, and mental fortitude that my students most easily identify with when they think back to the exercise on tangible and intangible aesthetics undertaken at the beginning of the course. They begin to see the four women in terms of their own family members.

The effect of Simone's sounds is felt, and therefore perceived, through motion. These motions shatter the stereotypes. The strength evoked by the plight of the elderly but efficacious Aunt Sarah resonates through each woman's story, each student's story to some extent. Follow along as Simone's Sound Motioning is examined.

She sings, "My back is strong / strong enough to take all the pain / It's been inflicted again and again and 'gain, 'gain, 'gain, 'gain, 'gain, 'gain, 'gain, 'gain, 'gain 'gain."[22] It is Simone's repetition of the word "'gain" in a (down-down-down-down-down-down-down-up-up-up-up-up-up-up) motion that penetrates the listener. Does Simone's Sound Motion walk well? That word can certainly be perceived as walking well; moving the heart or spirit from feeling low to feeling lifted.

Because perceiving sound is so intangible, it is difficult to describe in brief and understandable terms. Articulating perception of sound may be more easily attained in a scientific mode when one looks to established rules in Africana Aesthetics. Based on my knowledge, this is where the song and dance nexus becomes key.

When African Aesthetic algorithms like repetition, get-down, and Kinat[23] are applied to this kind of Sound Motioning, one gets closer to communicating what has been perceived. Repetition highlights an accountability for every note/sound[24] in the sense that each "'gain" could represent centuries of pain and perseverance, or breaking cycles of psychological bondage, or picking away at the locks that shackle the minds of many Black women with respect to standards of beauty, or literally the imagery of cat-o'-nine tails landing on the backs of enslaved Africans, or even the most banal contextualization of pain in romantic love stories.

Repetition serves to intensify the effect and leads to a climax. Simone's execution of this particular device exacts Africana Aesthetics in a manner that opens the door to exploring its aesthetic families, particularly rules found throughout the "African" and "Black" Aesthetic compounds. Both contain interchangeable modal rules and are enormous repositories from which those rules can and should be applied to African art forms. Movement, motion, the idea of walking become accessible constructs for students to use to communicate their perceptions.[25]

Also evident in Simone's Sound Motioning is a combination of West African dance notation-based "get down" quality and East African song symbolization-based "Kinat" characteristic.[26] The way she sounds out "'gain" in a down-down-down-down-down-down-down-up-up-up-up-up-up-up pattern lends itself to physical exploration of the movement pathway. Here, I make use of dance to engage my students in applied aesthetics. Not unlike the way I used song to commit movement to memory— Asante's "Circle of memory"—I call my students to the Pharaoh Stance, where they eagerly turn inward to that visceral place of intuit, and I ask them to mimic the Sound Motion with their bodies.

Their movements tend to be motions centered in the bending and straightening of knees. This very "get down" is reverently regarded in African dance (across the continent) as a modal pathway to divinity, conjuring both closeness to and reverence for the earth. Quite appropriately, too, the ascending element in this motioning bears witness to the "Kinat." This characteristic of Fellasha singing is effectively praxis where both singer and listener are brought closer to the Divine. As combined by Simone, the pathway can be likened to that traveled by the Divine chariot which is recounted so often in African American gospel songs.

I have found that with this explanation, my students begin to comprehend just how far-reaching the application of Africana Aesthetic rules can be. We begin to concern ourselves with Simone's use of the "repetition-get-down-Kinat" algorithm in terms of painting, sculpture, poetry, dance, and, of course, song. Their Pharaoh Stances, coupled with this kind of basic algorithm, expand intuit to encompass the seeing of sound, hearing of color, tasting of motion, and various combinations of sensory knowing as logical; analytically part of the perception process.

We are then able to explore aesthetic rules offered by Larry Neal, Zora Neale Hurston, Amiri Baraka (LeRoi Jones), W. E. B. Du Bois, Addison Gayle, Jr., Leopold Senghor, John S. Mbiti, Kariamu Welsh, Janheinz Jahn, Kwame Nketia, John Chernoff, Alexis Kagame, Langston Hughes, Katherine Dunham, and numerous others. The works put forth by these emissaries of African pattern, form, philosophy, design, mode, Nommo, cultural tradition, and hope help students have deep insights into a world of misery and majesty, circumstance and circumvention, pain and power. The Africana Aesthetic opens up probability of humanistic understanding. Sensory knowledge becomes a journey often employing repetition. For example, I again draw on the colorful costume of Pitchy Patchy in a Jonkunnu masquerade dance. The red strips of fabric in his outfit lead to pondering the importance of the color red to the Dahomean deity Shango, which leads to explorations of Shango's energy in the Quilombos of Palmares, which leads to identifying Shango rhythms in Hip Hop beats, which leads to exploration of Sound Motion in the words of commercial rappers and Hip Hop lyricists, which leads back to circular movement in Pitchy Patchy's cartwheels, which seem to be a powerful device in the lyrical fierceness of conscious lyricists and unconscious rappers alike, which can be likened to circular movement in B-boy floor (earth) work, and so forth. There is discovery of a oneness, of commonality in the experiences of African people worldwide, especially in the last millennium, where the duality of oppression and overcoming have found manifestation in artistic re-presentations.

Not only does the example, exploration, and explanation of Simone's Sound Motion open the way for analyzing African art forms, it also elicits a song and dance nexus by which Black Aesthetic themes of struggle, survival, and triumph can be cross-referenced with African Aesthetic proverbial wisdom such as the Ethiopian proverb, "Move your neck according to the music." In this place, space, matrix of culturally centered science, the perception of beauty in art finds itself governing perception of beauty in my students' lives. Armed with language like that of Thompson's reporting on "the cool," Hurston's "the Mule," Baraka's "Blues People," Du Bois' "Sorrow Songs," Senghor's "Negritude," McKay's "Home to Harlem," and Simone's "Four Women," my students begin to listen to themselves and each other. Motion commenced from an intuitive Stance, abets communication, centered on liberation.

CONCLUSION

By showing "repetition" in my use of words and phrases like "Africana Aesthetics," "Kugusa Mtima," "motion," "walk(s) well," "Pharaoh Stance," and "Sound Motion" a flow of ideas, moving through various levels of intensity climaxes in the phrase "Song and Dance Nexus." Within this discussion the process of aesthetic understanding is explored in terms of 1) selective perception, 2) intuit-based perception, 3) pastness-centered perception, and 4) applied form perception. In this way I chart a course for exploring Africana art, highlighting beauty in function or "Art for Life's Sake." Although function lies deep within the Sound Motion structure of Simone's "Four Women"—Aunt Sarah is literally the pastness of her future types—bending knees downward took us closer to her truth. The reverberation of her strength moves us upward toward presence of self and world.

The song and dance nexus is key in the playing out of this aesthetic puzzle—of motion and pattern and form and quality and rule and mode. Hearts are touched and epistemics are expanded and so much so that Alan Merriam's suggestion—"there is a growing conviction among students of the aesthetic aspects of culture that both their technical and broader behavioral studies must assume far wider application"[27]—is manifest in my classes. This way of perceiving and applying intuit, pastness, spirit, and care for beauty is often actively applied by my students in their medical, political, artistic, athletic, community service, leadership, and even legal professions.

Not only do we explore "Does it walk well?" but also we explore "From what circumstances does it walk well?" Simone's Sound Motion exhibits values of flexibility and vitality; the kind of values that become the kinds of skills necessary for navigating struggle, exacting survival, and achieving triumph.[28] These very values are the kind my students describe in their assessment of why their people are beautiful. We learn that what makes people beautiful is in close proximity with what makes Africana art forms beautiful.

NOTES

1. Marimba Ani, "The African Aesthetic and National Consciousness," in K. Welsh Asante, ed., *The African Aesthetic: Keeper of the Traditions* (Westport, CT: Praeger, 1994), 65–6.

2. I use the term "African people" in the sense of a philosophical definition of Africa that asserts "Africa is wherever African people exist" (Welsh-Asante, class lecture, 1996).

3. "African Art through African Eyes" elucidates the issue of the term "art" specifically in the Bamana culture of Mali. There is no such word or concept as art in the Bamana language, as is the case in many African languages. This leads to a noteworthy statement about cultural conditioning and the road to introspection, "what [Westerners] can learn on the way [toward self-critique] is that there are values, aesthetic disciplines, and forms of beauty which are quite distinct from [their] own and it is that understanding that has to be the key to looking at art from other countries [cultures]." A. Forna, S. D. Camp, J. Herman, K. Varnedoe, H. L. Gates, and C. West, *Through African Eyes* (New York: Public Media Home Vision, 1995). For this outcome, to be positive, it should be harmonized with a strong commitment to a *Maātian* empathy with and edification of Africana culture, heritage, and history for what it is in all of its beauty, and not for what Westerners wish it to be.

4. The spelling of this word "Africaness" varies and can include "Africanness" and "African-ness."

5. O. E. Uya, *African History: Some Problems in Methodology and Perspectives,* Monograph Series 2 (Ithaca, NY: Africana Studies and Research Center, Cornell University, 1974), 7.

6. W. Swindell, "Aesthetics and African American Musical Expression," in Asante, *The African Aesthetic: Keeper of the Traditions,* 175–94.

7. Yhema G. Mills, "Is it is or is it ain't: The Impact of Selective Perception on the Image Making of Traditional African Dance," *Journal of Black Studies*, vol. 28, no. 2 (1997), 139–56.

8. Pitchy Patchy is a lively (male) character, often cited as the most popular in Jonkunnu celebrations. His costume consists of brightly colored strips of cloth (fashioned after the warrior attire worn as camouflage by Jamaican Maroons) and a square hat or feathered cap adorned with mirrors and tinsel. Jonkunnu is most notably known as a Jamaican traditional dance with origins in West Africa; however, it is celebrated throughout the Caribbean. I learned about Jonkunnu and Pitchy Patchy when I was a teaching assistant to Kariamu Welsh in Kingston, Jamaica at the Edna Manley College of Visual & Performing Arts in 2005. The *Jamaican Gleaner* newspaper has covered the celebration, highlighting its various characters over the years. Research on this masquerade celebration tends to exist in the form of music compact disks.

9. "*Maāt* is a fundamental concept for understanding Egyptian philosophy and spirituality. The icon or image of *Maāt* was represented as a beautiful young woman with an ostrich feather on top of her head . . . Depictions of *Maāt* are numerous and correlate attributes including: a goddess, the personification of law, order, rule, truth, right, righteousness, canon, justice, straightness, integrity, uprightness, and the highest conception of physical and moral law known to the Egyptians." T. Obenga, *Icons of Maāt* (Philadelpha, PA: The Source Editions, 1996), 1, 5. *Maāt* is key in approaching the goal of evaluating beauty in Africana Aesthetics because the nature of beauty and good(ness) is encompassed in *Maāt*.

10. Diopian refers to the seminal Senegalese scholar Cheikh Anta Diop (1923–86), whose re-evaluation of the role of African (Black) people in world history and culture led to a corroborated theory about the influence of African civilization on the course of world cultures. Armed with a breadth of disciplines, including linguistics, history, anthropology, chemistry, and physics, he argued that Ancient Egypt civilization produced the origins of culture and science. His assertions about the Black origin of this civilization, particularly based on evidence from his carbon-14 dating tests that proved heavy melanin content in Ancient Egyptian pharaohs, have catalyzed efforts by and for African peoples to claim greatness of heritage and debunk issues of inferiority. Amongst his great works are: *Roots of Black Civilizations: Myth or Historical Truth* (1967); *African Origins of Civilization: Myth or Reality* (1974); *Precolonial Black Africa* (transl. 1987); *The Cultural Unity of Black Africa* (transl. 1990); and *Civilization or Barbarism* (transl. 1991).

11. Congolese scholar Theophile Obenga is trained in Philosophy, History, Linguistics, Egyptology, Philology, Prehistory, and Education. He holds three Master's degrees and has a PhD in Letters, Arts and Humanities from Montpellier University, France. Obenga's outstanding method for teaching African historiography includes the use of *Mdw N t r* (Ancient Egyptian hieroglyphics) as a means to teach ancient African philosophy and culture. Obenga worked with Cheikh Anta Diop to end cultural imperialism's long-lasting attempt to whiten ancient Egypt. Obenga has authored over 100 books and journal articles, mostly in French. Amongst his great works in English are: *Ancient Egypt and Black Africa: A Student's Handbook for the Study of Ancient Egypt in Philosophy* (1992); *Readings in Precolonial Central Africa: Texts and*

Documents (1995); *A Lost Tradition: African Philosophy in World History* (1995); *Icons of Ma'at* (1996); and *African Philosophy: The Pharaonic Period, 2780–330 B.C.* (2004).

12. Welsh was formerly known as Kariamu Welsh Asante and has authored numerous scholarly books and articles on African dance. A contemporary dance choreographer and scholar, she has been awarded a National Endowment for the Arts Choreography Fellowship, a 1997 Pew Fellowship, a 1997 Simon Guggenheim Fellowship, and three Senior Fulbright awards. Welsh created the Umfundalai (Contemporary African dance) technique in 1970, which incorporates movements, sounds, music, rhythms, and philosophy from African cultures worldwide. Amongst her single authored and edited works are: *Zimbabwe Dance: Rhythmic Forces, Ancestral Voices* (2000); *Umfundalai: An African Dance Technique* (1997); and *African Dance: An Artistic, Historical, and Philosophical Inquiry* (1996).

13. Molefi K. Asante, "Afrocentricity and the Critique of Drama," in D. P. Aldridge and E. Lincoln Jones, eds., *Africana Studies: Philosophical Perspectives and Theoretical Paradigms* (Pullman, WA: Washington State University Press, 2007), 212.

14. A. Bekerie, "The Ancient African Past and the Field of Africana Studies," *Journal of Black Studies*, vol. 37, no. 3 (2007), 455.

15. It must be stated that while my focus is on "motion," any one form of art can become canon for any other form of art in African artistic expression. I profess the motion sense as a primary means of establishing a canonical matrix that cross-references all African "art" forms. Consider Ron Wellburn's statement, "In this combination of music and the body, the wedding of impulses, we find soul in its most expressive and resilient terms. Black [artists] will waste their [artistry] if they do not give articulation to the spirit of the dance motion" (1971, 133). Ron Wellburn, "The Black Aesthetic Imperative," in A. Gayle, Jr., ed., *The Black Aesthetic* (New York: Anchor, 1971), 126–42.

16. Nissio Fiagbedzi, *An Essay on the Nature of the Aesthetic in the African Musical Arts* (Nissio: Fiagbedzi Publisher, 2005).

17. A. Alkalimat, *Introduction to Afro-American Studies: A People's College Primer*, 6th edition (Chicago: Twenty-first Century Books and Publications, 1986), 167.

18. Robert F. Thompson, *African Art in Motion: Icon and Act* (Berkeley, CA: University of California Press, 1974), 1.

19. Thompson, *African Art in Motion*.

20. Melanie Bratcher, *Words and Songs of Bessie Smith, Billie Holiday, and Nina Simone: Sound Motion, Blues Spirit, and African Memory* (New York: Routledge, 2007), 90.

21. Nina Simone, the "High Priestess of Soul," in part wrote the song to relate her issues of self-esteem as far as physical beauty is concerned. Among her hundreds of recordings, the corpus of her songs revolved around themes of protest and freedom and race and/or cultural pride (1993). Her original compositions are the Black Aesthetic manifest—she sang the words and sounds that acted as "a corrective means of helping Black [African] people out of the polluted mainstream of Americanism, and [offered] logical, reasoned arguments as to why we should [aspire to our own cultural pride]. H. W. Fuller, "Introduction," in A. Gayle, ed., *The Black Aesthetic* (New York: Anchor, 1971), xxii.

22. Nina Simone, *Four Women* (New York: EMI Publishing Co., 1965).

23. "Kinat" is from the Ethiopian Ge'ez language and means "upward *glissando*." A corresponding term is *aKina* and "both terms are derived from the verb *maKnat*, 'to raise up.'" A. Kebede, *The Roots of Black Music: The Vocal, Instrumental, and Dance Heritage of Africa and Black America* (Trenton, NJ: Africa World Press, 1995). "Get down" is central in Robert Farris-Thompson's analysis and description of West African dance. Both "get down" and "kinat" are motion-oriented rules or diktats for evaluating Africana dance and song, and can easily be applied to other Africana art forms.

24. "'Swing' every note and every color strong," as described by Robert Farris Thompson in *African Art in Motion*, speaks to the concept of "Ephebism" or "vital aliveness." Pointedly, there becomes a focus on the balancing of "full sonority and attack" of notes "phrased with equal strength, equal force, [thus] creating a youthful buoyancy and drive" (1974), 7.

25. That students become open to seeking out "repetition" in additional forms of art is both a cornerstone and a capstone in the building up of aesthetic reasoning.

26. While I identify specific geographic regions of the continent, it is well established that dance and music traits share great commonality across the continent. M. K. Asante and K. Welsh Asante, eds., *African Culture: Rhythms of Unity* (Trenton, NJ: Africa World Press, 1985).

27. A. P. Merriam, *African Music in Perspective* (New York: Garland, 1982), 133.

28. Anger, war, and Black Nationalism are focal themes in the Black Aesthetic and Black Arts Movement (Fuller, "Introduction"). They were also focal points in Negritude. Aesthetic families like Negritude and the Black Aesthetic profoundly inform this discussion on Africana Aesthetics.

CHAPTER 12

Perspectives on Womanism, Black Feminism, and Africana Womanism

Maria D. Davidson

University of Oklahoma

and Scott Davidson

Oklahoma City University

INTRODUCTION

Scholarly criticism always happens after the fact. From an historical distance, scholars wonder whether Phillis Wheatley[1] *intended* that some of her poetry should be read through the lens of irony, or whether Linda Brent[2] *intended* Harriet Jacobs to be her alter-ego or an expression of her actual self (or both).[3] In addition to being a possible obstacle to understanding, historical distance can also be an aid to understanding, as when it allows scholars to perceive commonalities that might unite a group of writers, artists or theorists. For example, looking back on the past, literary scholars now label George Gordon Byron, Percy Bysshe Shelley, and John Keats as British Romantic poets,[4] and philosophers now label Søren Kierkegaard, Friedrich Nietzsche, and Jean-Paul Sartre[5] as existentialists, even when these thinkers might not have associated themselves with one another. The same can be said for the category of Womanist literature. Scholars today regularly classify authors such as Anna Julia Cooper, Jessie Redmon Fauset, Zora Neale Hurston, Gwendolyn Brooks, and Toni Morrison under the heading of Womanist literature.[6] This naturally raises the question as to what leads these authors to be placed under this category, and whether these authors are indeed related to one another in important ways or whether this category is merely imposed on them by scholars.

Before addressing those questions, we should first consider some benefits to the scholarly work of categorization. Categorization is not necessarily negative, as if it were only a limit imposed on the potential of a theorist or writer. The use of categories can provide important insights into the past, allowing us to discern common themes, styles, and modes of inquiry among a group of thinkers or writers. For instance, the existentialist category, though it would not be accepted by many existential authors themselves, can help to highlight a set of common themes and preoccupations among those thinkers, such as the themes of absolute freedom and individualism. And although Byron, Shelley, and Keats never referred to themselves as Romantics, the word Romantic is "strictly applicable to . . . some aspects of the intellectual and cultural character" from 1800–30.[7] The work of categorization in some cases can also allow us to transcend the bounds of place and time in order to find affinities between thinkers or writers working in different historical and social contexts.

It is this latter feature of categorization that should be of special interest in this context, because it corresponds to the Afrocentric principle of Sankofa. In Sankofa, the attitude toward the past is one where the past does not remain in the past but comes to life in the present. In this way, the work of categorization looks back to the past in order to keep the names, scholarly work, and artistic productions of our ancestors alive by seeing how they are relevant to and alive within the present. So, in what we may call a Sankofic spirit, this chapter will first examine the meaning of the category Womanism and then turn to the work of several Black women writers, both past and present, in order to discern some of the key features that led them to be classified as Womanist authors. In exploring this issue, the chapter will address the following questions:

1. What is Womanism?
2. How does Womanism differ from Black Feminism and Africana Womanism?
3. What are some of the dominant themes in Womanist literature?
4. Who are some of the major writers in the Womanist tradition?

ALICE WALKER AND WOMANISM

The term "Womanism" was coined by Alice Walker in her groundbreaking work *In Search of Our Mothers' Gardens: Womanist Prose*. In the opening pages, Walker explains that the term "Womanism" is derived from "*womanish*." The opposite of being "girlish," which for Walker means acting in a way that is "frivolous, irresponsible, not serious,"[8] to act "womanish" is for a woman to go about her business in a bold and daring way. Walker traces the adjective back to a "black folk expression of mothers to female children, 'You acting womanish,' i.e. like a woman . . . usually referring to outrageous, audacious, courageous, or *willful* behavior. Wanting to know more and in greater depth than is considered 'good' for one."[9]

Walker's definition of Womanism is clearly rooted in praxis because it defines a Womanist in terms of what she does and how she does it. Another, more subtle element of Walker's definition of Womanism is that it also includes a Sankofic project, because it uses actions and events from the past to inform the present. More specifically, the origin of Womanism is rooted in the relations maintained between mothers and daughters. So, in addition to evoking bold and daring ways of acting, Walker's definition of Womanism highlights the importance of relations not just between mothers and daughters but between all women. A Womanist, as Walker notes, is:

> A woman who loves other women sexually and/or nonsexually. Appreciates and prefers women's culture . . . and women's strength . . . committed to survival and wholeness of entire people, male and female. Not a separatist . . . Womanist is to feminist as purple is to lavender.[10]

This analogy—"Womanist is to feminist as purple is to lavender"—is probably the most often cited phrase of Walker's discussion of Womanism. While the analogy is beautifully poetic, more importantly it illuminates Walker's view of the key differences between Black women and White women on issues related, for example, to agency and community. "Second-wave feminists"[11] were typically White, middle-class, well-educated activists and thinkers who were primarily driven by the desire to confront gender-based oppression and violence. This is represented, for example, by Simone de Beauvoir's groundbreaking work *The Second Sex*,[12] Betty Friedan's *The Feminine Mystique*,[13] and Luce Irigaray's *This Sex which is not One*.[14] In their introduction to *Writing on the Body: Female Embodiment and Feminist Theory*, Katie Conboy, Nadia Medina, and Sarah Stanbury suggest that de Beauvoir's scholarly legacy lies in "her application of the philosophical categories of Self and Other to the division of gender."[15] As a result, de Beauvoir and other (mostly) White Feminists were able to pinpoint the various ways in which women are identified with their bodies and come to embody difference, because they are "trapped in immanence, defined and evaluated by its bodily shape, size, and function."[16] Men, on the other hand, come to represent the agency of the self which is "associated with the mind, it is an entity that floats free of a body or appears superior to bodily functions."[17] We can then see feminism, in general, as an attempt to destabilize the *categories* of man/woman and subject/other in order to unveil new possibilities for agency among women.

However, in response to the work of White Feminists, Walker, along with other Feminists of color/Womanists, highlights the extent to which the experiences and concerns of women of color are excluded from standard White Feminist discourse. White Feminism's exclusive focus on gender-based oppression leads it to play down the broader types of oppression experienced by Black and other women of color. More specifically, by placing its primary focus on the effects of gender oppression, White Feminism tends to ignore the underlying effects of social, economic, and racial oppression. In a similar vein to Walker, many other Black women thinkers, including Patricia Hill Collins,[18] bell hooks,[19] Michele Wallace,[20] Carol E. Henderson,[21] Cheryl Wall,[22] and Hortense Spillers,[23] have further elaborated the exclusionary practices of White Feminist discourses. Together, their work documents the various ways in which second-wave feminist discourse defines the category of woman in terms of the standards of White women's experience.

In *Feminist Theory from Margin to Center*, bell hooks[24] points out the limitations of mainstream White Feminist critiques of gender from the likes of Betty Friedan, whose analysis, she argues, was limited to a "select group of college-educated, middle-and upper-class, married white women—housewives bored with leisure, with the home, with children, with buying products who wanted more out of life."[25] hooks, like Walker, wants to expand the Feminist Movement by rendering visible the experiences of the *other*, women of color—those commodified others "who are daily beaten down, mentally, physically, and spiritually—women who are powerless to change their condition in life." "They are," she continues, "a silent majority. A mark of their victimization is that they accept their lot in life without visible question, without organized protest, without collective anger or rage."[26] Alicia D. Boisnier also recognizes the exclusionary tendencies of White Feminism when she observes that:

Several theorists suggest that Black women are less likely than White women to identify as feminist. Hemmons (1974) posited that the women's movement did not specifically address issues central to the concerns of Black women, and Kelly (2001) reiterated that, even today contemporary feminism fails to be relevant to young Black women's lives. Therefore, although Black women may support the premises of the women's movement, they may not ultimately identify with being feminist.[27]

Not to be misunderstood, Walker's definition of Womanism does acknowledge the validity of White Feminist issues, especially those related to gender equality and the right to political participation. Yet her claim, which is echoed by other Black women scholars, is that White Feminist discourse is limited. In positing the notion of Womanism, Walker sets out to establish a standpoint from which Black women (and all other women) can articulate their own concerns and visions. Such a space for interaction and discourse intends to provide Black women with a platform to critique and confront what Patricia Hill Collins[28] refers to as the interlocking systems of oppressions of race, class, and gender. Importantly, the analogy "Womanist is to feminist as purple is to lavender" reminds us that even though all women have a gender in common, gender is not necessarily the *sole* determining marker in a woman's life. Black women in particular need a theory that speaks to this difference—a theory that speaks to their unique embodiment as both *women* and *Black* within a society plagued by sexism and racism.[29]

WOMANISM AND BLACK FEMINISM

Clearly, one of the key tasks of Womanism is to establish a discourse in which the unique experiences and concerns of Black women can be voiced. This is echoed in Toni Morrison's statement, "I write all of the things I should have been able to read."[30] Extending Morrison's statement, Alice Walker writes: "I write not only what I want to read—understanding fully and indelibly that if I don't do it no one else is so vitally interested, or capable of doing it to my satisfaction—I write all the things *I should have been able to read.*"[31] Although Walker provided an early theoretical foundation for Womanism—a discourse that she hoped would be inclusive and empowering—more recently a number of Black women theorists have expressed skepticism toward her notion of Womanism. This skepticism is rooted in several important issues, including the fact that some Black women are feminists but do not approach issues of race, class, and gender from a Womanist—which they may perceive as code for Afrocentric—position.[32] As a testament to the importance of this debate, the *Journal of Feminist Studies in Religion* dedicated an entire volume to a discussion of Womanism.[33]

In her essay "Must I be a Womanist?" Monica A. Coleman writes from the perspective of a younger generation and claims that she is more comfortable calling herself a Black Feminist than a Womanist. Coleman argues that, unlike her mentors ("godmothers"),[34] she always had strong examples of Black women working in the discipline of Religious Studies. Inspired by women like Katie Geneva Cannon, Coleman observes:

> I never once doubted that I could have a place in religious
> scholarship. I never felt the pain that no one was talking about
> my experience, my literature, or my role models . . . I've also
> been shaped by black feminists, and I believe that I'm a part of a
> generation of women who have grown up (intellectually) during a
> time that takes womanism as a given. I'm not sure I'm a womanist.[35]

Coleman thus speaks for a generation which, unlike Walker and other early Black Womanists, was able to encounter the myriad experiences of Black women in both literature and theory. This might be taken as a sign that Womanism has become a victim of its own success, because it is largely due to the efforts of that earlier generation that these examples were available to younger generations. For members of younger generations, then, it might seem that Womanism is the product of a bygone era and no longer relevant to the realities facing women today.

More deeply still, Coleman goes on to identify several theoretical shortcomings that she finds with Womanism. One of these is its inability to address issues like homophobia. Coleman writes: "without giving detailed attention to the issue of sexual orientation, womanists paint a picture of black women as sisters, other-mothers, girlfriends, and loving church mothers, when there is much more to the picture."[36] For this reason, Coleman is concerned that Womanism imposes an overly restrictive definition on women and the relations between women, and thereby creates yet another essentialist paradigm in which Black women now become the principal signifiers. To be sure, Coleman's concern about Womanism's turn toward essentialism is well taken, because every attempt to formulate a theory and discourse based on issues related to gender, class, race, and sexual orientation is always open to the charge of essentialism.[37] Yet, if one pays close attention to Walker's definition of Womanism, it is clearly not exclusionary or restrictive in the ways that Coleman would suggest for Walker writes that a Womanist is:

> Traditionally universalist, as in: "Mama, why are we brown, pink, and yellow, and our cousins are white, beige, and black?" Ans.: "Well, you know the colored race is just like a flower garden, with every color flower represented."

For Walker, then, it is important to note that a Womanist is a universalist who accepts all kinds of different women and all kinds of different relations among women.

While theorists such as Coleman might regard Womanism as representing the concerns of an earlier generation of women, many others seem to use the terms Womanism and Black Feminism interchangeably. Indeed, Walker herself seems to use the terms interchangeably in writing that a Womanist is "a black feminist or feminist of color."[38] In"What's in a Name? Womanism, Black Feminism, and Beyond," Patricia Hill Collins observes that "like Walker, many African American women see little difference between the two [i.e. Black Feminism and Womanism] since both support a common agenda of black women's self-definition and self-determination."[39] Does this merely come down to a question of semantics or is there a genuine difference between the two? In what follows, we want to suggest that the difference between Womanism and Black Feminism is more than mere semantics and that there are significant differences between the two perspectives.

The debate between Womanism and Black Feminism is, in many ways, reflective of the way in which academic discussions *by* Black women and *about* Black women have matured and become more nuanced over time. Echoing the discussion above of inclusion and universalism, Hill Collins writes: "current debates about whether black women's standpoint should be named 'womanism' or 'black feminism' reflect this basic challenge of accommodating diversity among black women."[40] To distinguish between the two perspectives, then, we will suggest that Womanism can be characterized as an "internal discourse," while Black Feminism is an "external discourse." That is to say that Womanism is a perspective that speaks primarily to a Black audience about relations among Black people. According to Hill Collins, it "seemingly supplies a way for black women to address gender oppression without attacking black men."[41] By contrast, Black

Feminism is an external discourse that places greater emphasis on the relations between Whites and Blacks:

> Disrupt[ing] the racism inherent in presenting feminism as for-whites-only ideology and political movement. Inserting the adjective "black" challenges the assumed whiteness of feminism and disrupts the false universal of this term for both white and black women. Since many white women think that black women lack feminist consciousness, the term "black feminist" both highlights the contradictions underlying the assumed whiteness of feminism and serves to remind white women that they comprise neither the only nor the normative "feminist."[42]

Again, the goal is not to present Womanism and Black Feminism as mutually exclusive categories. On the contrary, here Womanism and Black Feminism offer different but complementary positions on issues affecting Black women. The push to differentiate them should not be construed as antagonistic for "African American women's efforts to distinguish between womanism and black feminism illustrates how black women's placement in the hierarchical power relations fosters different yet related allegiances to black women's self-defined standpoint."[43] Walker's notion of Womanism is thus rooted in the unique, embodied, irreducible experiences of Black women *and* their relationship to Black culture.

WOMANISM AND AFRICANA WOMANISM

Before we examine the difference between Womanism and Africana Womanism, it is important to note that, in spite of their critical differences, these two perspectives are united by a commitment to articulating theories from the standpoint of Black women. What further unites them is the recognition that Black women in the United States, like Black women around the world, "constitute an oppressed group."[44] Given this fact, Black Feminists, Womanists and Africana Womanists all seek to create relevant and "activist response[s]"[45] to the disenfranchisement that Black women throughout the world continue to face. Nevertheless, their points of contrast with respect to issues of community, gender, and sisterhood can help to illuminate a range of possibilities and different opinions on how best to rectify the oppression of Black women.

While the various labels mentioned here may seem like mere semantics, they have the potential to divide Black women scholars.[46] This divisiveness is discussed by Nikol G. Alexander-Floyd and Evelyn M. Simien in "Revisiting 'What's in a Name?': Exploring the Contours of Africana Womanist Thought," where they offer the following observation:

> The uncertainty and controversy surrounding naming practices reflect a concern with differences among individual Black women who wish to emphasize the primacy of their racial identity, particularly nationalist, and others who do not. At the heart of this debate . . . is a struggle to authoritatively name a political identity for black women: Black feminist, womanism, or Africana womanism. Such a question forces Black academics, intellectuals, and activists to reconsider longstanding notions of race loyalty and the hierarchy of interest within Black communities relative to the prioritization of race, class, and gender.[47]

As with Womanism and Black Feminism, there are important differences between Womanism and Africana Womanism that need to be highlighted, differences that ultimately have political implications.

Africana Womanists tend to argue that Womanism, as articulated by Walker, is incomplete. First, this refers to the fact that Walker does not provide a detailed discussion of its purpose and goals. The argument for the incompleteness of Womanism is developed, for example, in Clenora Hudson-Weems' *Africana Womanist Literary Theory*, where she notes that:

> Alice Walker's "womanism" pronouncements—literally a page and one-half—does little more than present a brief commentary on the shade of differentiation between what Collins notes "alternately call[ed] womanism and black feminism.[48]

More substantively, Hudson-Weems criticizes Womanism for its lack of a diasporic vision which incorporates the experiences of Black women outside of the US. According to Ama Mazama, it was Hudson-Weems who "coined the term Africana Womanism in 1987 out of the realization of the total inadequacy of feminism and like theories (e.g., Black Feminism, African Womanism, or Womanism) to grasp the reality of African women, let alone give us the means to challenge that reality."[49]

At the core of Hudson-Weems' disagreement with both Womanism and

Black Feminism is the idea that both perspectives seem to operate on the very same Western paradigms which have historically led to the exclusion of Black women. These paradigms, first articulated by White Feminists, speak from the normative position of Western society and its values, such as individualism and autonomy. This renders them incapable of articulating an authentic standpoint for Black women. In order to adequately represent and reflect the lived experience of Black women, feminists should embrace an Afrocentric understanding of women instead, one that emphasizes Afrocentric values of relations and community. From this central point of disagreement, we can identify a key difference between Womanism, Black Feminism, and Africana Womanism with respect to the idea of *agency*.[50]

Agency from an Africana Womanist perspective is closely related to the Afrocentric notion of *nommo*. Molefi Asante defines *nommo* as "the generating and sustaining power of the creative word."[51] As expressed by Asante and other scholars operating within an Afrocentric paradigm, the primacy of spoken language over written language is an Afrocentric idea insofar as the spoken world has been the primary form of communication in African culture. Adisa A. Alkebulan explains:

> Understanding *Nommo*, the power of the word, is primary to an understanding of the universe. Naming is a creative act. What we cannot conceive does not exist. And every human thought that is expressed becomes reality, that is, is spoken into being. Once a person names it, it moves into existence. The power of *Nommo* through naming creates life.[52]

For Hudson-Weems, to be an agent is to exercise the ability to name and to define oneself. Hudson-Weems believes that "self-naming and self-defining" is "the *raison d'être*, the very foundation upon which the critical paradigm of Africana Womanism rests."[53] While this might seem to parallel the Western ideal of autonomy, closer scrutiny will reveal a difference here between Womanism and Africana Womanism.

Both perspectives connect the notion of agency to the ability to speak on one's own, in one's own voice. The speaking subject, from a Womanist perspective, is closely related to the Western idea of subjectivity where one asserts one's own individuality through one's ability to speak on one's own. By contrast, from an Africana Womanist perspective, agency is not tied to individuality but to the importance of community. Describing the important connection between voice and community, Hudson-Weems notes:

> But the voice of Africana womanism will not and cannot be silenced, and like the true Africana womanist, who has never really needed to "break silence" or "find voice," the expressed sentiments of many feminist, I have continued . . . to uphold the Africana womanist agenda and priorities within Africana historical and cultural contexts. Such contexts are reflected in our ongoing struggle for the human rights of our entire family—men, women, and children.[54]

This sentiment regarding the primary importance of commitment to one's own community is supported by the work of Nikol G. Alexander-Floyd and Evelyn M. Simien. In addition to the importance of speaking for oneself, they state that Africana Womanism rests on two further principles: first, the need for Black women to stay focused on their families; and second, the need for Black women to remain connected to their communities, which includes seeing Black men as critical partners in the struggle to end oppression and to rebuild strong communities.[55] This definition of Africana Womanism, accordingly, marks a clear break with both Womanist and Black Feminist scholars, insofar as Africana Womanism places a greater value on the importance of service to the community over the individual well-being of individual women. At this point, with the centering of Black female identity on the Black community and relations to Black men, there are two questions that Womanists and Black Feminists might raise in reply. First, is Africana Womanism truly diasporic or does it restrict women's experience by imposing an Afrocentric identity on them? Second, does Africana Womanism ultimately become a theory that is not rooted in Black women's own experiences but rather in the needs and experiences of others?

To the former question, it could be argued that Africana Womanism is not truly diasporic in its scope. Black women living on the African continent, like Black women in the West, are diverse. Just as Black women in the US have struggled to establish an all-embracing perspective that can unite the diversity of their experiences, we should not assume that all Black women on the continent will easily fit into one category or set of values either. To the latter question of whether or not Africana Womanism is a theory rooted in the experiences of Black women, it can be argued that Africana Womanism's focus on Black women's responsibility to their families and communities does not adequately define Black women outside of the confines of traditional feminine roles. In light of the assault on the Black family structure, one cannot deny the importance of the call for strengthening Black families. And certainly we can respect Vivian Gordon when she writes:

> To address women's issues, therefore, is not only to address the crucial needs of Black women, it is also to address the historic primacy of the African and African American community; that is, the primacy of its children and their preparation for the responsibilities and privileges of mature personhood.[56]

Nevertheless, we may want to be wary of an account of Black female identity that does not envision Black women outside of their traditional roles in families and communities. While it is certainly not wrong to choose to be a wife or mother, the concern would be that Africana Womanism may limit the options available to Black women when it criticizes other strands of Feminism for their emphasis on "independence and freedom from family responsibility."[57]

Having identified some of the key differences between Womanism, Black Feminism, and Africana Womanism, we will now apply what we have learned about Womanism to the work of some Black women writers who are often categorized under the heading of Womanist literature.

WOMANIST LITERATURE AND THEORY

The question "What is Womanist literature?" recalls the discussion that opened this chapter, where it was asked how a group of writers who do not share the same historical time period and who did not necessarily understand themselves as Womanists or their work as Womanist literature could be united in this category. The key to defining Womanist literature is not to regard it as a limiting or closed category. This means that although Zora Neale Hurston's work, for example, might be defined as Womanist literature, her work can also be examined from a Black Feminist or Africana Womanist perspective, among others. In literature, Womanism signifies a style of interpretation whose aim is to open up the text to greater meanings. To define Womanist literature, we might propose the following definition: "Womanist literature is literature written by Black, Western women and narrated from the perspective of Black, Western female character(s) and addresses the lives, struggles, relationships, and concerns of Black female characters in search of their own agency primarily through finding their own voice."

Some of the key features of this definition of Womanist literature would be as follows. First, this definition roots Womanist literature within a Western framework. This acknowledges that, although Womanist literary theory may be an appropriate way of analyzing Black women in the West, it may not suitable for all Black women in the African Diaspora.[58] Second, this definition emphasizes that Womanist literature is authored by Black, Western women, and in so doing, it highlights the role of Black Western women's literary production. Third, inasmuch as it is told from the perspective of Black Western female characters, Womanist literature explores the unique experiences and ways of engaging the world that are part of the Black female standpoint. This leads to the final, and perhaps most significant, part of our definition: the search for agency through finding a voice. What, perhaps, makes Womanist literature different from Black Feminism and Africana Womanism is its emphasis on the development of Black women's agency through the use of language. To be sure, Black Feminism and Africana Womanism are also concerned with issues of agency and voice, but agency is the central concern for Womanism and thus gaining a voice is the central theme in Womanist literature. To be more precise, Womanist scholars are less concerned with the ways in which racism, classism, and gender oppression inhibit the agency of Black women. Instead, they are much more interested in showing how Black women, in spite of and in defiance of oppression, have nevertheless been able to articulate and develop their own agency. As stated by Stacey M. Floyd-Thomas: "Womanism is revolutionary. Womanism is a paradigm shift wherein Black women no longer look to others for their liberation, but instead look to themselves."[59] Seeing the focus of Womanism in this way, we will now have a good starting point from which to develop a Womanist reading of Hurston.

Although much is known about the life of Zora Neale Hurston,[60] what may not be as readily known is that without Alice Walker and the great scholar Robert Hemenway, we may not have her works today. Walker has powerfully stated that:

> a people do not throw their geniuses away . . . if they are thrown
> away, it is our duty as artists, scholars, and witnesses for the future
> to collect them again for the sake of our children . . . if necessary
> bone by bone.[61]

This is exactly what Walker did after coming across Hurston's name while "auditing a black literature class."[62] Like the other excluded Black women writers such as "Jessie Fauset, Nella Larsen, Ann Petry, Paule Marshall," Walker experienced Hurston as a "verbal footnote, to the illustrious all-male list that paralleled them."[63] Though Hurston was a rather successful writer during the Harlem Renaissance, she died in near-obscurity in 1959. Eventually, Walker was compelled by her experience *with* Hurston and her love *for* her to locate Hurston's grave in a snake-infested, unkempt Black cemetery in Fort Pierce, Florida.[64]

What draws Walker and other Womanist theorists to Hurston is the articulation of a longing for a type of freedom that allows us to act as agents but preserves our rootedness in the Black community.[65] Walker calls this "racial health" and it provides "a sense of black people as complete, complex, *undiminished*, human beings."[66] Hurston is widely known today for her literary masterpiece *Their Eyes Were Watching God*, where the world is introduced to the book's protagonist, Janie Crawford. Janie stands as a symbol for the Black female who struggles against the forces of silence and oppression in order to be able "tuh find out about livin' fur theyselves."[67]

Hurston actually begins *Their Eyes Were Watching God* at the end of the story, where Janie is returning to Eatonville after burying her third husband, Tea Cake. Janie is greeted by her friend, Pheoby, to whom she relates her tale. By beginning the story at the end, Hurston gives Janie the opportunity to exercise the agency that she has won. This sense of agency—the ability to tell one's own story—is the interpretive key to a Womanist reading of the text. The beginning of Janie's story is not atypical. Like many women, Janie is married to an older man, Logan Killicks, whom she does not love. Yet, what makes Janie's story extraordinary is that she does not accept her fate. Exercising her agency, she leaves Killicks for Joe Starks. Starks turns out to be domineering, but his death provides Janie with the financial means to care for herself and an increased confidence in her ability to live as a single woman. More extraordinary still is Janie's third marriage to Tea Cake, a marriage that she chooses for herself. Janie gives up the comforts of her life and heads further South with Tea Cake where they work as seasonal laborers.

After their attempt to flee a hurricane, Tea Cake is bitten by a rabid dog. He does not seek medical treatment in time and Janie is forced to kill him after he attacks her. In killing the love of her life, a Womanist reading might say that Janie displays a self-love that is able to transcend her attachment to Tea Cake. Alice Walker and other Womanists thus see Janie as a woman who, in spite of society's many attempts to silence her, was able to maintain a strong sense of herself. This sense of self is punctuated by her use of language throughout the text—by talking back to her first husband when she tells him that she is thinking about leaving him; by telling her second husband what she thought about him on his death bed; or by defending herself in a court trial against a Black community that would have seen her executed for killing Tea Cake. Throughout all of these situations, Janie displays a willingness and ability to speak for herself.

The works of Toni Morrison provide another good example of Womanist literature. Novels like *Sula* and *The Bluest Eye* are less about traditional feminist concerns of gender and more about how Black women struggle to gain a sense of agency and maintain their connection to one another. This emphasis on the importance of connections between women can be tied to Walker's definition of Womanism, where to be a Womanist is to be "a woman who loves other women sexually and/or nonsexually. Appreciates and prefers women's culture . . . and women's strength." In the relationship between Sula and Nel, for example, a web of connection is spun between women who love one another profoundly but are driven apart. As Morrison implies, the relationship between Sula and Nel is both natural and necessary to their own survival. They both come from homes that are ultimately unconcerned about their being, and therefore they attempt to find wholeness in each other. Yet, they are complete opposites—whereas Nel is passive and accepts society's expectations of Black women, Sula rejects the order of things. Their relationship is thus necessary if any balance whatsoever is to be maintained. Naturally, the two women establish their own agency in very different ways. Sula, the bolder of the two, exerts her own agency in ways that are shocking and extreme. For example, in order to protect Nel and herself from a group of boys, she cuts off the tip of her own finger and warns the boys that if she could do that to herself, they do not want to see what she would do to them. Nel, the more passive character, comes to exercise her agency only at the end of the novel when she is finally able to articulate her love for Sula:

> "All that time, all that time I thought I was missing Jude." And the loss pressed down on her chest and came up to her throat. "We was girls together," she said as though explaining something. "O Lord, Sula," she cried, "girl, girl, girlgirlgirl." It was a fine cry—loud and long—but it had no bottom and it had no top, just circles and circles of sorrow.[68]

Morrison's emphasis on the search for agency and voice in female characters is also a central theme of *The Bluest Eye*. Frieda and her sister,

Claudia, become agents as "outrageous, audacious, courageous, or willful" little Black girls often do; they plant flowers to save the life of a child and a child who has no hope of being born. Frieda and Claudia realize that society, though troubled by what has happened to Pecola Breedlove, has given up on her. Young, ignored, and wishing that she had blue eyes, Pecola Breedlove is impregnated at the age of twelve by her father, Cholly, a brutal, broken, hate-filled man. It is only through Frieda and Claudia's actions that we see any compassion for the plight of Pecola and her unborn (never to be born) child. Frieda and Claudia claim their own agency by supporting another Black girl and displaying a commitment to her survival.

Finally, Walker's own work also exemplifies Womanist literature, especially her canonical text *The Color Purple*. Celie, like her ancestors, gains the ability to liberate herself and thus to become an agent through writing and reading. Literacy is her metaphorical sword and she uses it to cleave through the chains around her body her rapist step-father, violent husband, and a static Black community bound her in. In conjunction with literacy, Celie is able to form a bond with Shug Avery, who supports and comforts her—a bond that provides a safe place in which to encounter love. Viewed as an example of Womanist literature, Walker's novel chronicles Celie's struggles in her search for agency and her own voice. Although Celie undergoes perpetual assaults from those around her, this does not prevent her from becoming a fully actualized woman. Celie's self-actualization comes not in her decision to leave Mr., but when she asks Mr. whether her sister, Nettie, has sent any other letters. It is Mr.'s reply—"If they did, he say, I wouldn't give'em to you"—that leads Celie to curse him:

> I say, Until you do right by me, everything you touch will crumble
> . . . Until you do right by me, I say, everything you even dream
> about will fail . . . Then I say, You better stop talking because all I'm
> telling you ain't coming just from me. Look like when I open my
> mouth the air rush in and shape words.[69]

This highlights the fact that her basic struggle is not for freedom of movement but for the control of language. The emphasis on the theme of language and of finding one's own voice is what makes *The Color Purple* a prime example of Womanist literature.

CONCLUSION

Through this brief survey of the similarities and differences between Womanism, Black Feminism, and Africana Womanism, we have sought to indicate some important theoretical perspectives for articulating the experiences and concerns of Black women. These perspectives have a point of interest in common—the experience of Black women—but a close examination reveals some key philosophical and political differences between them. In light of these differences, it is important for students of Black Studies to be aware of the mistakes that can be made by grouping all Black women writers or theorists together under any one of these headings. To do so would be to conceal the very real and substantive differences between them, such as their differing views on the importance of gender and of African cultural experiences. Still, it would equally be mistaken to regard these positions as being at odds. Instead, this chapter encourages students of Black Studies to see Womanism, Black Feminism, and Africana Womanism as compatible and complementary discourses. Since each recognizes the importance of empowering Black women to give voice to their own experiences, the differences between them should be understood as different perspectives that provide equally important insights, and various aspects, of the depth and breadth of the Black female experience.

Womanism, Black Feminism, and Africana Womanism are not just theories set apart from practice; they are of the utmost importance to the real lives and experiences of Black women. These theories are developed out of the practical and lived experiences of Black women, and in turn seek to give a new significance and direction to those experiences. This call and response, this give and take, this unification of theory and practice, enable Womanism, Black Feminism, and Africana Womanism to impact not only the academy, but also the everyday lives of Black women. By studying these theories, students gain a better understanding of the lives and specific challenges that Black women face in their personal experiences and social interactions. Students also have the opportunity to connect these complex and varied experiences to enrich their own lives.

NOTES

1. Phillis Wheatley (1753–84) was the first African American to publish an anthology of poems. See *Poems on Various Subjects Religious and Moral* (New York: Cosimo, 2005).

2. Linda Brent published *Incidents in the Life of a Slave Girl* (1861) under the alias Harriet Jacobs. At the time of publication, Brent's book did not garner the public attention that was received by Harriet Beecher Stowe's *Uncle Tom's Cabin* or Frederick Douglass's *The Narrative of the Life of Frederick Douglass, An American Slave*. Subsequently, Brent and her book fell into obscurity and was "lost" for over 100 years until it and other works from writers like Zora Neale Hurston, whom we now consider canonical, were "rediscovered" by mainly Black women such as Alice Walker, who are dedicated to recovering Black women's literary production.

3. For a very interesting discussion of Harriet Jacob's *Incidents in the Life of a Slave Girl*, see Stephanie Li, "Motherhood as Resistance in Harriet Jacob's *Incidents in the Life of a Slave Girl*," *Legacy*, vol. 23, no. 1 (2006), 14–29; see also Jean Fagan Yellin's seminal *Harriet Jacobs: A Life* (New York: Basic Civitas Books, 2004).

4. George Gordon Byron (1788–1824), Percy Bysshe Shelley (1792–1822), and John Keats (1795–1821) were all leading poets in the British Romantic period.

5. Søren Kierkegaard (1813–55) Danish philosopher, Friedrich Nietzsche (1844–1900) German philosopher, and Jean-Paul Sartre (1905–80) French philosopher.

6. Anna Julia Cooper (1858–1964), Jessie Redmon Fauset (1882–1961), Zora Neale Hurston (1891–1960), Gwendolyn Brooks (1917–2000), and Toni Morrison (1931–).

7. David Perkins, *The English Romantic Writers* (San Diego, CA: Harcourt Brace Javanovich, 1967), 1. In his general introduction to the text, Perkins makes a similar point about issue of classification that began this section when he writes: "All historical labels are, of course, simplifications and fail to suggest the diversity of life, thought, and art in the period to which they are applied" (1).

8. Alice Walker, *In Search of Our Mothers' Gardens* (Orlando, FL: Harcourt, 1983), xi.

9. Walker, *In Search of Our Mothers' Gardens*.

10. Walker, *In Search of Our Mothers' Gardens*.

11. First-wave Feminists, such as Susan B. Anthony and Elizabeth Cady Stanton, fought against *de jure* inequalities faced by women and they also fought for the right for women to vote. First-wave Feminism ended when the Nineteenth Amendment to the US Constitution, which gave women the right to vote, was passed in 1920. Second-wave Feminism refers to activist who came of age in the 1960s. Second-wave Feminists believe that it is important to extend the rights won during the First Wave. These rights include women having a greater presence in the workforce, the right to safe and legal abortions, and the ending of discrimination in education. At present, we are experiencing Third-wave Feminism. Coming during the 1980s and 1990s, Third-wave Feminism is more interested in localized activism and making Feminism more inclusive of women of color and non-economically privileged women. See Rebecca Walker, ed., *To Be Real: Telling the Truth and Changing the Face of Feminism* (New York: Anchor Books, 1995); see also Daisy Hernandez and Bushra Rehman, eds., *Colonize This! Young Women of Color on Today's Feminism* (Emeryville, CA: Seal Press, 2002).

12. Simone de Beauvoir (1908–86) was a prominent French philosopher. See *The Second Sex* (New York: Alfred A. Knopf, 1993).

13. Betty Friedan (1921–2006) was a leading American feminist thinker whose work helped to define Second-wave Feminism. See The *Feminine Mystique* (New York: Norton, 1974).

14. Luce Irigaray (1932–) is a Belgian philosopher and feminist. See *This Sex Which is not One* (Ithaca, NY: Cornell University Press, 1985).

15. Katie Conboy, Nadia Medina, and Sarah Stanbury, eds., *Writing on the Body: Female Embodiment and Feminist Theory* (New York: Columbia University Press, 1997), 2.

16. Conboy, Medina, and Stanbury, *Writing on the Body*.

17. Conboy, Medina, and Stanbury, *Writing on the Body*.

18. Patricia Hill Collins (1948–) has written extensively on Black women's issues from a theoretical standpoint. For an introduction to her work, see her seminal *Black Feminist Thought: Knowledge, Consciousness, and the Politics of Empowerment* (New York: Routledge, 2000).

19. Gloria Jean Watkins (penname bell hooks 1952–) is perhaps one of the most prolific and widely read African American scholars today. For an introduction to her work on feminist issues see *Feminist Theory from Margin to Center* (Cambridge, MA: South End Press, 2000) and *Ain't I a Woman: Black Women and Feminism* (Boston, MA: South End Press, 1981).

20. Michele Wallace (1952–) is an influential feminist scholar who critiques sexism in *Black Macho and the Myth of the Superwoman* (New York: Verso, 1999).

21. Carole E. Henderson is a literary scholar and theorist. See *Scarring the Black Body: Race and Representation in African American Literature* (Columbia, MO: University of Missouri Press, 2002).

22. Cheryl Wall is a literary theorist who has done much to advance Black literary theory. See *Changing Our Own Words: Essays on Criticism, Theory, and Writing by Black Women* (New Brunswick, NJ: Rutgers University Press, 1989).

23. Hortense Spillers is a prominent literary critic and theorist. For an overview of her thought, see *Black and White and in Color: Essays on American Literature and Culture* (Chicago, IL: University of Chicago Press, 2003).

24. For an extended discussion of hooks' critique of white feminism, see Maria del Guadalupe Davidson, "bell hooks and the Move from Marginalized Other to Radical Black Subject," in Maria del Guadalupe Davidson and George Yancy, eds., *Critical Perspectives on bell hooks* (New York: Routledge, 2009), 121–31.

25. bell hooks, *Feminist Theory from Margin to Center* (Cambridge, MA: South End Press, 2000), 1.

26. hooks, *Feminist Theory from Margin to Center*, 1.

27. Alicia D. Bosinier, "Race and Women's Identity Development: Distinguishing Between Feminism and Womanism Among Black and White Women," *Sex Roles*, vol. 49, nos. 5–6 (2003), 212.

28. In *Black Feminist Thought: Knowledge, Consciousness, and the Politics of Empowerment* (New York: Routledge, 2000). Hill Collins shows the various ways in which race, class, and gender work together to negatively impact Black women's lives.

29. hooks has been outspoken on the need to develop a theory and discourse that speaks to the importance of both gender and race on a person's life. She asserts that "at the moment of my birth, two factors determined my destiny, my having been born black and my having been born a female." See *Ain't I a Woman*, 12.

30. Walker, *In Search of Our Mothers' Gardens*, 13.

31. Walker, *In Search of Our Mothers' Gardens*.

32. It is important to note that not all Black scholars work out of an Afrocentric framework; many are in fact critical of Afrocentrism. See Anthony Appiah, "Europe Upside Down: Fallacies of the New Afrocentrism," in *Perspectives on Africa*, ed. Roy Richard Grinker and Christopher Burghard Steiner (Cambridge, MA: Blackwell, 1997), 728–31.

33. It is important to note that much of the dynamic scholarship on Womanism has come from religion scholars like Katie Geneva Cannon, Ariasika Razak, and Jacquelyn Grant.

34. Monica A. Coleman, "Must I be a Womanist?" *Journal of Feminist Studies in Religion*, vol. 22, no. 1 (2006), 86.

35. Coleman, "Must I be a Womanist?" 85–6.

36. Coleman, "Must I be a Womanist?" 88.

37. For an excellent discussion of this issue as it relates to Black Feminism, see Ann duCille, "The Occult of True Black Womanhood: Critical Demeanor and Black Feminist Studies," in *Female Subjects in Black and White: Race, Psychoanalysis, Feminism*, ed. Elizabeth Abel, Barbara Christian, and Helene Moglen (Berkeley, CA: University of California Press, 1997), 21. See also Maria del Guadalupe Davidson's "Rethinking Black Feminist Subjectivity: Ann duCille and Gilles Deleuze," in Maria del Guadalupe Davidson, Kathryn T. Gines, and Donna-Dale L. Marcano, eds., *Convergences: Black Feminism and Continental Philosophy* (Albany, NY: SUNY Press, forthcoming).

38. *In Search of Our Mothers' Gardens*, xi.

39. Patricia Hill Collins, "What's in a Name? Womanism, Black Feminism, and Beyond," *The Black Scholar*, vol. 26, no. 1 (2001), 10.

40. Hill Collins, "What's in a Name?" 9–10.

41. Hill Collins, "What's in a Name?" 11.

42. Hill Collins, "What's in a Name?" 13.

43. Hill Collins, "What's in a Name?" 15.

44. Hill Collins *Black Feminist Thought*, 22.

45. Hill Collins, *Black Feminist Thought*.

46. It is important to note that tension exists about whether non-Black women can be Womanist, Black Feminist or Africana Feminist, or produce Womanist, Black Feminist or Africana Feminist scholarship. Trying to avoid the charge of essentialism, scholars such like Ann duCille has spoken about this issue (see "The Occult of True Black Womanhood"). It might stand to reason that to argue otherwise would be tantamount to establishing yet another exclusive paradigm which Black Feminists purport to reject; yet if the definitions are opened up to "others," does this reduce the effectiveness of the various disciplines?

47. Nikol G. Alexander-Floyd and Evelyn M. Simien, "Revisiting 'What's in a Name?' Exploring the Contours of Africana Womanist Thought," *Frontiers*, vol. 27, no. 1 (2006), 67–89.

48. Clenora Hudson-Weems, *Africana Womanist Literary Theory* (Trenton, NJ: Africa World Press, 2004), 5.

49. Hudson-Weems, *Africana Womanist Literary Theory*, 8.

50. To be clear, agency is also a foundational principle in Womanist theory, yet it is expressed differently. For those working from an Africana Womanist theoretical

position, agency is rooted in the Afrocentric process of self-naming or *nommo*. On the other hand, Womanist theory sees agency as the individual telling her own story and being independent, which leads us back to Walker's discussion of the origin of Womanism: "Black folk expression . . . usually referring to outrageous, audacious, courageous, or *willful* behavior . . ." See *In Search of Our Mothers' Gardens*, xi.

51. Benjamin R. Bates, Windy Y. Lawrence, and Mark Cervenka, "Redrawing Afrocentrism: Visual *Nommo* in George H. Ben Johnson's Editorial Cartoons," *The Howard Journal of Communication*, vol. 19 (2008), 279.

52. Adisa A. Alkebulan, "Nommo," in *The Encyclopedia of Black Studies*, ed. Molefi Kente Asante and Ama Mazama (Thousand Oaks, CA: Sage, 2005), 380.

53. Hudson-Weems, *Africana Womanist Literary Theory*, xix.

54. Hudson-Weems, *Africana Womanist Literary Theory*, 8.

55. Alexander-Floyd and Simien, "Revisiting 'What's in a Name?'" 70–1.

56. Vivian Gordon. *Black Women, Feminism, and Black Liberation: Which Way?* (Chicago, IL: Third World Press, 1987), viii.

57. Hudson-Weems states that: "Hence, Africana women have historically demonstrated that they are diametrically opposed to the concept of many white feminist who want independence and freedom from family responsibility." See *Africana Womanist Literary Theory*, 25. I would suggest that this statement may well be painting Feminists with too broad a brush.

58. This definition is not intended to be exclusive in any way. Diasporic Black women may use it if it accommodates their needs. What this definition ultimately seeks to do is respect the standpoint of diverse Black women.

59. Stacey M. Floyd-Thomas. *Deeper Shades of Purple: Womanism in Religion and Society* (New York: New York University Press, 2006), 1.

60. See Robert Hemenway, *Zora Neale Hurston: A Literary Biography* (Champaign, IL: University of Illinois Press, 1980).

61. See Hill Collins *Black Feminist Thought*, 2.

62. Walker, *In Search of Our Mothers' Gardens*, 84.

63. Walker, *In Search of Our Mothers' Gardens*, 83.

64. For a full accounting of this story, which is one of the greatest literary searches of all time, please see Alice Walker, "Looking for Zora," in *In Search of Our Mothers' Gardens*, 93–116.

65. It should be noted that some scholars have been critical of seeing Hurston's character Janie Crawford as an example of Black women's agency. See Jennifer Jordon, "Feminist Fantasies: Zora Neale Hurston's *Their Eyes Were Watching God*," *Tulsa Studies in Women's Literature*, vol. 7, no. 1 (1998), 105–17.

66. Jordan, "Feminist Fantasies," 85.

67. Zora Neale Hurston, *Their Eyes Were Watching God* (New York: HarperPerennial Modern Classic, 2006), 192.

68. Toni Morrison, *Sula* (New York: Vintage Books, 1973), 174.

69. Alice Walker, *The Color Purple* (Orlando, FL: Harcourt, 2003), 206.

CHAPTER 13

Theorizing African American Religion

Victor Anderson

Vanderbilt University

African American Religion, sometimes referred to as African American Religious Studies, is a critical discourse that focuses on African American religious experience. The adjective "critical" determines how the discipline is theorized. Theory, in this context, has three elements: (1) how the discipline is imagined; (2) articulated; and (3) socially constructed, that is how it is arranged in relation to other disciplines. African American Religion has long been included in the overall curricula in American Studies. Surprisingly, however, in several of the most recent anthologies on African American Studies,[1] Religion as a contributing core discipline in the field is absent or limited. In Norment it is absent, and it is defined exclusively by African American Islam in Marable's text. Bobo, Hudley, and Michel,[2] in comparison, devote an entire section to Blacks' biblical interpretation, Black and Womanist Theology, Haitian Voodoo, and Islam in America. While they sectionalize African American Religion, nevertheless, it remains undetermined as a core discipline in African American Studies. Originally published in 1982 and updated in 1993, Karenga,[3] a leading early theorist of Black Studies throughout the 1970s and 1980s, devotes an entire chapter to "Black Religion" as a core discipline within Black Studies, but not without extensive justifications.

The problem he faced, and which most recently was faced also by religious theorist Anthony B. Pinn,[4] was how the discipline can be theorized in a manner that highlights the variety of African American religious experience beyond a Christian hegemony in the study of African Diaspora religions and in North American African Christianity. Karenga organizes "Black Religion" along three traditions of Africa: Ancient African;

Christian; and Islamic. With each tradition, he highlights their internal varieties. Karenga's principal logic is what he calls an *Afrocentric* philosophy and pedagogy. *Afrocentricity* focuses "on the cultural and human quality of African thought and practice rather than on thought and practice as an ideological conception and standard of conduct. Rejecting the 'ism' becomes another way to avoid being labeled as simply another ideological posture."[5]

Pinn takes up the challenge and problem Karenga sets out. Separate from Karenga's Afrocentric pedagogy, Pinn has published extensively on Black humanism as a distinctive philosophy and pedagogy in African American Religion.[6] He insists that belief in god(s) is not the "litmus test for religion. In fact, for some African Americans, belief in god(s) is not the basis of their religious experience."[7] What counts are the "big questions" of human experience: "What is the nature of existence? Who am I? Why am I here? What sense can be made of collective pain and suffering?"[8] Theorizing African American Religion so as to "describe or present African American religious experience in ways that capture its complexity and diversity" beyond African American Christianity remains the ongoing project of African American Religion.[9]

Disagreements over nomenclature have always been an aspect of African American Studies (Black Studies, Afro-American Studies, African Diaspora Studies, etc.) and pedagogies (Africentricity, Afrocentrism, Afrocentricity). Typical disagreements also prevail in theories of African American Religion (Black Religion, African American Religious Studies, Black Church Studies, and Black Theology). The disputes usually come down to whether "Black Religion" or "African American Religious Studies" should have priority over both the content and pedagogy of the discipline, or whether "Black Church Studies" and "Black Theology" should determine the field. In what follows, I offer a short genealogy of this problem. Every attempt to theorize African American Religion involves acts of self-interrogation and self-articulation. They involve hermeneutical moves, which are subjective and intersubjective—subjective insofar as it is I, a religious thinker, doing the work; and intersubjective insofar as I circulate in a field of study that is already riddled with shared agreements and disagreements on which I take sides.

I am reminded of Michel Foucault's description of genealogy as a tool of criticism. "Genealogy," he says, "is gray, meticulous, and patiently documentary. It operates on a field of entangled and confused parchments, on documents that have been scratched over and recopied many times."[10] I begin with lessons learned from a preeminent scholar of African American Religion, Professor Charles H. Long, who theorizes the discipline within a phenomenological hermeneutic. He reminds us that with every attempt to discover the origin of a work of art or religious practices we are met with an "archaic silence" that is already broken by spoken existences and structured by endless speech-acts.[11] In this short genealogy, I can only mark out a world of happenings, events, and cultural and social moves that are already taken account of, taken for granted, linguistically determined, and theorized. I will proceed by way of five moves: (1) the ruptures of African life and civilizations through European contact and conquest of Africa; (2) formations of African American religious experience through the history and sociology of the Negro Church; (3) methodologies of the empirical sciences and the debates on the African presence in African American religious experience; (4) the Black Church Studies and Black and Womanist Theology; and (5) contemporary attempts to theorize the discipline within Black Culture Studies.

THE RUPTURES OF CONTACT AND CONQUEST

As the religious practices of African American peoples and as a discipline of study, African American Religion takes as its point of departure the ruptures of African life and civilizations through European contact and conquest and new formations of African religions in the African Diaspora. Two revolutions of the fifteenth and sixteenth centuries directly affected African culture and religion. The first was the advancement in maritime technology which made possible a slave trade in the Atlantic basin. The second was the economic development and deployment of the plantation system to the Atlantic basin, which made the slave trade highly profitable. Understanding these technologies of contact and conquest means that African American Religion is methodologically connected by historiographies beyond the history of religions in America, which include economic, political, scientific, and technological histories.

Historical methods are critical for understanding the effects that mercantilism and plantation economics had on the ruptures of contact and conquest of Africa. They also help us to appreciate the religious worlds that African people produced in the African Diaspora. With advances in maritime technology and plantation economics, "all the coasts of Africa were now open to European trade by sea," and with this, "the isolation of the Americas also came to an end," says historian Phillip D. Curtin.[12] Moreover, with "the Portuguese exportation of the Mediterranean plantation system to the South Atlantic basin, this revolutionized the economics of sugar production." This required a "cheap labor force to keep pace with European consumption and demand. The answer became the transatlantic African slave trade."[13] The foremost scholar of African American Religion in the late nineteenth and early twentieth centuries, W. E. B. Du Bois, in *Black Reconstruction in America*, describes this massive event in most striking terms: "The most magnificent drama in the last thousand years of human history is the transportation of ten million human beings out of the dark beauty of their mother continent into the new-found Eldorado of the West. They descended into Hell."[14]

In the ruptures of Sub-Saharan African life and civilization initiated first from the exportation of slaves from West Africa and later from Central Africa as well, African slaves, from wide geographical regions, transported aspects of their traditional religions to the Americas. These are usually referred to as African Diaspora Religions. Albert J. Raboteau described this phenomenon in his monumental work *Slave Religion: The Invisible Institution in the Antebellum South.*

> The gods of Africa were carried in the memories of enslaved Africans across the Atlantic. To be sure, they underwent a sea change. African liturgical seasons, prescribed rituals, traditional myths, and languages of worship were attenuated, replaced, and altered or lost. Still, much remained, and particularly in Latin America the gods lived on in the beliefs and rituals of the slaves' descendants. Candomblé in Brazil, Santeria in Cuba, Shango in Trinidad, and Voudoo in Haiti, all attest to the vitality and durability of African religious perspectives. And it should be emphasized that it is this continuity of perspective that is significant, more so than the fact that the cults of particular African gods, such as Shango or Elegba, have been transmitted to the New World. For new as well as old gods have come to be worshipped by Afro-Americans, but the new, like the old, have been perceived in traditionally African ways.[15]

Raboteau highlights one of the most enduring questions in the study of African American Religion. The problem is not to what extent African retentions survived the slave trade, but to what extent they can be identified as having enduring significance in African American religious experience.

THE NEGRO CHURCH: ITS WORLD SIGNIFICANCE IN HISTORY AND SOCIOLOGY

As noted earlier, disagreements over nomenclature are not just about nuances but also of substance, methods, and pedagogy. This is true in how we frame African American Religion/Religious Studies. One critical theorist of religion, William D. Hart, insists that the dispute over nomenclature is not trivially about nuances. For him, African American Religious Studies form the standard narrative in which "the black protestant Church is virtually coterminous with Black Religion. It defines Black Religion. Every other form of Black religious expression is normatively peripheral and culturally suspect."[16] Hart defines "Black Religion" by contrast:

> Black Religion is a consequent not an antecedent—primordial—reality, an artifact not an essence. Produced by people identified as "Negro," "colored," "black," or "African American," Black Religion emerged from a violent intercultural encounter under the conditions of conquest, slavery, and white supremacy. Black people transformed the traditions they encountered by "bluing the note" and producing a sound that was recognizable but different.[17]

Whether one theorizes Black Religion as the narrative of the Black Church and Black Christianity or as the politics of encounter, conquest, and self-making, as Hart does, the enduring question remains: to what extent has the *African presence*, as power and manifestation, contributed to the formation of African American Religion?

For most of the first half of the twentieth century, African American religious experience was almost singularly registered and understood as North American Christianity and its peculiar divide between white Christianity and the Negro Church. The Negro Church was celebrated as an epochal, messianic event, a moral light to the world, and Ethiopia's rising from its shadowy negation in world universal history. Confined to a shadowy existence in European world historical consciousness, which rendered Africa invisible to Europe's cultural formation of civilization, the Negro Church was imagined, articulated, and socially constructed as God's providential hand directing history toward its fulfillment in a kingdom of love and justice. Such a theorization evidences an understanding of the Negro Church as an epochal event of world historical significance, articulated in cultural, Ethiopian, and progressive millenarianisms in the nadir of post-Reconstruction and Jim Crow legislations, says American Religious Historian Timothy Fulop. These millenarian hermeneutics continue even in contemporary imaginings of the Black Church in America, which add to contemporary debates on the meaning and significance of the Black Church for Black cultural and social life.

Cultural millenarianism *imagines* freedom's great expectation articulated in images of the US as the "redeemer nation of the world" through forces of Western civilization, education, and democracy. Ethiopian millenarianism *articulates* a Pan-African "future golden age connected to a great African past accompanied by God's judgment over white society and Western civilization." And progressive millenarianism *socially constructs* the role of the church, evangelicalism, missions, and social reform as keys to the earthly kingdom of God, displaying great optimism in the power of Christianity to transform and correct the social ills of America.[18]

The work of African American historians and sociologists was to study the cultural significance of the Negro Church. Their interests were as apologetic as they were scholarly. This is not surprising for the religious and moral questions guiding African American Religion concerned the historical and cultural significance of the Negro Church, not as a Christian entity, but as a distinctively *Negro, Black* or *African* manifestation. Consider this problem in light of two contrasting millenarian formations. AME Bishop R. H. Cain expressed the negro problem in progressive optimism when he said: "Happy for the great country, happy for the negro and the nation when the great principles upon which our government is founded, when the genius of liberty as understood by the fathers, shall permeate this whole land . . . Then there will need be no more discussion as to what of the negro problem."[19] Consider next J. Augustus Cole's pan-African millenarianism, which highlights the Negro problem within African spiritual and moral superiority. For him, the Negro problem was construed as a moral endeavor, the "labor for one end," and to "keep the integrity of the race." He contends that "It is in the Christianity of the Negro that this destiny will be realized." He further argued that "in embracing Christianity the Negro has made a very sad mistake, which will always hinder his progress. When we accept Christianity from the white man, we do not regard it so much as the religion of Christ, as the "white man's religion." Consequently, "we have imitated the white man instead of imitating Christ, and we have retained both the white man's vices as well as his virtues."[20]

Mapping the spiritual, moral, and distinct contribution of the Negro Church—that is, Black Religion—to world universal history was the primary method of African American religious scholarship in the first half of the twentieth century. *Tracking* the social role of the Negro Church in racial uplift and democratic progressive social reform was the social contribution of African American Religion as a discipline. Both tasks define the works of eminent twentieth-century Black religious historians and sociologists such as Du Bois,[21] Carter G. Woodson,[22] E. Franklin Frazier, and C. Eric Lincoln.[23] Mapping the spiritual and moral contributions of the Black Church and tracking its social activism and advocacy continued well into the second half of the twentieth century with Gayraud Wilmore,[24] C. Eric Lincoln and Lawrence H. Mamiya,[25] R. Drew Smith,[26] and Stacey Floyd-Thomas, Juan Floyd-Thomas, Carol Duncan, Stephen Ray, and Nancy Lynn Westfield.[27]

WITH ETHNOGRAPHERS' TOOLS: THE AFRICAN PRESENCE IN AFRICAN AMERICAN RELIGION

With ethnographers' tools for observing practices, rituals, and ecstatic expressions of spirited life prior to Emancipation, Black religious scholars tracked the distinctive contribution of the African presence in African American religious experience in the spiritual and moral significance of the Negro Church. What spiritual, moral, and cultural influences does the African presence have, prior to Emancipation, on the institutional Negro Church? What religious meanings are expressed in spirituals, shouting, and dancing, which are all bearers of the African presence? These were the important questions of African American Religion. Again, Du Bois remains of critical importance for the continuing significance of these questions even in contemporary theories of African American Religion. Referring to Black folk religion, spirituals, shouting, and dancing, Du Bois contends that "these were the characteristics of Negro religious life as developed up to the time of Emancipation. Since under the peculiar circumstances of the Black man's environment they were the one expression of his higher life, they are the deep interest to the student of his life, both socially and psychologically."[28] As a scholar who tracks the significance of this folk tradition for Black religious thought, for Du Bois this meant mining this expressive culture to learn about the Negro mind: "What did slavery mean to the American savage? What was his attitude toward the World and Life? What seemed to him good and evil,—God and Devil? Whither went his longings and strivings and wherefore were his heart-burnings and disappointment?"[29] Du Bois concludes that the "answer to such questions can come only from the study of Negro religion as a development, through its gradual changes from the heathenism of the Gold Coast to the institutional Negro Church."[30]

Ethnography provided African American Religion with a method for disclosing the theological and moral meanings of Black Religion, the Negro Church, through analyses of Black folk religion. The spirituals, Black preaching, and surviving slave tales were of great importance. Black folk religion determined not only the cultural significance of the Negro Church, but also the whole of Black expressive culture. In the organic, expressive, and performed displays of Black folk religiosity, Black Religion constituted the soul of the institutional Black Church. It would also situate one of the most enduring debates in African American Religion. It is the debate on *Africanisms* in the Black Church. The debate erupted in the social sciences themselves, in sociology and anthropology, between Melville Herskovits and E. Franklin Frazier. Moreover, the debate also made the study of slave culture and religion central in African American Religion.

Robert E. Park and E. Franklin Frazier were members of the Chicago School of Sociology. They argued that transplanted Africans were geopolitically landless and unable to provide a conducive environment for preserving and cultivating a tradition of *Africanisms* or *African Retentions* in their religious experience when compared to the Caribbean Basin, including Brazil, where distinct African forms provide continuity with a continental West and South African past. This is called the "cultural deprivation and assimilation theory" and was no new idea for historians and sociologists of the late nineteenth and early twentieth centuries. However, Park and his student and onetime president of the American Sociological Association, Frazier, proffered its most virulent articulation. Park explains: "it seems to me, that the Negro, when he landed in the United States, left behind him almost everything but his dark complexion and his tropical temperament. It is very difficult to find in the South today anything that can be traced directly back to Africa."[31]

In 1939, Frazier made most explicit the ramification of Park's radical cultural deprivation and assimilation thesis in his famous book *The Negro Family*. In its starkest articulation, Frazier observes that "probably never before in history have a people been so stripped of its social heritage as the Negroes who were brought to America."[32] He continues that they so assimilated into American cultural forms that their prodigy "soon forgot the few memories that had been passed on to them and developed motivations and modes of behavior in harmony with the New World." Sadly, what is left are "fragments of stories concerning Africa, which have been preserved in their families. But, of the habits and customs as well as the hopes and fears that characterized the life of their forbearers in Africa, nothing remains."[33]

Responding to Frazier in 1941, Melville Herskovits published *The Myths of the Negro Past*, challenging the Park-Frazier thesis by correcting five myths supporting it and articulating a comparative method of ethnography that determines the African presence in the religious experience and imagination of African Americans. Comparing Black Religion in the US with Caribbean and West Africa religions, Herskovits argues that persistent African traits of practices and thought in slave religion and culture can be measured in contemporary Black Christianity. By targeting American "Negro Religion," "Black Religion," as the most decisive site for mapping "Africanisms" in Black cultural formation, Herskovits challenged the cultural deprivation thesis of Black cultural inferiority and acculturation. He argued that the cultural deprivation thesis was "a misrepresentation of the richness of the African cultural past and a denial of the tenacity of that culture in the life ways of Afro-American people."[34]

Under Herskovits' influence, scholars of African American Religion now contend that the African presence in Black Religion is located where one looks for it, and knowing how to decode its encoded signs in Black folk culture and slave religion is the clue to understanding the tenacity of the African presence in Black Religion. Tales, songs, spirituals, conjuring, root medicine, wit and humor, signifying, playing the dozens, dancing, ring dancing, shouting, call and response, clothing, material culture, even dialect and language all signify the African presence in Black Religion in the Caribbean Basin most distinctively, and in the US to a lesser extent.

It is the work of African American Religion to track, identify, and interpret these signifying practices in Black Religion and Black folk culture. These hermeneutical tasks constitute African American Religion as a field of study distinct from mainstream institutional histories of Protestant Christianity in America and Black Church History. Exemplary are the works of scholars such as Albert J. Raboteau,[35] Sterling Stuckey,[36] Lawrence Levine,[37] John W. Blassingame,[38] and Riggins R. Earl, Jr.[39] However, under the influences of the Black Power, Black Students, Black Arts, and Black Studies Movements, the enduring debate on African retentions becomes radicalized, as African American Religion travels from the Negro Church to the Black Church. The Negro Church metamorphoses into "The Black Church in America" and a Black Theology of Liberation.

FROM THE NEGRO CHURCH TO THE BLACK CHURCH: BLACK CHURCH STUDIES AND BLACK THEOLOGY

African American Studies is interdisciplinary and draws on new and expanding forms of criticism circulating throughout the humanities and social sciences. These new forms of criticism include literary criticism, critical historiography, critical theory, ideology criticism, critical race theory, and poststructuralism. With new critical tools, the discipline created a counter-discourse on hegemonic epistemologies that defined and subjugated Black experience under the representational force of White Supremacy. In this new discourse on race, the cultural significance of "Blackness" came to signify Black Power, Black Arts, Black Expressive Culture, Black Religion, the Black Church, and Black Theology.

The expressive elements of Black folk culture and Africanisms joined with a New Black Aesthetics in African American Religion. What was produced in 1969 and the 1970s was Black Theology, of which James H. Cone is the unsurpassed representative. In the preface to his 1986 edition of *A Black Theology of Liberation* (first published in 1970), Cone insisted that the theological problem of American culture is white racism. The task of Black Theology is to engage it by way of a new, revolutionary Black collective consciousness in light of the Black experience, Black history, and Black culture. This clearly put Black Theology into conversation with Black Studies, for Black Theology had now to show how its content and pedagogy were methodologically rooted in Black expressive culture. In Black Theology, the essential theological meanings of Black experience, history, and culture emerge on the survivalist culture of "the black community, the pain and joy it derives from reacting to whiteness and affirming blackness" and "the mythic power inherent in [its historical] symbols for the present revolution against white racism."[40] Black culture, arts, music, literature, and theology were symbolic-expressive vehicles of a Black Theology of Liberation.

Over the past forty years, Black Theology has advanced by means of both external and internal criticism by African American theologians themselves. A number of theorists, including Wilmore and Cone,[41] Dwight N. Hopkins,[42] Stephanie Mitchem,[43] and Victor Anderson,[44] have documented these challenges and changes. But perhaps the works of Womanist theologians have posed the greater challenges to Black Theology. African American women theologians such as Katie Cannon,[45] Jacquelyn Grant,[46] Delores Williams,[47] and many more, moved the discourse most directly into conversation with the critical methodologies of African American Studies, Black Cultural Studies, and African American Religious Studies.

In Womanist Theology and Ethics, gender, race, and class form constitutive categories of criticism. The discourse produces a Black Womanist consciousness that entails and mediates difference. Distinguished theologian Delores Williams, in *Sisters in the Wilderness*, sees such mediatory possibilities in Alice Walker's "Womanist" trope on which Walker framed her collection of poems, *In Search of Our Mothers' Garden*. Williams sees such mediations displayed well in Walker's *The Color Purple*.[48] In Walker's "Womanist" definition, Williams sees the promises of racial and cultural mediation over the hegemony of Black, male, clergy elites over legitimacy claims in African American religion. "For Black women's womanhood is their humanity. To devalue Black womanhood is to take away their humanity," says Williams. "This can be illustrated by focusing on some aspects of Alice Walker's understanding of Black womanhood suggested in her definition of a womanist."[49]

Womanist theology and ethics offer a comprehensive experiential matrix for the analysis of African American life that is tri-modal: racism, sexism, and classism, and most recently, heterosexism. Womanist theology accents the ways that their triple oppressions provide an angle of vision that anticipates some promise of transcendence and hope over the burdens that Black existence, whether male or female, is bound by unprecedented suffering and survival. In a word, Stephanie Y. Mitchem summarizes the significance of this work for African American Religion:

> Womanist approaches to theology aim to develop a variety of
> theological constructions in which black women are the main
> subject. Where is God in the lives of African American women?
> How do black women name God? [W]omanist theology is a place of
> discovery, in faith, that analyzes both politics and culture.[50]

A constitutive methodology of Black and Womanist theologies is what I have called elsewhere a "Hermeneutics of Narrative Return" to Black cultural sources of Black folk religion and experience.[51] In the narrative return to distinctively Black sources, the theologian returns to African traditional religions and slave narratives, autobiography, and folklore in order to accent the vitality of the Black Church and forms of cultural solidarities that transcend the individualism that drives our market culture and morality and that robs the Black community of moral vitality. Black theologian

Dwight N. Hopkins sees in slave thought a synthesis of "white Christianity with the remains of African religions under slavery."[52] African slaves maintained enough residual aspects of their former religions to establish an historically effective slave religion that was preserved and transmittable in an invisible institution: bush arbor theology. In that institution, these "remains" achieve some measure of coherence and a content that signifies a distinctive discursive site for the formation of a slave theology that achieves "remarkable clarity concerning the cultural dimension of their theology."[53] "Black theology is a continuation of that discursive tradition," says Black theologian James Evans.[54]

Black and Womanist theology is grounded by both the theologian's recognition that his or her project is historically derivative from the economy of slavery and expressive of the passions, feelings, and rationality that constitute the Black Church in the US. The hermeneutics of return projects a grand narrative that evokes a great cloud of witnesses whose heroic legacy of survival, resistance, and hope mediates the fragility of African American experience today and binds contemporaries in the need for a heroic Black faith.

While not a self-identified Black or Womanist theologian, philosopher and religionist Barbara A. Holmes has produced a remarkable body of work that creatively deploys this legacy of survival, resistance, and hope.[55] She produces a mode of Black cultural retrieval that unites the witnesses of African American faith, the cultural deposit of Black folk religion, and aspects of traditional African religions within the discursive site of religion and science. She contributes a refreshing significance of these Black sources for contemporary African American religious experience. In *Liberation and the Cosmos: Conversations with the Elders*, Holmes says:

> The conversations in this book take seriously the unfinished state
> of the liberation project and the need for imaginative solutions that
> will provide the fertile soil for new initiatives. My grandmother
> used to say, "If you don't see a way out, stand still." After a
> century of activism, the desire to do something, to advance the
> cause of freedom, and to liberate those still in bondage is almost
> overwhelming. And yet the path is unclear. It seems a perfect time
> to regroup, to keep an eye on world events, to help a neighbor close
> by and imagine the future. And this book revisits the quest for
> freedom using unique rhetorical tools that include the languages of
> cosmology, Africana thought, philosophies of liberation, and the
> impetus toward moral fulfillment.[56]

Holmes moves African American Religion toward a more rigorous engagement with Black Church Studies, Black Theology, and Womanist Theology and critical methods circulating throughout Black Cultural Studies.

A THEORY OF AFRICAN AMERICAN RELIGION WITHIN BLACK CULTURAL CRITICISM

In previous writings, I have offered extensive criticisms of the use of Black cultural sources in Black and Womanist Theology.[57] However, Black feminist critic Barbara Christian identifies a certain irony in the countercultural discourse of the new Black Aesthetic Movement, Black Power, and in Black Studies which I also see communicated in Black and Womanist Theology. She argues that as Black Arts theorists critiqued, not only the dominant literatures and representations of Black experience, which were overdetermined by assimilation, decadence, and pathology, but the Black experience by reversal was "re-theorized" by a new radical, militant, and Africanized Black consciousness. Within these cultural moves, race discourse recoiled, turning back on itself, replicating and reinscribing forms of Black identity that concretized into essentialist cultural images. Black expressive culture registered signs and symbols of a near "monolithism" and cultural monotheism. Christian says:

> It is true that the Black Arts Movement resulted in a necessary and important critique both of previous Afro-American literature and of the white-established literary world. But in attempting to take over power, it, as Ishmael Reed satirizes so well in *Mumbo Jumbo*, became much like its opponent, monolithic and downright repressive. Inevitably, monolithism becomes a metasystem, in which there is a controlling ideal, especially in relation to pleasure. Language as one form of pleasure is immediately restricted, and becomes heavy, abstract, prescriptive, monotonous.[58]

Black Culture Studies and its politics of race consciousness displayed not only a tendency toward "monolithism," but also a repressive "monotheism," says Christian. It formed an iconography of "Blackness" that raised the symbol to the divine and registered all other expressive modes of Black culture manifestations of Black Power, Black Cultural Consciousness, and

Black Religion (Black Folk Religion) in the image of the Black Church, and given ideological significance in Black Theology.

From the radical identity politics of the Black Power, the New Black Aesthetic, and Black Student Movements, the Negro Church, which was signified as such for a century, met its greatest challenges in this new climate of Black disenchantment with the perceived quietism of Black Christianity. The Negro Church was ripe for social, political, cultural, economic, and ideological criticism. The ideological critique of the Negro Church, along with the historical and sociological theories that funded its preeminence in African American Religion, now positioned Black Religion and Black Culture Studies along hostile trajectories with Black Church Studies and Black Theology. Black Church Studies was conceived of as "ideological" (i.e., theological), while Black Religion or African American Religion was "critical" (religious studies).

I want to insist that this divide more than any other factor is a major reason for African American Religion's marginal position in African American Studies. The divide produced two distinct imaginations, articulations, and constructions of African American Religion. With the first, African American Religion was theorized as a "theological discourse," And the second theorizes African American Religion as a "critical discourse." Two anthologies represent this contest well. First, in *African American Religious Studies: An Interdisciplinary Anthology*,[59] African American Religion is framed by rubrics of theological studies: origins, context and conceptualization; biblical studies; theological and ethical studies; historical studies; and missions and ministry. The majority of contributors are theological educators. The theological curriculum structures African American Religious Studies within the geopolitical constructions of the North American Black Church experience, nearly equating African American Religion with Black Church Studies. Wilmore contends that "the best religious scholarship in the Black academy is, perforce, 'believing scholarship,' accepting all the risks that such a position entails. It could not be other wise." He continues: "The centuries-old struggle for Black humanity in a racist environment has not encouraged the development of a dispassionate, armchair science of religion for preparing the leadership of the Black Church in North America."[60]

In *African American Religious Thought: An Anthology*,[61] West and Glaude theorize African American Religion within Black Culture Studies. Their organization is historical and interdisciplinary: Prehistory of African American Religious Studies; Theorizing African American Religion;

Slavery and a Black Religious Imagination; Black Destiny and the End of the Nineteenth Century; The Interwar Period: Migration, Urbanization and Black Religious Diversity; Black Religion and the 1960s; Black Theology and its Critics; and African American Religion and Cultural Criticism. In distinction from Wilmore, West and Glaude contend:

> With this historical periodization and these three extant categories in mind (politics, cultural criticism, and the study of a variety of black institutions that intersect with black religion), this volume aims to broaden our conception of the field and to take seriously the importance of interdisciplinary approaches to African American religious practices. History, theology, and what can be called cultural criticism remain constitutive subareas of the field. One of our major tasks is to urge that we think about these areas within a broader framework that is not reducible to theological claims.[62]

I think it fair to say that these two contested trajectories situate where African American religionists are in theorizing African American Religion. We find ourselves entrenched in the tensions that Hart maps out between "Black Church Studies" and "Black Religion," on the one hand, and on the other, "Black Theology" and "Black Cultural Criticism."

I want to conclude this short genealogy on theorizing African American Religion by suggesting a way forward beyond this divide and disciplinary hostilities. Elsewhere I put forward a methodological position, which I described as African American Religious and Cultural Criticism. My position takes for granted that cultural formations of African American Religion are directed toward satisfying basic human needs, ends, and values that Black producers of religion require for a fulfilled life. These needs, such as life, safety, work, leisure, knowledge, and subjective needs, such as friendship, peace of mind, integrity of conscience, and what Du Bois described as our spiritual strivings, are categorical. I call the cultural integration of these categorical and subjective needs, ends, and values Black cultural fulfillment.[63] African American religious and cultural criticism analyzes and critiques processes of successful cultural fulfillment and conditions by which it is either satisfied or frustrated in African American religious experience. It is not content with describing the dark side of our cultural formations of religion, without also affirming creative possibilities of the cultural fulfillment of Black people by seeing within African American religious experience possibilities for realizing our political, social, and spiritual strivings.

This work does not require of the African American religious and cultural critic commitment to any particular faith tradition, even while the critic makes interpretative and critical judgments about formations of religion in the lives of Black people by deploying theological and religious vocabularies in their work of criticism. Moreover, the critic need not be hostile toward theological interpretations of Black Religion as it circulates throughout Black folk religion and expressive culture. African American religious and cultural criticism, however, is guided by an iconoclastic rigor that robs every theory of African American Religion of totality, what Barbara Christian names, monolithism, and monotheism. The critic is suspicious both of Black cultural heroism and idolatries whether determined by Black expressive culture (music, art, poetry, and literature) or in Black Church Studies and Black Theology in which a distinct racial essence results. African American religious and cultural criticism discloses emancipatory aspects of individuality that make for difference within Black communities and which every Black person has a legitimate right to expect of cultural fulfillment. It is both iconoclastic and utopian.

Theorizing African American Religion within Black cultural criticism acknowledges that there are always political, social, and ideological moves in our theories of African American religious experience. There are always human and cultural ends, values, and needs that determine our theories of African American Religion. To acknowledge this is to stand with predecessors and contemporaries theorizing African American Religion in this genealogy. At its best, African American Religion imagines (sees connections), articulates (makes explicit), and socially constructs (creates and participates in) formations and fulfillment of human needs, ends, and values that circulate throughout African American religious experience.

NOTES

1. Nathaniel Norment, Jr., *The African American Studies Reader* (Durham, NC: Carolina Academic Press, 2007); Manning Marable, ed., *The New Black Renaissance: The Souls Anthology of Critical African-American Studies* (Boulder, CO: Paradigm Publishers, 2005).

2. Jacqueline Bobo, C. Hudley, and C. Michel, eds., *The Black Studies Reader* (New York: Routledge, 2004).

3. Maulana Karenga, *Introduction to Black Studies*, second edn. (Los Angeles, CA: University of Sankore Press, 1993).

4. Anthony B. Pinn, *The African American Religious Experience in America* (Westport, CT: Greenwood Press, 2005).

5. Karenga, *Introduction to Black Studies*, 35.

6. Anthony B. Pinn, *African American Humanist Principles: Living and Thinking Like the Children of Nimrod* (New York: Palgrave Macmillan, 2004).

7. Pinn, *The African American Religious Experience in America*, xvii.

8. Pinn, *The African American Religious Experience in America*.

9. Pinn, *The African American Religious Experience in America*.

10. Michel Foucault "Nietzsche, Genealogy and History," in *Language, Counter-Memory, Practices: Selected Essays and Interviews by Michel Foucault*, ed. Donald F. Bouchard (Ithaca, NY: Cornell University Press, 1977), 139.

11. Charles H. Long, *Significations: Signs, Symbols and Images in the Interpretation of Religion* (Aurora, CO: The Davies Group, Publishers, 1986), 67.

12. Phillip D. Curtin, "The Slave Trade and the Atlantic Basin: International Perspective," in Nathan I. Huggins, Martin Kilson, and Daniel M. Fox, eds., *Key Issues in Afro-American Experience* (New York: Harcourt Brace Jovanovich, 1971), 79.

13. Curtin, "The Slave Trade."

14. W. E. B. Du Bois, *Black Reconstruction in America 1860–1880* (New York: Harbor Scholars' Classics Edition, 1956; first published 1935), 727.

15. Albert J. Raboteau, *Slave Religion: The Invisible Institution in the Antebellum South* (New York: Oxford University Press, 2004; first published 1978), 16.

16. William D. Hart, *Black Religion: Malcolm X, Julius Lester, and Jan Willis* (New York: Palgrave Macmillan, 2008), 8.

17. Hart, *Black Religion*, 193.

18. Timothy Fulop, *African American Religion: Interpretative Essays in History and Culture* (New York: Routledge, 1996), 231.

19. Fulop, *African American Religion*, 233.

20. Fulop, *African American Religion*, 238.

21. W. E. B. Du Bois, The *Souls of Black Folk* (New York: Penguin Books, 1969; first published 1903).

22. Carter G. Woodson, *The History of the Negro Church*, second edn. (Washington, DC: The Associated Publishers, 1945; first published 1921).

23. E. Franklin Frazier and C. Eric Lincoln, *The Negro Church in America / The Black Church since Frazier* (New York: Schocken Books, 1974).

24. Gayraud Wilmore, ed., *African American Religious Studies* (Durham, NC: Duke University Press, 1989).

25. C. Eric Lincoln and Lawrence H. Mamiya, *The Black Church in African American Experience* (Durham, NC: Duke University Press, 1990).

26. R. Drew Smith, ed., *New Day Begun: African American Churches and Civic Culture in Post-Civil Rights America* (Durham, NC: Duke University Press, 2003).

27. Stacey Floyd-Thomas, Juan Floyd-Thomas, Carol B. Duncan, Stephen, J. Ray, and Nancy Lynn Westfield, *Black Church Studies: An Introduction* (Nashville, TN: Abingdon Press, 2007).

28. Du Bois, *The Souls of Black Folk*, 212.

29. Du Bois, *The Souls of Black Folk*, 212

30. Du Bois, *The Souls of Black Folk*, 213.
31. Johnnetta, B. Cole, "Africanisms in the Americas: A Brief History of the Concept," *Anthropology and Humanism Quarterly* , vol. 10, no. 4 (1985), 121.
32. Cole, "Africanisms in the Americas," 121.
33. Cole, "Africanisms in the Americas," 121.
34. Cole, "Africanisms in the Americas," 121.
35. Raboteau, *Slave Religion*.
36. Sterling Stuckey, *Slave Culture: Nationalist Theory & the Foundations of Black America* (New York: Oxford University Press, 1987).
37. Lawrence Levine, *Black Culture and Black Consciousness: Afro-American Folk Thought from Slavery to Freedom* (New York: Oxford University Press, 1978).
38. John W. Blassingame, *Slave Testimony: Two Centuries of Letters, Speeches, Interviews, and Autobiographies* (Baton Rouge, LA: Louisiana State University Press, 1977).
39. Riggins R. Earl, Jr., *Dark Symbols, Obscure Signs: God, Self & Community in the Slave Mind* (Maryknoll, NY: Orbis Books, 1993).
40. James, H. Cone, *A Black Theology of Liberation*, 20th anniversary edn. (Maryknoll, NY: Orbis Books, 1990; first published 1976), 27.
41. Gayraud S. Wilmore and James H. Cone, *Black Theology: A Documentary History*, Vols. 1 and 2 (Maryknoll, NY: Orbis Books, 1993; first published 1979).
42. Dwight N. Hopkins, *Introducing Black Theology of Liberation* (Maryknoll, NY: Orbis Books, 1999).
43. Stephanie Mitchem, *Introducing Womanist Theology* (Maryknoll, NY: Orbis Books, 2006).
44. Victor Anderson, *Beyond Ontological Blackness: An Essay on African American Religious and Cultural Criticism* (New York: Continuum Publishers, 1995); and *Creative Exchange: A Constructive Theology of African American Religious Experience* (Minneapolis: Fortress Press, 2008).
45. Katie G. Cannon, *Black Womanist Ethics* (Atlanta, GA: Scholars Press, 1988).
46. Jacquelyn Grant, *White Women's Christ and Black Women's Jesus: Feminist Christology and Womanist Response* (Atlanta, GA: Scholars Press, 1989).
47. Delores S. Williams, *Sisters in the Wilderness: Womanist God-Talk* (Maryknoll, NY: Orbis Books, 1993); and "A Womanist Perspective on Sin," in Emilie M. Townes, ed., *A Troubling in My Soul: Womanist Perspectives on Evil & Suffering* (Maryknoll, NY: Orbis Books,1993).
48. Williams, *Sisters in the Wilderness*, 52–6.
49. Williams, "A Womanist Perspective on Sin," 145–6.
50. Mitchem, *Introducing Womanist Theology*, 46.
51. Victor Anderson, *Beyond Ontological Blackness*, 93; and *Creative Exchange*, 53–72.
52. Dwight N. Hopkins, *Shoes that Fit Our Feet: Sources for a Constructive Black Theology* (Maryknoll, NY: Orbis Books, 1993), 15.
53. Hopkins, *Shoes that Fit Our Feet*, 19.
54. H. James Evans, Jr., *We Have Been Believers: An African-American Systematic Theology* (Minneapolis, MN: Augsburg Fortress Press, 1993), 2.
55. Barbara A. Holmes, *Race and the Cosmos: An Invitation to View the World Differently* (Harrisburg, PA: Trinity International Press, 2002); and *Joy Unspeakable:*

Contemplative Practices of the Black Church (Minneapolis, MN: Fortress Press, 2004); and *Liberation and Cosmos: Conversations with the Elders* (Minneapolis, MN: Fortress Press, 2008).

56. Holmes, *Liberation and Cosmos*, x.
57. Anderson, *Beyond Ontological Blackness; and Creative Exchange.*
58. Barbara Christian, "The Race for Theory," in Joy James and Tracey Sharpley-Whiting, eds., *The Black Feminist Reader* (Malden, MA: Blackwell, 2000), 18–19.
59. Wilmore, *African American Religious Studies.*
60. Wilmore, *African American Religious Studies*, xii.
61. Cornel West and Eddie S. Glaude, Jr., *African American Religious Thought: An Anthology* (Louisville, KY: Westminster John Knox Press, 2003).
62. West and Glaude, *African American Religious Thought*, xviii.
63. Anderson, *Beyond Ontological Blackness*, 27.

PART V

Commentary

CHAPTER 14

African American Studies: Vital, Transformative, and Sustainable

Jeanette R. Davidson and Tim Davidson

University of Oklahoma

INTRODUCTION

A frican American Studies is vital to the mission of the academy and transformative for students, educators, and communities. The discipline continues to evolve in the twenty-first century, is proven to be resilient, and should be sustained. The story of African American Studies has always been about finding a place to stand—securing a footing in the academy, finding a clearing (opening) for pedagogy, and being integral to the process of discovering, transmitting, and creating knowledge without the Black focus being assimilated, diluted or commodified by the (typically) White power structure within the academy.

Up to this point, much of the narrative of African American Studies is cast within the politicized frame of Black liberation and self-determination amidst White resistance and strategies that foster second-class citizenship or institutional vulnerability. But at its core, African American Studies is more than freedom as opposition; it is freedom as greater understanding and expression. It not only challenges the academy, but revitalizes it through its systematic enquiries into: (1) African modes of thought and traditions; (2) the international impact of the Diaspora; (3) American culture (past, present, and future); and (4) theoretical perspectives on race (forged experientially from the vantage point of the oppressed).

Maulana Karenga says the "very meaning of Black Studies" is "to speak African people's special cultural truth and make their own unique contribution to the flow of human history"—not just as a "variant discourse," but as a specific and unique field of study.[1] Kathleen Cleaver emphasizes how the original commitment to Black self-determination and liberation resulted in

> the push for academic recognition of our history and culture, brought about black studies programs through radical protest actions, promoted the Black Arts movement, insisted upon the values of our heritage, supported African independence struggles, and challenged American racist domination in political, economic and military spheres . . .[2]

This dynamic—resulting from speaking truth to power—remains and is a necessary ingredient of a vital university.

UNDERSTANDING THE DISCIPLINE'S RANGE

The various names used for the discipline—African American Studies, Black Studies, Africana Studies, Diaspora Studies, Pan-African Studies, African and African American Studies—describe departments or programs within universities that tend to be inter-, cross- or transdisciplinary,[3] but share common ground in research, historical perspective, service learning, and community involvement. Over time, several foci have developed in African American Studies in higher education with varying degrees of emphasis on diversity variables of class, gender, sexual orientation, and identity and varying political or cultural orientations. One result of a synthesized, interdisciplinary education like African American Studies is a well-rounded, contextualized scholar who thinks outside the boundaries of a singular discipline, which can be very useful in a complex world.

The development of African American Studies over the past fifty post-civil rights years has been impacted by several factors, including the (usually racially charged) history of the university in question: geographic location; choices made by faculty members within these units, related to philosophical stances and political ideology; and the organizational politics of making resources accessible. These factors have all influenced whether units within universities have flourished or withered.[4] In some institutions, African American Studies has departmental status, while some units are configured structurally as programs (with or without specific tenure lines for faculty). Some have very high visibility and considerable resources in faculty membership and financial support. Others have moderate resources. Many struggle with minuscule budgets and mostly part-time faculty members or members borrowed from other departments.[5]

On a theoretical level, there is critical, even fractious dialogue among some Black intellectuals and there are major competing paradigms regarding the proper perspective and content that African American Studies should take. The different voices reflect the energy and potential of the discipline.[6] Some departments or programs champion certain portions of the vast body of Africana literature and de-emphasize or ignore some of the material favored by other institutions and other intellectuals. Some studies are nationalist, others are pan-nationalist. Some are more contemporary, others more classical. Some focus more on the humanities, while others have more of a focus on the social sciences. Some are faithful to the original notion of Black Studies' ties to liberation and community activism. These various emphases are understandable when there is such comprehensive subject matter to be examined. The *sine qua non* of African American Studies is praxis—an intellectually rigorous human activity, emerging from Black traditions, experience, and culture that consists of "reflection and action" intended to "transform the world."[7]

To maintain viability and distinctiveness, the discipline needs, as Ronald Bailey puts it, a paradigm of "unity without uniformity"[8] and a consolidated framework that continues "to make the broad, social transformational contribution that we intended when we stormed the barricades to create the field."[9] Jacqueline Bobo, Cynthia Hudley, and Claudine Michel emphasize that African American Studies is fundamentally "expansive" and "inclusive" of many disciplines within the "social sciences, humanities research, and natural and physical sciences"[10] and is the "progeny of centuries of research that seeks to redress long-standing misconceptions of Black inferiority, African heritage, and cultural significance," but is unified in its purpose as "a socially engaged field of scholarly enquiry."[11] Leadership within the discipline needs to be savvy enough to position African American Studies in as adaptive a fit as possible within a given university, without compromising the subject matter and transformative purpose of African American Studies.[12]

Karenga identifies the classic core areas of the discipline as (1) Black History, (2) Black Religion, (3) Black Social Organization, (4) Black Politics, (5) Black Economics, (6) Black Creative Production (including but not limited to art, music, dance, and literature), and (7) Black Psychology.[13] Nell Painter notes that in recent years the discipline "has experienced extraordinary intellectual growth over the span of a generation" with "interdisciplinary work of stunning sophistication" and has grown into a "field that encompasses the histories and cultures of people of the African Diaspora, in particular, and the meaning of race and difference, in general."[14] Even though every department or program may not be able to provide a comprehensive portfolio of educational foci, the sustainable goal is to build on core content and continue to expand the multidimensional reach of the discipline, according to available human and economic resources within a particular university.[15]

FRAMING THE DISCIPLINE'S LEGACY

Robert Harris[16] describes four stages of intellectual development in the academy relating to Africana traditions, experiences of the Diaspora, and African American life. The first two stages pre-date formal African American Studies in predominantly White universities. The stages and approximate dates Harris details are:

1. early Black literary and historical associations in the 1890s through the 1930s, as well as W. E. B. Du Bois' research program on African American life at Atlanta University;
2. predominantly White political and sociological analyses of Black America from the 1940s into the 1960s;
3. the intellectual manifestations of Black power and Black consciousness within universities (accompanied by the morally persuasive power of the Civil Rights Movement within society as a whole)[17] in the mid-1960s into the mid-1980s; and
4. the process of legitimization and institutionalization of the discipline within the academy in the latter half of the 1980s to the present time (with the discipline becoming more theoretically refined and sophisticated).

In stage one (e.g. Du Bois, Woodson, Frazier) and stage three (e.g. Karenga, Hare, Davis, Asante) Black leaders took charge of the content and application of the discipline and developed scholarship. In stage one, educators in Black colleges and universities were so markedly separate from predominantly White universities that their work was not subject to the same censor and control as it might otherwise have been. Some Black scholarship during this period was supported through White patronage, and modes of thought were influenced by Eurocentric traditions and White cultural productions and authorship, but a significant amount of Black historical research and field studies was mostly ignored or dismissed as inconsequential by those outside of Black intellectual life who might otherwise resist and dismantle the efforts. In contrast, in stage three, Black educators initiated the change process in the academy and did so with much controversy and determination to present educational content that originated from and was meaningful to Black culture and experiences. White respondents and power-mongers (including corporate, political, and academic leaders) often strongly resisted the development of African American Studies within "their" universities and the clash of driving and restraining forces was dramatic. In stage three, Black scholar-activists pushed their way into the academy against the odds and in the face of great resistance, and the formal discipline of Black Studies—the term generally used at the time—was formed within a few predominantly White universities.

Stage two is not seminal to African American Studies as we conceptualize the discipline today, but it was dramatically influential in how academics in predominantly White universities approach the discipline. Widely disseminated information about African American experiences was produced by White academics operating from, as Harris puts it, a "Eurocentric focus" that "excluded people of African ancestry or studies them through a European filter."[18] In the final analysis, in stage two, Black culture and life were seen by many of these White scholars as problems created by racism and conditions of oppression and needing to be managed by White elites; or as culturally pathological and/or intellectually inferior; or as phenomena "over there," to be studied and improved upon by the wit and largesse of White progressives. Black scholars during this era were marginalized, to say the least. During this era, the intellectual thrust of the White academics, at its best, created pathos and at worst reinforced an image of Black people as a helpless, hopeless, hapless group and ignored Black scholarship and excellence. The unfortunate legacy today is that some White academics are still busy studying and making scholarly commentary on Black experience from either the allegedly "helpful" posture of the Left or the typically "hostile" posture of the Right.

Today, in stage four, personnel in leadership positions in predominantly White institutions still at times try to restrain the advancement of African American Studies as a central part of the organizational life of the academy. White academics (and some Black academics) also sometimes act to alter the achievements that were fought for and realized in stage three and beyond. The result is that Black scholars with a commitment to African American Studies must try to balance building the discipline's knowledge-base, community involvement, and research agendas while surviving organizationally as intact units within the academy. Just as in stage two, White educators still try to dominate the intellectual life of the university.[19] Even so, Black leadership now is often strong enough and African American Studies is legitimized enough to create its own driving force within the academy, but it is not easy and in most cases the structural inequities that are embedded in the university system prevail.

Unfortunately, the tangled legacy of racism still exists in the academy in the twenty-first century. Old, out-of-date, embedded messages still sometimes crop up when the subject matter is African American Studies as if it was still 1910 or 1960 (e.g., the scholarship is unimportant and should be ignored; the intellectual products are inferior; the advocates of these studies are troublemakers and always complain of inequities; "they" (i.e., Black spokespersons) are trying to take over; the instructors of African American Studies need to be vetted by faculty from traditional disciplines (i.e., generally White faculty) to ensure their credentials are up to standard and their presence on campus is not merely the result of affirmative action, etc.). Even so, there is a sufficient legacy of resilience and accomplishment and a destiny of promise from within African American Studies to suggest that White, Black, and other under-represented racial and ethnic groups in the academy can build the future university together on equal terms. To move forward, however, the old problems of White domination and negative stereotypes about Black scholarship need to be eradicated and more emphasis placed on solutions, parity, and solidarity as a community of scholars that finds its strength in diversity.

FACING STRUCTURAL INEQUITIES

Structural inequities that need to be addressed in the academy include but are not limited to: (1) a scant focus on African American Studies faculty and Black faculty in general regarding hiring, retention, promotion, and positioning with powerful roles within the university; (2) disregard or marginalization of the subject matter; (3) disparities in funding African American Studies compared to other disciplines; and (4) overview and control of processes and initiatives in African American Studies by uninformed or peripherally involved White faculty via committee structures external to the unit. Most of the structural inequities are so embedded in the academy that they go unnoticed by many White faculty (cf. Peggy McIntosh's concept of White privilege and "obliviousness"[20]) while being blatantly obvious to most Black faculty. Following are a few more details regarding these structural inequities.

On Faculty

Many students pass through predominantly White institutions without ever having a Black instructor. This is a serious social problem and one where African American Studies, if properly endorsed by the leadership of the university, can provide assistance. On the surface, hiring practices at universities appear inclusive of all races, but in practice Black applicants for tenure-track positions can be included in the first pool of qualified applicants, only to be systematically removed from the applicant interview process as the hiring cycle unfolds. Black instructors throughout the nation struggle for full inclusion in the academy as tenured faculty; tenure protects academic freedom and increases rights to participate in faculty governance (e.g., voting on new hires and other people's tenure, developing curricula, and being promoted to leadership roles). African American Studies represents a core group of scholars who should be a key part of the academy's development of Black human resources. There needs to be a critical mass of Black faculty to help attract other Black scholars to the campus.

On Subject Matter

Studying race relations and Black culture is sometimes critiqued by White academic colleagues as "ghetto" scholarship and results in a sense of workplace dissatisfaction when a person's research interests are devalued or treated as unimportant or less worthy of the academy. Black faculty routinely are faced with decisions on whether or not to leave an institution based on some of the hidden, racially biased, informal rules and negative judgments in departments and colleges and an unsupportive work environment. In the classroom, African American Studies is unevenly criticized by faculty members of other disciplines as not rigorous enough, partly because of its inter- or transdisciplinary approach, but mostly as a way of intimating that the subject is not serious enough or pertinent. This all too common inequity rests squarely on the shoulders of worn-out racial bias and provincial disciplinary reactions.

On Funding

Under-funded programs and budgetary restraints for African American Studies are more often the rule than the exception. Many chairpersons and faculty members do not find the university is truly supportive of their initiatives because their funding does not match that of other units. This manifests in too few faculty lines; less than preferred classroom sites; many times, "soft" (i.e., temporary) money is used to fund programs, program development, and faculty positions rather than "hard" money dedicated over the long term to the discipline.

On Overview and Control

Faculty governance within departments over disciplinary content is almost sacrosanct in the academy. To be sure, there are hierarchical management controls at the college and university level, but at the department level there is an understanding that faculty will exercise academic freedom and accept responsibility for their research and teaching. In contrast, on too many campuses, there remains an oversight mentality from inter-departmental reviews or committees as African American Studies develops its curricula and selects its instructors. Faculty members in traditional departments (history, sociology, fine arts, literature, etc.) often think they "own" certain subject matter (even if they do not emphasize or even include Black scholarship in their disciplines); and if they see African American Studies instructors successfully teaching content, which they then determine should be "theirs," they will try to co-opt it and insist they are "qualified" to teach it even when not culturally competent to do so. Similarly, when research, travel abroad, and teacher or student exchanges involve Africa, or countries heavily impacted by the Diaspora, or African American life, African American Studies faculty members are often not recognized as the obvious principal participants and expert voices in these matters.

These brief references to some of the inequities in the academy are not new. They have been brought up in university after university for decades. The issues generally are framed in terms of a demand for accountability and such moral notes are still legitimate; but the cacophony in the academy in reaction to yesterday's insistence on fairness, inclusion, and parity should not drown out what must be heard today. A deontological ethic (based on what is right) may not have been as persuasive in the past as it needed to be, but a teleological ethic based on consequences might result in greater recognition of the importance of African American Studies. White elitism, domination, and privilege will not continue to work in the real world. If the academy wants to be relevant, it must provide an example and leadership in broadening worldviews—including pride and more support for all levels of Black scholarship (as well as other racial and ethnic populations).[21]

Formally, if or when the academy finally decides to buttress African American Studies, this decision will translate into:

1. an increased number of tenured lines and departmental or program visibility on campus;
2. more financial support for programs and departments (e.g., faculty awards with honors; more fellowships, grant priorities, foundational and philanthropic support);
3. movement from program status to department status, with the increased autonomy that comes with that status;
4. expansion from undergraduate studies to master and doctoral programs, with research assistant support for graduate students; and greater locus of control coming from Black scholars, with cooperation from White academic allies who have an investment in African American Studies as a discipline rather than vested personal interests in their own projects (e.g., research in Africa or places of the African Diaspora).

Informally, structural inequities will be known to have decreased when there are no more reminders of the demonizing policing orientation of the past with White academics acting superior in reference to the discipline; the White pecking order on everyday matters throughout the academy is eradicated; and good things in African American Studies stay with the program or department (e.g., a popular dance class, a grant opportunity in an African setting, a campus-wide colloquium on race, creation of a community project, etc.) and are not seen as fair game to be commodified.

DEVELOPING INTELLECTUAL CAPITAL

Black intellectual capital is an important resource to be explored and developed. African American Studies rescues, reconstructs, and revitalizes vital truths of Black heritage and provides a much-needed revelatory perspective on contemporary experience at a national and international level. In so doing, it provides a clearer, more encompassing view, not only of Black culture and life, but of humanity as a whole. On one level, the discipline provides an academic antidote to counteract the bias and dominant narratives of White Supremacy and the Eurocentric inclinations that are so infused within the academy; but, just as sunlight is a good disinfectant, even more so it is necessary for life and growth. Thus, as an important part of any vital university system, African American Studies should be encouraged by power-brokers within the system to fulfill a key role in developing and investing in the intellectual capital of Black scholarship, thereby helping the academy thrive as it fulfills its true mission to be an expansive, universal community of scholars.

Three key themes regarding intellectual capital in African American Studies are: (1) the intellectual investment in students of all races and ethnicities that occurs; (2) the establishment of a socially elevated setting for Black intelligentsia; and (3) the kind of intellectual product that is often created.

On Investment in Students

Paulo Freire's message to educators[22] is to invest in learners' potential and to draw on students' collective knowledge and experiences. This is at the heart of African American Studies, particularly when the focus is on contemporary experience in African American life, or is on race relations in the United States. Freire sees effective pedagogy as different from depositing large sums of elitist knowledge into a poor learner's bank, with educators feeling good about themselves for their patriarchal munificence. Progressive instructors know that students need to be encouraged, inspired, and challenged by the content in the classroom and that the subject matter is meaningful to their life experiences.

The educator's legitimate domain is knowledge drawn from research and theory—and to some degree his or her subjective, lived experience. Effective pedagogy includes a scholarly presentation of facts and reality checks; descriptions of the subject matter in ways that students can appreciate and learn from the process; articulation of useful analytic keys for students to apply in real-world settings; and methods that facilitate students' deeper self-understanding. However, in addition to the academic content to be explored in the classroom, education must also "begin with the solution of the teacher-student contradiction, by reconciling the poles of the contradiction so that both are simultaneously teachers *and* students."[23] In African American studies, the "contradiction" that Freire references can be complicated further by the racial dynamic between the teacher and students. If the instructor is White and the students are Black (or from other under-represented racial groups), the dynamic is different compared with if the instructor is Black. All the other possible variants impact how the "contradiction" can be resolved too: if the instructor is African (Black or White), if the instructor is Hispanic, Asian, bi- or multiracial, gay or lesbian, traditional or alternative in lifestyle, is strongly identified with a religious group, has an accent that is different from that of the students, is interracially married with some experiential knowledge of African American life, has working knowledge of African countries by virtue of having lived, worked or researched on the continent, or is Black and from a colonized country or from a European colonizing country.

When the professor is Black and teaching Black students, those students may have a deep, tacit knowledge by acquaintance of the material under discussion, while students of other racial and ethnic backgrounds may resist the expertise of the instructor and wonder if the Black students are being unfairly advantaged. In a multiracial classroom, there will be students who do not have an immediate or tacit knowledge of the Black experience but have *parallel knowledge* of Black life and culture or *obscured knowledge* of race relations, based on their own lived experiences and (perhaps) racial privilege within society as a whole. In following Freire's approach, this means the Black instructor must be able to learn from every student without letting dominant White modes of thought or privilege prevail and then must help students move forward in their understanding of race, oppression, and privilege in a transformative way. This is not easy, but is part of the everyday challenge of teaching African American Studies.

In a multiracial classroom, something relatively intangible but recognizably valuable transpires when Black instructors invest in their students. That "something" is more than just helping students work through issues of privilege and bias on a cognitive level. Since there are so few Black faculty members in the academy, the Black African American Studies instructor may be the first and only Black teacher that students in predominantly White universities experience. The influence of that student-teacher relationship can be life-altering. The positive impact of a Black instructor discussing race and Black culture and life in a constructive and knowledgeable format is very valuable to the overall educational experience. Students of all races are likely to be socially influenced by the instructor's referent power and find points of psychological identification with their teacher, not to mention the value of recognizing a Black instructor's legitimacy and expertise as a member of the academy.[24]

The best teachers stimulate a student's intellectual curiosity by thorough and scholarly attention to the subject matter under discussion from a Black perspective. For many students, steeped in Eurocentric perspectives and believing that their perspective is a universal, all-encompassing point of view, the result can be liberating intellectually. African American Studies helps students think about who they are—their meaning, significance, place, and agency in the world. It is then that students are better equipped to move from reflection to action to make the world a better place.

Two typical classroom results from this approach to investing in students are improved critical thinking and emotional reasoning. Since the classroom is not a therapy setting, better critical thinking is probably a more recognizable objective for an instructor than enhanced emotional reasoning, but both are desirable.

In African American Studies, critical thinking:

- puts to use new data and observations about Africa, the Diaspora, and African American life;
- promotes a higher order of reflection, based on conceptual models within the field while examining Eurocentric assumptions;
- broadens points of view historically and contextually so that the predominant White accounts are not privileged;
- promotes insights about other racial groups and cultures;
- challenges media representations and stereotypes that shape race-based messages;
- helps reverse internalized prejudices and examines group norms, beliefs, and identities with a judicious eye; and
- reduces the tendency to be culture-bound (i.e., placing one's own group above others').

Improved emotional reasoning may be even more valuable than critical thinking for the majority of students in African American Studies. Talking about race stirs emotions, and concentrated studies on Black experience at least bring the subject from a suppressed and naïve consciousness to some level of externalized narrative. More than this can occur on an emotional level if instructors continue to nurture students' self-awareness and expand their worldview. Enhanced emotional reasoning can be measured when there is:

- a heightened awareness of one's emotional reactions and their effects when talking (e.g., about race, privilege, oppression, identity);

- a greater sense of self-control when negative emotions and impulses are triggered if someone in class is disagreeing or disagreeable;
- the ability to be more flexible and adaptive when new information is presented, some of which in African American Studies may genuinely shake basic presuppositions (e.g., about culture, history, politics, gender, poverty, etc.);
- clear evidence of having empathy and being able to sense others' feelings and perspectives in a respectful way, but not acquiescing to White dominant views or being tolerant of intolerance;
- motivation to do something constructive, based on what has been learned (whether locally or globally);
- a sense of classroom synergy as students develop a feeling of being together, irrespective of their differences; and
- some adeptness in constructive persuasion as students become more knowledgeable and articulate in their understanding of the discipline.

On the Vital Role of a Black Intelligentsia

If all that African American Studies accomplished for Black faculty is a political sanctuary and a niche to have collegial relationships with other Black faculty, it would be worth it for the university. African American Studies departments and programs provide more than this, however. And there is important work to be done. Sundiata Keita Cha-Jua emphasizes that African American Studies is an "intellectual and artistic socioeducational project" with a "dual purpose": "(1) to recover subjugated knowledge, that is, to reconstruct research and instruction on the Black experience; and (2) to rewrite the historic relationship between the campus and the Black community."[25] Marable cogently defines the intellectual work of African American Studies as descriptive, corrective, and prescriptive.[26]

African American Studies endeavors to make a difference to how Black people are understood and gain from the collective wisdom and genius of generations of scholars whose work otherwise is lost, ignored or forgotten. Karenga argues that if we allow just "the progressive Europeanization of human consciousness" without any other worldviews in the marketplace of ideas, then

> at least three things occur: (1) the progressive loss of historical memory [e.g., of the people of the African Diaspora]; (2) the progressive disappreciation of themselves and their culture; and (3)

the progressive adoption of a Eurocentric mode of assessment of self, society and the world, inducing cognitive distortion and deprivation and the destruction of the human richness we find in human diversity.[27]

The sad fact is that, even in the twenty-first century, many Americans do not equate intelligence with being Black. Yet Black intellectuals know that their work is undertaken not to prove that they are smart, but to "focus on contradictions in society, especially those of race, class, and gender, looking again not only for what is present and distorted in the discourse but also for what is absent and undiscussed, not only for codified ignorance but also for canonized illusion."[28] In prophetic form, Cornel West indicates that the future of a Black intelligentsia will be in "regimes of truth" that are "inseparable from the emergence of new cultural forms that prefigure (and point toward) a post- (not anti-) Western civilization."[29]

Because of the clash of Eurocentric and Afrocentric worldviews and centuries-long diminution of not only Black contributions to civilization, but Black capacity to contribute, the intellectual project of African American Studies is necessarily political. From Du Bois on,[30] the discipline has coupled information with transformation. Henry Louis Gates, Jr. is not a strong advocate of an activist agenda within the university, but he too asserts that the "tools of black studies scholarship could not be narrowly confined to the traditional apolitical approaches set by Euro-American intellectuals."[31] The historical roots of the discipline feed on the relationship of academic knowledge and social power, and, as Joy James states, the "future of black studies is tied to past and present political battles." James emphasizes that these battles should not be conceptualized as "political performances" within a sterile academic environment, but as intellectual work that addresses "critical issues for the future of black studies seeking political communities outside of academic carcerals."[32] Just as pedagogy in the classroom is geared to be transformative for students, the writings of Black scholars in the discipline are inclined toward transformation within communities.

On the Intellectual Product

There is no one way to conduct research in African American Studies, but there is a tradition that derives from an investment in the community (and now, more often, the broader international community of people of African descent) and the need for action.[33] Points to consider here include:

1. In James B. Stewart's words, "reservations about excessive commitment to quantification at the expense of conceptual clarity."[34] Numbers require context.
2. Rather than a collection of facts, there is an interest in the hermeneutical function of the facts—i.e., what the meaning and impact of the facts are for real people.
3. There is an attempt "to be careful of the fragmentation of knowledge" as Ronald Bailey describes it, because of the more effective and powerful method of bringing multiple levels of "knowledge creation in creating a better world."[35]
4. A "high valence" is "placed on artistic and humanistic modes of understanding"[36] because the emphasis is on people's lives and experiences, and the narrower confines of positivistic science can be reductionistic and miss the human narrative.
5. As Cha-Jua indicates, the intellectual product provides "relevant research for community activists and progressive politicians"[37] to support their efforts to confront everyday struggles in Black communities.

This unfettered, yet focused approach to scholarship is one of the reasons why African American Studies is presently pushing forward to include many new areas related to Africa and the Diaspora, the social sciences, contemporary culture, gender, sexual orientation, institutional and societal problems, theories and practice, policy and service delivery, and the study of African languages, to name only a few.

HONORING A TRANSGRESSIVE[38] IMPULSE

The question of "transgressing" is crucial to understanding the discipline's past and future. To what degree should African American Studies be militant, rebellious, stand firm, and press against White domination and elitism? As previously intimated, the academy did not welcome African American Studies in its infancy in the 1960s. Activists had to storm the gates of the ivory tower. In fact, if Black scholars and activists had not breached the boundaries of propriety and dominion set by White academics, it is very likely that the discipline would not exist in its present institutionalized form. As it is, African American Studies continues to fight for its integrity as a discipline in its own right; to challenge external efforts to turn the subject matter into "Black-lite" courses; to contend with empty promises to infuse other established disciplines in the university with Black intellectual contributions (realizing that this is not often done in any measurable, knowledgeable or sustained way); and to see faculty co-opted and courses poached by other departments once it is discovered that the subject matter attracts students. Often, the academy has resisted African American Studies, minimized its role through lack of funding; dissolved programs by acting as if other traditional departments will include Black content; or tried to reconstitute African American Studies as a minor area of ethnic studies to be examined from a Eurocentric perspective; or simply eliminated it.

Reflecting on her experiences as a Black intellectual in the academy, hooks describes the situation accurately when she maintains that "the university is basically a politically conservative framework which often inhibits the production of diverse perspectives."[39] While many pundits today conclude that the academy nurtures progressive indulgences, many administrators and teachers in African American Studies know that, in matters related to race relations and Black life and culture, there can be a "major backlash" in the academy "that seeks to delegitimize progressive pedagogy" from either the Left or the Right; indeed, there seems to be a tacit recognition by many in positions of university leadership, in hooks' words, that "the focus on difference has the potential to revolutionize the classroom" and many academics who resist change or educational reform "do not want the revolution to take place."[40]

Another theme that hooks develops concerns being at "home" in the academy. She argues that the very meaning of the term changes if the university system is functioning with a colonial mindset. "Within complex and ever shifting realms of power relations, do we position ourselves on the side of colonizing mentality? Or do we continue to stand in political resistance with the oppressed?"[41] hooks adds that the "experience of decolonialization, of radicalization" means that at times home is "nowhere" and the transgressive rebel will have to come to terms with "extreme estrangement and alienation" and will need to confront and accept "dispersal and fragmentation as part of the construction of a new world order that reveals more fully where we are, who we can become . . ."[42] Faculty in African American Studies need to take hooks' analysis seriously and make sure that our "home" in the university is not only somewhere, but somewhere we want to be, because she is right—it would be better to be on the margins and dispersed than on the side of White domination, ignoring the serious problems of racial supremacy in the academy and society.[43]

However, it seems in many cases now that our challenge as programs and departments of African American Studies is to make ourselves at home within the academy, without abandoning our commitment to free expression, without forgetting our past, with an allegiance to oppressed populations, and with responsibilities to the communities. As a discipline that is already established within the academy, we must assert "homeowner rights" and "homeowner responsibilities" for the way we want our discipline to function. Some departments and programs are relatively secure, while others experience great instability. For programs that are struggling, protests for inclusion are needed. For programs that are more ensconced in a particular university, the protests can be directed more toward protection of the subject matter and promotion of the discipline's agendas and modes of thought and to provide more solidarity to colleagues whose programs and departments are in jeopardy. Colonizers create circumstances that call for revolutions; once progress is made, as it has been with African American Studies, transgressive rebels need to secure their place ("home" in hooks' sense) and then continue to advance. The goal is an inclusive university and a constructive department.

Bailey suggests that there have been three stages of development for Black Studies since the 1960s: (1) *innovation*—a time of social disruption and activism embraced by scholars within the discipline; (2) *experimentation*—a period of disciplinary differences and ideological demarcation; and (3) *professionalization*—a mild-mannered, go-along-to-get-along shift motivated by self-preservation in the academy, with an inclination to perpetuate the status quo rather than fulfill its historical mission of social transformation.[44]

In keeping faith with the transgressive image, the stage of "professionalization" that Bailey describes needs to be reframed in those settings where the tasks of resistance have been compromised for ease of survival. The discipline has already established a sustainable place in the academy, but only if we continue to push for an indispensable and integral (not assimilated) Black presence and worldview within the university system (i.e., "innovation") and continue to develop frontiers of knowledge about Black culture and life (i.e., "experimentation"). We have no interest or need to "assimilate to succeed" or become "honorary Whites."[45] In fact, self-preservation is best served by continued institutional transformation, strategic social disruption, and more demarcation and expansion of the discipline's boundaries. The transgressive impulse of African American Studies needs to be sustained in the twenty-first century—not to be mired in discontent, but to stimulate change within the academy, to nurture growth of the discipline, and to serve better the Black community and oppressed populations anywhere. As Karenga puts it, "Our defense lies essentially in our development."[46]

Honoring the transgressive impulse today means we:

- *resist* commodification of Blackness, whenever White intellectuals try to function as owners, interpreters or overseers of Black ideas and images;
- *reject* the role of servant or hired-hand in the academy and assert ourselves in positions of power (intellectual and leadership roles, rather than being limited to administrative assistants, human resources, or service-oriented capacities);
- *erase* old, colonial, racist images through continuous, multi-dimensional, interesting, free expressions of Black culture and life;
- *affirm* our presence on campus as our home to be invested in and preserved, collectively and collaboratively, and through our physicality and bodily presence; and
- *transform* structures within the academy that perpetuate White domination and do so in a way that moves beyond complaint to reconstruction.[47]

VALUING TRANSCENDENT EDUCATION

The irony of the aforementioned descriptions of structural inequities, protests, and struggles within the academy is that African American Studies is, by its very nature, incredibly valuable to the academy. If all that African American Studies did was bring scholarly attention to an entire continent and the impact on the world as people moved and were removed from Africa, it would be worth the effort. If all the discipline offered was a deeper understanding of race in a country limited in its greatness by the seminal problem of racism, it would make a priceless contribution to the university and society as a whole. If all that was achieved was the creation of a vital connection between the campus and Black communities, the financial commitment of the university to the discipline would pay off in terms of the university fulfilling its mission to contribute to social well-being, commerce, and the development of human potential. If all that happened was an enhanced and integrated focus on Black culture, arts, humanities, philosophy, religion, and other creative productions, African American Studies would easily match the inherent value of many programs and departments across campus. If all that African American Studies could offer to the university was a place to encourage and to engage Black faculty and where Black students could experience a profound sense of being welcome and belonging on predominantly White campuses, the money supporting the initiative would be more wisely spent than many other initiatives to recruit and retain Black faculty and students.

There is a transcendent (surpassing, more than exceptional) dimension of education in African American Studies that may go unnoticed by external observers. Transcendence can be described in several concrete ways. The discipline (1) transcends the racial divide in the classroom; (2) transcends elitism through commitment to oppressed populations; and (3) is transcendent in terms of being guided by moral prerogatives.

On Transcending the Racial Divide

African American Studies crosses the color line by design. Although the study is focused on Black people around the world, students of all races come together in African American Studies classes, and though it is generally the case that Black faculty are the most likely teachers, faculty of various races and backgrounds do teach in the discipline. On predominantly White campuses, multiracial interchanges in the classroom often turn out to be consciousness-raising experiences for the participants just by virtue of being there in a setting with subject matter that is not White first and Black second or even invisible. As Painter says, "black studies offers the most hospitable setting for the pursuit of racial issues" partly because "most teaching about American history and culture still ignores racial themes," whereas academics in African American Studies are teaching from "a scholarship of struggle," with an intellectual mission "to correct erroneous and pernicious notions about African Americans" and Black populations in general.[48]

Marable says it is time to "redefine America" in a transformative way[49] and the classroom can be a microcosm where this change is generated. Marable uses the phrases "radical democratic multiculturalism" and "a transformationist cultural critique"[50] to describe a multiracial movement that is not bent on assimilation, or accommodation of privileged interests and values, or self-segregation, but is based on "collective efforts of Black people . . . to transform the existing power relationships and the racist institutions of the state, the economy and society."[51] Our contention is that the classroom can sow the seeds for this multiracial, transcendent objective. The emphasis on race modeled in African American Studies is meant to stimulate solidarity with oppressed people and promote social change. From this stance, by its very makeup, it demands egalitarian ideology rather than privileged perspective. It is not just a place to air various interests and compare ethnic styles and values, is not simply a venue to claim a cultural identity, and is not just an environment where various racial groups gather. It aims "to rethink the entire history of this country, redefining its heritage in order to lay claim to its future."[52]

On Commitment to Oppressed Populations

In a 1963 freedom rally, Martin Luther King, Jr. articulated a vision of brotherhood and sisterhood that resonates to this day in African American Studies, captured in the famous quote: "injustice anywhere is a threat to justice everywhere."[53] A sense of unity with the oppressed keeps African American Studies on target with its mission to vulnerable people in communities that exist outside of the relatively safe confines of the campus.

An academic-only approach to injustice and oppression is rightly criticized by activists who sense that "elitist" university accounts of "non-elite Black life" pale into insignificance when the problems on the street and behind the scenes are so intense, desperate, and multilayered (e.g., a growing penal industry with prisons full of poor people and over-represented by African Americans and other people of color with harsh sentences; immigration detention centers with insufficient protection of human rights; toxic waste sites near neighborhoods of color; workfare that keeps wages so low that social and health problems are guaranteed; the difficult circumstances and vulnerabilities of poor women, or youth without a sense of promise, or the pervasive discrimination levied against gay and lesbian people).[54]

The challenge built into the *raison d'être* of African American Studies is to insist that academic theorizing remains tied to the realities of Black lived experience and the struggles of all who are oppressed, and that students are inspired to be activists. Community-based projects connected to the campus through internships and service-learning classes provide an immediate interface between students and real-life situations. The impact on learning is transcendent. With effective teaching in the classroom, the activity in the community will be hands-on and mind-alert, with students better prepared both to question the power that dominates and controls oppressed people and to improve the environments that prolong their suffering.

On Moral Prerogatives

Marable writes that "Black Studies must project itself not just as an interpretation of reality, but as a projection of what should be and must become."[55] Students should not be reduced to consumers of an educational product, particularly not in African American Studies, where a moral mission undergirds the knowledge being pursued. Karenga describes one desired outcome of African American Studies to be a "mutual commitment to an ethics of sharing: shared status, shared knowledge, shared space, shared wealth, shared power, and shared responsibility for conceiving and building the world we want to live in."[56]

It would be unrealistic to think that every student who reads of colonial exploitation through the slave trade and of sacrifices made during the African American freedom movement, or is inspired by the ethical courage of Harriet Tubman and Malcolm X in the face of grave danger or by the deep understanding of womanhood from the spiritual encouragement of Mary McLeod Bethune or the righteous defiance of Angela Davis, or catches a glimpse of the moral bearing and perseverance of Frederick Douglass and W. E. B. Du Bois, or is moved by the poetic grasp of human pathos from James Baldwin or Maya Angelou, will fully embrace the moral prerogative of liberation so interwoven through African American Studies; but exposure to these and other great moral and intellectual leaders in the discipline should help to develop that more magnificent outlook. Then, that transcendent benefit of education becomes more a gift to be passed on than a commodity to be consumed.[57]

CONCLUSION

A strengths-based analysis of African American Studies suggests that the twenty-first century will be a promising time for sustainable growth of the discipline. That growth is likely to be based on the extensive intellectual development regarding Black experience at home and around the world in so many areas where the possibilities of scholarship are limitless and interdisciplinary; and hopefully the growth will manifest itself in a renewed commitment to an activist impulse for social justice, lest the discipline become more and more cerebral with less and less heart.

It is not surprising that African American Studies has struggled to gain support in the academy despite its salient and transformative dimensions.

Even though the academy is one of the best institutions in society, universities are still part of the greater social order which has been marred by racial inequality, domination, and privilege. This is the reality of American life, but the fight is not over and there is great potential for positive developments in universities across the nation. In a speech in which Martin Luther King, Jr. was celebrating the 1954 US Supreme Court decision to allow Black people voters' rights but many states were defiantly opposing the ruling, King set the tone for a solution to this profound human rights issue which applies to our lesser battles to advance and to sustain African American Studies within the academy:

> We must respond to every decision with an understanding of those who have opposed us . . . We must act in such a way to make possible a coming together . . . on the basis of real harmony of interest and understanding. We must seek an integration based on mutual respect. I conclude by saying that each of us must keep faith in the future.[58]

NOTES

1. Maulana Karenga, *Introduction to Black Studies*, 3rd edn. (Los Angeles, CA: University of Sankore Press, 2002), 27–8.
2. Kathleen Nell Cleaver, "And the Beat Goes On: Challenges Facing Black Intellectuals," in Manning Marable, ed., *The New Black Renaissance: The Souls Anthology of Critical African-American Studies* (London: Paradigm Publishers, 2005), 288.
3. Karenga describes "intradisciplinary foci" recognized as "separate disciplines when they are outside the discipline of Black Studies. But inside the discipline, they become and are essentially subject areas or fields which contribute to a holistic picture and approach to the Black experience. Moreover, the qualifier Black, attached to each area in an explicit or implicit way, suggests a more specialized and delimited focus which of necessity transforms a broad discipline into a particular field" (*Introduction to Black Studies*, 28). Stewart notes that the "multi-disciplinary or interdisciplinary status" can also be "only loosely connected collections of studies performed by specialists in different disciplines" (94) and encourages "Africana Studies proponents" to "endorse a unified social-science approach that synthesizes perspectives from various disciplines to identify as many factors as is feasible that affect a particular phenomenon and decipher how these various influences interact" (83). See James B. Stewart, "Social Science and Systematic Inquiry in Africana Studies," in J. Conyers, Jr., ed., *Afrocentric Traditions: Africana Studies*, Vol. I (London: Transaction Publishers, 2005).

4. The programs and departments referred to in this chapter are on predominantly White campuses throughout the country.

5. Kendra Hamilton comments that a focus on "high profile African American studies departments . . . and their 'stars' . . . offers a pretty distorted picture of what's happening 'on the ground' in the field," and that while "departmental status represents the pinnacle of academic success . . . it's also a fact that African American studies remains a discipline dominated by programs" often "trying to offer full course coverage with what's essentially part-time faculty." See "Under the Media's Radar," *Black Issues in Higher Education* (October 9, 2003), 32.

6. Marable writes: "The scholarship of African American studies must reflect the full diversity and conflict of theoretical perspectives that currently exist. No voices should be suppressed in the pursuit of knowledge." Manning Marable, "Introduction: Black Studies and the Racial Mountain," *Dispatches from the Ebony Tower: Intellectuals Confront the African American Experience* (New York: Columbia University Press, 2000), 24.

7. Paulo Freire, *Pedagogy of the Oppressed* (New York: Continuum, 1970, 1993, 2003), emphasizes that when education is focused on populations who have been marginalized and silenced, educators must bring together the full force of theory, research, experiential learning, and involvement with the community to achieve authenticity. He also argues that there must be "radical interaction" between the two dimensions of "reflection and action" because "if one is sacrificed—even in part—the other immediately suffers. There is no true word that is not at the same time a praxis. Thus to speak a true word is to transform the world" (87) Marable adds: "To have any practical relevance to the actual conditions and problems experienced by African-American people, Black Studies must conceive itself as a type of praxis, a unity of theory and practical action . . ." Manning Marable, *Beyond Black and White: Transforming African-American Politics* (London: Verso, 1995), 112.

8. Ronald W. Bailey, "Black Studies in the Third Millennium: Reflections on Six Ideas That Can Still (and Must) Change the World," *Souls* (Summer 2000), 88.

9. Bailey, "Black Studies in the Third Millennium," 77.

10. Jacqueline Bobo, Cynthia Hudley, and Claudine Michel, "Introduction," *The Black Studies Reader* (New York: Routledge, 2004), 3.

11. Bobo, Hudley, and Michel, "Introduction," 1.

12. See the interview in this volume, Chapter 6, where Marable discusses working with the strategic goals of the university.

13. Karenga, *Introduction to Black Studies*, 28.

14. Nell Irvin Painter, "Black Studies, Black Professors, and the Struggles of Perception," *The Chronicle of Higher Education* (December 15, 2000).

15. Karenga says that "Black studies . . . has shown a remarkable capacity for development and expansion in spite of its critics" and touts the advantage of a discipline that is "an open-textured and open-ended project" not held back by "long-term entrenched contentions grown hoary and semi sacred with age." See "Black Studies: A Critical Reassessment," in Marable, *Dispatches from the Ebony Tower: Intellectuals Confront the African American Experience*, 163.

16. Robert L. Harris, Jr., "The Intellectual and Institutional Development of Africana Studies," in Bobo, Hudley, and Michel, *The Black Studies Reader*, 15–20.
17. We agree with Lea Redmond and Charles P. Henry, "The Roots of Black Studies," in Conyers, Jr. *Afrocentric Traditions: Africana Studies*, Vol. I: "Histories of Black Studies often view its development as emerging from the Black Power Movement with no link to the Civil Rights Movement. At worst, they present civil rights and Black Power as opposites. Our analysis links the two movements together as essential to the formation of Black Studies" (165).
18. Harris, "The Intellectual and Institutional Development of African Studies," 18.
19. One development in the academy is a movement to include "White Studies" alongside Black Studies and other under-represented racial and ethnic groups. Karenga makes several strong points: "studies of 'Whiteness' as a concept as distinct from White supremacy as thought and practice of domination can end up psychologizing White domination in counterproductive ways. This begins with rediscovering and trotting out the old liberal argument that Whites are victimized like the people of color they victimize. This leads to comparative victimization discourse . . . it tends to diminish the necessary moral and social distinction between oppressor and oppressed . . . also, focusing on Whiteness as a concept can degenerate into a project that results in treating Whiteness as simply an intellectual problem of abnormal and contradictory thought and 'invention' rather than a social problem of domination, unequal wealth and power, injustice and unfreedom. The central problem is not White attitudes but White domination . . . [What is required is a] 'focus on concrete expressions of White power rather than on muddled and mistaken conceptions of self by White people . . . [There is a need to] focus not on Whiteness as a concept, but on White supremacy as a social problem, a problem of thought and practice which destroys human lives, human cultures, and human possibility and requires radical treatment on a global scale" (2). "[C]learly one of the main focuses of Black Studies and other ethnic studies is a critique of White supremacy—its origin, structure and functioning, as well as the possibilities of social initiatives to end it. In fact, in the four fundamental aspects of the Black Studies mission, the critique of White domination plays an ongoing role. These are: 1) the ongoing critical search for truth and meaning in society and history; 2) a radical alternative to the established order's ways of viewing and approaching the world; 3) a moral critique of constraints on human freedom and dignity, especially those based on race, class, and gender, 4) a critical contribution of correctives and models of possibilities toward creating the just and good society , and the maximum conditions for human freedom and human flourishing in the world" (3). See Maulana Karenga, "Whiteness Studies: Deceptive or Welcome Discourse," *Black Issues* (May 13, 1999).
20. McIntosh describes pervasive cultural patterns in society at large, and in the academy *per se*, that "over-reward" White constituents with "unearned assets" (1) and an illusory sense of having achieved success based on hard work and talent ("the myth of meritocracy") (9), while systematically leaving people of color in disadvantaged, less powerful positions. Peggy McIntosh, *White Privilege and Male Privilege: A Personal Account of Having Come to See Correspondences through Work in Women's Studies*, Working Paper No. 189 (Wellesley, MA: Wellesley College Center for Research on

Women, 1988). See also Jeanette Davidson, Tim Davidson, and Judy Crain, "White Skin and Sheepskins: Challenging the Status Quo in the Education of Helping Professionals," *The Journal of Intergroup Relations*, vol. 27, no. 4 (Winter 2000–1): 3–15.

21. Marable makes a corollary point if the academy does not move forward into the twenty-first century and does not more fully embrace perspectives other than the traditional White *Weltanschauung:* "if Black Studies does not consciously seek to transform these elitist institutions, which are essentially designed to reproduce the daughters and sons of privileged social classes and racial groups, African-American Studies programs and departments will inevitably atrophy, becoming marginal appendages of the closed university system." See *Beyond Black and White*, 115.

22. Freire, *The Pedagogy of the Oppressed*, esp. 72–6.

23. Freire, *The Pedagogy of the Oppressed*, 72.

24. See John R. P. French and Bertram Raven's classic discussion in "The Bases of Social Power," in Dorian Cartwright, ed., *Studies of Social Power* (Ann Arbor, MI: University of Michigan, 1959): 150–67 on social influence and various forms of power in helping relationships and other dyads (e.g., teaching in higher education). The same point can be made in reference to White instructors who seem knowledgeable about African American Studies, care about the subject matter, and relate positively to their multiracial students. But at this stage of the academy's racial evolution, the under-represented Black instructor (of every national origin) in African American Studies really can bring a dimension that is desperately needed to the educational experience of predominantly White institutions.

25. Sundiata Keita Cha-Jua, "Black Studies in the New Millennium: Resurrecting Ghosts of the Past," *Souls: A Critical Journal of Black Politics, Culture and Society*, vol. 2 (Summer 2000), 44.

26. Marable's fuller quote in *Dispatches from the Ebony Tower* is rich and worth repeating: "First, the black intellectual tradition has always been descriptive, that is, presenting the reality of black life and experiences from the point of view of black people themselves. Instead of beginning the logic of intellectual inquiry standing on the outside of the lived experiences of the people, the black intellectual tradition at its best has always presumed the centrality of black life. The scholar was a participant-observer who was challenged to undertake a thick description of cultural and social phenomena. Scholarship was therefore grounded in the very subjective truths of a people's collective experience" (1). "The black intellectual tradition has, second, been corrective. It has attempted to challenge and to critique the racism and stereotypes that have been ever present in the mainstream discourse of white academic institutions" (2). "And, finally, the black intellectual tradition has been prescriptive. Black scholars who have theorized from the black experience have often proposed practical steps for the empowerment of black people. In other words, there is a practical connection between scholarship and struggle, between social analysis and social transformation. The purpose of black scholarship is more than the restoration of identity and self-esteem: it is to use history and culture as tools through which people interpret their collective experience, but for the purpose of transforming their actual conditions and the totality of the society all around them" (2).

27. Karenga, "Black Studies," 165–6.

28. Karenga, "Black Studies," 167.

29. Cornel West, "The Dilemma of the Black Intellectual," *The Cornel West Reader* (New York: Basic Civitas Basic Books, 1999), 313. West develops many key concepts relating to Black intellectuals in this much cited text. His comment at the end of the chapter is instructive for many thinkers who want to avoid Eurocentric modes of thought in favor of Afrocentric ones (while recognizing their epistemological foundations, formally and informally, are laid in a Black and White world): "'The future of the black intellectual lies neither in a deferential disposition toward the Western parent nor a nostalgic search for the African one. Rather, it resides in a critical negation, wise preservation and insurgent transformation of this hybrid lineage that protects the earth and projects a better world" (315).

30. Stewart writes in "Social Science and Systematic Inquiry in Africana Studies: Challenges for the Twenty-First Century," that "despite his continuing commitment to the type of systematic inquiry [of the social sciences] by the first decade of the twentieth century, Du Bois had already recognized that social science studies were insufficient to alter broader patterns of social construction of race and patterns of political and economic domination. This realization led him to seek ways of integrating political advocacy and systematic inquiry" (88).

31. Henry Louis Gates, Jr. and Manning Marable, "A Debate on Activism in Black Studies," in Marable, *Dispatches from the Ebony Tower*. Marable makes his fuller point on politics in the academy by noting: "In truth, the ideal of wholly disinterested scholarship—in any field of research—will probably remain an elusive one. But it's one thing to acknowledge the political valence of even the 'purest' scholarship; it's another to demand of it immediate political utility the ideal of knowledge for its own sake . . . may be unfashionable, and even unrealizable; but it should command our respect all the same. For it remains the basic rationale of the university . . . those who would enlist the academy in the cause of activism must confront the awkward fact that the political views of academics can no more be regimented than their scholarly opinions" (187).

32. Joy James, "The Future of Black Studies: Political Communities and the 'talented Tenth'," in Marable, *Dispatches from the Ebony Tower*, 156.

33. Marable makes the valid point, in *Beyond Black and White*, that there "are Black Studies programs at major universities which are conducting impressive research projects, producing monographs on various aspects of the black experience. Yet, much of this work is abstract and disconnected; it is framed in a discourse which is literally indecipherable except to a small body of scholars. It replicates the stilted, obtuse language that characterizes much of the Western intellectual tradition" (112). The emphasis we make here is on activist, community oriented intellectual products with more of a utilitarian purpose.

34. Stewart, "Social Science and Systematic Inquiry in Africana Studies," 88.

35. Bailey, "Black Studies in the Third Millennium," 81–2.

36. Stewart, "Social Science and Systematic Inquiry in Africana Studies," 84.

37. Cha-Jua, "Black Studies in the New Millennium," 49.

38. This term is borrowed from bell hooks in one of her discussions about being marginalized as a Black scholar in the academy: "Making a space for the transgressive

image, the outlaw rebel vision, is essential to any effort to create a context for transformation. And even then little progress is made if we transform images without shifting paradigms . . ." *Black Looks: Race and Representation* (Boston, MA: South End Press, 1992), 4. W. E. B. Du Bois also observed: "education among all kinds of men always has had, and always will have, an element of danger and revolution, of dissatisfaction and discontent." *The Souls of Black Folks* (New York: Literary Classics of the United States, 1986/2009), 28.

39. bell hooks, *Yearning: Race, Gender, and Cultural Politics* (Boston, MA: South End Press, 1990), 7.

40. bell hooks, *Teaching to Transgress: Education as the Practice of Freedom* (New York: Routledge, 1994), 145. Studying transgressive activity within the discipline itself, Karenga observes that African American Studies is more likely to be "constantly confronted with challenges of the reactionary right" because programs and departments have a "commitment to raise and pursue issues of both intellectual and social significance"; he warns that the discipline needs to be ready for "the larger effort to contain, compromise and essentially defeat the ongoing struggle for an expanded realm of freedom both in the academy and the society." See "Black Studies," 162.

41. bell hooks, *Yearning*, 145.

42. bell hooks, *Yearning*, 148.

43. In the "Introduction" to *Dispatches from the Ebony Tower*, Marable notes that: "Fundamental social change is usually achieved at the boundaries of society and not from the center. The classical black intellectual tradition was largely constructed at the margins of white society, in segregated black institutions with close proximity to the daily struggles of African American people. It was no accident that the character of black intellectual work was frequently passionate, informed by the urgent tasks of black survival and resistance" (23).

44. Bailey, "Black Studies in the Third Millennium," 79.

45. hooks, *Yearning*, 189.

46. Karenga, "Black Studies," 163.

47. Davidson and Davidson, "bell hooks, White Supremacy and the Academy", 72–5.

48. Painter, "Black Studies, Black Professors, and the Struggles of Perception," 2–3.

49. Marable, *Beyond Black and White*, 124.

50. Marable, *Beyond Black and White*, 123.

51. Marable, "Introduction," *Dispatches from the Ebony Tower*, 19–20.

52. Marable, *Beyond Black and White*, 124.

53. Martin Luther King, Jr., *A Call to Conscience: The Landmark Speeches of Dr. Martin Luther King, Jr.*, ed. Clayborne Carson and Kris Shepard (New York: Warner Books, 2001), 69. In the speech referenced, which King delivered over fifty years ago in Detroit, he emphasized three areas of injustice: *de facto* segregation of public schools; employment discrimination; and housing discrimination based on race. He also tested out his "I have a dream" phraseology, made famous in the march on Washington, DC two months later, wherein he expresses the hope of greater social gains by the time his four children became adults. The fact that a half-century has passed and the social justice agenda of African American Studies is still aimed at many of the issues that

King addressed attests to the structural and institutional problems of race within the US.

54. See Joy James' account in "The Future of Black Studies: Political Communities and the 'talented Tenth'," in Marable, *Dispatches from the Ebony Tower*, where she argues that African American Studies needs to remain true to its activist roots and work to strengthen "radical political communities" (156)

55. Marable, *Beyond Black and White*, 116.

56. Karenga, "Black Studies," 168.

57. Marable, "Introduction," *Dispatches from the Ebony Tower*: "The classical scholarship in the black intellectual tradition suggests that knowledge exists to serve the social welfare of black people and, by extension, humanity as a whole. Therefore, knowledge should not be seen as a commodity, even in a capitalist environment" (5).

58. King, *A Call to Conscience*, 54–5.

Notes on the Editor, Contributors, and Interviewees

THE EDITOR AND CONTRIBUTORS

Leslie M. Alexander PhD is Associate Professor in the Department of History, The Ohio State University.

Victor Anderson PhD is Professor of Christian Ethics at the Divinity School and Professor of African American Studies and Religious Studies, Vanderbilt University.

Molefi Kete Asante PhD is Professor in the Department of African American Studies, Temple University.

Curtis J. Austin PhD is Director of the Center for Black Studies and Associate Professor in the Department of History, the University of Southern Mississippi.

Melanie Bratcher PhD is Assistant Professor in the African and African American Studies Program, the University of Oklahoma.

Mark Christian PhD is Associate Professor of Sociology and Black World Studies, Miami University, Ohio.

Jeanette R. Davidson PhD is Director of the African and African American Studies Program and Associate Professor in the Anne and Henry Zarrow School of Social Work, the University of Oklahoma.

Maria D. Davidson PhD is Assistant Professor in the African and African American Studies Program, the University of Oklahoma.

Scott Davidson PhD is Chair and Associate Professor of the Philosophy Department, Oklahoma City University.

Tim Davidson PhD is Associate Professor in the Department of Human Relations, the University of Oklahoma.

Perry A. Hall PhD is Associate Professor in the African and Afro-American Studies Department, the University of North Carolina, Chapel Hill.

Charles E. Jones PhD is Chair and Associate Professor of the African-American Studies Department, Georgia State University.

Nafeesa Muhammad BA is a graduate student in the African-American Studies Department, Georgia State University.

Tibor P. Nagy, Jr. (Ambassador) is Vice Provost of International Affairs at Texas Tech University and Adjunct Instructor in the African and African American Studies Program, the University of Oklahoma.

George Yancy PhD is Associate Professor in the Department of Philosophy, Duquesne University.

THE INTERVIEWEES

Danny Glover is an acclaimed actor in blockbuster movies, films that focus on the African and African American experience, and in television and theater projects. He is also know for his lifelong efforts as an activist and has received numerous awards for humanitarian and advocacy efforts.

Manning Marable PhD is the M. Moran Weston and Black Alumni Council Professor of African-American Studies and Professor of History and Public Affairs, and Director of the Center for Contemporary Black History, Columbia University.

Index